B. J. boyer

Cuddesdon, August '56.
SPCK grant.

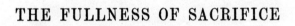

THE FULLNESS OF SACRIFICE

NUGENT HICKS

THE
FULLNESS OF SACRIFICE

AN ESSAY IN RECONCILIATION

BY

F. C. N. HICKS, D.D.

SOMETIME BISHOP OF LINCOLN

WITH A FOREWORD TO THE THIRD EDITION BY

J. A. DOUGLAS, D.D.

HONORARY CANON OF SOUTHWARK

LONDON

S·P·C·K

1953

To the memory of his friend
WILLIAM TEMPLE
Archbishop of Canterbury

K. N. H.

First Published by Macmillan and Co. Limited
Third Edition 1946
Reprinted by S.P.C.K., 1946, 1953

FOREWORD TO THE THIRD EDITION

On the face of it, this book is the product of life-long thought, study and research. Its value as an original and able contribution to scientific theology has received wide and ample recognition and must be assessed by others than myself. I am bold to write these few lines in preface to its third and posthumous edition simply to stress that which I think must be obvious to every reader of it. It is instinct with intense religious conviction. The theory and concept of sacrifice which are presented in it might have been merely the conclusion of an academic theologising. They are almost palpably the expression of the writer's inner life in Christ. It was in fact as a confession of faith, as I had it from his own lips, that Nugent Hicks wrote this book. From his undergraduate days the study of the rationale of sacrifice had obsessed him, not merely as an attractive field for intellectual exercise and for research but as a necessary and formative principle in his personal religious life. In that adventure his head and his heart were welded together, checking and helping each other. Busied to the limit as he always was and rejoicing in being a man of affairs, he was also by nature and habit a student and a teacher. His pastoral activities were his workshop, his library was his playground. But he was more than a man of affairs and a man of books. He was a man of prayer. The Eucharist was the power centre and focus of his prayer life, and from his undergraduate days the study of its rationale of sacrifice was for him a necessity of devotion. So to speak, he never prayed without visioning better the spiritual meaning of sacrifice and he never

v

studied the theology of sacrifice without praying more effectually and more fervently.

Over and above its value as a contribution to scientific theology this book is a very human document. Its shape and form as indeed its theses were without doubt largely influenced by the reason for which and the circumstances in which Nugent Hicks set out to write it. That he had had in mind the summing-up some day of the results of the investigation which had been the *parergon* of his strenuous life had indeed been the case. But it was not until just before and after having become Bishop of Gibraltar, when he became immersed in the contacts and problems of Anglican and Orthodox relations in particular, and of the Oecumenical Movement in general, that he addressed himself to this task. How he found time to get his materials into shape baffled those of us who knew the ceaseless strain of travel and of work under which he lived. But the urge was upon him, and though at some cost to health he carried it through.

For the resolution of all the antinomies, of all the theological differences and clashes of ecclesiastical division, he held that the first thing needful was mutual understanding of spiritual life and of mystical experience. And so, as under vocation in the service of Christian solidarity, overworked though he was with his manifold responsibilities, he never spared himself but gave every minute which he could find for it until he had completed it.

That Orthodox theologians should say that this book might have been written by one of themselves is not surprising; for, as it were congenitally, Nugent Hicks shared their mystical categories. That it was welcomed with equal and impressive gratitude, as he himself describes most modestly in his second preface to it, by Protestant Evangelical theologians of every Church and kind was patent to all who took part in the Edinburgh Faith and Order Conference of 1937.

At a small gathering of his intimate friends some months after his death, Archbishop Temple summed up the matter by describing it as an *eirenikon* of abiding power and forecast that, as time passes, it will become a classic for those who pray and labour for the Reunion of Christendom.

December 24, 1944.   JOHN A. DOUGLAS.

PREFACE TO THE FIRST EDITION

THE choice of a title for his book must always be one of an author's most serious difficulties. For my title I can at least claim that it makes clear one of the limitations under which I have deliberately worked. I have not attempted to write another treatise on the Eucharist, as such. I venture to say this explicitly, because it is, in fact, the bearing of a true idea of sacrifice upon eucharistic controversy that I have, quite frankly, had in mind throughout. That is, however, not the same thing as a treatment of eucharistic problems as a whole.

Nor, indeed, do I aim at a full treatment of sacrifice, either historically, as a factor in the general study of religion, or in its moral or doctrinal significance.

I have tried to show, with what degree of success the reader must judge, the part which the idea of sacrifice played in the formative period of the Christian religion, and what the content and character of that idea originally were. And I have done this because I hope that I have also succeeded in showing that it has been from the gradual departure from the original conceptions of sacrifice that a great part, if not all, of the eucharistic controversies of the last four centuries, and some, at least, of our present-day difficulties about the Atonement, have arisen.

I am conscious that little, if any, of what I have to say is original. My main thesis as to the true content of sacrifice is familiar enough to theologians. But it seemed to be

viii

worth while to bring together, with a continuity which
can only be found in one volume devoted to a single side
of a great and complex subject, what is for the most part
only to be found in fragments in books dealing with
special periods or special departments of theology. I am
conscious that, in making this attempt, I am writing
about matters that, in each period or department, are
the province of specialists. But the following of a single
thread, or line of thought, from primitive times to the
present day, may perhaps, in an age of specialisation,
have its value. And what has encouraged me to make the
attempt is the conviction, based on many years of teaching and explanation, and on constant listening to discussions, even among experts, on the subject of the Eucharist,
that what is quite generally known by specialists can
be wholly new even to those who have a reasonable
degree of theological knowledge, and still more to the
great majority of ordinary Christians. I remember, in
particular, one informal gathering at which, very briefly,
I spoke on the lines of what I have written in this book.
One of my hearers, a pronounced and definite "Evangelical", now called to his rest, who was one of the small
minority who voted against the new *Prayer Book* in the
House of Clergy, told me afterwards that if that was what
was meant by the eucharistic sacrifice he could go with
me all the way. And another hearer, who is one of the
leaders of the "Anglo-Catholic" group who also voted
against the *Prayer Book*, told me that I had at the same
time also adequately stated the "Catholic" view of the
sacrifice. I mention this because the incident is typical of
many; and if, with my own inadequate equipment for the
task, I have ventured to restate many things that have
often been said before, and to put together what seems,
at least to me, to be a connected statement of the true
conception of sacrifice, my justification must be that so

many of those who have heard it by word of mouth have asked me to put what I had to say in writing.

A Vicar of Brighton and a Bishop of Gibraltar have not many opportunities for the quiet study which should lie behind such a book as this. I can only ask my readers to forgive such inevitable deficiencies as must be found in what is written in the intervals of a busy life. I know that there is much that should be dealt with in a full treatment either of sacrifice or of the Eucharist which will not be found here. But an author, after all, chooses his own subject, and may impose his own limitations upon it.

I hope that I may at least claim that, in writing about a subject which has provided material for endless and even bitter controversy, I have said nothing that can add to bitterness or accentuate divisions. My purpose in writing will at any rate have been largely achieved if I have succeeded, in however slight a degree, in helping to exorcise the controversial spirit, and to lead those who think that they are bound to differ from another to ask themselves whether, after all, there is need for one great controversy to continue.

I have attempted to acknowledge my direct obligations to other writers in the notes. But there must be many to whom I am as much indebted, but whom I have followed unconsciously or subconsciously. I will only ask these to accept a general acknowledgment of what I owe to them. Among them, I know, are teachers, pupils, and friends whom I cannot enumerate, but whom I do not forget.

Two debts of gratitude cannot be repaid by mere references in footnotes. No one who studies the developments of eucharistic theology in any of its aspects can ever adequately express the gratitude due from himself or from other workers in the same field to Dr. Darwell

Stone for his *History of the Doctrine of the Holy Eucharist*. We may, individually, find ourselves differing from some of his conclusions; but we are bound to pay our tribute to him for having given us what is at the least an astonishingly complete and many-sided book of reference. It is as such that I have ventured to use his book, and in that spirit that I offer him my tribute. One other debt is of a more personal kind. The Rev. S. C. Gayford's book on *The Christian Sacrifice*, published a few years ago by Messrs. Methuen, has not, I venture to think, attracted the notice or received the recognition which it deserves. But my obligation to him, if it becomes evident to any who take the trouble to compare our two books, is profound; and it does not begin with the publication of his book. We began our common interest in the subject while we were students together; we pursued it independently while he was teaching at Cuddesdon and I at Oxford; and we continued it during five years of comradeship while he was Vice-Principal, and I was Principal, of Bishop's College, Cheshunt. What I owe to him, especially in the part of my book which deals with the Old Testament, I cannot specify in detailed references. I can only hope, so far as we have dealt with the same material, to popularise a subject of which he has made himself a master.

I wish to thank most cordially various friends who have helped me by reading what I have written before publication; in particular Dr. A. E. J. Rawlinson, Archdeacon of Auckland, for reading the whole book, the Rev. Leslie Owen, Warden of the Bishop's Hostel, Lincoln, and Professor A. Guillaume, of Durham University, for help with Part I., Dr. Edward Lyttelton for reading Part III., and the Rev. W. T. V. Langley, Chaplain of Bishops' College, Cheshunt, for verifying references in Part I. And I owe warm and special thanks to my old teacher and friend, Dr. Lonsdale Ragg, not only for reading the whole book in proof, but still more for having relieved me, at a time of year when my work demands incessant travelling, from the labour of compiling the Index.

I cannot close without a tribute, or an acknowledgment, of another kind. I do not know whether to call it an expression of gratitude, or an act of "piety" in the sense of the Latin word *pietas*. This book, for whatever it is worth, could not have been written, in the circumstances under which I have worked, in my parishes and my diocese, for the last six years, without the ready access to books and the facilities for quiet afforded by St. Deiniol's Library at Hawarden. That Library was Mr. W. E. Gladstone's noble gift to the Church. The time may not have come, as yet, for a permanent and final estimate of his place as a statesman in our national history; to the older among us the controversies in which he played his great part are too near for a dispassionate judgment; and to the younger, for this generation at least, he may be little more than a name. But to those who use his Library he is, and will remain, a living inspiration, in his personal devotion to the Church and his whole-hearted love for sound learning. And I know that I speak not for myself alone, but for all who, like me, have learnt to use and to love his Library, when I say that we wish anything that may be good in our work to be regarded alike as a homage to his memory and as a witness to the undying power of a consecrated and abiding life. Nor can I omit a word of warm personal thanks to the two Wardens of the Library during these years, the Very Rev. J. C. Du Buisson, Dean of St. Asaph, and the Rev. C. R. N. Blakiston, now Headmaster of St. George's School, Jerusalem, and the Sub-Warden, the Rev. Edgar Vincent, for constant help of all kinds.

I may perhaps add that, for simplicity's sake, I have used throughout the abbreviation "I" for the periphrasis "the present writer". I trust that in this respect simplicity — and brevity — will not be mistaken for egotism.

N. G.

May, 1930.

PREFACE TO THE SECOND EDITION

THIS edition is, necessarily, not more than a reprint, except for a few corrections in detail, which will, I hope, not alter the paging of the first.

I have re-read, with care, the different reviews of the first edition which are in my possession. I have to acknowledge in them very considerable kindness; and I wish that I could have expressed my sense of the value, as I see it, of some of the criticisms that have been made. That might have been possible if this second edition had given me the opportunity of attempting to clear up mis-understandings by the rewriting of certain passages. But all that I can say on these matters must be confined to a preface, and I am sure that that should be short.

I am not trying, therefore, to answer my critics in detail. A good many of their observations, indeed, do not meet the main argument of the book, and the answers can, in some cases, I think, be found, if desired, by a careful re-reading.

I may, perhaps, say, in general, that I have never wished to suggest that sacrifice, as a category of thought, must be regarded as the only form in which Christian doctrine or morals can be approached or formulated. I should go no further than to urge that it is still, in spite of the movement of the modern mind, one of the chief lines of New Testament teaching and of the traditions and controversies of the Church, and that so far as it takes us it needs careful reconsideration. With that limitation, on the other hand, I am still confident that such a reconsideration will show that, when fully allowed for, it does carry us, in its fundamental principles, both further and deeper, alike in doctrine and in morals, than its unhappy controversial history has allowed us to see (pp. 3-5).

I welcome, in this connection, in particular, the whole of Chapter xxi of Dr. O. C. Quick's recent volume on *Doctrines of the Creed* (Nisbet, 1938), in which he deals with Theories of the Atonement. My book was expressly devoted to a study of sacrifice, especially in its bearing on the Eucharist. It did not aim, in fact, at a complete treatment of the latter subject, and it was for that reason that there was no full treatment of the problem of the Eucharistic Presence itself. What I said about the Atonement was necessarily partial and incomplete. I should, myself, be the first to say that no one theory of this great truth could ever exhaust its meaning. The different so-called "theories" are not exclusive. Each is more of a metaphor than a theory. None of them, separately or together, ought ever to claim to be explanations. Each, on the other hand, has some aspect of the truth, and each may help the others.

Dr. Quick certainly vindicates the place of the priestly "religion" as well as of the prophetic in the Old Testament *præparatio evangelica*; and while showing how the familiar contrast between "subjective" and "objective" interpretations alike of the Old Testament preparation and of the New Testament gospel breaks down on analysis, he deals with the four main "theories" of the Atonement which lead into one another and are mutually supplementary—i.e., the "Subjective," the "Classic or Dramatic," the "Juridical," and the "Sacrificial." I could wish that my readers would study the whole chapter (pp. 216-237).

I can understand, in particular, some having thought that in laying stress, as I have done, on what followed the Cross in the work of redemption, I may have seemed to underestimate the centrality of our Lord's Death in the emphasis that I have laid throughout upon His Life. But I cannot agree with that judgment. One of my recent critics, for instance, the Rev. A. M. Farrer, in his essay on "Eucharist and Church in the New Testament," in *The Parish Communion*, edited by the Rev. A. J. Hebert (S.P.C.K., 1937), seems to understand me as saying, simply, that blood means not death, but life. That never meant, in my mind, anything but the blood poured out. The whole power of the blood, however that may be interpreted, can only be its power as surrendered in death. Theologically, to use Mr. Farrer's distinction, neither I, nor the many writers whom I could quote as interpreting "blood" in sacrifice in the same way, have ever suggested that the blood means, in his words, "life simply, to the exclusion of the death through which it has passed." To us, the whole power of the "precious Blood" is that it makes the saving work of the Cross an ever-present fact. Historically, we are still content to rest upon the key-passage in Leviticus (xvii, 11)—"the life of the flesh is in the blood"—as well as upon other evidence of the same kind; and we do not feel that the gap between Leviticus and the New Testament is too considerable for that assumption, if the date of Leviticus is post-exilic. It might, of course, be different if the date of that book were Mosaic, but I can hardly suppose that that is Mr. Farrer's argument. Here I cannot but refer to Dr. C. H. Dodd, on Romans, in the Moffatt N.T. Commentary (Hodder and Stoughton, 1932), pp. 54-56 (on Rom. iii, 25). He shows the true meaning of our Western word "propitiation" in its Greek equivalent (ἱλαστήριον), through its sacrificial setting, and deals also with the use of the word "blood" in Rom. iii, 25, as in Rom. v, 9, using, as I have done, Lev. xvii, 11, and other passages. Thus, he says, "when Paul speaks of the blood of Christ, he is thinking of His life as laid down in self-dedication to God." Thus He was obedient unto death, even the death of the Cross (Phil. ii, 8), and "the language of sacrifice expresses figuratively a reality which is personal and ethical."

I may have overstated Mr. Farrer's criticism of what I have myself written, but, in any case, I am glad that he has given me an opportunity of dissociating myself from any who may use the common interpretation of the blood as the life to minimise the essential place of the Death of our Lord in His Sacrifice.

What I am much more concerned about is Dr. J. K. Mozley's review of this book in the *Journal of Theological Studies* (Vol. xxxiv—1933; pp. 294-304). That is a review of which any author might be proud, and for which I am profoundly thankful. I only wish that I could meet its very helpful criticism by the full answer that it deserves. It is so fair that I wish I could only take blame to myself if, in dealing, almost incidentally, with the Atonement, I have made it appear, in the stress that I have laid upon the after-effects of the Cross, that I regarded the Atoning Death as only important *per accidens*. I have already made plain, I hope, that the whole secret of the Atoning Sacrifice is the surrender of the Life, and that means the Cross. I am bound to say that when Dr. Mozley says that "in the Epistle to the Hebrews alone is there an exposition of the work of Christ as the fulfilment of the old Jewish sacrificial system," everything turns on what he means by "exposition." If he means full and careful exposition only, that may be true, but much of the most valued teaching of St. Paul and of the other New Testament writers is incidental and allusive, and there are many passages which use the category of sacrifice in direct illustration of aspects of our Lord's redeeming work outside the Epistle of the Hebrews—such as those to which I have referred on pp. 233 ff. below.

Let me add that at the Edinburgh Conference on Faith and Order in 1937 I was given the opportunity, in the section to which I was attached, on the Sacraments and the Ministry, to deliver, first by word of mouth and then in a short paper, reproducing, by request, in writing what I had already said, to repeat the substance of the argument set out at length in this book. That paper was ordered by the Conference to be printed, and will appear very shortly, I understand, in its full Report. What struck and touched me most, since my purpose has from the beginning been eirenic, was the sympathetic reception that my statement had from the representatives of various European, British, and American Christian bodies; it has been an encouragement that goes too deep for words to find—not formal approval, for that stage was never reached or asked for—but brotherly understanding and general agreement from Swedish, French Protestant, Presbyterian, Congregationalist, Methodist, as well as Orthodox and other friends.

NUGENT LINCOLN:

August 1938.

CONTENTS

xix

PART I

THE OLD TESTAMENT AND AFTER

CHAPTER I

THE JEWISH SACRIFICIAL SYSTEM IN OUR LORD'S TIME

I. *Introductory*

"SACRIFICE was a language used by all men, but understood by none." So Dr. Glover, somewhat pessimistically, summarises the situation in New Testament times.[1] The following pages are not intended to be either pessimistic or censorious; but I believe it would be at least as true, if not more true, to use the present tense, and to say "Sacrifice is a language used by all men, but understood by none". For the language is still used. We cannot get away from it, if we would. The experiences of recent years have only given it a firmer hold on the hearts of men. Its range goes far outside the circle of purely theological or ecclesiastical ideas. It belongs to everyday language, and as such it is a witness to an undying faith that there is, somewhere and somehow, even if not here or now, a solution to the problem of evil, that death is not the last word, and that waste is not the true value of that which in the right spirit men surrender.

Yet there is perhaps no word more loosely used. It would be interesting to examine the senses given to it in current literature or in everyday speech: such an examination would show clearly enough how singular, though how common, is the assumption that what everyone speaks about everyone must understand.

My purpose, however, is to examine the use of the word sacrifice, and of sacrificial terms and ideas generally, in

---

[1] Glover, *Jesus in the Experience of Men*, p. 63.

3

their bearing upon Christian faith and life at the present day. Here, most certainly, whatever our inclinations—and it is often said that the category of sacrifice has no value for the modern interpretation of Christian thought—it is a subject of which we are bound to take account. Whatever sacrifice means, or has meant, it has given us a large part of the traditional statements of the faith. The problems of the Atonement and of the Eucharist are as central for the Christian world to-day as they have ever been. And both, rightly or wrongly, perhaps in excess, perhaps not, have been constantly interpreted in terms of sacrifice. Do we know what we mean either when we assert or when we deny the sacrificial character either of the Eucharist or of our Lord's atoning work? Or, knowing perhaps what we mean ourselves, can we be sure that in passing judgment on the opinions held by our predecessors or our contemporaries we know equally what they have meant, or that they in turn understood their predecessors?

The following pages are written in the belief that there is no question which more urgently requires examination; that on examination it will be found that the meanings commonly ascribed to sacrificial terms have in fact changed from time to time without any clear or conscious recognition of such change; and that much of the controversy which hampers us to-day, and which has divided Christendom in the past, is due not to ultimate differences of belief but to a misunderstanding of terms.

The terms, or at least some of them, and the sacrificial ideas which they have been intended to express, have come down to us from the New Testament. Our first need, therefore, is to find out what sacrifice meant in the New Testament—to our Lord, and to the writers of the books in which we have the record both of His life and teaching and of that interpretation of it which became the rule and norm of subsequent Christian belief.

Such an attempt is not easy For, in spite of traditional Christian language, large parts of the Christian world do not now think in terms of sacrifice: and in those parts which do so think sacrificial ideas are inevitably coloured, and in a sense limited, by past controversies. The recoil from the idea of sacrifice, in fact, whether in connection with worship or as to the Atonement, is as controversial as the belief in it—controversial not necessarily in a bad sense, but in the far more binding sense of loyalty to the more immediate past. Yet what we have to do is to get back behind such controversy to the New Testament itself. And even then we have difficulties enough. It is not only that the New Testament books are hardly ever systematic attempts to set out doctrine. We shall not expect to find in them formal statements on questions classified and systematised by the thought of later times. But as regards sacrifice we have to reconstruct for ourselves a whole life, a way of thinking, that is totally unlike our own. For religion, whether for better or for worse, was in ancient times, both among the Jews and in other nations, sacrificial in a sense which it is extraordinarily hard for us to recapture. If this is perhaps too large an assumption to make at the outset, it will at any rate be agreed that the ancient world was familiar with what may be called the *technique* of sacrifice in a way which is wholly unknown to us in modern times. What no one understands to-day, everyone was in touch with then. Much therefore will be taken for granted in first century literature which we have to refashion and supply for ourselves. We have to ask what lay behind the New Testament: to recover its background: to see what religion, as a living system, was assumed to be by first-century Jews. And that means that to understand the New Testament we must go back to the whole of the formative influences that made the religious life of the Jewish people what it was in our Lord's day.

We shall see that these influences reach back to very primitive beginnings. We are accustomed, and rightly, to distinguish Semitic, Hebrew, Israelite, and Jewish stages: these are great landmarks which for purposes of classification divide the history; and they are more than mere landmarks: they represent distinct changes or advances in the

whole religious outlook. But behind them all there is a
real continuity. The later religion did not cease to be
Semitic in its fundamental character, because at various
periods in its growth it became more and more distinct
from the other forms of religion which had descended
from the original and common Semitic type. And no
stage in the development is without its significance for
the content of what we find in later times. The past is
always alive. It is also comprehensive. We shall have to
remember that ancient life did not fall, as modern life has
come only too much to do, into stereotyped and easily
distinguishable departments. What we are tracing is at
every point as much a racial or a national, as a religious,
history. Issues that we distinguish as social, political,
or intellectual are all part of the content of a single
whole. Israel while it was a nation was also as such what
we call a Church, and when it had become more of a
Church, in post-exilic times, had still not ceased to be a
nation.

And the life, or the religion, was Semitic, not European.
I shall not anticipate here what we shall have before us
at every turn as we go on; but it can never be unnecessary to insist that the difference between our own ways
of thinking and those of the Old Testament should be
borne in mind. Our temptation is to recreate, or to read
into the language and thought of the Jews at whatever
period of their history, ideas and habits of mind which
were entirely foreign to them. And as there is much in
our points of view which is not to be found in theirs,
so there is much in theirs which is foreign to us. It
is the natural tribute which we pay to great men in
the past to assume that they anticipate us, and that
the problems to which they are addressing themselves
are ours.

I need not say more at this stage by way of caution.
What we have to do is to trace the continuous life as it
comes down from early times to the period of the New
Testament; to recognise it all as fundamentally Jewish;
and to see our Lord, and the New Testament writers, such

as St. Paul and St. John,[1] as what they were, as well as
the great leaders of Old Testament thought and life. We
must not interpret them as speaking or thinking like
modern Catholics, or Protestants, any more than as the
teachers of a modern undogmatic ethic. They were,
happily, none of these things. They were Jews. Their
horizon was that of their own country, and of their own
day. Their native language was Semitic, and their forms
of thought followed on the whole the genius of Semitic
speech, and not that of contemporary Greeks or modern
Europeans. Behind them lay an organised life—and they
knew no other—which was at once a religion and a
national tradition. It rested on the Old Testament, but
on much besides that. In our day we have learnt the
value, for the understanding of the New Testament, of
that large tract of Jewish history of which the Old Testament, except for one or two of its latest books, and a
few parts of the others, gives us no information. Much
had happened in the religious life of the Jewish people
since the close of the period of the prophets, and for this
we have a considerable amount of evidence in the literary
material which survives. But beyond the books to which
our Lord and His contemporaries had access, there was
the religious and social life of the community. We persist
in making His religion, as we do our own, the religion of
books. It is true that it is only from books, for the most
part, that we can reconstruct; but a reconstruction there
must be if we are to see Jesus as He really lived, as boy
and man. We must make Him real to ourselves as a child
of synagogue and temple, as well as of the village home,
and the open-air life of the Galilean hills. For what He
gives us is not only a system of teaching, though He does
give the elements of that; not only a religion, though He
gives that far more truly than a system of teaching; but
above all a life. He taught; He prayed and worshipped;
but above all He was a living Man. There went into His
life, to make Him what He was, as a man of Palestine of

---

[1] I shall not be misunderstood, in the use of St. John's name in this connection, as prejudging the question of the authorship of the Johannine literature.

His own day, all the varied and informal influences and elements which go into the making of any one of us. It is these, as well as our formal teaching, that make Him and us what we are.

To say this is, of course, not to say that there was not that in Him which made Him able, and His followers after Him in their measure, to handle what He and they received with a freedom that in His case was His own and that they received from Him. He had the creative originality, explain it as we may, which made Him not the slave, but the Master, of the life which He inherited. He made it a new thing. But creativeness and originality do not mean, under the conditions of human life—and it was under these conditions that the Son of God did His work —the producing first of a *tabula rasa*, the making of a void in order that it may be filled. However complete the change which He effected, there is no gap. He accepted what He found; He regarded it as the divinely ordered preparation for Himself; He built out of the existing materials. He assumed the history and traditions of His people. It was to His own home that He came, though His own people rejected Him.[1] It was that that He re-created.

What then was the background of His life and teaching, so far as our own immediate subject is concerned? For this purpose we must select. We wish to understand His attitude to, and teaching about, sacrifice, and in such a way as to be able to understand further how His first followers built upon what He gave them, and, further still, how the later Church built upon the teaching and life of New Testament times.

It will perhaps be best to attempt in the first place a sketch however brief of the actual system of the Temple worship in our Lord's day. To do this is not to prejudge its value for good or for evil, or His attitude towards it. When that has been done, it will be possible, by looking back over the history of its growth, to elucidate some of its meaning, either explicit in His day, or only potential.

[1] John i. 11.

I shall endeavour in the next place to estimate its position in the religious life of the Israelite people, both in primitive times and under the covenant relationship with the national God: both as criticised, or opposed, by the prophets and as an accepted method of contact with God.

In addition to this examination of the sacrificial system proper, I propose to suggest some considerations as to certain of the recurring religious conceptions of the Old Testament, the bearing of which on the main subject will, I hope, become clear in the examination of New Testament results.

II. *The developed sacrificial system in the time of our Lord*

I begin, so far as the background of New Testament life is concerned, at the end, and not at the beginning, for two reasons.

(1) For our immediate purpose it is this that matters most. What we have to know is, quite simply, what in fact happened in the sacrifices, and sacrificial ceremonial, to which the Jews of the first century were accustomed. They had not what we understand by the historical sense; they were not interested in origins, and had no methods such as those of the historical and literary criticism, or archaeological or anthropological research, to which we owe so much. When they spoke of sacrifice, or used sacrificial terms, it was of contemporary usage that they were thinking. The investigation of the past history of the sacrifices has its value as illustrating meanings and possibilities which to them may not have been explicit, but which were nevertheless inherent in the acts: for one marked feature of all ancient sacrifice—in fact, as we can see, its supreme danger—was the ease with which correct performance was emphasised at the expense of the apprehension of its inward meaning. But the historical view of the system is necessary for the interpretation of New Testament presuppositions. It was one of our Lord's most

marked characteristics that He was able to go back over the intervening centuries to aspects of Old Testament life which had been obscured or forgotten—to revivify, and reinterpret—and there is *a priori* no reason why we should not be prepared to find Him doing this with the idea of sacrifice, if there were elements in it in its earlier and fresher days that could yet be charged with a new meaning and therefore had a permanent value of their own. And, further, it was in the course of the historical development that views were formed as to the sacrificial system which undoubtedly were taken up and used in the New Testament; if we are rightly to estimate these views and the subsequent use of them, it can only be in relation to the circumstances of the times when they were expressed.

(2) It was said by Dr. Moberly [1] that "it is only possible to reach real definitions retrospectively". He was speaking of the true meaning of sacrifice and priesthood as discoverable in the Old and in the New Testaments respectively. "The Old Testament itself is only really understood retrospectively. Of course, all that is in the Old Testament is relevant. The New Testament will interpret it all. But the Old Testament is not determinative of the meaning of the New. What things mean in the New Testament is their true meaning. It is only from *that* that you can go back and find out how all the Old Testament had been (however blindly) leading up to the different elements of the fullness of the truth." [2]

This is, I think, true, *mutatis mutandis*, of the final form of the Old Testament system as compared with its earlier stages. However some parts of the significance may have been lost, it is in the full development that we can see, made explicit, what was only implicit, and so elementary as to be sometimes difficult to recognise, in the more rudimentary beginnings.

Our authority for the system as finally developed is in the main the priestly document in the Pentateuch. The parts of this relevant to our purpose [3] are Exodus xxv.-

---

[1] Sanday (ed.), *Sacrifice and Priesthood*, p. 6.   [2] *Ib.* p. 74.
[3] Driver, *Introduction to Lit. of O. T.* pp. 37 ff., 42 ff.

xxxi. 18 a, which may be a later addition to the main body of the Pentateuch legislation, and Leviticus i.-xvi., Leviticus xvii.-xxvi. being a separate code, with characteristics of its own which give it the name—Law of Holiness—by which it is generally known, and having more affinity with the corresponding chapters in Ezekiel (xl.-xlviii.) than with the Pentateuch.

What follows does not profess to be a detailed account. I take only certain outstanding features as being immediately relevant to my purpose.

The sacrifices are commonly classified in various ways, according to the material offered (animal and vegetable offerings), the offerers (public and private sacrifices), or the purpose. The third is here the most convenient. The division is a familiar one into three classes: the piacular or atoning sacrifices, the burnt-offering, the peace-offering. In all three there is a common underlying plan, the understanding of which is of the first importance for a grasp of the whole system.

I. The offerer "draws near" with his victim. So technical does this act become that the causative form of the verb "to bring near" is regularly translated "offer" or "present" in R.V., and the substantive "that which is brought near" is *corban*, familiar to us from the New Testament (Mk. vii. 11), which is translated "oblation" in R.V. with only one exception. The act of approach reappears in Hebrews x. 22 ("let us draw near with a true heart in fullness of faith"), and has passed into the English Liturgy in the words of the Invitation: "Draw near with faith."

II. The offerer laid his hands[1]—or leaned or rested them—on the head of the victim. This was formerly interpreted as an act of substitution—by a reading back into the Old Testament sacrifices of "substitution" theories of the Atonement; but such an explanation breaks down if only for the reason, among others, that the victim is still holy. The better explanation is that it symbolised "the solemn and deliberate appropriation

[1] Driver, note in Sanday (ed.), *Priesthood and Sacrifice*, pp. 39 and 40.

of an object coupled with its assignation to a particular purpose"—the transmission "of power to represent another". So Robertson Smith[1] says, "the imposition of hands is not officially interpreted by the Law as a transference of sin to the victim, but rather has the same sense as in acts of blessing or consecration, where the idea no doubt is that the physical contact between the parties serves to identify them, but not specially to transfer guilt from the one to the other". Or[2] "the purpose of the imposition of the offerer's hand . . . was not the transference of guilt from him to the offering . . . it simply represents the *dedication* of the animal to God upon the part of the offerer".

III. The victim is killed by the offerer, the sinner. The only exception to this, viz. on the day of Atonement, proves the rule: for then the High Priest slaughters the victim as himself one of the sinners for whom he is offering it.

In view of modern and popular misconceptions of sacrifice it is necessary to emphasise this rule by inverting it: the one person who does not (with the apparent exception just noted) kill the victim is the priest. The killing is the offerer's—the sinner's—own act.

IV. It is at this point that the specific work of the priest begins. The blood is in all early religions, not Semitic only, regarded as the life, and it is hardly too much to say that for a proper understanding of Hebrew and other sacrifices, the principle laid down in Leviticus xvii. 11 is central: "For the life of the flesh is in the blood: and I have given it to you upon the altar to make atonement for your souls: for it is the blood that maketh atonement by reason of the life".

The uses made of the blood vary in the different classes of offerings. But in substance the principle is the same. It is taken by the priest into the presence of God. This may be done by pouring it round, or dashing it against, the altar: or in more intimate ways: generally speaking the more important, far-reaching, or effective the act of

---

[1] Robertson Smith, *Religion of Semites*, 2nd ed. p. 423 (quoted below as *R. S.*[2]).

[2] Burney, *O. T. Conception of Atonement as fulfilled by Christ*, O.U. Press, 1920, pp. 18, 19 (with the rest of the passage).

atonement desired, the nearer is it taken to the Divine presence, until on the Day of Atonement itself it is taken by the High Priest through the veil into the Holy of Holies and sprinkled upon and before the mercy seat (Lev. xvi. 14).

V. The flesh—or part of the flesh—of the victim (here again the rules vary with the different kinds of sacrifice) is placed upon the altar and burnt with the holy fire. Here there are two points of vital importance—the character and purpose, and the meaning, of the burning. The character is shown by the words used. The Hebrew special term for the burnt-offering is " 'ōlāh"—probably = "that which goes up"; and the word for the burning is the word used for burning incense, קָטַר ḳaṭar (indeed it supplies the word for incense itself קְטֹרֶת ḳeṭoreth), not the word used for burning to destroy (שׂרף saraph). The offering is not destroyed but transformed, sublimated, etherealised, so that it can ascend in smoke to the heaven above, the dwelling-place of God.

The meaning of the burning appears most dramatically in the story of Elijah's sacrifice on Carmel (1 Kings xviii. 38). It is God's acceptance of that which is offered. In accepting, He transforms it into a condition in which it can enter into His life. So the fire of the sanctuary originally "came forth from before the Lord" (Lev. ix. 24), and once on the altar it was to be kept burning continually (Lev. vi. 13).

VI. Lastly, in the sacrifices other than burnt-offerings, in which the whole victim was consumed on the altar, a certain portion was eaten. In the peace-offerings it made the sacrificial meal for the offerers: in the piacular offerings it was reserved, on account of its special holiness, for the priests, except on those occasions when their own sins were atoned for and it was therefore too holy even for them (Lev. v. 13; x. 16-20).

These six actions appear to follow on one another in an orderly and logical sequence. The value and significance of this we shall see later: it will suffice here simply to recapitulate the ideas which underlie the process.

The offerer, then, makes his own approach to the

presence of God: it is his own free act. He identifies himself
with the victim in the pressing on its head of his hands:
what happens thereafter to the animal happens symbolically to himself. He kills the animal: "the soul that
sinneth, it shall die": the death is his own death, accepted
by him as the consequence of sin. The life is now set free:
it is for this that the death was effected: and as set free
it is taken by the priest into the presence of God. The
atonement—at-one-ment—has been made; and the substance of the offering, the flesh, can now be offered, and,
so offered, God accepts it by His fire, and, in accepting,
transforms it. In the common meal on the flesh of the
victim, now that atonement has been effected, the life of
the offerer has been brought before the face of God, and
his offering made and accepted, God and man become at
one, and man finds his fellowship with man.

I have summarised the process in this way for clearness'
sake, although there are various features in the different
acts, besides those emphasised already, which require
further notice.

In the first place, the division between piacular sacrifices and the other two kinds is not an absolute one. There
is a strong piacular element in the burnt-offering, and
apparently some in the peace-offering. This does not affect
the point of the classification, because the piacular element in the second and third kinds of sacrifice is probably
a survival from the earlier period before the need of a
special class of atoning sacrifices was felt. It is an element of the history of Hebrew sacrifice which remained in
the system as fully developed.

Of far more importance are the characteristic features
of the piacular offerings.

The chief of these is their incompleteness. Sins, under
the system of the Jewish law, were distinguished as sins
done with a high hand, and sins of a less serious kind,
such as those of inadvertence. The former had no atonement by sacrifice. They put the sinner outside the
covenant: and the sacrifices were for those still within it.
The latter "comprehended all sins done not in a spirit of

rebellion against the law or ordinance of Jehovah, sins committed through human imperfection, or human ignorance, or human passion; sins done when the mind was directed to some end connected with human weakness or selfishness, but not formally opposed to the authority of the Lawgiver".[1]

However the distinction may be defined, it is in its main lines clear and fundamental. In the one case—that of sins which placed the sinner outside the covenant—the primary idea is that of God as righteous. It is these sins with which for the most part the prophets were concerned; and the view that was held of them was that they brought out the character of the righteous God in the two opposite aspects of anger and of mercy. His primary quality is mercy: but sin, unrepented and deliberate, must draw upon itself His anger. That anger means punishment (Is. xl. 2: "she hath received of the Lord's hand double for all her sins"). But punishment is followed—may be followed—by mercy. It may be because God's own honour, as the God of Israel, is involved. He will forgive "for His name's sake". Or some member of the sinful people identifies himself with the mind of God; acts for Him, as Phinehas did when the Israelite sinned with the Midianitish woman (Num. xxv. 10-13: "Phinehas ... hath turned my wrath away from the children of Israel, in that he was jealous with my jealousy among them, so that I consumed [them] not in my jealousy"): or intercedes for the people, as Moses after the sin of the golden calf (Ex. xxxii. 31 f.). Or it may be done simply out of God's inherent mercifulness (Ps. lxxviii. 38: "But he, being full of compassion, forgave their iniquity, and destroyed them not: yea, many a time turned he his anger away, and stirred not up all his wrath"). This forgiveness—however caused—is called by the same word as the ceremonial forgiveness, or atonement. To atone is *kipper*, to cover.[2]

---

[1] A. B. Davidson, *Theology of the Old Testament*, p. 315.

[2] See Brown, Driver, and Briggs, *Heb. Lexicon, s.v.* כפר; and G. B. Gray, *Sacrifice in O. T.* pp. 67 ff. The different interpretations of the original meaning of "*kipper*" hardly affect the distinction between "forgiving" sins and "forgiving" the sinner.

In this case it is God who covers: and what is covered is
the sin (Ps. lxxviii. 38: "but he, being full of compassion,
forgave their iniquity", quoted above, is in the original
"atoned", *i.e.* "covered their iniquity", so Ps. lxxix. 9):
or perhaps the idea of covering the sin may pass into
that of God's face being covered so that He does not see it
(Ps. li. 9: "Hide thy face from my sins").

On the other hand, the dominant conception of God
in the Law is that of His holiness. And the Law, as illustrated by the legal passage in Ezekiel (chs. xl.-xlviii.)
assumes something of an ideal condition for the people.
They are, *ex hypothesi*, within the covenant. The last
eight chapters of Ezekiel describe the life of the restored
community. God is present with His people in the Temple.
And holiness in this sense, as the dominant attribute of
God, embraces, as Dr. A. B. Davidson says,[1] besides the
moral attributes such as righteousness and power and
majesty, something that may be called an aesthetic
quality. There is the feeling in Him that there is in men,
of shrinking from what is out of place, repulsive, or unclean. Hence sin is viewed as uncleanness: and in the
legal atonement, for which the same word is used as in
the judicial, or extra-ritual, it is the sinner who is
covered, not the sin. The difference may seem strange:
but the meaning appears to be that before the eye of the
King or Judge the sin is something done by the sinner—
external, in a sense, to himself: before the eye of the Holy
One, the sinner personally is unclean. Thus, quite unexpectedly, the apparently trivial, superficial, group of
ideas which at first seem to characterise the imperfect
atonements of the Law, as against the full and gracious
atonement by the mercy of God, come to penetrate to a
deeper and more permanent conception of sin, while the
other conceptions pave the way for the conception of
sins as concrete external acts: and we almost arrive at the
paradox that after all in this respect the prophetic view
prepared the way for the later conception of law, and the
sacrificial principles for the later conception of grace.

[1] *Op. cit.* pp. 347 ff.

But in practice the Old Testament leaves us with an unsolved enigma: on the one hand, the demands of God's righteousness in their fullness, without, except for such cases as those of Moses and of Phinehas, clear indications of a method by which His anger might be turned into mercy; and, on the other hand, a definite conception of the atoning power of the life laid down, but of such power as strictly limited in its operation. The two conceptions appear to meet in Isaiah liii. There the most complete picture of atonement for sin is described in the language of the piacular offerings. It was reserved for the New Testament in this as in other respects to find the full value and meaning of this chapter as interpreting and combining the separate lines of Old Testament history and teaching.

In any case the use of the word *kipper* for both kinds of atonement may at least be an indication that there was a feeling, of which, except in Isaiah liii. and perhaps also in Psalm li. (see below, pp. 85 f.), no explanation could be given, that there could ultimately be only one method for the forgiveness of sins. The God of the Law is after all the God of the prophets, and in the bitter experience of the decline and fall of the Jewish monarchy, and of the captivity in Babylon, there emerged, as the fundamental conviction of prophet and priest alike, the fact of human sin, and the fact of God's desire that it should be atoned for.

I have dwelt at some length upon the incompleteness of the atoning sacrifices, because in the light of subsequent developments we are always confronted with a double fact. There is, on the one hand, already in the Old Testament a singularly complete method of access to God. The six actions of the sacrifices show this; but, on the other hand, it is always easy to overestimate the spiritual value of it. The whole point of the Christian attitude to the Law must always be that, though it was our schoolmaster to bring us to Christ, it stood condemned to fail, and to fail utterly. The blood of bulls and goats cannot take away sin.

Of the distinction between the sin and the guilt, or trespass, offering it is not necessary to say much. Broadly speaking, it was that the former, the sin-offering, was for offences for which no concrete reparation could be made; and the latter for cases which admitted of such reparation. It is perhaps worth noticing, as either suggesting that the difference between the two was not regarded as considerable, or indicating that the Priestly Law was still only in course of its development, that the lamb in Isaiah liii. is regarded not as a sin- but as a guilt-offering, and that in Leviticus iv.-vi., where the law of the two offerings is laid down, the lamb is assigned to the sin-offering (of individual members of the people) and the victim in the guilt-offering is a ram.

The fundamental feature in the sin- and guilt-offerings is undoubtedly the use of the blood. It is not the death that atones, but the life (Lev. xvii. 11 above). The death is vital to the sacrifice, because it sets free the blood, which is the life. But the victim is, in a true sense, operative, not as dead, but as alive "as it had been slain": not as νεκρόν but ὡς ἐσφαγμένον.

Once more, in this connection, we meet the limitations of the system. An element of the communion meal remained in the sin-offering and still more in the peace-offering. But it was severely restricted. In all sacrifices the blood—the life itself of the divine food—was wholly forbidden to the Israelites. Here and there, as when on some occasions the priest dipped his finger in the blood or in the putting of the blood on the door-posts at the Passover, there is perhaps an unacknowledged survival of the unrestricted personal appropriation of the blood of primitive times. But the eating of the flesh alone made that stage of the sacrifice, as communion, almost wholly inoperative.[1] And, in the sin-offerings, even this was restricted, as stated above.

The reason for this is significant. The flesh of the sin-offering is holy. What was eaten by the priests was to be eaten "in the place of the sanctuary, seeing it is most holy"

---

[1] But see below, pp. 36 f., 93-96.

(Lev. x. 17). The part which was not eaten, or burnt, was to be carried without the camp, and burnt there, but the bearer was to wash his clothes and his person—under the rule for contact with what was holy (Lev. xvi. 27 f.). It is this principle which makes it clear that the victim does not become sinful by the imposition of the offerer's hands. On the Day of Atonement two goats are used. One is taken by lot as the sin-offering, and, as we have seen, is holy. It is the other over which the High Priest confesses the sins of the people ; and this is the scapegoat which is sent to Azazel in the wilderness, to carry the sins away (Lev. xvi. 21, 22).

Just as in the sin-offering the characteristic feature is not the death of the victim but the liberation of its life, so in the burnt-offering the significance lies not in its destruction but in its transformation. It is difficult to over-estimate the harm that has been done to the ordinary ideas about sacrifice by the use in the translations of the Hebrew text for this offering of the words ὁλοκαύτωμα, holocaust,[1] "burnt-offering". These familiar words, inter-preted inevitably by the overwhelming later association of burning with the purpose of destruction, suggest exactly the wrong conception of the 'ōlāh. Provided, however, that the character of the burning is understood, "burnt-offering", and, still more, the comparatively rare term kālīl (Dt. xxxiii. 10; Ps. li. 19) translated "whole burnt-offering", do suggest another important feature, viz. that the whole of the flesh was in this case consumed on the altar. There was nothing left over for a sacrificial meal. The significance of this emerges in the study of the historical development of the various sacrifices (see below, pp. 40 f.).

The significance of the peace-offering lies in the fact that it is a meal. Its various forms were the votive offer-ing, the free-will offering and the thank-offering, into the distinctions between which for our immediate purpose it

---

[1] The English translation has given to the ordinary mind exactly the wrong emphasis on these words: it should be on the first half, and is generally put on the second: *whole* burnt-offering, not whole *burnt*-offering.

is not necessary to go. There can be little doubt that as it
is the oldest of the Hebrew sacrifices, so it carried with it,
at least in its history, the tradition of an original purpose
of communion with the deity. How far, if at all, the idea
of communion remained explicit in the later period will
be considered later.[1] What does remain is the fact that
it is inseparably bound up with the idea of praise (LXX
περὶ αἰνέσεως) and thanksgiving. In fact, in Philo and in
Aquila the word εὐχαριστία (eucharist) is frequently used
to describe it.[2] Whatever it had lost, it preserved and
emphasised the old spirit of joyfulness in the worship of
God in contrast to the more sombre feelings of penitence
and guilt which belonged to the piacular sacrifices, and
the thought of fear, of securing the Divine favour, and of
self-surrender, in the burnt-offering.

I have not attempted to give separate descriptions of
each of the three kinds of sacrifice. Apart from the special
characteristics of each, of which something has been said,
the primary feature is the general plan on which the whole
system is framed. This appears in all three kinds—the
drawing near (of the offerer), or bringing near (of the
victim), the imposition of hands, the killing, the dealing
with the blood, the burning, the meal; except for the
variations, already noticed. Of these the only one of importance in this respect is the limitation of the last stage:
it does not occur at all in the burnt-offering, and it is
severely limited, and on certain occasions, as has been
said, does not occur, in the sin-offering. But such omissions meant less in practice than appears when they are
merely tabulated, as must be done in modern studies of
them, for classification and for description. In the living
system—and it is always that which we must have, in
imagination, before our eyes—the sacrifices were, as a
rule, not offered separately after the later developments
had been reached. Before the exile, burnt-offerings and
peace-offerings were generally offered together (*e.g.* 1
Sam. x. 8); and when the system was complete the three

---

[1] Pp. 93-96.
[2] MS. note by Dr. Hort, printed in *J. T. S.* vol. iii. pp. 594 f.

are found together (Ex. xxix. 14, 18, 28; Lev. viii. 14-17,
18-21, 22-32, etc.). There was always a burnt-offering with
the sin-offering, and the two, or the three, always followed in the same order—first the atonement, then the
offering, then the meal. Thus the complete action of
sacrifice is constant.

Of the non-animal sacrifices the chief was the offering
of cereals (R.V. meal-offering), to which the general term
minḥāh, meaning a present, or gift, came to be appropri-
ated. It is therefore an act of tribute. It consisted as a
rule of fine flour, mixed with oil, and frankincense, and
salt. A portion of this was known as the memorial
(*'azkārāh*), and was burnt upon the altar—the intention
being to bring the offerer to God's remembrance (cf. Is.
lxii. 6; and for the *minḥāh*, see Lev. ii. 1-16). What was
not burnt was eaten by the priests as something "most
holy". No leaven was to be used in the meal-offering—
leaven and honey both being excluded on the ground
that the fermentation already in the leaven and the fermentation to which honey was liable signified death—
again a mark of the intense feeling of life as contrasted
with death running through the sacrifices. So also the salt
used in the *minḥāh* and in the other offerings was the
symbol of life and permanence.

There should be mentioned also, though only for completeness' sake, the drink-offering which was poured out
at the burnt- and peace-offerings; but in the Hebrew
system it played only a small part as compared with its
frequency elsewhere.

The purpose of the non-animal offerings taken together
seems to have been that of providing in the sacrifice a
meal for the god which must therefore be furnished as
the offerer's own meals would be. This conception survives in the Hebrew system in the expression "the bread
of God" (Lev. iii. 11; xxi. 6, 8, 17, 21; xxii. 25). So also the
altar is the table of the Lord in Malachi i. 7, 12; and con-
versely the table of the shewbread—another form of the
cereal offering—appears to be called the altar in Ezekiel
xli. 22.

The whole course of the sacrifices was regarded as belonging to the covenant system. We have seen that the latest form of them—the atoning sacrifices—presupposed the covenant; and each kind in its different way was a method of restoring, acknowledging, or renewing and enjoying the covenant relationship. Sacrifice was, in fact, to the Jewish mind an essential feature of a covenant. To the modern mind a bond or agreement seems to have no imaginable connection with sacrifice; but if the ancient system is to be understood, it must be realised that when a Jew thought of a covenant he thought of a sacrifice. This seems to be implied by the Hebrew word for making a covenant, which is *kārath*, to cut. How a covenant was "cut" appears in detail in the story of God's covenant with Abraham in the midst of the divided animals in Genesis xv. 9-21. The same action is referred to in Jeremiah xxxiv. 18 f.: " ... the men that have transgressed my covenant, which have not performed the words of the covenant which they made before me, when they cut the calf in twain and passed between the parts thereof; the princes of Judah, and the princes of Jerusalem, the eunuchs, and the priests, and all the people of the land, which passed between the parts of the calf". Here, in fact, the description is fuller than in Genesis, where nothing is actually said of Abraham's passing between the severed parts. Jeremiah's emphatic repetition of the passing between the parts shows that it was part of the process of confirming the covenant; and there can be no doubt that the same thing was understood to have occurred in Abraham's case. The point is a small one; but it is worth a passing notice, because it illustrates vividly the way in which the isolated mentions of sacrifice and sacrificial acts in the general literature of the Old Testament (as contrasted with the detailed instructions in the actual code, though even these are incomplete and often allusive) rest upon the assumption that the whole of the methods are commonly understood. The writers are writing for, or speaking to, people to whom the sacrificial system was a living reality. For what is mutually under-

stood, and familiar to all from their childhood, a reference is all that is necessary. We can never press omissions; if it had not happened that Jeremiah had spoken
in this way in this passage no one would have suggested,
on the evidence afforded by the Old Testament, that the
passing between the parts was an essential element in the
proceeding. Or, if it had been suggested, the story of
Abraham's covenant would have been quoted as evidence
to the contrary.

I have stressed this point, because it bears upon a
further feature of the sacrificial making of a covenant
which has been minimised by some authors, among whom
is Dr. A. B. Davidson in his article on "Covenant" in
Hastings' *D. B.* vol. i. It would appear from various instances that the culmination of a covenant sacrifice was
the sacrificial meal. Two cases of this occur in Genesis. In
chapter xxvi. 26 ff. Isaac makes a covenant with Abime-
lech. They agree upon the terms—"and he (Isaac) made
them a feast, and they did eat and drink. And they rose
up betimes in the morning, and sware one to another. . . ."
Here Dr. Davidson says that the feast was no part of the
covenant ceremonies because it preceded the oath: but
in the early days it appears to be clear that meat was only
eaten at sacrificial meals; and in any case, in view of the
regular practice, for which there is good evidence, it
seems hardly possible to press the detail of the story as
regards the order of events.

The other case is the covenant between Jacob and
Laban in Genesis xxxi. 44 ff. Here the order of the pro-
ceedings is clear. Laban and Jacob both swear; "and
Jacob offered a sacrifice in the mountain, and called his
his brethren to eat bread: and they did eat bread, and
tarried all night in the mountain. And early in the morning Laban rose up, and kissed his sons and his daughters,
and blessed them: and Laban departed, and returned
unto his place." Here Dr. Davidson says that the meal
was not a covenant meal, because Jacob only gave it to
his own brethren. It is, of course, a question of interpretation; but it is safer to assume, if the details of the story

are to be pressed at all, that Jacob negotiated with Laban personally and summoned his companions and dependents for the ratification; after which, not before, the two parties separated. (So Dr. R. W. Moss in Hastings' *D. B.* 1909: art. "Covenant".)

But the classical case of a covenant, with express information about its ratification, is that of the covenant at Sinai. Here (Ex. xxiv. 1-11) the account is precise. The blood is sprinkled—the regular technical term for the use of the blood in sacrifice—spirted—upon the altar and upon the people. Moses offers burnt-offerings and peace-offerings: "and they beheld God, and did eat and drink".

The Passover, again, in some of its features a sacrifice of a primitive type,[1] is essentially a sacrificial meal. And its primary purpose is to commemorate the deliverance from Egypt, the beginning in history of the covenant relationship between God and His people.

One further point should be mentioned. In all the sacrifices there is one constant element. The animals to be offered were limited to the domestic [2]—those which shared man's life, and into the tending of which he put his work. Similarly there were no wild products of the earth in the non-animal offerings. Here again they must be something into which man's own life had passed—to the form, at least, of which he had contributed by his labour. There is, therefore, in every offering an ethical element. So David says to Araunah (2 Sam. xxiv. 24): "neither will I offer burnt-offerings unto the Lord my God which cost me nothing". Cost is the essential of sacrifice; and with all the failures of the Old Testament system, alike by historical precedent and by sacrificial rule, there was a sense in which man, in offering, offered himself.[3]

---

[1] *R. S.*[2] p. 344 f.
[2] The Babylonian, on the other hand, offered wild animals.
[3] It is in this chapter, from p. 11 onwards, that my obligations to Mr. Gayford's book, *The Christian Sacrifice*, to which I have referred in the Preface, have been closer than elsewhere.

CHAPTER II

In speaking of the sacrificial meal I have more than once used the word communion. It is a convenient term, because "feast" to us has no sacrificial significance whatever; but in fact the question must be faced whether the Jewish peace-offering really conveyed the idea of communion at all. It is doubtful whether any finally satisfactory answer will ever be found; for it is mainly to prehistoric times we have to look for the materials for it.

In any case the study of Jewish sacrifice gains by being taken historically. I have hitherto only attempted to sketch some of the features of the whole system as it was in its final form, and references to earlier stages in the history were incidental. I propose now to examine some of the more significant facts which seem to emerge from the system as seen in its growth.

"The origin and rationale of sacrifice are nowhere fully explained" in the Old Testament.[1] Like other fundamental beliefs and institutions, it is taken for granted. But the beginning illustrates the end, just as the end often reveals the beginning. There may survive in a later system traces of what was originally there, or atrophied parts, which seem to have lost the capacity of being used again, until some new force revivifies and reinterprets the whole. Further, it is not always to be expected that with primitive forms, and with survivals from them, we should find conscious expressions of their meaning. Robertson

---

[1] *R. S.*[2] p. 3.

25

Smith pointed out [1] that here, as so often is the case, we tend to apply our own ideas, or to expect to find them applied, to circumstances entirely different from those of the age in which we live. We think more of the inward meaning than of the outward act: ceremonial only has value to us as interpreted. We go further, "religious duties being presented to the learner as flowing from the dogmatic truths he is taught to accept". That is no doubt true enough of the modern attitude; I should add only too true. We do, in fact, tend to damage our own religion by assuming as its foundation principle the intellectual acceptance of a given intellectual position: quite unconsciously in most cases, no doubt, but none the less truly, we try to erect a religion on the basis of a philosophy. And we are surprised that the religion, in its devotional expression or as a motive force for character, is all the time cold and lifeless in itself, and has lost the power of stimulating. It is not infectious. And with this disqualification unrecognised, and indeed misread as an actual advantage, we try to form opinions about earlier and less advanced religions. The truth often is that where we assume the power to criticise we ought really to be learners. Ancient religions were crude, barbarous; from our standpoint, immoral or non-moral; based at the best on a perilous admixture of the false with the true: but they were religions, and ours may have gained all the advantages which they had not but have lost itself.

We need to remind ourselves, therefore, both of the inevitable difference of standpoint and of our own disadvantages before we can estimate the meaning of ancient religious institutions; and, in the first place, as I have suggested, it is not always right to expect to find meanings for actions such as we instinctively expect. For religion—whatever its form—is a life: a way of living. It rests, not upon abstract definitions, but upon a felt contact between man and God. No one would estimate the goodness of a child by the things which he says about his parents—nor even by the things which he says to them: we observe

[1] *Op. cit.* p. 16.

what he does, and the feelings and dispositions which he shows. So in religion, whether primitive or developed, what matters is what a man is; and what he does shows what he is and what he feels. The earlier we go in human history, the less self-conscious the stage of human development that we are studying, the less shall we expect to find men expressing, or able to express, or even thinking of expressing, the meaning of their acts. And a large part of the value of the study of primitive religion lies just in this, that in the old age, or disillusioned middle life, of human history we can put ourselves to school with its childhood. Because we shall find there crudities and ineptitudes it does not follow that we shall not also find something that we may well recapture for ourselves. The grown-up man has his lessons to learn from the nursery. "Except ye turn, and become as little children, ye shall in no wise enter into the kingdom of heaven."

Such considerations as these apply to most of the ancient observances; but there are others that have an especial bearing on the question of the value of survivals such as that of the sacrificial meal. At every point, on a question of survival, we have to bear in mind the contrast between East and West, and between the conditions of ancient and of modern life. To the duration of traditions and observances such contrasts make all the difference. The habits of modern life destroy memory: not only its hurry, its multiplicity of experiences, its loss of the vacant spaces for quiet thinking, but the instinct for written memoranda in private affairs, and for the making of careful records in public life, all tend to destroy our belief in tradition. No one can fail to recognise this who observes the difference even in our own day between the life of towns and the life of the more or less untouched parts of the country: there tradition still lives, and with an accuracy at which, when it can be unexpectedly tested, we are innocently surprised. And in the East memory and tradition hold a place which no child of a European civilisation of yesterday can easily picture for himself. We cannot measure the survival force of Eastern customs

and institutions by our Western standards. Our tendency
in the West is easily to think that things must be too old
to be true. There, in the East, nothing seems too old to be
true. Which of these, after all, is the greater or the more
damaging superstition?

Yet again, the fundamental difference between ancient
life—both in the East and elsewhere—and modern lies in
the singleness of the former; and this from several points
of view. Ancient society was a single unit. The individual
as such neither was realised, nor realised himself. Thus
memory, habits, beliefs, feelings are racial. We must
measure time, in prehistoric and even in historic periods,
in units far larger than the single generation of which we
naturally think. The span of life is that of the race, of the
community, not of the individual member of it. And,
further, the life lived is undifferentiated. We shall not
find citizenship and religion in water-tight compartments.
They were one. There is no distinction between State and
Church. Every community is a whole, and acts as a whole
for all purposes. Nor is there a division between this world
and the next. So far as the unseen is realised it is as part
of the life lived on earth; no other is known: and we cannot
say that an act, or a custom, is not religious because it
does not carry beyond what we should regard as an
exclusively material sphere.

It is to conditions such as these that we pass when we
study the beginnings of Hebrew religion. We are in a
field of inquiry where at every turn our own presuppositions, even if we shrink from calling them prejudices, dis-
qualify us from forming a fair judgment. And, in spite of
the mass of material which the modern study of primitive
cults has given us, we are in a region where, with every
precaution against our own disqualifications, inferences
are precarious.

It does appear, however, to be established beyond doubt
that in the first place early Semitic religion bears very
strong resemblances to other religious phenomena now
recovered from the life of early man in all parts of the
world, and in the second place that Hebrew religion has

the strongest affinities with the religions of the kindred peoples of the Semitic stock. And if we wish to arrive at the meaning, to catch the inner spirit, of the later Jewish religion, there are reasons, not always apparent to the modern Christian, why these affinities should be carefully, and indeed sympathetically, examined.

There is no modern believer in God, whether Christian or non-Christian, who is not a monotheist. We take it for granted that in this respect at least we are all on common ground. But even within the circle of definite Christianity and still more, so far as European thought is concerned, outside it, this belief in one only God is actually derivable from two quite different sources. The ancient world was polytheistic. Either a body of gods, a pantheon, was accepted, as in Greece and Egypt, or, as among the Western Semites, each race or nation worshipped its own god as one among the many individual gods of its own and neighbouring nations. We call this monolatry, and it is a matter in these days of common knowledge that the Israelites until the time of the eighth-century prophets were monolaters and not monotheists.[1] It was at first from the teaching of the prophets, and later, and effectively, through the discipline of the Babylonian exile, that the Jews came to believe that Yahweh, the God of Israel, was the only God of the whole world. But monolatry is after all only one form of polytheism, and the pantheon another. In Greece and in Israel alike polytheism broke down and disappeared. But the change was effected in totally different ways.[2] In Greece monotheism was philosophical in origin; in Israel ethical. Or, in other words, the Greeks arrived, by reflection on the order of nature, at the conviction that the gods as formerly believed in were not the key to the problems of life. And, in this conviction, the gods, though their cultus remained, even with the philosophers, as a matter of civic order and inherited tradition, were doomed to disappear. The One God was not their gift, but man's discovery. Thus,

---

[1] Or at least the *people* were: great leaders such as Moses or Elijah may have been monotheists.   [2] Hamilton, *People of God*, vol. i. chap. iii.

for whatever the ancient gods were still worth, the traditional religions of all nations came to have just the same degree of sanction: they were all equally true, or equally false, and essentially on the same level. The One God was proved discoverable by processes of reasoning, and, wherever these originated or were followed, was therefore equally within the reach of all men.

On the other hand the Hebrew prophet was only carrying out the inherited tradition of his race—inherited at the least from the days of the Mosaic Covenant, if not from earlier times still—in regarding the religion of Yahweh as something given, not discovered. I shall have something to say later, in another connection, as to the full force of the idea of Revelation as attaching to the nature and character of the God of Israel; but it will suffice to say here that the whole way along the line of Hebrew development the idea of God is something with a continuous historical past behind it. At whatever point, and in whatever way, the religion of Israel became fundamentally different—as it did—from that of the kindred Semitic peoples, there was no breach with the past. El, or Elohim—God as known to Hebrews and other Semites alike—became known, at some stage, it may be, and perhaps to the patriarchs, as El Shaddai. It was the same God, only more fully known as the God of power—God Almighty. At another stage—that of the covenant—the same God makes Himself known as entering into a special relation to Israel which is described in Hebrew fashion by a new name, Yahweh. Yahweh *is* simply "Elohim saying to Israel אהיה" (I am, *i.e.* I will be, or I will become); "And Elohim saying אהיה is Elohim of Israel".[1] The next, and the most vital, transition in Hebrew history is the move from the belief in Yahweh as the God of Israel only to the belief that He is the God of the whole world. But he remains Yahweh. He is still the God of Israel, the God of Abraham, of Isaac, and of Jacob, the God who redeemed them from bondage, and gave them the Covenant and its Law. He will, indeed, now "reveal Himself to all

[1] A. B. Davidson, *Theology of O. T.* p. 58.

mankind, but it is only as God of Israel that He is known, and it is only therefore through Israel that He can reveal Himself to them". "Hence when He finally redeems Israel, His glory appears to all flesh."[1]

These two conceptions of monotheism are fundamentally different. Each illustrates, and derives help from, the other. No one would wish to deny the debt which Christian theology owes to Greek philosophical ways of thinking. But where they should only have illustrated, criticised, and confirmed, they have been allowed in some measure to transform. On the surface, as I have said, the modern world is in agreement that if there is a God, He must be one. It does not seem to matter how the conviction is arrived at, provided it is there. But the study of origins makes it clear that the origin does affect the character of the belief. Where the mental affinity is with the philosophical monotheism of the Greeks, discovered, not revealed, the interest in and the study of ancient religions has the spirit of the philosopher's attitude to the old polytheisms which they undermined. They all mean something, and they all have some value—some more and some less—for the moral and social effects which they had in their day upon the course of human development. They have their place—and a vitally important place, it may be—in the history of morals, of sociology, of organised human life, but not in the history of the convictions by which we live. From this point of view the primitive Hebrew religion is only one among many. It has no vital message, no living force, to-day. The part of it which survives is the part in which it seems to coincide with, or to overlap, the intellectual conviction of the unity of God. The rest is only of interest to the scientific student, and is part of the outworn fabric which the enlightened world has discarded.

But the Christian religion did, in fact, emerge from the Jewish. It claims to be, in its essence, the true development, the further revelation, of the faith and the God of the Hebrews. It is their conception of monotheism upon

[1] *Op. cit.* p. 38.

which it rests. And from this point of view the study of
primitive religion is a totally different thing. It is still
religion: it is vitally linked up with the whole of our experience. Whatever the Israelites did at any stage of
their historical development, whatever the prehistoric
Hebrews practised, is all part of our inheritance. And
what was akin to their religion is akin to ours. Experiences shared by them with the other Semites; instincts,
and feelings after God, which were common to the
Semites with other races of the primitive world, belong to
us as they did to them. So also, as we know, does each
differentiation as it comes—whatever it was that gave
the Semitic type of religion its superiority over others,
whatever it was in turn which made the early Hebrew
religion different from the Semitic, each fresh revelation
which enabled Israelite leaders to transform or to throw
off parts of their inheritance. We have inherited both the
continuities and the revolutions: both elements are ours.
For these men never, at any stage, left the God of their
fathers; they took what they found, and in their hands
it was "transfigured and endowed with a higher significance".[1]

I have dwelt at length on these preliminary considerations, because it is more on our attitude to the evidence,
than on its bulk, that our impressions of it must be
formed. There has been much dispute as to the earliest
form of sacrifice practised by the Hebrews. There is no
doubt that in the historical stage they had already
arrived at the burnt-offering. The great covenant-sacri-
fice in Exodus already alluded to consisted of burnt-
offering and peace-offering. The record, whatever it is
worth as actual history, of Abraham's sacrifice of Isaac,
and whatever its precise significance, places at that time
what looks like the classical example for later practice
of the truth that the God of Israel does not desire human
sacrifice. But if Robertson Smith is at all right in his
account of the origin of the "fire-sacrifice" of which the
later burnt-offering is the familiar presentment, that

---

[1] Hamilton, *op. cit.* Intro. p. xxxvi.

story marks a transition from its earliest form; so that the Hebrew records do at least take us back to its first stages, whereas the sacrificial meal simply appears throughout as an understood and accepted institution. However this may be, the point remains that the Old Testament records leave us, apart from this case, almost without guidance as to the question of historical priority between the two types. They leave the door open, or almost open, for the theory that sacrifice originated as a gift, and the theory that it originated in the sacrificial meal.

For further guidance we must go behind these records. It is here that we pass into the questions of primitive practice. We begin with the known fact that in practically every quarter of the globe religion as it emerges as such in a recognisable form is bound up with sacrificial practice. And this practice has one marked feature. For whatever reason, it centres upon a solemn act of eating and drinking. Sir James Frazer has collected from all directions material which supplies evidence of this, whether in the death of the corn-spirit or in the periodical slaying of the king; and in one form or other the eating and drinking, whether of flesh and blood, bread and kindred substances and wine, or of other things, seems to have been regarded as an act of communion with the god. Problems of totemism and magic lie behind these acts, but of the acts themselves, both before the dawn of history and in historical times, there is no doubt. Robertson Smith took the view that to some extent totemism, as being almost world-wide, must have prevailed, and that there is evidence that it did prevail, among the primitive Semites. But, unless his use of Arab practices as evidence for early Semitic habits is misleading, there seems little doubt of his main contention, that the sacrificial meal, whatever the explanation of it, was the earliest Semitic, as it is the most universal, form of sacrifice.[1]

[1] For a recent discussion on the difficult question as to whether sacrifice originated in a gift to God or in the idea of communion with God, see G. B. Gray, *Sacrifice in the Old Testament*, chapters i.-iii., especially p. 54. What is essential for our purpose is the principle that the blood was the life and that there was a

D

In all probability the key to the development of sacrifice is the development of society. The primitive Semitic unit according to Robertson Smith is the kin unit of the clan—originally reckoning its descent from the mother and later from the father, just as in some cases the Semitic deities appear to change from the female sex to the male. The bond of unity was the blood which made them of one flesh. And within this unit there were included, certainly the god of the clan, and probably its domestic animals. The evidence for the latter is of various kinds: there are creation legends which represent the creating god as making both men and animals out of a mixture of clay with his own blood: there is the undoubted sacredness of the animals, and their ownership, not by private individuals but by the clan as a whole. With this went the limitations on their killing. The clan-blood might only be shed by the clan (thus the Hebrew method of execution, when an offender had to be separated from the community, was by stoning, every member taking his part in the act): and the animals were only killed by a corporate act to which the god was made a party. Thus sacrifices are, in the first place, acts of fellowship between the god and members of the clan; and—later—are used for covenants, to create a blood brotherhood with individuals to be admitted into the clan or with other clans, though this second covenant use may only belong to the time when the original clan-unit system was breaking down. In every case the blood is life released in order to be communicated. This connection of blood with life appears in the case of water: for in a largely waterless country perennial springs and streams were parts of the divine manifestation due to divine agency, and the life-giving character of the water was ascribed in many cases to the blood of the god having mingled with it. Thus the familiar idea of "living water"

kinship, if only at first what we should now call "physical", between the god and his worshippers. The main question in dispute seems, however, to be as regards the ultimate origin of sacrifice: not as to the fact that at some prehistoric stage —in the beginnings of Hebrew religion before the later development of the burnt-offering—there was a meal with "sacramental" significance. See E. O. James, *Sacrifice and Sacrament*, Mowbrays, 1927, pp. 1-7.

in the Bible has a subconscious connection from the first
with the idea of the community life, both divine and
human, as blood: it is part of the circle of ideas out of
which, from its ultimate beginnings, the later religion
grew, with its characteristic principle of the communication of a single life to the whole community.

It is in this primitive stage that the idea of Divine
fatherhood takes its rise. The god is father of the clan, but
in a physical sense which was later transmuted into a
spiritual. The fatherhood rested obviously on the idea of
the blood bond of the common life: and the same idea was
expressed in the figure of the branches of a tree springing
from the single root—again, a conception which, used by
all Semites and common in the Arabian poets, was to find
its development in later days both in the Old Testament
and in the New.

So also the idea of the sharing of a common life appears
in the Arab phrase "our blood has been spilt"[1] meaning
the blood of an individual: and the Hebrew "I am your
bone and your flesh" means the same thing, "flesh" being
used for "clan" or kindred group: once more a phrase, or
an idea, to be watched in view of later language.

The question may be asked, and should be asked, as
to the essential point of significance in the sacrifice. It
appears always to be the use of the blood. Robertson
Smith shows cases of the primitive idea of atonement by
individuals as opposed to the clan which illustrate this:
here there was no slaughter, because slaughter as such, as
we have seen, was a corporate act: but the "individual
seeks to establish a physical link of union between himself
and the deity . . . either by the use of his own blood in a
rite analogous to the blood covenant between private
individuals, or by other acts involving an identical
principle"[2] such as the offering of hair or clothing. So in
the public act of sacrifice the central point is not the
slaughter but the application of the blood, and the sharing
in the life.

The act of communion is at first complete: the blood is

[1] *R. S.*[2] p. 174.   [2] *Ibid.* p. 320.

drunk and the flesh eaten: and part of the blood is shed
upon the stone or altar as the god's share. The progressive
modification of the act of communion can be traced among
the Hebrews from prehistoric times down to the Deuteronomic age, and even later. The flesh was at first eaten raw
while still "living": later it was cooked, but always within
a specified time, which is prescribed in the Levitical code.
The eating of it cooked was in itself a move away from the
directness of the original communion: it was inevitable as
life became less barbarous, but it helped in the growth of
the idea of an ordinary feast at the expense of that of
communion. Further, in very early times—before the
history, in the proper sense, of Hebrew sacrifice begins—
the blood was no longer drunk—it was too holy: just as
in the later fire-sacrifices the entrails, which were regarded
as especially the seat of life in the body, were always burnt
upon the altar and not eaten. It may be well here to
anticipate so far as to trace the further shrinking of the
communion practice. In the burnt-offering itself—though
commonly followed by the peace-offering—there was
none: and as the burnt-offering developed so largely in
later times the original relation of the act of eating to
the act of sacrifice as a whole was further altered. One
supremely important change took place when the Deuteronomic reform established the principle of a central
sanctuary. Until then sacrifices were possible for every
local community; the old custom had continued, that meat
was only eaten as part of a sacrifice: every meat meal was
sacrificial. But with the centralisation of all sacrifice the
sacrificial meal, instead of being part of the constant home
experience of every Israelite, could only take place in
Jerusalem, and passed out of his life except on the comparatively rare occasions when he went up to the Temple
for the feasts. The evidence for this lies in the fact that as
a corollary of the reform the Deuteronomic law has to
provide permission for flesh meals when the appointed
place of sacrifice is too far:[1] only with the significant

[1] Deuteronomy xii. 20-25. Hence the special Jewish method of killing
animals for food, which continues to this day.

reservation that the blood is the life and is therefore not
to be eaten, but poured out on the ground like water.
Lastly, in the piacular sacrifices, though there is still some
eating—by the priests when offering for other people—
and even then it is only part of the victim that they may
eat—the restriction on the ground of holiness is in full
operation: the people may not eat because the meat is
holy: the priests may not eat when they offer for themselves: and the parts that would have been eaten are
burned outside the camp as holy things.

It is worth while to recapitulate the ideas which are
found in this early stage: we have had the eating and
drinking of the communion meal: the use of the blood as
life: the purpose—to convey life: and such less essential,
but incidentally significant, links with later language as
the living water, the tree and its branches, and "flesh" in
its collective sense.

Round the whole institution, then, gathers the feeling of
the family spirit. Intercourse with God is free, natural,
and joyous: there is no sense of sin, and no fear: there is
the strong communal spirit of the one flesh, or, as we
should say, body, made up of the father and his children.
It is the unsophisticated stage of human history—with
all that to us seem conditions of roughness and coarseness and barbarism, it is care-free and happy. And whatever, from its rich store of early traditions, the sacrificial
meal seemed to have lost in later history,[1] it never lost
the spirit of rejoicing and of thanksgiving. That the
Psalms testify to, and it was preserved to the end.

How, and by what stages the two later forms of sacrifice were developed is, and must probably remain, ob-
scure. What we do know is that זֶבַח (zebaḥ), the regular
word for slaughtering in sacrifice, is always kept for the
peace-offering, and that מִנְחָה (minḥah), the other general
word for offering in the sense of gift, is the special word
for the meal or cereal offerings. The slaughter of animals
may, and probably will, begin in a nomadic life: the offering of cereals belongs to an agricultural : and the use of

---

[1] See below, pp. 71 f.

these two words points (1) to the tradition of a time when all slaughter sacrifices were peace-offerings, and (2) to the priority of the idea of a sacrifice as a meal to that of a sacrifice as a gift.

Robertson Smith's theory of the burnt-offering is that it is derived from a piacular use of the original type of sacrifice, and the question is too elaborate to be discussed here. It is probable, as I have said before (p. 14), that there was never a time when there was not some piacular element in the burnt-offering, and even some in the sacrificial meal: for ceremonials to maintain kinship must have also served the purpose of restoring it when it was not irretrievably broken. In this case the situation would be exactly parallel to that of later times when, as we have seen, the whole department of piacular sacrifices was confined to the atoning for the less serious sins, and sins done with a high hand (perhaps the phrase itself is a relic of the days of primitive and simple violence) excluded from the covenant and the family relationship between Yahweh and His people.

But the fact that emerges from the later history without any question is that the burnt-offering, piacular as it may have been in one aspect, was established for many centuries before the need was felt for such an emphasis on sin and atonement that a special class of sacrifices must be devised, as distinct in their way from the burnt-offering as the latter from the peace-offering. And as our main concern is with the ultimate meaning of the sacrifices, it is this stage that matters most. What we have to see now is the place of the burnt-offering in the historical development.

I said above (p. 34) that in all probability the key to the expansion of sacrifice is the growth of society. The clans, as time went on, combined into groups; and as the blood relationship was understood to be the bond of social unity such combinations of clans would be brought by extensions of the blood covenant or otherwise under the same god. We can see the process of combination between larger groups taking place in the Book of Judges,

which is a history of the steps towards the achievement
of national unity. There tribes combine into local groups
under the stress of temporary emergency, and at first the
groups dissolve when the stress is over. Later, in the case
of Gideon's judgeship, there is a combination of several
tribes, though not of what was afterwards the whole
nation, which continues after peace, and is within reach
of becoming a hereditary monarchy. In the first Book of
Samuel the process is complete. What would be the effect
on the conception of God? In older days the unit was not
indeed what we should call a family, but a clan of the
same blood to which the god was father—though in fact
there is a sense in which, in modern language, "family" is
the only word to use; it is a large family, under a leader in
the position of a father, with an unseen leader greater
than he, and thought of in terms of fatherhood also. As
the clans combine into groups, and the groups into a
nation, the earthly leader becomes a king. God, the unseen leader, greater than the earthly, will in His turn also
be thought of as a King. We have seen that the sacramental, or communion, side of the old sacrifices tended
to grow less in evidence; and we have now a motive for
another use of sacrifice which may have been either one
cause or the effect of such lessening, or merely have
grown up side by side with it for other reasons. If men
are going into the presence of their father they expect to
find him in the freedom and familiarity of the common
meal: the time comes when God is still father, and His
table is still open to His children; but He is now not
Father only, but also King; and, before He can be met
face to face, familiarly, at the meal, His kingship must
be recognised in homage. He has a claim upon the service
of His subjects. They will bring Him gifts. They will
"intreat his favour" (Ps. xlv. 12, "And the daughter of
Tyre shall be there with a gift; even the rich among the
people shall intreat thy favour"). So Saul says to Samuel
as an excuse for his premature sacrifice: "I have not in-
treated the favour of the Lord: I forced myself therefore
and offered the burnt offering" (1 Sam. xiii. 12). And it

becomes a rule in the Law: "none shall appear before me empty" (Ex. xxiii. 15).

As the subjects of a king naturally brought him cattle, grain, and other fruits of the earth as their gifts, to enable him to discharge his duties of hospitality; so the worshippers brought their cattle, their fine flour and oil and wine, to God—these were the materials of the burnt-offering, and the meal- and drink-offerings which accompanied it. They were, as we have seen, the bread of God; and the altar, on which He accepted them, was His table. And they went up into His presence in sweet smoke—an anthropomorphism which runs all through the Bible from the story of Noah's sacrifice after the Flood ("and the Lord smelled the sweet savour"—Gen. viii. 21) to the "odour of a sweet smell", ὀσμὴ εὐωδίας, of the sacrifice and offering of Christ (Eph. v. 2).

The burnt-offering, then, was an act of homage, a rendering of service. It meant cost, the sacrifice of the offerer's self, obedience: "Lo, I come to do Thy will, O God" is its highest expression. It meant also fear: something of the naturalness and freedom of the old approach had gone. It was at once an advance and a retrogression: something was lost, and something was gained—a fuller and wider conception of God brought with it a removal from His immediate presence which the weakened sacrificial meal could not counteract. And in another strange way there seems to have been loss and gain. Robertson Smith suggests[1] that in this phase of sacrifice a new idea comes in with the change in social conditions. The breakdown of the small clan unit and the formation of larger units such as the nation meant also the breakdown of the old communal method of owning animals. They became individual property: and individual sacrifices have become possible: indeed it may be that it was this that led to the burning of the whole sacrifice upon the altar: sacrifice need no longer be a communal and mutual act; the victim was something which had belonged exclusively to the individual offerer, and once offered ceased to be his

[1] *R. S.*[2] pp. 390 ff.

property and became entirely holy as given to God. But with the new possibility of private sacrifice there came a materialising of the relations with God: such and such things had to be done to secure favour: the connection could be established quantitatively, and the level of personal religion had fallen. The act of approach became concrete and calculable—a matter almost of payment rather than of inward disposition. That was a loss, and it is easy to see in the light of later history in what direction it led. But with the loss, if this theory is true, there must equally have come a gain. For it marks a moment when, perhaps for the first time, the individual stands, if on his own merits, still for his own sake, before God. It is only a beginning, but it is a beginning charged with possibilities only to be realised when the actual breakdown of the attempt to buy the favour of God with external and measurable and costly offerings drove the man back upon those first principles of his own relation to his God, which the prophets tried to teach but only the personal experience of the failure of the old system could bring home.

Thus the burnt-offering illustrates the ultimate paradox of the Jewish religion. The Old Testament gives us at every stage an advance, step by step, to a conception of God, and of man's duty to God, to which our Lord had almost nothing to add that was in itself new. But at each of these steps it also advances nearer to its ultimate failure. In the earliest stage its theology is rude and simple: its vision of God is limited: its morality is what we should call immoral: and there is no problem that defies an answer. Religion is easy; duty is simple and straightforward: the relations with God are happy and natural. But the vision grows: the ethical standards are raised; and religion means fear, and comes to be externalised. The answer to the human heart is given, and at the same time withheld; and the whole process ends in a deadlock. It has no solution in itself. There is at last only one Way along which Truth and Life can be made one—Christ, the Way, the Truth, and the Life.

The kingship, one effect of which upon the development of sacrifice I have traced, also operated in another way on its social side.[1] The king saved the weaker members of a community—not in the Hebrew society alone—from the tyranny of powerful clans, or of aristocracies. It meant, on the whole, in spite of all its failures, a larger and stronger and more equitable conception of justice. It created an ideal: and an ideal which, once transferred to God, could in a real sense, under Hebrew conditions, prepare the way for that teaching of His perfect righteousness which was to mean so much with the prophets.

It is at this point that we enter upon the last stage of the sacrificial development. The piacular sacrifice, as a separate class, does not, as we have seen, appear until after the Exile. We find it for the first time in Ezekiel's anticipation of the reconstructed covenant-community in the last nine chapters of his prophecy. How was the change brought about? Once again, it comes, in a sense, with the growth of the social unit.

I have spoken above, but only incidentally, of the *differentia* which at one stage after another made the religion of Israel, while it remained like, yet so fundamentally unlike, the religions of neighbouring and kindred nations. Something happened which changed the Semitic fatherhood of God by nature into the Hebrew idea of His fatherhood by grace. It was He who made man in His own image; the image was His gift. With the other Semitic gods the covenant union had not to be made: it was only maintained. With Yahweh the covenant was made; and it was made by a movement from His side. It is this movement of God towards His people—this Divine initiative—which is the distinguishing mark of Hebrew religion in the historical period. And it is expressed, as the character always was expressed, in the Hebrew custom, by His name.

Hebrew scholars tell us that whatever the original derivation of the sacred Name may have been, its meaning as conveying the Hebrew idea of God's nature was

[1] *R. S.*[2] pp. 73 ff.

that which is expressed in His revelation of Himself to
Moses. "I AM hath sent me unto you"—"I AM THAT I
AM"—like many other translations that have become
established, has much to answer for. It suggests to our
minds a metaphysical conception of God's unchanging
Eternity. But the Hebrew word is in the "imperfect"
tense—the tense of a continued not a completed action,
and therefore often requiring to be translated by our
future. And the word itself means not "being" absolutely,
but "being" in relation to someone, or something, else.
It is γίγνομαι rather than εἰμι—"become" rather than
"be". He manifests Himself as "I will become"—אהיה—
and when He is spoken about it passes into the third
person—יהוה—"He will become".[1] "He will become what
He will become." There is in this the double aspect of the
personal God in which at length all the antinomies—
infinite and finite, invisible and visible, beyond comprehension and intimately known, even eternal and temporal
—find their solution. He is a Person—and the J document does not hesitate to be anthropomorphic—Who can
enter into personal relations with His servants. He makes
Himself known to them; they are in living touch with
Him: they can speak to Him face to face as a man speaketh
with His friend: that is one side. And the other is that He
does not tell them what He is. There is no positive description of Him by any one of the attributes by which
we should ordinarily attempt to express our idea of God.
It is only that as they continue in His service, allow themselves to be redeemed and shepherded and fed and ruled
by Him, they will come to know Him more and more; or
rather—not that they will find out more, but that He will
become more to them. It is the Name of Revelation. It
means, if it means anything, that the religion of Yahweh
is to be one of perpetual progress. Moses knew Him; but

---

[1] Driver, *Genesis*, pp. 408 ff. "This is certainly the sense that must have been
attached to the name *Yahweh* by the Israelites from the time when Exodus iii.
14 was written. The possibility cannot, however, be excluded that the intention
of Exodus iii. 14 is to attach to the name a special theological sense, and that
originally it may have had some other meaning": such other meanings are discussed by Driver in what follows. So Burney, *Gospel of the O. T.* p. 31.

Samuel knew Him better, and Isaiah better still, and Jeremiah, and the rest, each in their turn; but to each the first, and the ultimate, truth always was "He will become what He will become": you do not know it yet: there is far more that you and your successors have to learn.

It is suggestive to compare with such a name as this the names of other, typical, Semitic gods, such as Baal or Molech. Both of these describe the god positively, under one of his obvious attributes. He is owner of the land, and therefore lord of his people (Baal), or king (Molech = Melech, by an alteration of the vowels, in contempt, to those of *bosheth*, "shameful thing"). Here the name gives no leadership. The people of Baal think of him as lord; and they can only derive their ideas of what lordship means from the human lords and owners known to them in their daily experience. If these are coarse and licentious, coarseness and licentiousness become parts of their idea of the character of the heavenly Baal. The people of Molech think of him as king, and they must form their ideas of the kingly character of God on the earthly types of kingship that they know; and if these are cruel and bloodthirsty, Molech will be cruel and bloodthirsty too. The character of such gods must be a reflection of the characters of their people. Religion follows the movement of human life, instead of leading it. It has nothing to give. It is only what man makes it. There is no progress in such communities, but only, as the history shows, retrogression and decay.

I hazard this comparison of Yahweh with Baal and Molech for what it is worth; but apart from comparisons there can be no doubt, from the positive knowledge that we have of the course of Israelite religion, that the essence of the faith in Yahweh is this "givenness" of a constantly self-revealing God. Nothing else will account for the confidence which those of His servants who were nearest to Him, who could say that Yahweh had spoken to them, showed in the face of personal trouble and of otherwise irremediable public disaster. Nothing else gives us the reason of the constant lifting of the conception of God, and the corresponding conceptions of human life and duty, which is the history of the prophets who were the religious leaders of Yahweh's people. Whether it is right or not to say, as has been suggested above (p. 42), that the kingship prepared the way for the prophetic teaching of the absolute righteousness of Yahweh, there is no doubt that this is the first great feature of their theology. And with it went what was, at least as regards historical effectiveness, their supreme revelation, the belief that Yahweh is not only the God of Israel, one among many national gods, but the One God of all nations and of the whole world. I need not give the evidence for the fact of this development in detail: it will be sufficient to refer to Jephthah's argument with the Amorites: "Wilt thou not possess that which Chemosh thy god giveth thee to possess?" (Judges xi. 24); to David's complaint to Saul: "They have driven me out this day that I should not cleave unto the inheritance of the Lord, saying, Go, serve other gods" (1 Sam. xxvi. 19); to Naaman's request for two mules' burden of earth in order that in Damascus he may have a piece of Yahweh's soil on which to worship Him (2 Kings v. 17); or, perhaps strangest of all as coming from the pen of the prophetic historian, to the story of the king of Moab's sacrifice of his eldest son to Chemosh on the city wall—with the result that "there came great wrath upon Israel" (R.V.m.)—the wrath of Chemosh, which drove the invading armies out of his territory (2 Kings iii. 27).

To accept this transition as established by the historical evidence is not, of course, to deny the moral superiority of the religion of Yahweh in earlier days. That had been its mark from the moment when the religion of Israel became something distinctive from the neighbouring kindred cults. It was inherent, as we have seen, in the conception of the Divine character implied by the Covenant Name. But as long as the other gods had, at least in the popular mind, a real existence, it was impossible to make the difference effective in everyday religion and morality. The conquest of Canaan by the

Israelite tribes had never been more than partial. In their nomadic state they possessed, and brought with them into their new home, a religion adapted to their old conditions. They had yet to learn how to practise religion as a settled agricultural community. They were accustomed to using the title Baal of any god, and therefore of their own, as is shown by the names Meribbaal and Eshbaal, changed by the later instincts of monotheistic belief into Mephibosheth and Ishbosheth. And they settled down among the Canaanites who worshipped God—or their local deities—under the name of Baal. They found observances in the local Baal cults of the same kind as their own; they shared the Semitic character, with its tendency to sensual indulgence, as well as the Semitic religious traditions and customs. Yahweh had always been worshipped wherever there had been theophanies. There was no tradition of a single central sanctuary. Bethel and Beersheba and Mamre were already sanctuaries consecrated by memories of the Israelite past. It was small wonder therefore that they hardly knew whether they were worshipping Yahweh or Baal; or that they either frankly acknowledged the belief of their Canaanite neighbours in the local Baals—who after all had seemed to guarantee for the country in the past the blessings of agricultural life—or found it easy to worship their own god under the name of Baal, with the calf-image so natural to their primitive habits and traditions, with the *mazzēboth*, the *ashērim*, and all the traditional accompaniments, ceremonial or immoral, of the local sanctuaries.

It was the prophetic teaching which struck the first really effective blow at all this. In doing it, it revolutionised not merely the accepted ideas of theology and of morality, in that abstract sense into which it is the habit of the modern mind to isolate them, but the whole conception of the worship and ceremonial of the traditional Law or Torah. It was the best side of the teaching of the prophets—and indeed the central truth which they proclaimed—which led directly to those further developments of the sacrificial system which we are considering.

The immediate cause of the change was the revolution which this teaching produced in the content of the idea of holiness. Holiness always had been a quality attaching to the idea of deity. As such it belonged not to gods only but to persons and places and things which were in touch with the divine. It operated in what was practically a physical way, as if by contagion. The meaning of the word is doubtful, but most authorities are agreed that it carries primarily the idea of separation.[1] The gods, as such, were separate from men; and the persons and places and things which became permanently or temporarily connected with them were separate also. It was a ceremonial, or physical, rather than what we from our later point of view should call a moral quality. And indeed as applied to all gods as such it could have no "moral" content. If Yahweh, as a god, was holy, so were Molech and Baal and Chemosh; so were all the gods of the Babylonian pantheon. And whatever immoral qualities belonged to any or to all of them were consistent with the quality of holiness.

Once, however, the other gods ceased, for the prophets, to exist, the whole content of the idea of holiness was changed. It had meant only that each god was separated —as if physically, in the sense that he was above them, in the heavens—from his people. But the idea was inherent in that of Godhead. Yahweh, therefore, as God, must still be Holy; and the Holiness of the only God is therefore a new kind of separation. He is above, removed from, contrasted with, all men, and all the conditions of earthly life. At once its meaning includes what it could not have included before. He is contrasted with all forms of imperfection, moral, as well as ceremonial. I must quote at length a passage from a book by the late Mr. I. Abrahams,[2] because it exactly illustrates what I had

---

[1] So cf. Sifra on Leviticus xix. 2 (quoted by I. Abrahams, *Studies in Pharisaism and the Gospels*, 2nd series, p. 150): "Be ye holy—be ye perushim" (separated), "even as God is parush" (separated).   [2] *Op. cit.* pp. 150 f.

already written, and adds to it the weight of modern Jewish authority. "And then, since separateness means aloofness from the foul, the unchaste, the cruel, the term 'holiness' came to concentrate in itself the whole of the perfect life as Israel understood it; life perfect ritually, morally, spiritually. The word *Kadosh* grows ever richer in significance with the ages. Ritual cleanliness, dietary abstinences, communal separateness, detestation of the grosser indulgences and vices and moral licentiousness, the inspiration to purity of thought, action, and belief— in brief, the hallowing of life, and of the martyr's sacrifice of life for the hallowing of God—all these ideas, and more, accumulated round the Jewish conception of *Kedushah* (holiness). 'It is', as Dr. Kohler well says, 'holiness which permeates the thoughts and motives of life, and hence it is the highest possible principle of ethics.' And since the Pentateuch has chosen to put the Imitation formula" (Mr. Abrahams is writing on the Imitation of God) "in terms of holiness, it is therefore quite natural that the Jewish commentators should connect Leviticus xix. 2 with Genesis i. 26. The formula of Imitation is ' Be ye holy, for I am holy'; and, 'created in the image of God', man imitates God by stretching upwards to the Holiness which resides in Him."

It is so customary in our day to depreciate the spiritual value of the Priestly side of Jewish religion that it is well to note that the new conception of holiness to which we have come enables the Priestly document in Genesis i. 26 to lift the older, anthropomorphic, conception of God in the J part of the prophetic history into that which we know to be its corollary, the theomorphic conception of man. It is only that which in the end saves the anthropomorphism inevitably attaching to a personal God of revelation from cheapening and lowering the idea of the Divine. God mixes in human life only that in the end He may enable man to mix in His.[1] He stoops in order to raise us to Himself. The God of revelation is, as such, the God of redeeming love.

[1] Cf. part ii. ch. iii.

The cardinal merit of the new idea of holiness was that it was progressive. It defined God, not by what He is but by what He is not. The prophets of the eighth century, if they had sought for some positive attribute by which to lift the contemporary view of His character, might have used Righteousness, as in fact they did. But the meaning which they attached to it could only be their own. It would have been an advance for the moment, but like all advances the time would have come when it would have limited the idea of God's character. It would have become retrograde. Yahweh could never be Yahweh unless there were yet more revelations lying ahead, and His people had to be ready to receive them. In fact, no positive attribute can be found which can fully describe God. For every such attribute is limited to the ideas already existing in the mind of man, and a Being so described can only be a reflection of human ideals. He can be conceived as an intellectual idea: He cannot be known as a Person; and still less can He be worshipped as God.

The new Holiness thus expressed for the Hebrew mind the necessary thought of God's transcendence. In so doing it provided a conception which could make room for every fresh revelation of His character. The religion of the Holy God could never stand still. So Dr. A. B. Davidson says, "What God was is not expressed. And always as the conception of God enlarged and clarified, more was felt to lie in the expression *Kadosh*" (holy); "and the calling of a people who was His was felt to be more elevated."[1] It is in this way that the Holy, Holy, Holy of Isaiah's vision becomes the highest expression of the Church's worship on earth, and the formula of the perfect worship of Heaven.

One word of caution should be added here as to the prophets' use of the word in its new sense. It is often said that they distinguished two meanings: the moral, and the aesthetic or ceremonial; or, rather, that when they used the word, they used it in the moral sense alone. So Dr. Davidson[2] says of Amos' phrase "profane my holy

[1] *O. T. Theology*, p. 258.   [2] *Ibid*. pp. 147 f.

E

name" (ii. 7), of an act of physical sin; so, more startlingly,
of Isaiah's confession of uncleanness in his vision (vi.
5-7), where he compares Isaiah i. 16: "Wash you, make
you clean; put away the evil of your doings from before
mine eyes . . .". I quote him as an example of a common
tendency. But the tendency is after all unhistorical. It
means that we are reading back into the Jewish past the
preconceptions of our own times. To us, as a result of our
religious and intellectual history, worship and character,
faith and morals, are ideas entirely separable. The arena of
common life, in which character is made or marred, is not a
sanctuary, or has no living connection with the sanctuary.
And the sanctuaries themselves of large parts of modern
Europe are not so much places of worship as of teaching,
and of subjective religious emotions which become an end
in themselves. We need, not only as historical students,
in order to read the Old Testament records aright, but
for our own sakes, to recapture the Hebrew outlook. To
Isaiah what was morally wrong was unclean. It was in the
sanctuary that he found his sense of sin, and it was from
the sanctuary that he carried his message. There was no
separation between religion and ethics, between worship
as it ought to be, and indeed as it was, and life.

Such was the new Holiness. It was a conception which
was bound in the end to affect the law of worship as well
as the ideals of character. The Deuteronomic reform was
its first result. Ineffective as that was, it achieved a principle which made it possible for the Yahweh worship of
the whole nation to become morally pure. As we have
seen, it threw still more into the background the use of
the sacrificial meal. But the time had long gone by when
the religious value of that institution in primitive times
could be set against its corrupting influence when practised as part of the worship of the local sanctuaries; and
even that religious value had been largely lost. What
could be saved was saved; the sacrificial meal, confined to the Temple celebrations, did at any rate maintain its setting of joy and thanksgiving, its eucharistic
character; and it was the joy no longer of local orgies

but of the pure and uplifting gladness of the Temple
Psalms.[1]

But the efforts of Josiah, though they established the
principle of the central sanctuary, came too late. All that
they did was to leave a foundation upon which Ezekiel
and the later codifiers of the Temple traditions could
build in better times. The mass of the people, the political
leaders, the priests as a body, and many of the recognised,
or professional, prophets failed to respond. It was only
in the downfall of the kingdom of Judah, and in the discipline of the Exile, that the seed sown bore fruit. The
prophets had stated a problem. They had laid down (see
above, pp. 14 f., 45) God's righteousness as an absolute
standard, and set over against that the national death
that lay in the national sins. They had also lifted the central conception of the sacrificial approach to God—that of
his holiness—into a position which covered all that they
meant by His righteousness, and, in fact, potentially
went far beyond even their own standards of that. The
problem that they left behind them was a practical one.
Could a way be found by which the new holiness, now
identical with righteousness, might be achieved? The old
holiness could be secured, or preserved, by simple acts
performed in the course of the traditional sacrifices. It
was a quality, as we have seen, barely more than physical.
And but little moral meaning need attach to the process
by which it was reached. Burnt-offerings and peace-offerings, and the traditional regulations of everyday life,
were sufficient in themselves. The old system was hardly
self-conscious over penitence or atonement. It took them
in its course, and such as their problems were it provided
all the solution that they needed as it went along. The
old holiness made no serious demands upon the conscience.

But the new teaching, and its acceptance when the
time came, had changed all that. We have seen that the
beginning was made in the conviction that Yahweh was
the God of the whole earth and not of His own land alone,

[1] But see pp. 93-96.

and that that conviction carried with it the sense of His moral perfectness. It broke down the old belief that His action was limited to His own territory. That belief had had the force of a charm. As long as it persisted the corollary to its limitation of Yahweh to Israel was the sense that, come what might, the national existence of Israel was secure: that nothing could overthrow the national monarchy, or the House of Yahweh Himself. And on this belief those who refused to listen to the prophets' call, who would not recognise their new standards, or their new theology, were able to rely, until the actual fall of Jerusalem. But the holiness of a God, Whose scope was limited to their own kingdom, made no demands upon character. Their security was comfortable, as long as the social unit with which they were concerned was no more than the single nation, which had in its day succeeded to the clan. But the catastrophe which overwhelmed the kingdom and the Temple, and drove them into Babylon as exiles, gave them a new experience and a new horizon. They had yet to find, as they did find, that outside their own territory, and with no central, or any other, sanctuary, they remained the people of God. Yahweh was still their God by the waters of Babylon. But while they rediscovered Yahweh's faithfulness to His people, they found themselves in a wider life. They discovered that real access to God in spirit could be achieved by them as individuals as well as in corporate acts. And in this experience the truth of the prophets' doctrine came home to them as it never could have done while they were bound within the circle of their old life. The unit over which Yahweh—still their own God, and the God whom they had always known—was King was widened. It was now no longer the nation but the race. And with that the sense of His requirements was deepened and extended as it had been with the prophets. Still imperfectly, but at last in a real sense, the experience of the individual, which grew in the prophets from Jeremiah to Deutero-Isaiah, was brought home to the ordinary man. The problem of the prophets became the problem of priests and people alike.

And it was this problem which the development of the piacular sacrifices was an attempt to answer. From Ezekiel onwards the system must make a conscious attempt to solve it. That is the meaning of its appearance at this point.

It was only an attempt. As we have seen, it did not solve the problem. But its fundamental value is far greater than its achievement. It witnessed to, it made imperishable in the customary life of the Jewish community, the final opening out of the revelation of Yahweh in pre-Christian times. The first Semitic, and the primitive Hebrew, worshippers had desired that intercourse with God which we call communion, and they achieved all that they knew themselves to need on the easy terms of the common meal. Their Israelite successors were taken a great step further when they were taught that God was more than the simple father of a family clan, that He was not less than their heavenly king. And before they could dare to meet Him in the sacrificial feast they recognised this new truth by giving Him their homage and their service—their own selves—on the altar of burnt-offering. The Jewish nation, when it ceased to be a kingdom and became a Church, knew at last that the King of Israel was the Holy God of the whole race of mankind; and as each individual saw himself, as Isaiah had done, in that presence, he was forced to say, "Woe is me! for . . . I am a man of unclean lips, and I dwell in the midst of a people of unclean lips". And it followed that before either individual or nation could do homage to their King, both the one and the other must acknowledge and seek atonement for their sins, as coming into the presence of the Holy God.

The ultimate goal is still the same: but before it can be reached the truths given by experience must be recognised; hence the invariable order: first sin-offering, then burnt-offering, and finally peace-offering. The logical, or moral, order is, quite naturally, the reverse of the historical.

It is this then that marks the double character of the

atonement sacrifices. They represent at once an achievement and a failure, as does every other critical development in the history of Old Testament religion. They recognise and testify to the greatest truth which that religion achieved. They fail to meet the need which it had created.

CHAPTER III

THE PROPHETIC VIEW OF SACRIFICE

OUR knowledge of the sacrificial system, so far as the books of the Old Testament are concerned, comes of course in the main from the Priestly and the older documents in the Pentateuch, and from the last nine chapters of Ezekiel. These are the sections of the literature which are expressly concerned with setting out the system, the former as codifications and regulations, at various stages, of the existing customs, the latter as an ideal reconstruction for the time when the covenant-people should be restored.

But outside this formal presentation we have in the rest of the Old Testament references of every kind, explicit and implicit, to the practices of worship, to its purpose and meaning, and to its corruptions. And these, taken together, are of the first importance when we try to estimate it historically, as regards the place which it held in the life of the people, and morally, when we wish to understand how our Lord and the New Testament writers must have looked at it. They will also help us to estimate the degree of theological, or of religious, meaning which could be consciously given to its characteristic actions, or could be recognised in the light of later experience as being unconsciously attached to them.

Such references are in the main incidental. There is hardly a passage which can be called a systematic treatment of the subject. Every passage depends for its meaning partly on its context in the book in which it occurs, and often mainly on the historical circumstances to which it belongs and our knowledge of the contemporary conditions of life in which it finds its setting.

Thus many of the passages—those that contain reflection upon the cultus and are not merely narrative statements or descriptions—become mainly a question of interpretation. And in estimating interpretations we have to bear in mind the fundamental difference between the Semitic way of expressing thought and our own. It is not only a question of the difference between the modern and the ancient mind, though there are ways in which from certain points of view, as we shall see, this bears vitally upon our subject. But the differences between Hebrew grammar and syntax, and those of the European family of languages, classical and modern, express a profound difference of mental attitude. We reason where the Hebrew sees. Our languages, with their careful structure of clauses depending upon each other, express connected thought: the Hebrew, with its co-ordinate clauses, gives concrete word-pictures. It does not work out an argument in the connected way which is essential to our mind: it throws out vivid expressions of single thoughts which we have to combine. Thus the thought has to be translated as well as the language: the modern interpreter has to supply the links: and, though Hebrew syntax admits of scientific study, and in that sense we depend on the verdict of Hebrew scholars, there is much more room for the subjective element in interpretation, and indeed much more need of it, than when we are dealing with ancient literature in a language kindred to our own.[1] We have in some sense to supply the scheme which makes the sequence of thought coherent, and enables us to interpret it in the terms of our more logical habit of mind.

[1] See Dr. G. A. Cooke in Peake's *Commentary on the Bible*, p. 35: "In syntax Hebrew belongs to a primitive stage of development; it has no elaborated system of expressing the subordination of sentences, it simply co-ordinates them by the conjunction 'and'; the subtler connections have to be supplied by thought. Imagination also plays a large part in the use of the tenses. The perfect and imperfect do not determine the date, but only the character of an action as complete or incomplete" [that is, in the mind of the speaker]; "the date must be learnt from the context".

Thus interpretations of Old Testament sayings are likely to vary very greatly from one another; the interpreter builds much that is his own on very scanty materials. No one who has read modern commentaries on Old Testament books can fail to have observed this. And it cannot be helped. But it means that with Old Testament interpreters, as indeed with interpreters of the New Testament, but even more so, we have to look to the *provenance* of the writers.

This is not an easy point to bring out in this particular connection—and less easy still for one who cannot profess expert knowledge of the Old Testament. No one—certainly not one who can never hope to be more than a learner—can in these days fail to acknowledge the debt which is owed by all Christians, of whatever way of thinking, to the work of those who in modern times, and in the modern critical method, have made the study of the Old Testament possible for us. They have opened its treasures in ways which make us feel that without them it would have been a sealed book. They have revealed the inner meaning of the development of its religion. They have thrown light on its history in ways too many to particularise. They have given us new insight into the methods of Inspiration, and, with the methods, into the secret of the way in which God was all the time working His purpose out. To criticise, or even to seem to criticise, their work seems ungracious and ungrateful. But what I wish to say will not be said in that spirit. It will not, indeed, be criticism. It is, I think, a statement of fact, and not one which carries, or should carry, any depreciation with it.

What we have to remember, then, is that, with the exception of a few leading English and American scholars, the great bulk of the modern work on the Old Testament, and indeed the initiative in the whole, is owed to men who would trace, and be proud to trace, their spiritual ancestry and their own theological outlook as Christians, to the bodies which sprang in the full sense from the Reformation. Their spiritual homes are founded on a protest, which included, but went farther than, the specific form of protest which belonged to the Church of England.

It was a protest of a threefold kind. In the first place, it was largely an appeal to private judgment, and to that extent a breach with tradition. That breach was indeed made in the interest of truths which seemed to be, and indeed were, as I at least should acknowledge, in their place and in their time, vital: and I hope to show later that, in one respect at least, so far as my present subject is concerned, given the accepted use of a certain class of terms at the time of the Reformation, it was inevitable. But it meant the forming of a habit, by the fathers of the Reforming movement, which was bound to grow with subsequent generations, of a large independence of view as regards the inherited traditions of pre-Reformation and "Catholic" Christianity, both in the West and in the East. The need has therefore not been felt, in many respects, of testing results by their coherence with historical presentments of faith and practice.

In the second place, the protest was largely, if not against institutionalism in Christianity as a whole, yet certainly against what many thought, and perhaps rightly thought, the excessive institutionalism of the mediaeval Church. And in this institutionalism one feature stood out prominently in the elaborate character of the traditional worship, with its danger of externalism and formalism. And, further, this particular feature was identified, through and through, with the language of priesthood and sacrifice. The comparison was inevitable, to those who began, or were brought up under, the recoil from these conceptions, of the mediaeval system with that of the Old Testament. Christ, it was said, and it is still said to-day by those who take this point of view, came to abolish forms and ceremonies, altars and sacrifices, and a human priesthood.

And, in the third place, the protest was even more a doctrinal one than an institutional. And in the doctrinal questions upon which these Reformation bodies took their stand none stood out more clearly—it would almost be

true to say none was more central—than the whole problem of priesthood and sacrifice. It was not only the
expressions of the doctrine of priesthood and sacrifice in
the public worship and the ordered life of the Church
which were challenged, but even more the doctrines
themselves. The Reformers adopted, and not without real
justification, the principle, at least as regards the ministry
and the sacraments, that these were gone for ever from
the Christian Church. Christ indeed was our High Priest,
and His sacrifice the groundwork of salvation; but in very
loyalty, as they believed, to Him and to His work the
priesthood of the ministry and the sacrifice of the altar
must be put away. Thus the Reforming bodies were
largely committed to a view of the Ministry which made
it before all things a ministry of the Word, and, if of the
sacraments also, then in such a sense as to remove from
the Eucharist much, if not all, of the tradition of sacrifice
which had gathered round it.

Once more in modern times the Reforming tradition,
true to the first principle of its protest, has moved in
many quarters beyond the position of the original Reformers. That movement was, no doubt, inevitable, once
the principles were granted. But it has meant that in our
times the whole idea of Christ's own Priesthood and of
His Sacrifice has ceased to hold the position that it did.
Where it has not been abandoned it has largely fallen
into the background. What is challenged to-day is not the
extension of His Priesthood to that of the Church or of
the ministry, or the inclusion within the terms of His
Sacrifice of the worship of the Church, but the whole idea
of sacrifice as applied to the Atonement. Christ does, or
did, His work more by His teaching or by His example.
The Jesus of history is more than the Christ of dogma.
Liberal Protestantism, and the habits of thought which
have in a measure succeeded to it, have less value for the
priestly and sacrificial side of the Old Testament even
than the traditional Protestantism of the Reformers.

It is the Reforming outlook, and the outlook of the
modern schools of thought which have grown out of it,

that characterise most of the modern work on the Old
Testament. And the Old Testament, more than any other
branch of theological study, is a field in which the ordinary
man is in the hands of specialists. Much that is said about
it is therefore taken for granted, and it is not always that
we bear in mind the distinction which I have drawn above
between the material and the interpretation put upon it.
It is for the material that we are really in the experts'
hands; but the principle of private judgment itself, and
the duty of independent thinking, leave us free to form
our own judgments about the interpretation. To say this
is not in any way to suggest that work on the Old Testament has not been honestly scientific and scientifically
honest: it is only that each worker must be, the whole
time, himself.

What has happened with much of the accepted interpretation is that those who have given it to us have had
to fill in gaps; have had to translate thoughts as well as
language; and in doing so they have naturally and rightly
given us what is their own. They have a tradition to
which they wish to be loyal, a side of truth to which
they must witness; and it is not surprising that in the
old relations between the prophets and the Law, hier-
archy and sacrifices, they have seen the modern issues
of Word and Sacrament, of preacher and priest, of
Protestant and Catholic—even of rational thinking and
superstition.

None of these things are said without much truth. No
one need be concerned to defend abuses and degradations,
if there were such, of Catholic faith and practice. If the
history of sacramental worship and the priestly office in
mediaeval and other forms of Catholicism has called up a
comparison with the bad features of the Old Testament
system, that is a disaster for which those who were
responsible for it must bear the blame, and which those
who believe that they play an essential part in the
Christian system must acknowledge, and of which they
must be content to bear the consequences.

All this has been said, I hope, not controversially, but

only with the desire to clear the issues, and to claim a freedom for other interpretations which may be equally loyal to sound criticism and to true history. And it is not said with any desire to minimise the truth or to challenge the rightness of what undoubtedly is expressed in the prophets and elsewhere. When their protests are undoubtedly against the magical use of religious ordinances, against the divorce of religious acts from character, against the lowering of religious standards or the refusal of new light, they are still living protests for to-day: if the same things happen the same things need to be said.

The incidental references to the sacrificial system that we find in the Old Testament—apart from those that are merely narrative or statements of fact—fall into two groups. There is one group of what may be called depreciatory passages. In the other fall those which show what the system meant in its better, or perhaps in its normal, working, to those who used it in the right spirit.

What is needed for the weighing of the meaning of the passages which are not in themselves clear is, first, a knowledge of the system, both in its full technique as ultimately developed and as it was at that particular moment in the history of its growth: of these the latter is, if anything, the more important, and it was partly for that reason that I dwelt upon the history, and upon the principles involved in it, at length. Obviously the background of the general history is often a determining factor, as well as the history of the literature that may be referred to. And, lastly, there is for each writer his own personal equation—his origin, his point of view, his temperament.

When all is said that can be said on these points there must still in many cases be a large margin for the interpreter. If he is one who does not see any reason for laying stress on the institutional side of religion; still more, if to him the problem of religious origins is one mainly of ethical principle or even only of intellectually apprehended truth rather than of the mystical element, as it may well be, we do not therefore depreciate his reading of the passage. We only take note of his presuppositions, and if ours are different we substitute our *a priori* element—it may be no more than that, or it may, conceivably, be a definite element of truth that he had been unable to contribute—for his.

This essay is written frankly from the point of view that there is, in every religion that is to be effective, and to respond to the conditions of human nature, both a mystical and an institutional element, as well as morality and an intellectual grasp of truth. Truth and morality are vital: but neither can truth ultimately be apprehended nor character achieved on any but directly personal lines. That is to say, that religion is from first to last the contact of persons with persons; of man corporately, and of individual men, with God; in an experience both communal and direct to the individual; and, as a corollary to this, a linking, on the basis, and as part of the essence, of this experience, of man with man. Man knows himself best when he knows God best, and knowing himself means at once the sense of the ultimate value, the incommunicableness, of his own individual soul, and that he sees himself as part of a living whole. Loving God means the right kind of self-love, and loving one another.

Such, I believe, was in fact the character of the Old Testament religion, which it never lost: it revealed truth, and it set a standard of character: and it did both by the intercourse of the personal God, first with the people as a whole, and then with the people and with individuals alike. It was a religion of personal contact both individual and corporate, both "Evangelical" and "Catholic", and never true to itself unless it was at the same time profoundly ethical.

Of the passages in some sense depreciatory of the sacrificial system some may be dealt with summarily and as a whole: some will require more detailed examination.

There are first many passages where sacrificial worship is indeed denounced, but where the context makes it

plain that it is the worship of other gods, such as the
local Baals—or, if the worship of Yahweh, at least that
form of it which approximated so closely to the methods
of the Baal cults as to be hardly distinguishable from
them. These are the passages which do not need to be
particularised: examples of them may be found in several
chapters of Hosea, where they appear as instances of the
spiritual adultery of Israel, of which the unfaithfulness
of Hosea's own wife is a symbol (Hosea ii. 5, 8, 13, 17;
iv. 13; xi. 2; xiii. 1). Sometimes it is foreign rites, such as
the worship of the host of heaven (Zeph. i. 4 ff.; Jer. vii.
18, viii. 2), as well as of the Baalim. Or in Jeremiah we
have again the image of the unfaithful wife (ii. 2 ff.); Baal
worship (ii. 8), with its immoralities (ii. 20-28), and its
strange ascription of fatherhood to the images, instead
of to Yahweh (*ib.* 27)—a passage which illustrates exactly
the old Semitic idea of the god as father of, and therefore
of one blood with, his clan (see above, pp. 34 ff.)—I only
give examples. Or again Ezekiel (vi. 3, 9, 13; xx., etc.);
and in his case there is evidence of yet other cults, such as
sun worship (vi. 4, viii. 16); women weeping for Tammuz
(viii. 13 f.); and perhaps Egyptian observances (viii.
7-12). All these are brought again under the figure of the
faithless wife (vi. 9). Some are more, some less, explicit:
but they form a large and distinct class of attack upon
cultural observances of the wrong kind. They are so
manifestly directed against forms of worship which were
against the spirit and letter of every successive code of
the Law that it would not have been worth mentioning
them here if it had not been that when not examined
carefully some of them at least seem to add force to the
common feeling of the prophets' hostility to sacrifice as
such.

Of crucial importance are the passages which have
become classical as evidence for the feeling of the prophets against the actual worship of Yahweh as by sacrifice. Amos, Hosea, Micah, Isaiah, Jeremiah, and certain
Psalms are all quoted as decisive on this point. I propose
to take each of these singly.

Amos was a herdman of Tekoa in the Judaean wilderness. His language about the system which he denounces is strong and bitter. "I hate, I despise your feasts, and I will take no delight in your solemn assemblies. Yea, though ye offer me your burnt offerings and meal offerings, I will not accept them: neither will I regard the peace offerings of your fat beasts. Take thou away from me the noise of thy songs; for I will not hear the melody of thy viols. But let judgement roll down as waters, and righteousness as a mighty stream" (v. 21-24). Nothing could, indeed, be more emphatic, or more sweeping. But what is it that he is denouncing? Is it sacrifice as such, or is it some particular form of sacrifice? The answer is clear from the book as a whole. It is the worship of Yahweh as practised, not at Jerusalem but in the Northern Kingdom. It was at the time when Jeroboam II.'s long reign had brought unexampled prosperity, and with prosperity the social evils which follow it. Amos' attack was upon the sanctuary at Bethel—the king's sanctuary and a royal house (vii. 13). It was, in the first place, consecrated to the worship of Yahweh under the form of a calf. The older Northern prophets, Elijah and Elisha, were concerned with the service of Yahweh as against that of Baal, and we do not gather that in the stress of that conflict they had anything to say about the manner of Yahweh's worship. What they had to establish was His claim to be the national God. But to a Judaean such worship would have been corrupt from its foundation. It meant the subordination of religious purity as witnessed to in the Temple to the interests of political expediency. Jeroboam I. was the great Erastian of the Old Testament. And, further, Amos was, like the prophets who succeeded him, a monotheist: to him there is one God, and He a God of absolute righteousness. Under the corrupt conditions which he saw in the prosperous kingdom of the North there was the old conception of the mere need of external actions as such to secure the ends of worship, and this was aggravated a thousandfold by the flagrant immorality and unrighteousness of the worshippers. They were the sins

of over-civilisation: and he denounces them from the
threefold point of view of a Judaean, a monotheist of the
new kind, and a rough solitary from the desert. We cannot eliminate from his point of view his own personal
history. It may well be that in his own lonely life he had
less regard for any outward cultus than he would have
had if he had been accustomed to corporate worship of
any kind. But he could not have been ignorant of it: and
his strongest language is not against sacrifice as such but
against what to him must always have been the wrong
form of worship, and against such worship as offered in a
spirit inconsistent with any true meaning.

One passage is indeed said to reveal his views on past
history in the sense that he denies that in the wilderness, when Israel really allowed itself to be led by Yahweh
(ii. 10), sacrifice was offered at all. "Did ye bring unto
me sacrifices and offerings in the wilderness forty years,
O house of Israel?" (v. 25). The meaning of the question
is confessedly difficult, and must be affected by the sense
of the next verse, which is almost impossible to recover.
But the argument would seem to be, "You think that
whatever your character the mere correct offering of
sacrifices will preserve Yahweh's favour now: do you
suppose that even in the wilderness, when He redeemed
you and led you for the forty years, it was the sacrifices
that forced His favour?" The difficulty of supposing that
Amos really commits himself to a historical statement
that in the golden age of Israel's history there was no
sacrifice is insuperable. On the one hand, he knew, and
accepted, the Book of the Covenant: he twice reproves
the worshippers at Bethel for disobeying it (ii. 8; cf. Ex.
xxii. 25-27; and iv. 5—a ceremonial disobedience, in the
offering of leavened bread, expressly forbidden in Ex.
xxiii. 18); and this code assumes sacrifice and enjoins the
great festivals. On the other hand, such a statement is
flatly contrary to the picture which the whole of the earlier
records give of early times. The idea that there was a
time when Israel and Israel's ancestors did not offer
sacrifice, but that the sacrifices were instituted at the

F

beginning of the forty years' wanderings, belongs not to the period of Amos but to that of the Priestly code. To take the suggested meaning of the passage is to suppose that Amos is contradicting a historical fact by anticipating an unhistorical statement that was not made till between two and three hundred years after his time.

Hosea's references to contemporary worship are, as we have seen, numerous. Many of them are concerned with the cult of the local Baal sanctuaries (see above, pp. 62 f.). Beyond this it is clear that he combines with the love of a Northern Israelite for his own country a strong feeling against the separation of the two kingdoms: "I have given thee a king in mine anger (of Jeroboam I.), and have taken him away in my wrath (of Hoshea)" (xiii. 11; cf. x. 8). In the later days, after the political and religious life of the northern kingdom has been swept away, the children of Israel will return to Yahweh their God and David their king (iii. 4, 5). He attacks the calf worship of Samaria (viii. 5, 6). Bethel is several times changed from Bethel (house of God) to Bethaven (house of vanity). Such is the attitude of the whole book. The hostility is to a worship that is both corrupt and in its origin unjustifiable, and that Hosea sees in a setting of gross immorality; and to priests who are condemned, not because they sacrifice but because they sacrifice in the wrong spirit and manner: they do not teach the law of their own God (iv. 6). It is in harmony with this general attitude that the famous passage in Hosea vi. 6 must be interpreted: "I desired mercy, and not sacrifice; and the knowledge of God more than burnt offerings": cf. iv. 6, "my people are destroyed for lack of knowledge". It is the wrong spirit and the wrong method upon which Hosea concentrates, as the verses following show: Hosea's message—in fact his own special revelation—is that of loyal love ("leal love": G. A. Smith)—whether, in the first place, of God to man, as Hosea learnt it in facing the problem of his own married life, or, in the second place, of man to God and of man to man; there can be no acceptance of sacrifices which show no knowledge of this, which are breaches of the

covenant between God and His people, such as are per-
petrated throughout the kingdom from east to west—in
the bloodshed in Gilead, and the highway robberies by
the bands of priests on the way to Shechem (vi. 7-9).

Micah, who follows Hosea, and whose work was done
in the reign of Hezekiah and perhaps continued into that
of Manasseh, is, like Amos, a countryman. He has, as
such, a natural bias to a strong view of city life; and it is
with the evils, mainly social and economic, which attend
the growth of city life and of that type of civilisation and
prosperity throughout history that he is concerned. It is
uncertain whether his book is a literary unity or not: here
I can only assume that, whatever may be the case with
individual passages, the historical background is in the
main that of Micah's own time. What is wrong with the
nation as he sees it is, on the one hand, the old trouble of
the corrupt form of Yahweh worship: he speaks of the
images and idols of Samaria, under the familiar simile of
the wife's unfaithfulness (i. 6, 7); again of graven images,
mazzēboth and *ashērim* (v. 13); as well as of witchcraft and
soothsaying—not with him and Isaiah alone the signs of
a decadent civilisation—(v. 12): and, on the other hand,
of the concentration of property in the hands of the rich
and the oppression of the poor; of the corrupting influence
of money in judges, prophets, and priests (iii.; vi. 9 ff.;
vii. 1-6). It is the tradition of Omri and Ahab that he sees
continued. This is the background upon which stands out
the great passage in vi. 1-8. Yahweh pleads with Israel:
"O my people, what have I done unto thee? and wherein
have I wearied thee? . . . (Israel's answer): Wherewith
shall I come before the Lord, and bow myself before the
high God? shall I come before him with burnt offerings,
with calves of a year old? Will the Lord be pleased with
thousands of rams, or with ten thousands of rivers of oil?
shall I give my firstborn for my transgression, the fruit of
my body for the sin of my soul? (The prophet's answer):
He hath shewed thee, O man, what is good; and what doth
the Lord require of thee, but to do justly, and to love
mercy, and to walk humbly before thy God?" There is no

question about the moral grandeur of this saying; but to have its full force it must be seen, both as first uttered and as interpreted for later use, as relevant to actual life. Sacrifices after all—the sacrifices of the old Law—are only one form of external religious practice: and the value of Micah's words lies just in this, that they apply not to those external ordinances which happen to take the form of sacrifice alone, but to all. In all these there is the danger of moral inconsistency between the outward and the inward, and wherever such inconsistency appears Micah's saying applies in its full force. To say that it was directed against sacrifice as such, even if the context suggests it, is either disastrously to limit its application, or to say that where sacrifice has ostensibly ceased religion is no longer in danger of externalism. The real believer in Micah's principle will hesitate at either of these consequences. And does the context suggest such an interpretation? The prophet's own conception of God is that of a dweller in a sanctuary. If He manifests Himself as Judge it is from His holy temple that He comes (i. 2)—doubtless in this passage the heavenly dwelling-place; but it is a temple, not a throne. The fundamental idea of God is based upon the Presence in the Holy of Holies in the Temple at Jerusalem: the sin of the people is an offence against the holiness of the sanctuary, in the sense, both new and wider, of the prophetic monotheism, but, like all Old Testament religious ideas, continuous with the old, and that holiness covers all that is meant by righteousness. And the form in which Israel's question is put (vi. 6, 7) indicates clearly that it is not sacrifice as it ought to be understood, but sacrifice as it was understood, that is in view—the mere abundance of offerings, as if their value lay in their quantity, and the fundamentally impossible extension of this wrong principle to its logical conclusion in human sacrifice. It is not indeed impossible that the reference to human sacrifice should date this passage in the reign of Manasseh, and make it, in the first place, a protest against the degradations which marked the worship of that king's reign. But in any case the contrast is between doing justly, loving mercy, and walking humbly with God, and sacrifice not as rightly used but as misused and misunderstood.

There is perhaps no passage in Isaiah which is claimed in so unqualified a way as condemning sacrifice as such. The position appears to be the same as that in the three prophets whom I have already discussed. It is an age of elaborate outward observances upon a background of moral failure: there is the same trust as in Micah in external quantity rather than in moral quality: the people rely upon the multitude of their sacrifices (i. 11); upon the numbers which attend the Temple (i. 12). Their oblations are vain—"oblations of vanity" (i. 13): their assemblies and their solemn meetings are not what they should be: what Isaiah sees there is "iniquity and the solemn meeting"(ib.). Nor is it only the sacrifices and the festivals that are unacceptable; so also are the prayers: "And when ye spread forth your hands, I will hide mine eyes from you: yea, when ye make many prayers, I will not hear: your hands are full of blood" (i. 15). The passage, if it is taken in the unqualified sense so often assumed for it, proves too much. What Isaiah has to say about sacrifice is exactly parallel to what he says about prayer. Yet no one has ever thought of suggesting that, because prayer can be formal and hypocritical, prayer as such is to be abandoned.

It seems, therefore, to be not the Temple worship, but the wrong spirit of the Temple worship, that Isaiah has in mind. And the whole of his attack upon the social and moral evils of his age is an illustration of what he means. Such an age could not be genuine in even the right religious observances: and behind and around them there are the usual wrong forms of worship: "their land is full of idols" (ii. 8, 20); and there are the sacred terebinths and the sacred springs (i. 29, 30).

Side by side with such passages as these must be set the attitude of Isaiah himself to the Temple and to the worship of the future. It was, after all, in the Temple that he received his call: it is from the Temple and its associations that he draws his sense of sin as uncleanness, as incompatible with holiness: "Holy, Holy, Holy, is the

Lord of hosts. . . . Woe is me! for . . . I am a man of unclean lips, and I dwell in the midst of a people of unclean lips"; and it is with a coal from the altar that he is cleansed (vi. 3-7). And in i. 16 the two conceptions of sin are set side by side, not in contrast with, but as illustrating, each other. "Wash you, make you clean" gives the idea of sin as coming under the category of holiness; the sinner himself must be put right: "put away the evil of your doings from before mine eyes" is, as we have seen above (p. 16), the characteristic idea of sin before the Righteous Judge, Who in His mercy "covers" not the sinner but the acts of sin.

So the future is described in terms of the Temple and of its worship: "the mountain of the Lord's house shall be established in the top of the mountains, . . ." and it is the goal of the nation's pilgrimage (ii. 1-4 ; Micah iv. 1-3). So the restored people will be holy (iv. 3); and the Shekinah will be seen over the very assemblies that in his own day were marred by their iniquity (iv. 5); and a wedding canopy will be spread (ib.), under which the Bridegroom can enter with His Bride. So also there will be the peace-offerings with their rejoicing (xxx. 29). Zion will be "the city of our solemnities" (xxxiii. 20).

Jeremiah raises the most difficult problem. Is he opposed to the whole sacrificial cultus as such—whether rightly used or wrongly? Or is it only wrong applications of it that he is thinking of? The question turns largely upon his attitude to the Deuteronomic reform. The book upon which this reform is based is certainly contained in our present book Deuteronomy; but it is agreed that parts of the latter are additions, and that the actual book found in the Temple in 621 B.C., upon which Josiah took action, is, at the least, our chapters xii.-xxvi., and perhaps xxviii. Dr. Driver (*International Critical Commentary*, Deuteronomy, p. lxv. ff.) believes that chapters v.-xi. belong also to the original book and perhaps (p. lxxii.) also chapters i.-iii., which in any case cannot have been written long after the main part of the book.

What Deuteronomy does is to bring within the area of law what the earlier prophets had worked for. We have

seen that they attacked, in the main, two evils: on the one
hand, the corruptions inherent in the worship of the local
sanctuaries—whether of the Baalim, or of Jehovah-Baal
—and especially the immoralities attached to this worship; and, on the other hand, formalism in all worship,
whether local or central. What they saw so clearly was the
wrongness of the old idea, belonging to the earlier and
monolatrous, and therefore non-moral, view of holiness
as a quality of the sanctuary, that specific outward
actions, as it were, compelled the favour of God, and that
God was in a sense bound by His side of the covenant
to give, in the long run, an absolute and unconditioned
protection to His country, His shrine, and His people.
Further than this, it appears that there was no attack on
cultus in itself: it was only on cultus as wrongly used. No
one, indeed, in the old days—and this is really true of at
least the whole Old Testament point of view—ever conceived of a religion which did not express itself in outward acts of worship: it is questionable whether such a
conception is found anywhere, in the line of Hebrew,
Jewish, and Christian development, until a quite recent
period in the after movements of the Reformation.

The practical result of the Deuteronomic application of
the principles of the prophets was of course, in the first
place, the suppression of the local sanctuaries. This
appears to have been attempted before, by Hezekiah; and
it is only a revolution, under Josiah, in the sense that it
was done with a new, and a sudden, completeness. But in
theory it was the natural outcome of a movement which
had been in progress since the establishment of the Temple
worship at Jerusalem. Like other vital changes in the long
course of the history of the Old Testament religion, it
made no breach of continuity with the past. But the
change was none the less far-reaching. It operated in two
ways, as did all the great advances that had preceded it,
as well as the further development, after the Exile, of the
piacular type of sacrifice. It was, on the one hand, indubit-
ably a great and necessary advance. It cleared away, in
intention and, largely, in effect, once for all, the old and

fatal entanglement of the worship of Yahweh with that of the Baalim. As long as that continued there was no hope of eliminating the immoralities of worship native to the soil of Canaan, or of bringing the actual worship of Yahweh into line with the new monotheism of the prophets. On the other hand, while there was this incalculable gain, there was also a loss, and a real one. It took religion out of the daily home life of the people. There was as yet no synagogue system to serve the double purpose of local prayer and teaching and of providing a constant link between the local communities and the worship being offered in their name and by their delegates at the central sanctuary. With all its faults, the local feast—and all local feasts were sacrificial—was a free outburst of happiness. And there is something self-conscious and almost pathetic in the reiteration in the Deuteronomic law of the injunction to rejoice at the Temple feasts, and especially at the peace-offerings. The writer goes out of his way to tell the people that this new form of religion is to be just as happy and natural as the old. But with all this the new law must have left as its first legacy to the Temple worship an added strangeness and a greatly increased danger of formalism. The very increase of the sanctity and moral worth of the Temple increased the tendency to treat it in a magical way. It had become so unique; the presence of Yahweh had become so concentrated in it, that it was inevitable, until, and indeed even after, the experiences of the Exile, that Isaiah's promises should be taken in the wrong spirit, and it should be assumed that the mere existence of the house of the Lord was assured and was itself a disproof of anything that a prophet like Jeremiah, or any of his successors, could say.

But the second legacy of Deuteronomy was of a different kind and went far deeper. The whole book takes up Hosea's gospel of love. The secret of keeping the covenant and its laws is in the heart: because Yahweh loved Israel, Israel must learn that love is the fulfilling of the law. "Oh, that there were such a heart in them, that they would fear me . . ." (v. 29). "Hear, O Israel; the Lord our

God is one Lord: and thou shalt love the Lord thy God
with all thine heart, and with all thy soul, and with all thy
might. And these words, which I command thee this day,
shall be upon thine heart . . ." (vi. 4-6). So God's love is
the motive for Israel's loving Him and keeping His commandments (vii. 7 ff.): or, again, taking up the words of
Micah (vi. 8): "And now, Israel, what doth the Lord thy
God require of thee, but to fear the Lord thy God, to walk
in all his ways, and to love Him, and to serve the Lord thy
God with all thy heart and with all thy soul . . ." (x. 12).
Circumcision must be a new circumcision of the heart
(x. 16); "therefore thou shalt love the Lord thy God . . ."
(xi. 1, also 13). These passages are all from chapters
v.-xi., which may not belong actually to the book used in
621, but there is the same thing in xiii. 3, which does.
"The Lord your God proveth you, to know whether ye
love the Lord your God with all your heart and with all
your soul. . . ."

We have seen above (pp. 17, 51) that the Old Testament
never solved the problem of achieving righteousness in
terms of holiness. That was left for the New. But in
Deuteronomy we are still in a transition period. Yahweh
is indeed in theory the only God; but the people at least
had yet to learn that truth, and the achievement of the
central sanctuary was only one stage in the preparation
for it. Jeremiah had a further contribution to make, in his
teaching that the Temple was not in the last resort in-
violable; but it is at least possible that even he had not
cut himself altogether free from the old idea that it was
only in Yahweh's land that Yahweh could be worshipped
(Jer. xvi. 13). Both the Deuteronomic writer and the
great prophet were living in stormy times of change; and
we cannot expect complete consistency from either. It is
an unimaginative criticism—and an unhistorical—which
looks to them for clear-cut definitions, or the calm working
out of abstract theories from a detached and dispassionate
standpoint.

Such, in rough outline, was the situation created by the
publication of the Deuteronomic law-book. It is in the

light of this that we have to try to understand Jeremiah.
What was his attitude to the life of his own time?

There is first his own "personal equation". We know
what was his attitude to the old local worship of Yahweh
or Yahweh-Baal, with its corruptions. But his personal
history may well have left him with something more than
this unqualified hostility. At any rate it demands some
consideration. He was brought up at Anathoth, in a family
of priests. These priests had in all probability exercised
their office at the local shrine. He would therefore have
known the old system in all its aspects. And these were,
as we have seen, not all bad. There was, besides the superstition and the moral corruption, a thoroughly human
and happy side to it—the side of fellowship and friendship. It is part of the tragedy of Jeremiah's later life, not
only that he was lonely and persecuted—that is hard for
any man—but that he was especially the sort of man who
longed by temperament for what was denied to him. He
must have looked back with yearning to the old, happy
days before he had had to cut himself off from his family
and friends; and the old social life was inextricably bound
up with his family traditions of the old worship. He would
not be the saint that he is if he had not felt the drawing
of the old life on its better side. And this old life had a
past, and a distinguished past. His own line of priests
descended from Abiathar. They had behind them the
prestige and the sanction of the heroic age of David. If we
wish to see Jeremiah the man, we have to remember the
outlook in which he was brought up. Does he, in later
life, say hard things about the Temple worship, and find
himself in bitter opposition to its priesthood? Can he
separate himself altogether from his family traditions?
The line of Abiathar had been cut off for centuries from
access to the Temple at Jerusalem. The line of Zadok had
during that time occupied its place. Was Jeremiah, a
descendant of Abiathar, likely to think too well of the
Jerusalem priesthood? We cannot eliminate such a pre-
judice from the prophet's mind—just because he is, above
all the other prophets, so profoundly human and natural.

And the reforms of Josiah only threw up into greater prominence the family of Zadok. It is just here that we have the poignancy of Jeremiah's life history. He sides with Deuteronomy against his own family: and he is by inheritance out of touch with the leaders in the Deuteronomic party. Anathoth plots against his life; and for Jerusalem he has never had real sympathy. He is alone, just because he is loyal—loyal both to his own upbringing and to his God.

What then, in brief, is Jeremiah's teaching?

In the first place, he shares, without doubt, the attitude of Deuteronomy to all the abuses of worship—both those of the local sanctuaries, and those of the foreign cults introduced by Manasseh. His book is full of evidence of this.

Further, he carries forward the Deuteronomic insistence on a religion of the heart. To him it is a new covenant going deeper than anything in the past in the method of its sanction. The contrast is not actually with the covenant in its Deuteronomic form, but explicitly with that made in the wilderness: but the point of the contrast lies not in the substance of the covenant, but in the manner in which, on the side of the people of God, it is apprehended. It is still a covenant with the people: but it becomes individual also:[1] "they shall all know me, from the least of them unto the greatest of them" (xxxi. 31-34). That is, with less emphasis on individual apprehension, the idea of Deuteronomy: and Jeremiah elsewhere uses the Deuteronomic idea of the circumcision of the heart.

Thus it would appear that, on one side of the Deuteronomic reform, Jeremiah is with it. There are two passages which are discussed in this connection—xi. 1-8 and viii. 8. The interpretation of these must ultimately depend on the general view of Jeremiah's relation to Deuteronomy. xi. 1-8 appears to record a definite charge to Jeremiah to preach "this covenant"; the substance of the message, which refers in so many words to the

[1] Peake, Jeremiah (*Century Bible*), *ad loc.*

original covenant at the period of the Exodus; and an instruction to the prophet to go round and deliver it in the cities of Judah and in the streets of Jerusalem. It is, however, disputed whether the verses which refer to the Exodus period (4, 5) should not be omitted, and in that case the passage becomes an explicit statement of Jeremiah's support of Deuteronomy. The probability is, however, that too much is made of the distinction between one covenant and another. The principle of the covenant really remains the same throughout—that of the Exodus, that of Deuteronomy, and even the content of the new covenant, are only successive forms of the same fundamental principle that Israel is Yahweh's people, and Yahweh is Israel's God: on His side the initial act of love shown in His redemption from Egypt and in all the history, and on theirs, acceptance of His conditions—first as an act of simple obedience (Jer. xi. 7, "Obey my voice"), then as the outcome of a right heart, and of Israel's love (Deut.), and ultimately as that of an inward obedience, springing from the heart, both corporate and individual (Jer. xxxi. 31-34). In this case the passage in chapter xi. must mean, whatever its detail, that Jeremiah worked with the Deuteronomic reform and supported its restatement of the covenant.

Jeremiah viii. 8, on the other hand, has often been taken as a definite attack upon Deuteronomy. "How do ye say, We are wise, and the law of the Lord is with us? But behold, the false pen of the scribes hath wrought falsely." It is perhaps safe to say that this passage may mean anything. It is just one of those isolated statements which will fit into any theory. If, on other grounds, it can be shown that Jeremiah's teaching is all the time fundamentally inconsistent with that of Deuteronomy, it will mean that that book owes its false teaching to false scribes: it has no claim to be trusted as a true exposition of the real Law. If, on the other hand, Jeremiah was at least in some respects with and not against the new book, it can quite as easily be taken to mean that there were other interpretations of the traditional law of the scribes'

own making; and that it is these which Jeremiah attacks.
That there was scope for the growth of new interpretations is shown by the later development of the Priestly
code: and that there were many things in the Temple
tradition just before the Exile with which Jeremiah could
not have agreed is equally clear.

We have seen that Josiah's reforms gave two impulses
to the now centralised religion, one intentional and good
—the insistence on the acceptance of the Law from the
heart—and one unintentional and bad—the inevitable
growth in the dependence on the outward sanctuary,
with all that that meant of formalism and moral inconsistency. With the one Jeremiah was in entire sympathy,
and indeed it was the foundation of his own greatest
teaching: the other led directly to his revolutionary
attack on the Temple system. The passages in which we
have this are xxvi. 1-6, vii. 1-15. "Trust ye not in lying
words, saying, The temple of the Lord, the temple of the
Lord, the temple of the Lord, are these" (vii. 4). This
verse gives the key to the prophet's attitude. The "lying"
theory is, as we have seen, the "magical" view that
Yahweh is so bound by His covenant that nothing that
Israel does can prevent Him from maintaining the in-
violability of His house. Both passages are in fact conditional, and not absolute, predictions of its overthrow.
Thus xxvi. 4, "if ye will not hearken unto me"; vii. 5, 7,
"if ye throughly amend your ways, . . . then will I cause
you to dwell in this place". If they become absolute, it
is only because Jeremiah knows that the people will not
hearken or amend. It is formalism that he denounces,
and even now not formalism alone. He has in mind in
this very passage the Baal worship, and the strange gods
introduced by Manasseh (vii. 9), and later in the chapter
the abominations in the Temple, and the fire-offerings of
children in the Valley of Hinnom (vii. 30, 31). The
Deuteronomic reform had in fact, where it succeeded, increased formalism—the reliance on the external without
the internal—and it had, further, at least since the death
of Josiah, not even succeeded. The people are rejecting

the Law, both in spirit and in letter (vi. 19, xvi. 11), and
Jeremiah calls them back to the old paths (vi. 16). His
attitude is precisely that of Stephen, and indeed of our
Lord. St. Stephen was charged with teaching against
Moses, and the whole of his speech, even in the part about
the Temple, is a plea that it is not he who has been disloyal to the Law but the Jews—what they are doing in his
time, and what they did to Christ, is of a piece with what
they have done all through their history: "ye do always
resist the Holy Ghost; as your fathers did, so do ye, . . . ye
who received the law as it was ordained by angels, and
kept it not" (Acts vii. 51, 53). So our Lord vindicates the
sanctity of the Temple, against those who profaned it in
His day, in Jeremiah's own words, "Is this house . . .
become a den of robbers in your eyes?" (Jer. vii. 11); " ye
have made it a den of robbers" (Mk. xi. 17).

It is surely mere speculation to say what line Jeremiah would have taken if there had been no formalism
and no corruptions. That situation did not exist. What
did exist was enough, and more than enough, to cover all
his language, even the strongest. He says, and he may
well say, that under such conditions the sacrifices are so
useless that they may well, for all that God will care,
actually eat the flesh of the burnt-offering as well as that
of the peace-offering—for sacrifice so offered is no sacrifice (vii. 21): but he also says, as Isaiah does, that prayer
for such people is no use (vii. 16; xi. 14; xiv. 11), even the
prayer of such intercessors as Moses and Samuel (xv. 1),
or the fastings and prayers which they may offer for
themselves (xiv. 12). Once again the contention that it is
sacrifice as such that cannot avail proves too much: for
the language would in that case carry a denial of the
efficacy of prayer, and the best prayer.

Indeed, in one passage, towards the end of his ministry,
in Zedekiah's time (xxxiv. 13 ff.), he actually quotes
Deuteronomy as giving, on one point then at issue, the
substance of the covenant, "with your fathers in the day
that I brought them forth out of the land of Egypt"—
the very words in the crucial passage, vii. 22 ff., in which

he is supposed to have denied the Divine sanction of
sacrifice at all in the golden age in the wilderness. The
meaning of xxxiv. 13 ff. is clear when taken with the
words in chapter vii. He puts the Deuteronomic law on
the same footing of obligation as the commands given at
Sinai: and Zedekiah's special covenant for the release of
the Hebrew servants is a particular application, and renewal, of Deuteronomy. Each covenant—each re-enact-
ment of the whole or part—is in substance and spirit the
same as the other. And the heinousness, in Jeremiah's
own view, of the breach of Zedekiah's covenant is aggravated by the fact that it was made in the usual way
by the covenant sacrifice (xxxiv. 18). So too the new
covenant of the heart will be "cut", as all Hebrew covenants were (xxxi. 31-34: "make" is always in Hebrew
"cut"). Thus vii. 22 ff. cannot be interpreted as a denial
either of the history or of the principle of sacrifice: that
question is not raised; for as we have seen the thought in
the whole of chapter vii. is of sacrifice, and cultus, as
wrongly used, not of sacrifice as such. All that vii. 22 ff.
can really be said to mean is (1) that, as regards sacrifice,
perhaps it is meant to imply that it was not sacrifice which
was originally ordered at Sinai: that is historically true,
and the contrary view was only stated in the unhistorical
record in the Priestly code of later date; in Jeremiah's
time the available history and tradition was that sacrifice
had been practised from the earliest times; (2) that, supposing the later Priestly tradition was already to some
extent formed, and that the ordinances of worship bulked
as largely as, or more largely than, the moral law in the
common idea of the original covenant, the truth is that
if you are to sum up in one word what Yahweh said to
Israel at that time, the word would be "Hearken"—or
"Obey" (xi. 4)—and not "sacrifice".

So interpreted the passage exactly agrees with the
famous saying of Samuel—"Behold, to obey is better than
sacrifice and to hearken than the fat of rams. For rebellion
is as the sin of witchcraft, and stubbornness is as idolatry
and teraphim" (1 Sam. xv. 22, 23); that is, the formal and

insincere sacrifice is as bad as the corrupt and idolatrous: one has as little value as the other.

To suggest that an Israelite—certainly an Israelite of Jeremiah's period—could have thought of forty years of national history as having passed without sacrifice is to read back into the Old Testament an idea entirely foreign to it, but familiar enough in modern times. Is it, for instance, easy—to take one point alone out of that ancient life—for us to visualise a society in which meat meals and sacrifice meant the same thing? Yet that was the rule until the Deuteronomic legislator expressly permitted flesh to be eaten at home without sacrifice because the local sanctuaries and sacrifices were to be abolished; and to suppose that there were forty years without sacrifice is to suppose that for forty years the Israelite people ate no meat at all.

There is indeed one passage (xvii. 19-27) in which a future restoration is promised under a Davidic kingship in which "They shall come . . . bringing burnt-offerings, and sacrifices, and oblations, and frankincense, and bringing sacrifices of thanksgiving, unto the house of the Lord" (26). Most modern critics assign this to a post-exilic date, on the ground that Jeremiah could not have set so much store by the Sabbath—the restoration is conditional on a proper keeping of the Sabbath—or have written in this way about sacrifice. The argument is frankly *a priori*. Driver (*Introd. to Lit. of O. T.* p. 258) says: "The style is . . . thoroughly that of Jeremiah"; and Peake (*Cent. Bible*, Jeremiah, *ad loc.*) though he adopts the later date, agrees with this. Driver, with characteristic fairness, admits on the one hand that as regards Sabbath and sacrifice it is "not in the usual spirit of Jeremiah"; but on the other hand, "although no doubt Jeremiah speaks disparagingly of sacrifice offered by impure hands, it may be questioned whether he would have rejected it when (as is the case implicitly in xvii. 26) it is conceived as the expression of a right heart".

Of the same type as this is another restoration prophecy in xxxiii. 1-13, where again there will be the voice "of them that bring sacrifices of thanksgiving into the house of the Lord". And, once more, though there is more unanimity in the rejection of Jeremiah's authorship than is the case with verses 1-13, there is xxxiii. 14-26. Here we have the Davidic king, "the priests the Levites", and burnt-offerings, oblations (*minḥah*) and "sacrifice" (peace-offering). The last of these passages is omitted in LXX; and as all three passages are so much challenged it is perhaps better to draw no conclusions from them. Yet xxxiii. 18 uses a phrase of Jeremiah's time, "the priests the Levites"; and the enumeration of sacrifices in xvii. 26, xxxiii. 18, is also pre-exilic (*i.e.* there is no mention of sin- or guilt-offerings in what appears to be intended as a complete list); and as such it fits the conditions in Jeremiah's time but not those of P. Of "the priests the Levites" Peake's explanation is that the post-exilic writer "avails himself of the archaic mode of expression"; and presumably the same would apply to the lists of sacrifices. Driver (*Introd.* p. 262) appears to accept Jeremiah's authorship for the second and third passages as well as the first; and I am emboldened by this to suggest that to think themselves back by the exercise of the sense of what we call history into the conditions of the past is not, at the least, what would be considered a leading characteristic of post-exilic writers who have accepted the Priestly code; and indeed to ask whether the refusal of these passages, or perhaps the two first, rests on the *a priori* convictions of modern scholars, however eminent, or on real evidence from the accepted writings of Jeremiah and the established history of his period.

However this may be, it remains to be said that, after all, the value of sacrifice, at whatever period of its development, lies for us admittedly in its inner meaning. That meaning did attach to it, as we shall see below, in all its different forms—piacular, burnt-offering, peace-offering. And in the truest sense Jeremiah does undoubtedly show in two significant passages that he translated his own deepest experiences into terms of sacrifice. In the plot against his life at Anathoth he saw himself as a lamb

G

that is led to the slaughter (xi. 19); and in this—as well as in the spirit of the lament in xv. 15 ff.—"for thy sake have I suffered reproach"—he prepares the way for the servant who is the sacrificial Lamb in Isaiah liii. And indeed, if the text of xv. 16 f. is to be relied upon (LXX differs), he passes on in that passage to language that is typical of the meal of the peace-offering: "Thy words were found, and I did eat them; and thy words were unto me a joy and the rejoicing of mine heart. . . . I sat not in the assembly of them that make merry, nor rejoiced: I sat alone. . . ." He had found his own food from God—and it is in the inner meaning of the peace-offering that he expresses himself, though in the outward form of it he could not share.

And, perhaps more significant than any passages in which he used technical language, we have his use of three figures in which the fundamental conception underlying sacrifice from the beginning is contained—*i.e.* those of Israel as the bride of Yahweh, Yahweh as the Father of Israel, and Israel as the Vine (Jer. ii. 2; iii. 4; ii. 21). These are not new figures. But they stand for the old belief out of which sacrifice arose, and of which it is, in all its stages, the expression, that God and man are one flesh and that the life of God, whether shared as by a father with his children or as by the root and branches of a single tree, is the life of man.

Three passages in the Psalms remain to be considered: Psalms xl. 6-8 ; l. 8-15 ; li. 16, 17.

(1) Psalm xl. 6:

> Sacrifice and offering thou hast no delight in;
> Mine ears hast thou opened:
> Burnt-offering and sin-offering hast thou not required.
> 7 Then said I, Lo, I am come;
> In the roll of the book it is written of me;
> 8 I delight to do thy will, O God;
> Yea, thy law is within my heart.

The first question that arises here is as to the translation of the last line of verse 6. The Hebrew word for the

"sin-offering" of our version is חֲטָאָה *haṭa'ah*; and in every
other passage in which it occurs the meaning is "sin" not
"sin-offering". The word for sin-offering is the intensive
plural *haṭṭa'th*. Dr. Briggs therefore (*I. C. C.*, Pss. vol. i.
ad loc.) translates "burnt-offerings with sin". Besides the
linguistic reason for this there are others, literary and
historical. The rest of the passage suggests Deuteronomy—
"a roll of a book"; "mine ears hast thou pierced" or
digged, E.V. "opened", in order to make that "hearing"
of God's law possible which is so characteristic a phrase
of Deuteronomy; and "thy law is within my heart" like
the law of Deuteronomy and the new covenant of Jeremiah. If, as many suppose, this language dates the Psalm
in the seventh century, it belongs to the time before sin-
offerings were part of the sacrificial system. Thus (*a*) the
literary affinities with Deuteronomy and Jeremiah, and
(*b*) the consequent seventh-century date, confirm the
translation "with sin" as against "sin-offering". And in
this event the verses are, in so many words, not a condemnation of sacrifice as such but only of sacrifices offered
in the wrong spirit.

On the other hand, if the translation "sin-offering" is
kept, in spite of these difficulties, the Psalm may be post-
exilic. In that case it belongs to a period in which the
abuse of sacrifices could indeed be recognised, as it is in
Malachi, but which does accept the whole system as a
necessary part of the restored religion, and the usual
interpretation of verses 6, 7 must be given up.

Lastly, the translation "sin-offering" may be kept,
with the seventh-century date, in spite of the historical
difficulty. Even in this case, however, the affinity of
language and thought with Deuteronomy and Jeremiah—
with the two taken together—should be decisive. The
interpretation here must be governed, not by any theory
of Jeremiah's views taken alone but, in the first place, by
the meaning of Deuteronomy. What this Psalm does (and
it is of supreme significance) is to set over against the
wrong spirit in which the sacrifices were then being
offered the true spirit of all sacrifice, whether the

imperfect sacrifices of the old Law, or the perfect sacrifice
of Christ. Sacrifice, of whatever kind, is, if rightly understood, just one expression of "Lo, I come to do Thy will,
O God".

(2) Psalm l. Verses 8-15 and verse 23 must be taken
together. God tells His people that it is not any failure to
offer sacrifices that He reproves them for, but the misunderstanding of their meaning—apparently both because
they think that He is affected by the quantity of them,
and because they imagine that they are His food in a
material sense. What He does desire is the offering of "the
sacrifice of thanksgiving" and the paying of vows (verse
14): it is "the sacrifice of thanksgiving" that glorifies Him
(verse 23). The question here is—what is the antithesis? Is
it between all external acts of sacrifice on the one hand,
and the metaphorical offering of thanksgiving on the
other, without any material embodiment? or is it between
sacrifices offered in the old spirit, as charms compelling
God's favour in a magical way, and with the old, gross
idea that the god actually ate, in a physical sense, what
was given to him, and the sacrifices really offered out of
the desire of the heart in a thankful spirit?

It is again a question of the Old Testament use of
language. The Hebrew word for sacrifice in verses 14, 23
is *zebaḥ*, the regular word for the slaughter sacrifice *par
excellence*, the peace-offering: and the whole expression
"sacrifice of thanksgiving" is the ordinary one for the
peace-offering as such—meaning a sacrifice offered in a
thankful spirit. Are we to follow the regular use of the
Hebrew words—to which these are parallels both as
regards sacrifice (*e.g.* Ps. iv. 5, "sacrifices of righteousness") and generally in the Hebrew way of expressing
what we should express by an adjective? Or are we to
transfer a metaphorical use of sacrifice characteristic of
modern ideas into the Hebrew mind? Most interpreters
undoubtedly choose the latter; but the justification for
their doing so on the grounds of Hebrew usage, as distinguished from an *a priori* view as to what the Hebrew
writers are likely to have meant, does not seem clear.

And in verse 14 of this Psalm "offer unto God the sacrifice of thanksgiving" stands as a parallel to "pay thy vows unto the Most High"; and it is difficult to see that, if the latter is the concrete act of fulfilling a vow, as it appears to be, the sacrifice of thanksgiving is not equally concrete (Briggs, *I. C. C.*, Pss. *ad loc.*).

The setting of the sacrificial verses in this Psalm points to the same interpretation as that of Psalm xl. Verse 5 ("Gather my saints together unto me; those that have made a covenant with me by sacrifice") assumes sacrifice as the normal sanction of a covenant; and verses 16-22 make it clear that those to whom the sacrifice verses are addressed are living in sin: the view of sacrifice that is condemned, therefore, is one that is both formal or magical and material. The Psalm says nothing about sacrifice as properly offered, except, if the view taken above is the right one, to hold it up as an ideal.

(3) Psalm li. Verses 16, 17 are familiar:

16 For thou delightest not in sacrifice; else would I give it:[1]
   Thou hast no pleasure in burnt-offering.
17 The sacrifices of God are a broken spirit:
   A broken and a contrite heart, O God, thou wilt not despise.

Once more there is a linguistic question. Verse 17 may mean that the sacrifices acceptable to God *are* a broken spirit, though in that case "the sacrifice of God is a broken spirit" would be more natural; or it may mean sacrifices offered by a broken spirit, like sacrifices of thanksgiving in Psalm l. 14, and sacrifices of righteousness in Psalms iv. 5 and l. 18, as explained above (Briggs, *ad loc.*): it is not the mere outward offering of *zebach* or of *'olah* that counts, but the spirit of penitence and contrition in which they are offered.

The Psalm as a whole is one of the greatest post-exilic attempts to bring together the two conceptions of sin of which I have already spoken. There are the transgressions to be blotted out (verse 1), and the iniquities (verse 9): the Psalmist asks God to hide His face from his sins

[1] R.V.; or, as in R.V.m., "that I should give it".

(verse 9). That is the sin against God as a Righteous
Judge—which He atones for by covering the sin, in the
sense in which sins are objective realities, as it were external to the sinner. But on the other side—and it is this
which predominates—the sin is an offence against God's
holiness, and the language of forgiveness is not only that
of the cancelling of an outward act, but still more that
of the cleansing of the unclean sinner: "Wash me, . . .
cleanse me (v. 2). . . . Purge me with hyssop (v. 7, with
which sacrificial blood was sprinkled : Lev. xiv. 7 ; Ex.
xii. 22; cf. Heb. ix. 19): . . . Wash me and I shall be whiter
than snow. . . . Create in me a clean heart, O God (v.10). . . .
Cast me not away from thy presence; and take not thy holy
spirit from me (v. 11)." It is the language of the sanctuary.
The sinner is unclean, and needs the atoning blood; though
at the same time the Psalm, like Isaiah liii., reaches, or
nearly reaches, the New Testament solution of the problem of atoning for all sin—the sin to be forgiven includes
blood-guiltiness (verse 14), the sins with a high hand for
which the Old Testament sacrifices were powerless; for it
sees the holiness of God brought into the sinner by the
indwelling of His Holy Spirit.

It is in this context that the two verses especially in
question must be taken. The Psalmist's religious life
centres in the Temple and its associations of holiness,
of atonement, and of cleansing: and if he transcends, as he
does, the sacrificial standard of his day, it can only be a
question whether he is thinking of that standard in its
better, as well as in its worse, contemporary use, or only
in its worse. If the interpretation, suggested above, of "the
sacrifices of God are a broken spirit" is right, it will be the
latter; if not, it may, but we cannot say must, be the
former; and if it is, he is not abandoning the category of
sacrifice, but anticipating the New Testament in raising
it to a higher and a really effective level.

I have purposely omitted, up to this point, any reference to the last two verses of the Psalm, because—though
on the *a priori* ground that their spirit is inconsistent
with the earlier part—they are so commonly assumed to

be a later addition. But if the Psalm itself is an expression
of corporate penitence—Israel being spoken of collect-
ively in the first person singular—there seems no reason
why the prayer for forgiveness should not end with a
prayer for national restoration, in which the redeemed
and forgiven community shall once more offer sacrifices
—not now the mere external acts, but sacrifices that
spring from a righteous heart—that will be truly acceptable to God.

These passages are partly practical, and, in the Psalms
especially, partly theoretical—if anything in Hebrew
religion can be said to be "theoretical" at all. The prophets are dealing, from beginning to end, with the actual
circumstances of their time. They are speaking to their
own contemporaries, and meeting their own problems.
Much of the modern interpretation of them seems in a
strange way to have passed back, unconsciously enough,
into the old habit of regarding them as having spoken
not for their own times but for the future. They were,
not so long ago, imagined to have been speaking of the
events, and providing the interpretations of the events,
of the first Christian century. That view was taken because the early Christians, quite naturally, read back into
their still living words their own presuppositions, and it
has become easy to see the error which the first Christians made. It is not so easy to guard against the habit
of mind that caused the error. But "why beholdest thou
the mote that is in thy brother's eye, but considerest not
the beam that is in thine own eye?" The physician may
have need to heal himself. The instinct to read our own
ideas into the past is not so easy to eliminate; and the
prophets are now taken as having spoken for and anticipated the convictions of, not the first, but the nineteenth
and twentieth centuries A.D.

Does the evidence which has been examined justify this?
If we summarise it, there are certain points in the prophetic teaching and in the kindred teaching of the Psalms
which seem beyond all doubt to emerge from the passages
which are in a sense depreciatory or critical of sacrifice.

In the first place, there is unqualified condemnation of everything that was either inconsistent with the sole worship of Yahweh, or not on the line of the true development of that worship: under this head come all the passages which refer to the worship of definitely foreign gods; and, coming nearer home, of the Canaanite Baal as such; to the blend of Yahweh- and Baal-worship in the local sanctuaries, or even the worship of Yahweh as such along the lines of a genuine, though not the best, Israelite tradition in the greater sanctuaries of the Northern Kingdom. These pass into one another and into the next type in such a way that passages really dealing with the last, as in Amos, sometimes seem as if they might be attacks on the Temple worship itself: but the context makes it clear that they are not. The worship that they are attacking has all the time more or less of something fundamentally wrong in its outward embodiment.

Secondly, the worship itself may be on the right lines, but like all outward worship, sacrificial or other, it may be formal and external. The inner meaning of sacrifice is always ethical: it is the expression of the desire of the heart to do God's will. Wherever the prophets or the Psalmists felt that it meant less than that, wherever they saw it pass into mere reliance on outward acts, they said, without qualification, that obedience and mercy were better than sacrifice.

Again, the whole movement of Hebrew religion is one of growth; and like all growing things it was always changing, but, equally, always the same. The prophets came, like Jesus, not to destroy but to fulfil. They inspired, watched, protected its growth. And there came the time when the Psalmist had to say that the old idea that the burnt-offering was the bread of God did not mean that God ate bulls' flesh or drank the blood of goats. "My flesh is meat indeed, and my blood is drink indeed." . . . "It is the spirit that quickeneth; the flesh profiteth nothing: the words that I have spoken unto you are spirit and are life." Jesus is not contradicting His own teaching but interpreting it. In precisely the same way the Psalmist or the prophet warns his contemporaries off the wrong interpretation in order to open their minds to the right. They are not cancelling the past, but completing it.

And, lastly, there is in some at least, if not all, of the writers of these passages, from Isaiah in the earlier period to the Psalmist of the 51st Psalm at the end, a strong underlying dependence on the religion of the sanctuary. That belongs throughout to the idea of holiness, and its correlative idea of sin as needing cleansing and atonement. And there is growing desire to meet the claims of righteousness in terms of holiness—to find a way of atoning for blood-guiltiness by the blood of sacrifice—which leads their teaching as a whole to pass from the negative to the positive, from the destructive to the constructive. The moral abuses of the old sacrificial meals, the hollowness of the quantitative material use of the burnt-offering, the failure of the piacular element in the old sacrifices to meet the demands of absolute righteousness and of the new holiness—these are unsparingly and deservedly denounced. There is no salvation along these lines. But there is something in the peace-offering rightly used which makes it the supreme expression of thanksgiving and the secret of the highest joy that God can give to man: the burnt-offering does express, and in expressing is meant to inspire, the perfect surrender of the will to God; and they begin—now with an almost premature clearness and success, and now with a practical efficiency that in its very elaboration spelt its own failure, in the development of the special class of piacular sacrifices after the Exile— to feel after a solution of the ultimate moral problem of holiness and sin which the Old Testament religion in the end failed to find, but for which it left all the materials for our Lord to gather up and use.

Both these elements—the critical and the constructive —remain throughout the rest of the pre-Christian literature. From the reconstitution of the Jewish community after the return from Babylon the Temple worship is in the main accepted. The post-exilic prophets may criti-

cise it—as Malachi does (i. 6-14, etc.), but they assume it,
as indeed do Zephaniah, Nahum, and Habakkuk before
the Exile (Zeph. i. 7 f.; Nah. i. 15; Hab. i. 3: the prophets'
complaint is not against the system of the Torah, but
only that the system is not allowed to work). The main
work of Haggai and Zechariah is to inspire the rebuilding
of the Temple. Ezekiel, just as in his early chapters he
has, like the older prophets, denounced the abuses of
worship, in his closing section sees in a vision the whole
community reconstructed on the basis of the religion
and service of the sanctuary. Deutero-Isaiah's central
figure is the Servant of Yahweh; and "Servant" of God
means, in accordance with one of its constant uses, worshipper as well as slave: worship is service, and service
is worship. It is this inherent meaning of the term that
makes the ultimate development of the Servant idea
in Isaiah liii. so far more natural than would appear at
first sight to the modern reader. The Servant's life of
service is an approach to the altar. The prophet passes in
one picture of him after another from the collective idea
of the service of the whole nation, through that of the
faithful minority of the nation, to the last great passage
in which the religion of the Old Testament finds its
clearest expression of the individual. And in this the
Servant becomes identified, in the meaning of his
sufferings, with the sinners for whom he dies: the Lamb
offered in sacrifice for their sins has an atoning power
which the sin- and guilt-offerings never had; and out of
his death comes the achievement of the purpose of sacrifice in the satisfaction, for him, and, as must be implied,
for those for whom he has suffered: he has been both the
victim and the interceding priest, and suffering and intercession alike bring him to the portion with the great and
the dividing of the spoil with the strong, in which as
servant and worshipper, victim and priest, he merges
into the figure of the King.

Here, now less explicit and now more, there are the
fundamental ideas of the three kinds of sacrifices—sin-
offering with its atonement, burnt-offering with its wor-

ship of self-dedication, and peace-offering with its enjoy-ment of God's gifts. The ideals of the worship of Yahweh as the Holy God and of the service of Him as the Right-eous King are brought together, and both conceptions are lifted to the level at which the New Testament interpreta-tion of Jesus has made them practical and real.

This chapter is not, in date, the latest expression of the Old Testament attitude to the sacrificial worship, though in substance it is the highest development to which it attained. The later chapters of Isaiah, probably written by a different hand and at a later date, while in height of conception they do not reach its level, give pictures of the restored worship, and of its implication in the gathering of the Gentiles, that, like chapter liii., go beyond any-thing realised in the Jewish Church of the return, and lead on to the city of God at the end of the New Testa-ment. But they contain illustrations, and in one case something that may be a real extension, of the last Servant passage. As in the earlier Servant pictures the whole people is the Servant, and in the last the individual Ser-vant in his service becomes a priest, so now the whole people are priests (lxi. 6). And in the most striking passage of all the whole history since Israel became the covenant people is made a history of Yahweh's work for them as Saviour (lxiii. 8), Shepherd (*ib.* 9, 11), Redeemer, (*ib.* 16), Father (*ib.* 16), God in His heavenly sanctuary (*ib.* 15), manifesting Himself by His Presence to His people on earth (*ib.* 9), and in all this He is afflicted in all their afflictions (*ib.* 9). God, the Saviour, Shepherd, and Re-deemer, is after all like His servant. The sufferings of His people are His.

CHAPTER IV

LATER VIEWS OF SACRIFICE

No account of the evidence of the Old Testament as to the meaning and use of the sacrificial system would be complete without at least some mention of the Psalms. The whole Psalter has indeed been called the hymn-book of the second Temple: and the phrase is true to the extent that a large number of the Psalms were appointed for use in the Temple worship. It is to them that we must go if we wish to form an idea of this worship at its best. The evidence to be obtained in this way is often forgotten because of the excessive emphasis that has been laid on the depreciatory passages in the prophets and Psalms which have been examined above. But whatever the ultimate meaning of these passages may be, a sense of proportion is required. For one Psalm which may be depreciatory there are perhaps twenty which were used in the Temple services, or refer to them in the opposite sense.

I do not propose to examine the references to worship in detail. It will be enough to say in general that the daily and Sabbath sacrifices, and the special sacrifices of the feasts, were all celebrated with the singing of fixed Psalms and Psalm-like passages. Some of these are general acts of worship—none more complete than Psalm lxxxiv.; and with this may well go Psalms xxix., xxx., xlviii., lxviii., xcvi., xcix., cxiii.-cxviii. (the Hallel sung at the great feasts), cxli. Others have special links with different kinds of sacrifices. Psalm xx. and Psalm lxvi. are Psalms of the burnt-offering—and both assume its ethical meaning: in the former God answers the prayer of His worshippers, and accepts burnt sacrifice from them as being those who do not trust in chariots or horses but make mention of the name of the Lord their God: in the latter the answered prayer is that of those who fear God and can declare what He has done for their soul: "If I regard iniquity in my heart, the Lord will not hear". Psalm xx. couples with the burnt-offering the 'Azkārāh or memorial of the meal-offering (verse 3); and Psalm xxxviii., a prayer for deliverance from suffering (one of our Penitential Psalms) is headed (R.V.m.) "to make memorial", and was probably assigned for use with the 'Azkārāh (at which the Levite choirs officiated as well as at acts of praise and thanksgiving). (So also Ps. lxx.)

Of far greater importance are the many Psalms linked either expressly or in thought with the peace-offering. This type of sacrifice originated as we have seen in the idea of communion with the Deity; but as time went on it tended to lose its original significance. With the introduction first of the burnt- and then of the sin- and guilt-offerings it no longer summed up the whole meaning of sacrifice: and with the suppression of the local sanctuaries it became a comparatively rare event in the life of the ordinary worshipper. That it remained the most joyful of the sacrifices is beyond doubt, if only from the constant expression of this in Deuteronomy: and it is probable that, not only the actual phrase "sacrifices of thanksgiving" but all outbursts of rejoicing and thankfulness in Psalms that have anything to do with the Temple should be referred to it. What is doubtful, apart from the Psalms— and corresponding passages for which the Psalms may supply the necessary connection of thought—is how far, if at all, the peace-offering retained in later times any sense of communion. That it did suggest the thought of the food and drink given by God—and that in a definitely spiritual sense—and, with food and drink, life, seems to become clear from an examination of the language of many of the Psalms. There is, first of all, the group of what Cheyne calls the "guest Psalms". The worshipper is a guest in God's house. The idea is both a parallel with and a contrast to the same idea in the worship of the heathen Semitic deities. There too the worshipper was a guest; but the contrast lies in the moral significance. To be a guest of Baal meant sensual indulgence and gross immorality: to be a guest of Yahweh meant the character described in Psalms xv., xxiv. 1-6. That stands out as of primary significance. And in the thought of Yahweh's guest there is a further meaning. The guest (*gēr*) is the stranger who is admitted to the privileges of hospitality and protection. These things are not his by right but as a gift. And the Israelite as Yahweh's *gēr* is reminded of the Covenant: what he received from God is not what God is bound to give but the free act of grace on God's initiative. It is in this sense that the peace-offering, perhaps alone among the sacrifices, does stand for the receiving of grace—something is conferred by it, while the atoning sacrifices, for instance, can only register, and accept, a state that already exists. The gift is described, as we have seen, in terms of food and drink, of the satisfaction of the yearning for God and His presence which is naturally expressed as hunger and thirst; and the result of it is life. So Psalm xxiii.—even if we do not accept Cheyne's attractive emendation of "in the presence of mine enemies" in verse 5 to "within thy courts", and still more clearly if we do— shows God's shepherding of His people as culminating in the table that He has prepared for them. So in Psalm xxxvi. 7, 8, 9:

How precious is thy lovingkindness, O God!
And the children of men take refuge under the shadow of thy
    wings.
They shall be abundantly satisfied with the fatness of thy house;
And thou shalt make them drink of the river of thy pleasures.
For with thee is the fountain of life:
In thy light shall we see light;

and in Psalm lxi. 4-8 to dwell in His tabernacle for ever, and, as in Psalm xxxvi., to take refuge in the covert of his wings, means life in the perpetual singing of praise to His name, and the daily performance of the singer's vows —(the votive-offering, a form of the peace-offering). Or, in

Psalm lxv. 4 there is God's initial act of choice, the technical "approach" to the altar, the making of God's house a spiritual home, and the satisfaction with its goodness. Or, again, the peace-offering is definitely a eucharistic meal:

Psalm xxii. 25 f.:

> Of thee cometh my praise in the great congregation:
> I will pay my vows before them that fear him.
> The meek shall eat and be satisfied:
> They shall praise the Lord that seek after him:
> Let your heart live for ever;

as it is in Psalms xxvi. 6-8, 12 and xxvii. 1, 4-6. These three passages together combine the ideas of the worship as a corporate act—one of its fundamental principles—of its moral requirements ("the meek"; "they . . . that seek after him"; "I will wash mine hands in innocency"; "thy face, Lord, will I seek": Ps. xxvii. 8)—of the offering as an act of thanksgiving—of the gifts that God gives ("shall eat and be satisfied"; the "beauty" or "pleasantness" of the Lord—"not merely the outward beauty of the sanctuary and its worship, but the gracious kindliness of Jehovah to His guests"[1]); of the life (xxii. 26), and the light and strength (xxvii. 1) that the gifts bring with them.

So the two Psalms xlii. and xliii.—songs of memory and hope—are centred upon the worship that is remembered and longed for, and the longing is thirst: "My soul thirsteth for God, for the living God".

I need not add quotations; but they could be supplied from such Psalms as liv. 6, lvi. 12 f., lxxxi. 10, lxxxvii. 7 (unless Dr. Briggs' different rendering for "fountains" is right), xcii. (the Sabbath Psalm), xcv. 2, 7; c. esp. 3; cvii. 9, 17-22; cxvi., cxviii. Even Psalm cxix., which has perhaps no direct reference to Temple worship, is after all the Psalm of the Law of God, and not only does the Law in any case include sacrifice, but the Psalmist himself has the thought of God's feeding him, at least as a metaphor

---

[1] Kirkpatrick, Psalms, *ad loc.* (xxvii. 4).

(verse 103: "How sweet are thy words unto my taste! yea, sweeter than honey unto my mouth"), and the thought of the free-will offering (verse 108): the whole spirit of the Psalm is that of the spirit of the true burnt-offering, "Lo, I come to do Thy will, O God"; and, in the last verse, in his penitence he is a lost sheep and God is his shepherd —a thought which we have seen already, and shall see later, to be inseparably bound up with that of God's feeding His people. Or, lastly, both in Psalm ciii. and in Psalm cxi. we have the sequence of God's dealings with those who praise Him: in Psalm ciii. 3-5 He forgives—heals—redeems—"crowneth thee with lovingkindness and tender mercies, . . . satisfieth thy mouth with good things"; and in Psalm cxi. we have God as praised in corporate worship: His honour (verse 3), majesty (verse 3), holiness (verse 9)—the righteous God (verse 3), Who gave the Law (verse 9), Who redeemed His people (verse 9), Who hath given meat unto them that fear Him, (verse 5), Who will ever be mindful of His covenant (verse 5)—God to whom the memorial, the *'Azkārāh,* is not made in vain.

The teaching of the Psalms defies tabulation, and in those which I have quoted and to which I have referred there has been abundant evidence of the ethical character of the Temple worship: and in this connection Psalms iv. and v. might be quoted also—the whole Psalm in either case, summed up perhaps in iv. 5, "Offer the sacrifices of righteousness"; and v. 4, "Thou art not a God that hath pleasure in wickedness"; and v. 7, "In thy fear will I worship toward thy holy temple"; and the latter half of Psalm xix., with its summary of the moral meaning of the Law—the Law that was ceremonial as well as moral. The worshippers might fall below these standards; but they were the standards of the writers of the Psalms and of those who appointed so many of them for use at the Temple sacrifices. The sacrifices themselves could not but fail in the end; but the Psalms, as well as many other passages in the Old Testament, give us beyond a shadow of doubt what was their intention.

They played their part, and a high part, with the prophets in the spiritual preparation of the people of God.

There remains something to be said about the Wisdom
Literature. References to sacrifice are few and incidental,
and they do not add anything material, except by way
of illustration, to the evidence furnished by the prophets
and the Psalms.

The passages for the most part say what is found in the
other writers about the moral background of the sacrifice. Thus (Prov. xv. 8):

> The sacrifice of the wicked is an abomination to the Lord:
> But the prayer of the upright is his delight.

Or (xvii. 1):

> Better is a dry morsel, and quietness therewith,
> Than an house full of feasting with strife.

(R.V.m.: Heb. "the sacrifices of strife"—interesting mainly as
showing how easily in the untechnical English translation a definite sacrificial reference may be missed.)

Or (xxi. 3):

> To do justice and judgment
> Is more acceptable to the Lord than sacrifice.

(Apparently the strongest anti-sacrificial passage, though when
set side by side with the two previously quoted it clearly means
"than sacrifice without justice"), as in xxi. 27:

> The sacrifice of the wicked is an abomination:
> How much more, when he bringeth it with a wicked mind?

(R.V.m.: "when he bringeth it to atone for wickedness.")

Ecclesiastes simply accepts the system, and says what might
be expected, as Proverbs does, about sacrifices unworthily
offered: v. 1, "Keep thy foot when thou goest to the house
of God; for to draw nigh to hear" (*i.e.* in the right spirit
—cf. Deuteronomy's use of "hear") "is better than to
give the sacrifice of fools; for they know not that they do
evil": so v. 4, "When thou vowest a vow unto God, defer
not to pay it; for he hath no pleasure in fools; pay that
which thou vowest". The latter passage almost certainly
refers to the votive offering (Dt. xxiii. 21-23; Burton,

H

I. C. C. ad loc., only refers to verse 21, and on the strength of that verse says that there is no reference to sacrifice; again this shows how little some commentators grasp the constant sacrificial meaning of words apparently un-technical. Dt. xxiii. 23 fixes the meaning of a vow: "That which is gone out of thy lips thou shalt observe and do; according as thou hast vowed unto the Lord thy God, a freewill offering, which thou hast promised with thy mouth").

Or again, Ecclesiastes ix. 2: "All things come alike to all: there is one event to the righteous and to the wicked; to the good and (R.V.m. to the evil;) to the clean and to the unclean; to him that sacrificeth, and to him that sacrificeth not: as is the good, so is the sinner". In this depressing saying there is no doubt that the author takes it that the right kind of man does offer sacrifice.

Ecclesiasticus has two passages, one (xxxiv. 18-26) on unacceptable sacrifices and one (xxxv. 1-11) on acceptable. The former is a warning of the uselessness of sacrifices offered by men of the wrong character, and of trusting to the mere number of sacrifices—against formalism and materialism: and the warning is extended to unreal prayer as well as unreal sacrifice. Two verses (21, 22) bring out in a striking way the naturalness, to a Jew brought up on sacrifices, of identifying blood with life: "The bread of the needy is the life of the poor: he that depriveth him thereof is a man of blood. As one that slayeth his neighbour is he that taketh away his living; and as a shedder of blood is he that depriveth a hireling of his hire."

The second passage is a remarkable illustration, and a warning that is perhaps not unneeded, of the danger of assuming that apparently anti-sacrificial passages are always meant to be taken literally. The first two verses are:

He that keepeth the law multiplieth offerings;
He that taketh heed to the commandments sacrificeth a peace offering.
He that requiteth a good turn offereth fine flour;
And he that giveth alms sacrificeth a thank offering.

If these verses stood by themselves, as they might easily have done, they would have been taken as an unqualified statement that good actions are a sufficient substitute for actual sacrifices: but verses 4-11 are positive instructions to offer sacrifices of different kinds, and make it clear enough that as in xxxiv. 18-26 bad character is said to invalidate sacrifices, so in this passage good character is the first requisite: it is not that if a man is good he need not offer, but that if he is good his sacrifices are acceptable: "well begun is half done". The lesson of this passage might well be remembered in other and better-known cases where the author has not happened to add enough to make his meaning clear. On the other hand, both here and in vii. 7-10, where, in insisting on atoning sacrifices being prompt and having spiritual reality behind them, he seems to speak of prayer and almsgiving as having a parallel position with sacrifice, there may be the beginnings of the later Rabbinic point of view which in the end developed into a theory of prayer, almsgiving and fasting as representing the actual sacrifices (see below, pp. 106 ff.). But in Ecclesiasticus that stage has not been reached; the point is rather that there must be real character with the sacrifice.

The writer of Ecclesiasticus clearly accepts sacrifice and the Temple worship as part of the recognised system to which the wise man is loyal: in vii. 18-36 he summarises duties attached to various relationships of life—friends, wife, servants, cattle, children, parents, the poor, the dead, mourners, the sick; and in one section, to God and to His ministers the priests. It is possible that in the emphasis which he lays upon taking a full part in the duty of providing maintenance for the priests there may be evidence of a neglect of this duty already beginning: the centralisation of worship even before, and still more after, the dispersion made the complete working of the sacrificial system, and with it especially its ordinance of a priesthood passing by descent, impossible on the practical, as in the end it proved unavailing on the religious side.

More striking from the point of view of the place of

sacrifice and of the ideas underlying it in the religious life is the passage about Wisdom's feast in Proverbs ix. 1-6. Apart from the direct Christian use of this in later times in reference to the Eucharist, what it brings out clearly is the conception of God as giving what He gives to man in the form of food and drink; it is not teaching to be apprehended with the mind, or rules of conduct to be obeyed by the will, but ultimately a life to be incorporated with man's life. Here Wisdom, whom the Lord possessed in the beginning of His way, the Wisdom who is Divine, and almost the Divine Word of the Fourth Gospel, builds a house in order that the feast which she gives may be continual.[1] In LXX "she hath killed her beasts" of verse 2 is "she hath slain her offerings": and whether this is the right text or no, it undoubtedly gives the sense of the passage: the feast is a sacrificial one as all Hebrew feasts once were, and as all feasts in the house of God were in later times; and the sacrificial food gives *life*—the ultimate aim of the whole sacrificial scheme. Thus viii. 35—leading up to this passage: "whoso findeth me findeth life"—cf. xiv. 27, "the fear of the Lord is a fountain of life", etc. with Psalm xxxvi. 8, 9.

It is true that the Wisdom Literature taken as a whole lays no especial emphasis on sacrifice. The system is accepted as part of the established order. Its obvious danger, in later times, was that of formalism—of a dependence upon the prescribed external acts as in themselves sufficient; and to this the writers, like the Prophets and the writers of the Psalms, were, as is to be expected, alive. But the lack of emphasis must not be overpressed. The historical origin of the "wise man" and his characteristic way of teaching lies far back before the exile: and, though it was the form of Jewish religious teaching which was most naturally adapted to the assimilation of foreign elements, and therefore in later times could use Babylonian or even Greek ideas, it was essentially Hebrew or Jewish in character. It cannot be too completely detached from its context in the religious life of the people—the

[1] Toy, *I. C. C.*, Proverbs, *ad loc.*

life of the Temple worship and the Psalms. Its tendency
is to exalt the Torah, the Law, into something which is
almost as much a primeval condition, or instrument, of
the Divine life as Wisdom: and in fact there is almost an
identification of the two (*e.g.* Ecclus. xv. 1, " For he that
feareth the Lord will do this [seek Wisdom]; And he that
hath possession of the law shall obtain her"; so xix. 20; xxi.
11; xxiv. 23, 25): and in the Book of Wisdom, Wisdom
is again identified with the Holy Spirit (i. 5-7), and again
with the Word of the Lord (ix. 1, 2). Wisdom and the
Torah alike feed man; and their great gift is life.

Thus the Wisdom idea embodies or contains the full
scheme of religion; it is not a non-sacrificial way of conceiving of religion, but a way of conceiving the whole
religion, with its sacrificial aspect included with the rest.
Similarly there is no stress laid on the Messianic hope—
in fact there is perhaps less evidence with regard to it
than there is with regard to sacrifice. Yet contemporary
and later evidence make it clear that neither the Messianic
hope nor the Temple system had lost their significance.

On the other hand, with the later parts of the Wisdom
Literature we have passed into a period which for historical reasons was bound to be one of transition. In the days
before the Exile the religion of Israel was limited not in
its theology only but geographically to the land of Israel.
The Exile brought a new problem—that of the service of
Yahweh outside His own land; but in the light of the
promised return it was an interim problem only. The
restoration, and still more the reorganisation of the
Jewish nation as a Church on the soil of Palestine and
round the Temple, which is associated with the name of
Ezra, had, in theory at least, eliminated the temporary
difficulty of the Exile. The ideal constitution of the people
of God assumed the possibility of the Temple system as
the sufficient and normal expression of religion. But the
ideal could no longer, in fact, be realised. There were the
Jews of the dispersion to be provided for, as well as the
difficulty of making the Temple worship real even within
the limits of Palestine itself—the old difficulty created by

the Deuteronomic law of the central sanctuary. There were, it is true, some efforts in Egypt at re-creating Temple-centres elsewhere than at Jerusalem, presumably without the old dangers attaching to local sanctuaries such as those of Yahweh-Baal in Palestine. But these efforts had no lasting success, and played no real part in later developments. What did provide in a measure for the new need was the new system of the synagogue. Thus in the centuries immediately preceding the Christian era the working system of the Jewish religion is no longer simple but complex. There is on the one hand the living Temple worship and on the other the synagogue. The books of the Apocrypha and the pseudo-epigraphic literature give abundant evidence of the part which the former played in Jewish life not only in Jerusalem but in the dispersion as well. The desecration of the Temple by Antiochus Epiphanes and its recovery and rededication by Judas Maccabeus were, in a sense, the central events of the Maccabean history; and it is round it and its services that the national life is centred.

There are two remarkable passages, separated perhaps by an interval of 100 years, which, as descriptions, give a vivid impression of the solemnity and dignity of the worship—the famous 50th chapter of Ecclesiasticus in praise of Simon the son of Onias, and the less known and less vivid account in the Letter of Aristeas (chs. xcii.-xcix.) of the scene at the great sacrifices: "the orderly and silent service"; "the most complete silence reigns so that one might imagine there was not a single person present (. . . though there were actually 700 priests at work . . . besides many other attendants). Everything is carried out with reverence, and in a way worthy of God"; (after a description of the High Priest Eleazar's vestments) "their appearance created such awe and confusion of mind as to make one feel that one had come into the presence of a man who belonged to a different world"; (. . . everyone will be equally affected . . .) "at the thought of the sanctity which is attached to each detail of the service". Such passages indeed have no doctrinal bearing. But it seems worth while to bring them to mind, because without them it is easy to leave out such a side of the Temple system when we try to reconstruct it. We cannot readily connect the wholesale slaughtering, and the associations of what we know of the noise of an Oriental crowd, and the exaggerations which Christian writers have perhaps made of the business side of the Temple life,[1] with the perfect order, the alternations of profound silence with the music of the Psalms, which these writers reveal to us. There was something at the least of the spirit of true worship and of religious reality besides the formalism and other bad sides which to our minds too often and too readily make up the whole of the picture.

And the same type of literature reveals much in the way of spiritual significance. Some of the pseudo-epigraphic books have nothing to say about the Temple—whether because the writers depreciated it or because they assumed it we cannot say. But others are explicit enough.[2] The religion, ideal or actual, is one of the sanctuary, where God dwells in the midst of His people, "and they shall be my people in truth and righteousness" (Jub. i. 17). Confession of sin, present and past, will bring in the life of the new covenant, with the circumcision of the heart; and with that God will create in them a holy spirit, and will cleanse them, and will be their Father and they shall be his children (ib. i. 22-24). So the old law of the blood holds; it is not to be eaten (ib. vi. 7-14), and it is with blood that forgiveness will be pleaded for before the Lord (ib. 14).

Or again, in the sanctuary, God feeds His priests from His table (Jub. xxxi. 16—the table of the Lord is not only the table from which the Lord receives His food, but also that from which He feeds men: so Test. XII Patr. Jud. xxi. 5; Lev. viii. 16); just as in the first and the second Temple—the home both of the sheep (= Israel) and the Lord of the sheep—they offer a full table before Him (Enoch lxxxix. 50, 72, 73), but in the second Temple the bread of God was polluted and not pure (either because of

---

[1] I. Abrahams, *Studies in Pharisaism and the Gospels*, 1st series, xi. pp. 82-89.
[2] The quotations from these books are taken from Dr. R. H. Charles' translation in *Apocrypha and Pseudepigrapha of the O. T.*

the early post-exilic failures of the restored worship before
the Samaritan Temple was built or for such reasons as
Malachi has in mind in Mal. i. 7, etc.): and after the judgment God will still be feeding His people from the tree of
life (Enoch xxv. 4, 5, cf. Test. Lev. xviii. 11, etc.).

And the earlier ideas of the once separated aspects of
the life of the people of God begin to converge. The God
of the sanctuary, as we have seen, in communicating His
holiness to the people of the new covenant—holiness, the
quality of the sanctuary, as gathering up the moral content of the new obedience—becomes their Father (Jub. i.
22-24), and in the Holy Place where as God or as Shepherd He feeds the elect He is also the great King (Enoch
xxv. 4, 5). So on the side of human life the Messiah of the
Testaments of the XII Patriarchs is first priest—then
prophet and king—sinless, walking in meekness and righteousness (T. Jud. xxiv. 1) : and this priesthood is a
different one to that of Moses or that of Aaron and his
descendants; it is called by a new name (the priesthood of
the Most High God, *i.e.* that of Melchizedek—Test. Lev.
viii. 14). All the possibilities that Christians believe to be
realised in Christ begin to open out: He will be Teacher,
Judge, and King, the Light of the World, bringing peace
to all the earth: in Him the angels of the glory of the
presence of the Lord shall be glad: "the heavens shall be
opened, and from the temple of glory shall come upon
him sanctification, with the Father's voice as from
Abraham to Isaac. And the glory of the Most High shall
be uttered over him, and the spirit of understanding and
sanctification shall rest upon him. For he shall give the
majesty of the Lord to his sons in truth for evermore; and
there shall none succeed him for all generations for ever.
And in his priesthood the Gentiles shall be multiplied in
knowledge upon the earth, and enlightened through the
grace of the Lord; in his priesthood shall sin come to an
end, and the lawless shall cease to do evil": there is
hardly a word of the whole passage (Test. Lev. xviii. 2-14)
which might not be quoted.

Or the thought of atonement through blood is developed until it becomes effective; and it passes into the language of ransom, "Make my blood their purification and take my soul to ransom their souls" (4 Macc. vi. 29): the martyrs "became a ransom for our nation's sin; and through the blood of these righteous men and the propitiation of their death the divine providence delivered Israel" (*ib.* xvii. 21, 22). Indeed the idea of propitiatory sacrifice extended in later times from earth to heaven. Test. Lev. iii. 5, 6: "In [the 6th heaven] are the archangels, who minister and make propitiation to the Lord for all the sins of ignorance of the righteous; offering to the Lord a sweet smelling savour, a reasonable and bloodless offering"—an idea which, as Dr. Charles says (note on Test. Lev. iii. 5), must already have been familiar to the Jews because the earthly altar and tabernacle in Exodus were made after the heavenly pattern.

There are other more detailed points which bring out the significance of the sacrifices—*e.g.* in the "law section" (prob. 130–70 B.C.) of the Letter of Aristeas the High Priest explains the restrictions of the burnt-offerings to tame animals: "for he who offers a sacrifice makes an offering also of his own soul in all its moods". Thus the burnt-offering, as well as the sin- and peace-offerings, has its moral and religious background.

Side by side with the Temple system there are the synagogues. Both for the country Jews of Palestine, and still more for those of the dispersion, these provided a regular organisation for worship for those who could not be present at the Temple. In a sense they are a preparation for the survival of Judaism after A.D. 70; and it is often assumed that the synagogue worship was therefore of a kind fundamentally unsacrificial. There is truth in this, but not the whole truth. There was, naturally, no actual sacrifice. The law of the central sanctuary made that impossible. The problem had therefore to be faced of the participation in the sacrifices. And there were, in fact, three ways in which this was done. In the first place, individuals could journey to Jerusalem, be present at the public sacrifices, and offer their own. They might do this often or only occasionally, as circumstances permitted. But once at least in his lifetime each man would try to make the pilgrimage. In the second place, there was a definite organisation of the people, priests, Levites, and laymen alike, into twenty-four divisions, each of which was corporately responsible for the Temple worship for a set period. Representatives of each of the three classes went to Jerusalem on behalf of the rest; and while they were there the remainder followed in reading, in thought, and in prayer in their local synagogues what was being done on their behalf at the Temple. Or, thirdly, there was a movement of the utmost significance in the direction of the spiritualising of the actual sacrifices. The concrete acts of the Temple worship were performed in a liturgical setting of prayer and praise, and where sacrifice itself, in the technical and external sense, was impossible it came to be felt that the worshipper could identify himself with the moral meaning of the sacrifice by the spiritual acts corresponding with it. We have seen something of this tendency in Ecclesiasticus (xxxv. 1-3; vii. 7-10): keeping the law, departing from unrighteousness, or, more specifically, prayer and almsgiving are as acceptable to God as if the sacrifices which were the outward expression of such a character had been actually offered (cf. above, p. 99). But at the transition stage, of which the writer of Ecclesiasticus is a witness, there is no inconsistency between inward and outward. It is not suggested that sacrifices are futile or to be abandoned in favour of something inherently different. On the contrary, their moral significance is emphasised; and if the way is being prepared for the ultimate abandonment of the outward acts prescribed by the Law, that abandonment is by way not of the reversal, but of the fulfilling, of its requirements.[1] The synagogue worship in its traditional form has never been non-sacrificial; still less, anti-sacrificial. While the Temple

---

[1] For what follows, see M. Gaster in *Enc. Rel. and Eth.* vol. xi., "Sacrifice" (Jewish); and Oesterley and Box, *Religion and Worship of the Synagogue.* It is noteworthy, in view of the ordinarily accepted views about synagogue worship, that Dr. Gaster says at the end of his article: "The subject has not been dealt with anywhere else".

sacrifices continued, there was, as we have seen, at least
in the Palestinian synagogues, a definite and deliberate
attempt to participate in it, so far as was possible at a
distance, both by the system of delegates and by the
following of the Temple acts by those whose delegates
were acting for them there in the local synagogue. When
the Temple worship came to an end in A.D. 70 the Jewish
nation did not abandon the idea of sacrifice. They re-
verted to the attitude of Ezekiel during the Babylonian
captivity. The sacrifices are suspended, not abolished.
Ezekiel provided the people, against the time of the
promised return, with a careful picture of the restored
Temple and its sacrifices. So one of the six *sedarim*, or
orders, of the Mishnah—in which the oral tradition of
the first two centuries A.D. is recorded—is *Koddashim*
(holy things) recording all kinds of details as to the practices of the sanctuary, and including *Middôth*, a treatise
giving accurate measurements of the Temple. These are
preserved not out of mere antiquarianism, but as a guide
to future reconstruction.

So the devout Jew prays three times a day in the
'amidah: "Mayest Thou bring back the sacrifice to Thy
holy house, and the fire-offerings as well as their prayers
receive with favour". Or in the *'amidah* of the *musaf* or
additional service of Sabbaths, new moons, and festivals,
corresponding to the additional sacrifices on those days
in the Temple: "May it be thy will, O Lord our God, and
the God of our fathers, that thou mayest bring us up
with joy to our country, and then we will perform before
thee all the obligatory sacrifices, the permanent ones
according to their order, and the additional ones accord-
to the law". And there is the unconquerable optimism of
the formula used even now at every Passover meal: "This
year here—next year in the land of Israel! This year as
slaves—next year free."

And until the restoration, the sacrifices are offered in
spirit. Prayer, almsgiving and fasting, which to the
modern mind seem to have no connection with sacrifice,
are not substitutes for the ancient ordinances so much

as attempts to preserve them by rendering their inner and spiritual meaning. The two latter are the sacrifice of substance—even in quite a material sense—and prayer is definitely linked up with sacrifice on the principle laid down in Hosea xiv. 2. Further, the recital of the passages in the Law prescribing each sacrifice is preserved at the corresponding hour or season in the synagogue services as accepted by God in place of the act of sacrifice; and the Rabbinic tradition found, in a legend of Abraham, the authority for the practice: Abraham asked, "What will happen if they will no longer be able to bring such sacrifices?" and God's answer was: "Let them recite it before me, and it will be for me like unto the sacrifice".

Thus the modern conservative synagogue congregation is in fact in the same relation to the outward sacrificial acts as were the similar congregations away from Jerusalem before the destruction of the Temple. They took part in the outward acts, from which they were separated only by distance of space, in precisely the same way as that in which their modern successors enter into the spirit of acts from which they are separated by the distance of years. The actual sacrifices cannot be performed, but they are continued in spirit, in a setting equally of reminiscence and of anticipation. And death itself is interpreted sacrificially. It has its bearing on atonement. In Rabbinic teaching it is a sin-offering. The deaths of individuals are thought of as atoning for their own sins (Sanh. 44b), or for the sins of others (Sukk. 20a; Yᵉbamôth, 70a). The Talmud says: "The death of the high-priest is an atonement" (Jer. Yomā vii.; Makkôth 11b)—hence the permission for the slayer to leave his city of refuge on the death of the high-priest (and cf. the saying of Caiaphas about our Lord's death, which the writer of the Fourth Gospel, with his intimate knowledge of the Jewish mind, regards as the kind of thing that would come naturally from him as high-priest).

It is only in the quite modern "Reform" synagogues that this link with the sacrificial system has been broken. In them the sacrificial passages from the Law, and the prayers for a literal restoration of the sacrifices, have been dropped. Whether this is an improvement of traditional Judaism, or a legitimate development of it, it is not for a Christian to say. But in any case it does not represent the traditional attitude to sacrifice. And it is much to be desired that the undeniable attractiveness and, still more, the spiritual value of the writers of the new school of Liberal Judaism should not lead the interpreters of Christian origins to regard them as authoritative on questions of earlier Jewish doctrine, or as necessarily more likely than the conservative Jews to be able to throw light on the problems of the New Testament. What we need to visualise is the actual state of religion in Palestine in our Lord's time, and especially the part played therein by the sacrificial idea. For this the tradition of the synagogue is of first-rate value. And it shows conclusively that there is no such sharp antithesis between synagogue and Temple worship as is commonly supposed. It is true that the synagogue system enabled Judaism, as a living system of religion, to survive the catastrophe of A.D. 70. But that was not because sacrifice had already been repudiated in the synagogue. It was because it had in that form of worship a real life of its own; and in the later synagogue that life continued. The spiritualising of sacrifice became not its abrogation, but its justification: as its outward practice became less possible, its moral meaning stood out more clearly. And it is with its moral meaning, not with its ceremonial machinery, that the Christian view of sacrifice is concerned.

Our review of the sacrificial system and of the attitude towards it of the writers of Old Testament and other books, as well as of its place in Jewish religion in New Testament times, has necessarily dealt with details of the observances. But at every point these details are seen to express or to imply conceptions going to the root of religious and social life. And in the last resort what matters most is not details of ceremonial or of technique, but the general ideas which they illustrate. It is, in effect, the whole of Hebrew religion which we have been considering. And it is with the whole that, for New Testament purposes, we are concerned. It is not only that in order to find the true content for such a saying as "I came not to destroy but to fulfil" we are bound to ask what is in fact the inheritance which the first-century religion of Palestine had received from the past: we cannot interpret the Christian attitude to that inheritance until we know what in all its aspects it actually was; but even more than that, we have to go back into its history. For, as has been said above, our Lord's creativeness and originality consisted very largely in the freedom with which He was able to deal with the inheritance. He is not tied to contemporary interpretations of it, to this school of thought, or that. He is independent. He is able to go back over the old ground and to pick up what has been lost, or to bring into the light of day what has been overlaid. What He is, or does, or says is what would have had a meaning for all the great epochs of Hebrew history: the great leaders of the nation would have recognised it as their own. There is therefore nothing in the long past which is not relevant, or may not be relevant, to the interpretation of the New Testament. The God of Jesus is the God of Abraham and Isaac and Jacob, because as He sees the past it is not dead but alive: God is not the God of the dead, but of the living.

The outstanding feature, therefore, of the past is its continuity. What had come down by inheritance was a life, not a system or succession of systems. It was something practical and concrete, not a mere mechanism or a set of theoretical and abstract principles. It was wholly personal. There was a mechanism and there were principles; but the two were held together, and made operative, in the felt experience of a continued life. It was personal; but in its early stages without any self-consciousness, and even in its latest forms without those elements of introspection and analysis which have given to us the thoughts that such a word as personality naturally conveys. Its personal character was on the practical side: it was a life of intercourse between God and man,

and between man and man, and therefore always a
corporate life. As in all early stages of society, it was at
first wholly corporate. It was only later that the individual
as such began to emerge, and even then only in an incomplete and half-realised way. It was, as we know, only
through the Christian experience that the full value of the
individual over against the society was apprehended. On
the side of inheritance, what Christianity receives from
the past is life as lived in a society.

And this society goes back without a break to the
beginnings. What links generation to generation, what
makes the Jewish people of the first century A.D. one with
the Israel of the kings and prophets, with the people who
were redeemed from Egypt, with the families of the
patriarchs, and, unconsciously, with the prehistoric
beginnings of the Semitic clans, is the life shared by God
and man, the experience of belonging to the same God,
Who had given the life and maintained it. And that life
was only known in the society—clan, tribe, nation—
kingdom—Church—whatever the names by which we are
able to classify its various forms and stages. We can
indeed call the life in its Godward aspect religion. But the
very word religion to us means something specialised—a
department of life rather than the whole; and the use of it
for at least the earlier phases of the Hebrew life, if not for
the later as well, is fruitful of misunderstandings. We
think of religious life as distinguished from social or
political: of practices and ideas as spiritual or unspiritual;
and we cannot help it. But the concrete beginnings of
what, in our language, we have to call Hebrew, or Semitic,
religion belong to a period when the range of human
experience was limited in a way that we can hardly
reproduce in our imagination. None of our words help us.
We might say that the sphere of ancient life was almost
wholly material: but by the use of the word material we
suggest the exclusion of the spiritual, and in that sense
what we say is misleading. Or we may say that the experiences were of this life only without any thought of life
beyond the grave; and again we suggest something

approaching a negation. Or we may try to describe what was done or believed in terms of morality: and the only words that we can find for much of it suggest what we call immoral or non-moral: we imply a repudiation of what had never been faced, a denial of what had never as yet been asserted. What we have to try to reconstruct for ourselves is a society in the common life of which each and all of its members found everything which life, for them, could mean. That society included, as we have seen, God; and perhaps the domestic animals owned by the society as well. The experience of the daily, common life was its horizon, and the common life of God and man, whatever it was understood to be, was contained within that horizon. We have to look through the large end of the telescope: and if "what once were guessed as points we now know stars", it is as points that we must expect to find them, and we who are accustomed to the stars shall not always recognise our stars in the points from which they grew; the picture will be clear, but so reduced that its details become unrecognisable. The germs of what are to us religious, social, political, moral ideas are there; they will not look "religious" or "social" or "political" or "moral" to us; but they are germs none the less. There are ruling ideas—not yet known, in the first stages, as ideas at all—which are there from the beginning, and which last all through history: they are expressed in acts and institutions of which the underlying meaning becomes clear as time goes on, and the possibilities of which are developed, but which are none the less valuable because they are first found in a primitive society. The acts and institutions continue, and we find that they are the link between the present and the past. They carry on into a later period the fundamental character which has made the common life what it was from the beginning. That character it never loses. Every fresh development, every advance in spirituality, in morals, in organisation, recasts what was already there, extends its scope, but uses what it finds; it fulfils, but it does not destroy.

And we find that it is round life, in its origin and its

maintenance, that these ideas are gathered, and such a life—and it is indeed the only life that is possible for man—as is expressed in a visible society.

Thus the earliest is that of the family or clan; and whatever else God may be found to be, He is from the beginning the father. It may be that in our later language we have to say that it is at first a material conception of physical fatherhood, but early man knew no other kind of fatherhood and no life but that which we call the natural; and therefore his idea of fatherhood can no more be said to exclude than it can be said consciously to include what we mean by the Fatherhood of God in a spiritual sense. The one thing that matters is that the thought of God's fatherhood is wrought into the fibre of religion from the first; and the fact is none the less true, and its value none the smaller, because in later times spiritual realities began to be conceived and the old theories of the manner and character of the fatherhood had to be reconstructed to cover the new experiences.

And fatherhood, in a natural and therefore limited sense, meant the further ruling idea that the unity and the continuance, as well as the origin, of the common life of the family lay in the blood, as its manifestation or embodiment was found in the flesh. Both these words therefore survive as the word father does from the primitive vocabulary to the later: flesh, as we have seen, carries with it the sense of our common humanity as shared; and blood is life, in a sense always growing as the range and implications of what life is found to mean stretch out ever more widely into the spiritual and moral and eternal. And in the conditions of primitive life in the East, water —the perennial water of an unfailing spring or stream— is so inevitably bound up with the maintenance and the renewal of life that it is linked up in thought with God as giver of life, and even in theory therefore with His blood which is his life; it is "living water"; it carries something of the God with it; it has His holiness; it is His gift, just as are the fruits of the earth whose cultivation it makes possible. It is by food and drink that man lives,

I

and food and drink, therefore, are first and most simply
the content of what God gives to man, and as the measure
of what God gives becomes extended to gifts far out-
reaching bodily food and drink the old language continues. There is more in this continuance than what we
call "metaphor". Life in its widest sense has to be appro-
priated by assimilation, spiritual and mental, just as life
in the merely physical sense by the assimilation of bodily
food. Hence such passages as we have found in the
Psalms; hence the constant thought of the Law of God as
food; hence, as we shall see, the Christian conception of
truth. It is only when truth has been de-personalised—
and therefore in a measure de-Christianised—and the
processes of conveying and apprehending truth confined
to the mind as mechanised and abstracted from the rest
of the functions of the living personality as a whole, that
we feel that the language of eating and drinking has become inappropriate, and we have to apologise for its
use by calling it a metaphor. We have allowed our life
to become disunited: we try to carry out its functions in
artificial independence of each other along different roads,
and to regain touch between the roads we have to build
bridges which need never have been necessary.

Even in the Old Testament times this happened, to
some extent, with the food idea derived from the old
common life: just so far as the sacrificial meal survived
as an institution, but failed to retain even as much as
what had been its content in the older days, the language
which had belonged to it could be used in what was for
the moment a non-sacrificial sense. But the underlying
thought was fundamentally the same. The experience of
the meal at the table of God was always capable of re-
covering its full content. And the food language as used of
spiritual experience and of the conveying of truth was
derived from, and was only a restatement of, the original
instinct which regarded everything that went to maintain man's life as given to him as food and drink by God.

The ideas of God's fatherhood therefore, of the significance of blood, of living water, and of food and drink

as representing or summarising what God conveys to
man for the maintenance of his life, come down from
early times, with the sacrificial meal; and the same
thought of the common life as shared is also found alike
in Arabian and in Hebrew literature in the figure of the
tree. Cf. John xv. (the Vine).

The nomadic stage of Hebrew life left another way of
thinking of Yahweh which has already been noticed incidentally, but which deserves special emphasis. When
He led them through the wilderness He did for them
what in after times they thought of as the work of a
shepherd for his sheep—leading (Vulg. *regere*) as the King
led His people (Ps. lxxviii., etc.), and feeding them—as
with the manna, the bread of God, which, like the flesh of
the sacrifices, had to be eaten within a specified time.
Throughout the later history the idea of the shepherd
is bound up with the idea of the food which the shepherd
gives, as well as with that of pastoral care.

And with the Covenant there comes the foundation for
the thought so familiar in the prophets that Yahweh and
His people are bound together as husband and wife.
Under this conception we find linked together the two
ideas, so often regarded as separable, of worship and character: unfaithfulness in the worship of the national God
means unfaithfulness to moral ideals which distinguish
His servants from those of other gods.

With the growth of society, as we have seen, the idea of
God as Father, though it is not lost, grows into that of
God as King: and with this growth we have passed into
the specialisation of functions which inevitably accom-
panies it. Originally the patriarchal chief had represented
God in all the varieties of His work. He was all that in
later history was included in the separate offices of king,
and priest, and prophet. Later, the priestly functions
became separated from those of political leadership; and
the divining office of the priest developed in one direction
through the work of the seer into that of the prophet, and
in the other into that of the priest as, on the one hand,
guardian and teacher of the divine tradition, the Torah,

and, on the other, as the practices of worship became more elaborate and ultimately more centralised, as the necessary officiant at the sacrifices. Specialisation, as always, means both gain and loss. The ideal of each office was immeasurably advanced: but there comes a point when the tide turns, and the ultimate perfection of each is looked for in the merging of the functions which had to be separated in order to be developed. It is always Yahweh Whom each represents: and it is Yahweh Who is always the leader, the revealer, the giver of life; the father and husband in union with Whom alone the common life finds its meaning; the Shepherd Who redeems and leads and feeds; the God of the sanctuary Whom they fear and to Whom they are at the same time drawn, for Whose presence they must cleanse themselves, to Whom they must give themselves in homage, and from Whose table they are fed. Their life, however highly organised, is still one, in the one God, and its departments, as the ultimate meaning of each is more clearly seen, tend to merge into one another. So in Isaiah liii. the Servant fulfils the Messianic hope in His sufferings as victim and His intercession as priest; and in Zechariah vi. 11-13 the prophet means at the least—if the English text has to be abandoned which makes Joshua in his own person both priest and king— that the king and the priest work side by side in perfect harmony. Ultimately the achievements of the Maccabean priest-kings brought the king- and priest-conceptions still nearer together, and the Messiah in the Testaments of the XII Patriarchs is priest even before he is king, and prophet also.

Each of these functions, as we have seen, was bound up with the growth of the idea of sacrifice. Kingship added to the meal homage and service: "Lo, I come to do thy will, O God": the offering becomes that of the worshipper's self. And kingship again perhaps gave the experiences of judgment and righteousness which the inspiration of the prophets turned into the belief in the sole Godhead of Yahweh, and the absolute righteousness of the king who was the perfect judge: and out of that came the new conception of holiness and the last effort of the sacrificial system to provide atonement.

The prophets in fact developed the sacrificial effort in proportion as they reached the highest point in the growth of their own office. The period from the eighth to the sixth century B.C. is the period of the culmination of Old Testament religion on the one side as on the other. It was the age of the greatest of the prophets; it was also the age of the completion of the system of the Temple worship. What came afterwards on either side was not formative or original: the later prophets had little, if anything, to add to the teaching of their predecessors, and Ezra and the restorers of the sacrifices were only elaborating the principles laid down by Ezekiel. The end of the period is the turning-point of Old Testament history.

For the Old Testament—or, to speak more correctly, the whole pre-Christian experience of the chosen people— does not solve the problem of life. Its function is to discover it and to state it. That is the keynote of the whole history, and the centuries of the downfall of the two kingdoms, of the Babylonian captivity, and of the Return, or rather the preparation for the Return, are the crucial, the formative, the greatest period in the history just because it was in them that the last elements in the problem were discovered, and it could be stated as a whole.

The God of the clan and the common meal became the God of the kingdom and of the single sanctuary. Each stage carries with it an essential part of the full idea of His nature; and each brought its practical difficulties and its moral problems. With the prophets we have the ultimate form which, in the Old Testament, the problem took. God as King and Judge on the one hand makes a claim of perfect righteousness, and on the other hand as God of the sanctuary a claim of perfect holiness. The sacrifices could only embody the latter side of the problem: they could not solve it; and prophecy stated, equally without solving, the former side. There were attempts at the solution—in the developed system of the piacular sacrifices in the one direction, and in such conceptions as those of

Isaiah liii. and Psalm li. in the other, as well as in the feeling after a merging of the kingship and the priesthood, and even the prophetic office, of which I have just spoken. But the New Testament opens with a system of self-confessed failure in all three directions. The kingly ideal and the priestly ideal had not been realised, and the best that the Jewish mind could make of them was to look back with pathetic longing to great figures in the past which had, if for the moment only, seemed to embody what was hoped for in the one or the other. The last of the prophets was hourly expected, and he came in John the Baptist. The Baptist is the last word of prophecy, and the secret of his work is to acknowledge that he has no solution of his own. He is the greatest of all the prophets, and yet he that is least in the kingdom of heaven is greater than he.

This is the position at which our Lord gathers up the threads of the history. He has the whole of the past to justify and to redeem. The immediate problem is the last —that of redemption from sin; but in it all the others are gathered up. It has been a long road by which the people have been led. At every halting-place there are at once a record of an advance, and the debris of what was left behind. He has to secure the whole advance and to recover what is lost. It is not enough to do the one without the other. The dry bones must be made to live; and in coming back to life to fit into their places and fall into line in the army of the kingdom. The whole must be co-ordinated: the separate activities combined; the manifold ideas brought together. Nothing must be wasted. What had died out must be revived; what had lost its meaning must be reinterpreted.

We can see from what has been already said something of what the situation was which we find dealt with in the New Testament. Every gain had meant a loss. The primitive sacrificial meal lost its freedom and spontaneity each time that the sacrifices were lifted on to a higher level. The naturalness, the home feeling and the fearlessness of the earliest religion had gone, and it was necessary at the time that they should go for the sake of a higher con-

ception of God and for the purifying of His worship. The
burnt-offering had in the earliest days reached its highest
effort in human sacrifice; and again that had to go if the
character of God were to be understood: but even the
cruelty of human sacrifice had a truth in it without which
the later burnt-offering could never again be so real an
offering of self. It did mean that what God desires is
quality not quantity of offering; the dedication of human
life and not the externalised giving of the imperfect substitute of animals. Once more the later burnt-offering
itself, if it marked the development of private property,
at once made the individual, as opposed to the community, to begin to count for something before God, and at
the same time materialised and commercialised the idea
of offering. The Deuteronomic reform carried further
still the removal of religion from the home while it cleared
it from the corruptions of the local sanctuaries. And,
lastly, the final development of the sacrifices, the piacular,
if it meant more truth about the character of God, meant
also more fear and more difficulty of approach. With the
new holiness there came, in the sacrificial worship, a new
futility.

With all this gain and loss there went the great ideas
that we have traced in their connection with the society's
life: God is the Father of His children; the Husband of
His Bride; the root of the Tree of which His people are
the branches. He is their King and Judge; the God Whom
they worship, and Who feeds them, in His sanctuary;
and alike as leading and as feeding, the Shepherd Who
redeemed them from Egypt and has guided them through
all their history. The secret of that history is life, once
given, often all but lost, and always needing to be restored; its vehicles are the bread of God and the water of
life, and its instrument or embodiment is the blood.

And the final problem, as we have seen, arises when
monolatry becomes monotheism, and the content of
Holiness is extended to cover Righteousness. The achievement of the prophets is that they did not destroy religion,
but lifted it. If they had not been what they were they

would have turned religion into ethics: for there is
nothing specifically religious in the idea of satisfying a
righteous judge. As it was, they kept their ethical teaching
within the sphere of the service of God. It never occurred
to them to make it anything else. Their moral advance,
like all the previous moral advances of Israelite and
Hebrew history, expressed itself in terms of the living
contact with God. It becomes a question of fitness for
His presence; and being in His presence means worship.
Thus the last, as the first, word of the Old Testament
history is God. What determines its character is His
Nature. And the one word which stands for the ultimate
idea of the Divine is Holy. It is in this conception of
Holiness that in the end the problem of the Old Testament is both stated and, in the New Testament, solved.

It has been well said that Holiness is more than an
attribute of Godhead; it is its essence. At the beginning,
when the horizon of life is confined to what we should
call its material experiences, holiness shows itself in ways
that are hardly more than physical. It stands then, as it
stands now, for the idea of the separateness of God, which,
in all human experience, both repels and attracts: God
is desired just because, or in so far as, He is feared, and
feared in proportion as He is desired. A being who could
only be feared, or only desired, could not be loved, and
would not be God. It is after all only another way of saying that He is both immanent and transcendent; or that
He is the Person Who is always revealing Himself, and
yet always still to be revealed. And in its most primitive
form His holiness is something that is communicated like
a contagion. God cannot help communicating Himself:
that is His Nature. The places in which He dwells, the
things which are His, the persons who are in contact
with Him, share the quality. It is both to be sought for
and to be dreaded.

It is this idea of Holiness which conditions the whole of
man's intercourse with Him; God would not be God if it
were not for the sanctuary and the experience of the
sanctuary, which finds Him both elusive and expansive.

"There is mercy with Thee: therefore Thou shalt be feared" is but one of many expressions of the paradox which is from first to last the only satisfactory statement of the truth.

And the progress of the religion of Israel is the progress of the revelation of this Holiness. There are times—most markedly in the great advance made by the earlier prophets—when the sanctuary idea falls behind other conceptions in moral content. What they did was not to abandon, but to develop it, from the pre-moral, or the non-moral, habit of the earlier forms of religion into the moral, and in doing so they found, as we have seen, a formula which once and for all secured the vitality and the progressiveness both of religion and of morality itself.

What they did not do was to make the new conceptions effective. Righteousness at its best, taken by itself, was ultimately bound to remain an external standard of morality, and it became the strength not only of the moral law regarded as outward ordinance, but, in Christian times, with all its sublime moral achievement as in the Puritan type of character, of those forensic ideas of the Atonement which cannot ultimately satisfy the conscience or the heart. Holiness was in itself, once it became moralised, a question of the heart. It meant the sense of the presence of a God Who is both worshipped and communicated. For that character belongs to it from the beginning. It is still a "contagion"; "religion is caught, not taught". But it has to become a contagion of spirit to spirit as well as of body to body: not of spirit only, for there is no reason why in becoming spiritual it should cease to be also material. It has to be communicated to the whole life of man. And that is what, apart from isolated anticipations, the Old Testament could not do. It looked for the new covenant of the heart; and after the Exile it found the New Testament formula, though it could not make it effective, in the idea of the Holy Spirit of God and of His indwelling Wisdom. The sacrifice had to be made real: a real atonement, a real offering of the human will, a real communion in which God could dwell

in us and we in Him. The sanctuary had to be opened out
to people as well as priests, the peoples of the world to be
admitted to the sanctuary life of the people of God. The
righteousness of God had to be brought into human life
and to be made ours.

And it is this that in the New Testament is achieved.
Its achievement is the fulfilling of the ancient sacrifices;
it is the taking up of all the fundamental ideas of the Old
Testament life: but it is all this by the gift of the Spirit of
God's Holiness. That and that alone makes the people of
God into His spiritual House: not a kingdom only, but
priests: with a life that is only true worship because it is
service, and is service because it passes into worship. All
life, in the holiness of the Christian people as such,
becomes part of the life of God.

PART II
THE NEW TESTAMENT

CHAPTER I

INTRODUCTORY

OUR summary of the past has ended with an anticipation. Can the claim be justified that the New Testament solves the problems bequeathed to it? What is the nature of that solution? Has the Church in later times always been true to it? Those are the questions before us, and to which this book attempts at least to suggest the materials for an answer.

I have attempted to show that an objective study of the history gives us a "background" for the life and teaching of our Lord, of which sacrifice, and "cultus" generally, form an integral part. His inheritance from the past is a "life", which, whatever its other features—in our modern analysis we may think of it also as national, social, ethical—is fundamentally not only "religious" in the more technical and abstract, and therefore artificial, modern sense, but is itself religion. It is a religion, or an attitude to God, which includes all those elements which we tend to-day to think of apart from religion. And this religion is one which for Jews of our Lord's time—for the best as well as the worst—was essentially sacrificial.

The modern world, as we know, is not only unfamiliar with the ancient method of sacrifice, but is unwilling to accept sacrifice itself as a category of religious thought. The reasons for this are manifold. It will be one purpose of what follows to illustrate the loss of familiarity. It is only in recent times that there has been in the scientific sense a historical spirit. And it is only in the same period that the materials for historical reconstruction have become available. We cannot blame Christendom of the first eighteen centuries for losing its hold—if it did lose it —on the knowledge of what may be called the technical language of sacrifice. And it is, as I believe, mainly through this loss that the modern recoil from the idea of sacrifice has arisen. For the recoil has been on its best side a protest against what have seemed to be non-moral, or even immoral, and unspiritual ideas of religion. The ancient system of sacrifice has been thought both to rest upon a mere act of substitution, and to reduce the intercourse between God and man to the terms of what is on the whole a cultus that is both external and material. On the first of these assumptions rests the view of the Atonement which sees in it no more than a supreme moral example; and Dr. Rashdall's great work,[1] if his premises as regards sacrifice are sound, is a noble protest on behalf of the perfect goodness of God. On the second rests the whole of the contemporary fear of externalism and "magic" in the use of sacraments—a fear which expresses itself either in the attempts to explain away the sacrificial and sacramental thought of St. Paul and Hebrews and the Johannine writings, or in the more modern view that ascribes the teaching of St. Paul to elements borrowed by him from mystery religions and denies a place for the germs of it to the authentic records of our Lord.

Such protests as these are in the interests of real morality and of real religion, and it is as such that they should be met; for immoral conceptions of God, and magical uses of the sacraments, can be allowed no place in theories of Christian doctrine or in the practices of the religious life. They represent the modern recoil at its best, as a protest on behalf of truth, and it is only in attempts to explore the truth that they can be answered. But there is another side to the recoil. "Cost is an essential of sacrifice": "the goodness and severity of God": "there is mercy with Thee: therefore Thou shalt be feared"; these sayings sufficiently point to its nature. The tendency may be frankly that of indifference either to religion or to

---

[1] *The Idea of Atonement in Christian Theology.*

morality. Or it may be religious in its setting, and moral in its intention, but the outcome of emphasis on the immanence and not also on the transcendence of God: and in that case the answer to it must be that whatever it achieves it is not the religion of Jesus in which it can claim to find its setting, or the character of Jesus which it will reproduce in human life.

How far then, and in what sense, does Christianity embody the ultimate principles of sacrifice?

That is a wider question than is sometimes asked in the treatment of sacrificial problems. What has been said in Part I. will, I hope, indicate that there should be more in such treatment than a mere searching for, and illustration of, technical terms. We tend to look in the New Testament, for instance, only for what is called "sacrificial language". But a search even for that, by itself, cannot come first. We must begin by knowing what sacrifice is, or, more strictly, for New Testament purposes, what it was, in the first place, and so far as the Synoptic Gospels are concerned, to our Lord and other Jews, and, in the second place, for the history of the Apostolic Church, to the Christians for whom the other books were written. It is only so that we can be sure of knowing what words and ideas come, or do not come, within the scope of sacrifice. For it is not a matter of words only. The study of Hebrew and Jewish sacrifice shows us that the whole conception as it was in our Lord's day on the one hand gathered up the history of Israelite development, and on the other hand left the vital moral and religious problem of Hebrew religion still to be solved.

We have, it is true, found what may be called the *technique* of the system. It is nowhere systematically treated. The passages in the Law which describe it are not only of varying dates, so that they show it in successive stages of its formation, but even when taken as separate "codes" are not "codes" in the sense of a methodical and complete statement of its rules. Even in P. a working knowledge of the system is to a large extent assumed. And outside the Old Testament this assumption is even more marked. We have three treatments of it, to which we turn in vain for completeness. Philo gives summaries of its chief features, and his interpretations, passing, though they often do, into allegory, are of real importance, and at least show the spiritual value which he set upon it. Josephus gives hardly more than a summary. The Mishna contains the teaching of Jewish scholars and theologians of the first and second centuries, some of whom had actually known the Temple worship as a living system, and the rest of whom were linked to it by the retentive memories of at most only two or three generations: but here more than anywhere, except in the New Testament, it is taken for granted that the principal rules are understood; what is dealt with is almost entirely the minor problems of procedure which in the text of the Levitical law were left to be worked out in practice.

But of the main points of the technique there can be no doubt. They remain to us, as it were, as the grammar or A B C of sacrificial language. Behind the technique lie the principles of which I have spoken. These, as we have seen, have a wide range. They cover not only such principles as were understood, with more or less clearness, to be directly involved in the cultus itself, but also what would sometimes be regarded as wider principles represented in the language and the teaching of religion as a whole.

For the study of the problem in the New Testament technique and principles alike are needed—the name and the thing. But from first to last it is the thing that matters, whatever name is given to it. Christian theology and worship might, if it were thought well, drop the use of all technical terms or invent new ones, so long as both preserve the underlying truth and character which those terms have hitherto attempted to express. The value of the principles is permanent; the value of the terminology is historical; but we need the latter to group and check our principles.

The purpose of this book is to suggest a way of looking at two distinct, but related, problems, of which Part II.

will be mainly concerned with the first, and Part III. with the second. Part I. has been an attempt to give the materials for the treatment of both.

The first problem is that of the place, if any, which the idea of sacrifice—whatever the terminology employed—holds in the undoubtedly historical part of the tradition of our Lord's work and teaching. Is it there at all? Those who distrust the traditional belief about the Atonement, and the tendencies of a definitely sacramental religion, would say that it is not. Many others would accept it in relation to our Lord's redeeming work—most commonly in strict connection with His death—and would either repudiate it altogether or give it only a very limited application in connection with the sacraments, and especially—since it is here that controversy naturally arises—with the Eucharist. For both the question ultimately turns on the Synoptic story. It has, of course, been held that the whole of the "orthodox" interpretation of Christ's person and work, and of what may be called, un-controversially, the "Catholic" conception of Church life, dates from the second century. But the attempt of the "Tübingen" critics to justify this by a re-reading of New Testament history and a uniformly late dating for the New Testament literature has failed. Those who hold to the idea of sacrifice as an accepted view of our Lord's work, but refuse it for the Eucharist, attempt to justify both acceptance and refusal from the language of the Epistles, as well as of the Gospels. But modern criticism is forcing us, willingly or unwillingly, to recognise all that is essential in the sacramental side of later Christianity in St. Paul and in the Johannine writings. However it came, it was taught by St. Paul. And the familiar answer to-day is that St. Paul imported it into the primitive Palestinian Gospel from the mystery cults. Or, if the mystery solution is not accepted, some other reason must be found: and Dr. Rashdall, precluded as he is by his theory of sacrifice from allowing it to be derived from the true tradition about our Lord, suggests that it arose, perhaps at Antioch in the earliest days, from a natural but wholly illegitimate

K

application of the fifty-third chapter of Isaiah to the historical fact of Jesus' death.

Before any of these answers to the first problem can be tested, we must examine the Synoptic tradition itself. If we find the essentials of sacrifice there, it becomes unnecessary to account for their introduction, by St. Paul or anyone else, at a later stage. It is therefore with the Synoptic tradition that we are most concerned. What follows, upon sacrificial lines, in the Epistles and Apocalypse, is not of such primary importance at this stage. Its value will lie, like that of all developments, in illustrating and expanding the principles already there. It should be found to provide evidence for the scope and rationale of the sacrificial idea. But its main value, for my immediate purpose, will be in its bearing on the second problem (Part III.).

We shall pass, that is, from the stage in which we look for the basic principles, for the essence, of sacrifice, and for little, if any, of the technique which was formulated in the Jewish system, and partially, at least, reappeared later in the Christian, to the stage in which technical language, and what may be called expressly sacrificial ideas, begin to emerge. Our task then will be to test the later New Testament use of such language and ideas, and to see if it conforms to the ABC worked out in early sacrificial history and used and understood by the contemporaries of the New Testament writers. Our study of the New Testament therefore, beginning with principles, will lead us to what should be the normal expression of such principles on the side of technique. It is with the after history of this expression, as the New Testament leaves it to the post-Apostolic Church, that Part III. will be concerned. There, in the light of later confusions and the resulting controversies, we shall take the category of sacrifice for granted. The question will be whether the classical—Jewish, New Testament, even pagan—norm was adhered to: if not, how and when it was departed from, and with what results in doctrine and practice. And finally we shall, I hope, be able to estimate the bearing of this history, from the point at which we leave the New Testament to our own day, upon the eucharistic problems which we have inherited. We shall be able to see whether controversy must be the last word, or whether the spirit and the language of sacrifice, of which we have seen the beginnings in Jewish history, and which we have found vitalised in the New Testament, may not lead us out of controversy, not into "compromise for the sake of peace," but into "comprehension for the sake of truth".

I have spoken above of "the undoubtedly historical part of the tradition of our Lord's work and teaching". Those words are perhaps too confident. For with our present knowledge of the literary history of the first three Gospels there must always be a margin of the record as to the validity of which our own religious standpoint will be the decisive factor in our judgment.

Let me say, then, briefly, that I accept the broad results of modern criticism of the Synoptic Gospels: for my purpose it may perhaps be sufficient to say that I assume that they are first-century documents; that, when all allowance is made for the history, so far as we can recover it, of their composition, for the existence of oral traditions gradually reduced to writing and combined, for differences of temperament or of circumstance in those who contributed towards their ultimate form, they convey in their main outline, and, even in detail, with almost surprising consistency, a single picture. It would be easy, but it is unnecessary, for me to take as my basis of assumption, some one modern statement of results, such as that of Canon Streeter in his *Four Gospels*, or such as the more general summary given by Dr. Headlam in chapter i. of his *Life and Teaching of Jesus the Christ*. But I do not think I need say more than that what follows is written with critical results in view.

There may, indeed, be cases, whatever view of the literary history be taken, and however "conservative" the trend of recent critical work may seem to be, in which "doctrinal" developments really belonging to the thought of the Apostolic age are unconsciously read back into records of actual sayings of the Lord, or into the narrative portions of the record. We must be alive to such possibilities as these in the use which we make of the Synoptic story in its present form. Where crucial passages have been weightily challenged on doctrinal grounds they must not be used on a first survey of the material.[1] It is only if, and when, such a first survey may seem to justify their doctrine that they may be taken into account.

But, when all is said and done, a margin remains, in which what may be called "objective" certainty may perhaps never be assured. It is therefore fair that a writer should make his own position clear, not only as regards the documentary hypothesis upon which he works but as regards his own doctrinal standpoint. Let me say, therefore, that I write as one who believes whole-heartedly, on grounds both of traditional authority, and, so far as a man may dare to say it, of reason and of personal faith, that there is, in the last resort, no distinction to be established between the "Jesus of history" and the "Christ of dogma". I believe that the Jesus Who lives, with whatever imperfections of portraiture, in each of the first three Gospels and their sources, lives, unchanged but better seen and more fully known, in the teaching of the Epistles, and after them in the combined record and avowed interpretation of the Fourth Gospel, and in the rich symbolic pictures of the Eternal Sanctuary and City of the Apocalypse. I believe that He lives with a reality, a fullness, and a directness, intensified but not created by, and far transcending that of, the written records, in personal contact with the members of the society which He founded. The Gospels, after all, give us only what He "began both to do and to teach". Long before, and ever since, those Gospels were written, or their sources began to take written form, He continues His work, of action and of teaching, by His spiritual presence in the Church. It was from that Church that the Gospels came.

The real question as to the validity of the ultimate con-

---

[1] *E.g.* in this connection especially Mark x. (the λύτρον passage), and the narratives of the Institution.

sensus of the Church in the later Apostolic age upon the
Person and Work of our Lord must turn on the verdict
of historians as to the extent and effect of the different
movements within the earlier Apostolic society. If it can
be shown that in different centres, and under different
influences, vitally inconsistent beliefs were held—that
the Jerusalem interpretation of the school of James, for
instance, was wholly incompatible with the liberal interpretation of St. Paul—the weight to be assigned to primitive interpretation as a whole is seriously diminished. If,
on the other hand, whatever the exaggerations of followers may have been, the evidence points to a fundamental agreement on principles between the great leaders—
between St. James, St. Peter, and St. Paul[1]—there emerges
what I venture to think is a principle which must be behind all analysis of documents and in the end govern our
attitude towards the study of our Lord's earthly life. The
old contrast between the "Jesus of history" and the
"Christ of dogma" rests largely upon an unscientific view
of history. It assumes that there can be recovered, behind
the views which His followers formed about Him, the
actual words and acts, untouched by interpretation, of
the Master Himself. It is a natural and a tempting aim.
But is such a result, in the last resort, either possible or
rational? What we desire, for the purposes of scientific
history, is the original materials. That is agreed: everyone desires, or should desire, that history be scientific.
But the question is: What, in the nature of the case, are
the original materials?

It is, in fact, impossible, with any teacher, to recover
his exact spoken words. If he writes, it is, up to a point,
another matter. But if, like our Lord, he does not write a
word, the ultimate material for history is not the actual
saying, by itself. Such a thing does not in fact, and never
did, exist. The moment of speech is also the moment of
hearing. And hearing, so soon as we pass from the
physical reception of the sound by the ear, becomes also
an act of the hearer's mind. As it is heard, an opinion is

[1] See, *e.g.*, Streeter, *op. cit.* pp. 511 ff.

formed about it; a judgment is passed; it belongs no longer to the speaker only but to the listener also. From the first moment, what exists is the speaker's saying as understood by the hearer. That is true even before conscious thought on the hearer's part. It becomes still more true, quite apart from deliberate acts of reasoning, with every stage of the processes of memory, and even more of expression. And what is true of words is in its measure true of actions also. What is done can never be recaptured, except, up to a point, by the soulless image of a photograph. It exists as seen, as felt, as interpreted. And what counts most is often what is least readily expressed in conscious thought at all. The strongest impacts of one living person upon another reappear in the personality of the recipient; in his ultimate attitude to him from whom he receives the impact; in a life that, for better or for worse, more or less deeply, has been, by each experience, changed.

And in the case of our Lord's disciples, what would have been true, to some extent, even of His passing contacts with ordinary people is enhanced in two ways. In the first place, each of them had a contact with Him that was not occasional and accidental but continuous. It was probably for two years, more or less, that they were with Him. It was the contact of what must have been almost daily companionship. What went to form the impression which He left upon them was incalculably greater in mere extent than the isolated fragments of speech and action which the records have preserved. "There are also many other things which Jesus did, the which if they should be written every one, I suppose that even the world itself would not contain the books that should be written." That is Oriental hyperbole; but it pictures a profound truth.

And, in the second place, each disciple does not stand alone. We have only glimpses of their talk with one another; and the very fact that such of these talks as are recorded are nearly always to their discredit is itself, indeed, an evidence of trustworthiness. None of them mattered, in his own eyes and in those of the others, if there was a risk of the Master being misunderstood. But these stories only illustrate what we know must have been the case. They must have pooled their experiences and their conclusions. They must have had a common mind on the main issues, and as a body have known that mind. Once the air had cleared; once, first by the Resurrection, and then by the gift of the Spirit, they had been given a key to what had before been dark and baffling, they are found acting together. There are differences still, for they remain themselves: differences of character and of outlook. But they know, on the one hand, Whom they have believed, and, on the other hand, whom they can accept into their company. They give the right hand of fellowship first to James and his brothers, and then to Paul and Barnabas.

It is therefore in the common mind of the earliest Church, as it assimilates new elements from opposite directions, that we really find the ultimate materials for the history. If we try to go behind that common mind, the adventure may indeed be rewarded here and there by new light thrown back upon the earliest Church's faith itself; but it is precarious. Jesus after all left all that He said, or did, or gave, in the keeping of these men. We may think that He might have chosen better interpreters, but He preferred children and sinners: and the legacy that He left the world He entrusted deliberately to simple men of very ordinary character. Can we understand Him better than they?

It is, in any case, with this primitive Christian society that all soundly scientific work begins. The modern literary and historical criticism of the Gospels has, like all young things, tried its strength in all directions, and not within its own proper province alone. But as it becomes more mature, it does its work in its own place; and there it is of inestimable value. Within its province it rightly becomes our guide; it makes the first authors, known and unknown, live to us; it recreates lost pages of first-century history; and it enables us to judge of those differences of temperament and circumstance which give the books a meaning otherwise not to be discovered.

I propose, therefore, with the reservations already noted, but assuming, for my present purpose, the substantial trustworthiness of the Synoptic record as a whole, to examine some of the typical and central ideas of the story there told. We shall consider, at this stage, fundamental principles, without, at first, any obvious reference to what is commonly understood to be the conception of sacrifice. It will appear, I hope, now more clearly and now less, that in much of our Lord's central teaching, and in some of the outstanding features of the Synoptic portraits of Him, we are nearer than we normally suspect, not to the technical language of sacrifice, and certainly not to direct association with the contemporary Jewish cultus, but to its underlying principles, both in the theology of salvation and in the moral content of practical life. After that it will be possible, I hope, without forcing the evidence, and without any need, for the purposes of argument, to overpress the language of the records, to estimate our Lord's use of technical sacrificial language, slight as it is, and His general attitude to the Temple side of contemporary religion.

The message of the Gospels is one both of ethics and of religion: of a religion of which the content in human life is ethical; of an ethical system in which the first and the last word is God. There have been non-ethical attempts at religion, and non-religious systems of morals, and there have been phases of Christian interpretation on both these lines. But the test of what is or is not the Christianity of Christ must ever remain the double nature of its outlook. It must mean character; it must frankly issue from, and lead to, God. That is to say, it is morality in terms, not of abstract ideas, but of personal contact. The Christian life differs from other lives, of which the moral content may be in theory at least almost the same, in that it starts from, and is dedicated to, God. The Christian acknowledges his moral failures as personal acts of unfaithfulness to Him, a child's disobedience to its Father, a subject's disloyalty to his King, a citizen's lack of citizenship and of the sense of public duty in a Body which is not an abstraction or a mere aggregate, but Christ, and therefore as needing personal forgiveness. His efforts to live the moral life are the response of a child's love, the willing personal service of a subject, the discharge of the duties of fellowship and brotherhood to the Body corporate; the seeking for a life with, and in, and from God in which the things of time and space are here and now transfigured into the values of the unseen and the eternal.

Sin and its forgiveness; dedication or offering; union with God; these are the content of the life of sonship and of citizenship. There can be no dividing line between the religion of the sanctuary and the ethical character of everyday life, unless, here in one way and there in another, there come phases in which through the weakness of human nature either efficiency of worship appears valid apart from character, or, in the inevitable recoil, character is vindicated for the time at the expense of a formal worship. Holiness and righteousness are therefore intended to meet. Their spheres are neither mutually exclusive nor accidentally overlapping, but identical. The same life which in one set of passages is summed up in "Thy Kingdom come", and in another as the doing of the Father's will, is all the time the hallowing of the Name. The need of man is not only for the forgiveness which he at once receives and owes, nor only for the protecting care of the Father's hand, but also for the food which God, the Author and Perfecter of all life, alone can give.

It is under such forms as these that the essential teaching of the Synoptic Gospels is found—the teaching that is both essential and undisputed. For our Lord there is no morality without religion and no religion without morality. God is both Father and King, as well as God; but exposition alike of Fatherhood and Kingdom is sometimes so much concerned with the ethical content of life as for mere lack of stress to seem to ignore theology.

I have attempted to indicate what appears to be at

least one classification of the Synoptic teaching, or at
least three outstanding conceptions under which much of
that teaching falls. It is immaterial whether as a classification such a division is exhaustive. What will not be
disputed is that at least the first two—sin and its remedy,
and the dedicated life of service—are conspicuous elements in the Synoptic record. The third—which I have
called union with God—is more obviously an element in
the Johannine teaching, as it is also in St. Paul's. But I
hope to show that it does also represent an essential part
of the Synoptic teaching. I propose therefore in the three
following chapters to examine some of our Lord's sayings
in the first three Gospels, under these heads, without any
presupposition as to their ultimate bearing on the more
technical side of sacrificial doctrine.

CHAPTER II

WHAT is the teaching of our Lord, in the Synoptic record, as regards the reconciliation of sinners? We start with the universally admitted teaching of repentance and forgiveness, of which the supreme examples are in the parables of the Prodigal Son and of the Pharisee and Publican. But the beginning lies in Mark i. 15: "The time is fulfilled, and the kingdom of God is at hand; repent ye, and believe in the gospel"—no doubt a summary of much typical teaching, as well as, chronologically, the prelude to the rest. It is a call to repentance, and to faith, in the light of all that the earlier history has meant. Equally central, and equally primary, is the petition for forgiveness in the model prayer; but this goes one step farther—and it is a significant step; for it requires God's character in the penitent sinner: he must be ready to forgive if he is to be forgiven. So also does the parable of the Unforgiving Servant. This general teaching about repentance and forgiveness is not indeed, even professedly, complete. Our Lord is not necessarily saying how the sinner begins to repent. In the story of the Prodigal Son that is, strictly speaking, irrelevant; for the broad lesson is obviously "if you repent you will be forgiven", and no more. The point of the story does not lie in the circumstances which caused the self-exiled son to turn his face homewards, but in the fact that he did so turn it and in the Father's reception of him. Yet even in the story, so told, there are two indications of facts other than that of his actual return. In the far country he feels the consequences of his sins; he suffers.

And all the time the Father is looking for him; there is
the yearning of the Father's heart, the will that he should
return, which in a human father would be effective prayer,
and in the Divine Father is what we call prevenient grace.
So in the parable of the Unforgiving Servant the fact of
suffering has become the fact of punishment and is an
essential part of the story. And in the parable of the
Pharisee and the Publican the setting is the Temple. The
Publican, as well as the Pharisee, goes to the Temple in
his need, to take some part in what is done there. The
contrast is not between repentance and forgiveness in
themselves, and repentance and forgiveness by some
special method: the method—that of the Temple provision for the purpose—is assumed, and the contrast is
between sincere and insincere ways of using it.

Even in this that is commonly assumed to be the
simplest form of the teaching on recovery from sin, there
is no sign of the unprompted, uncaused, spontaneous,
repentance which is all too commonly taken for granted.
God's hand is seen in suffering that may be called punishment; in love that goes out in yearning for the sinner; in
the gift of His own character; in the use of established,
though, as they had proved, inadequate, means of grace.

Something is required beyond the mere change in the
sinner's heart. And there is evidence enough that that
something is spoken of, not only as ultimately due to the
Father, but as also due to the direct action of our Lord.
In the story of Zacchaeus (Lk. xix. 1-10), once the contact
has been made between Him and the sinner, the initiative
is His. His is the crucial act: He breaks tradition by going
to the publican's house. It is under the impulse of that act
that Zacchaeus makes restitution, or, in effect, offers a
genuine sacrifice. And the verdict is of what would be
called to-day "objective" reality: "this day is salvation
come to this house". "The Son of man is come to seek and
to save that which is lost".; that is the inner truth of the
whole. It is He Who seeks: it is He who saves: the lost is
sought, is found. Zacchaeus has not saved himself; he is
saved.

The story of the Prodigal Son, again, does not stand alone. It is only one of a group of three parables all dealing with the same subject. And of the three it is the last (Lk. xv. 11-32). The primary truth comes first, described in varying settings, each with its own suggestion, in the parables of the Lost Sheep (Lk. xv. 3-7) and of the Lost Coin (Lk. xv. 8-10). The two first give us God's action in saving sinners; and only when that has been made clear do we get the accompanying, or resulting, change in the sinner's heart. Together the three parables mean that in the recovery from sin two things happen, and not, as we are often told, one. The Shepherd goes after that which is lost, finds it, carries it on his own shoulders, rejoices. In the second parable God's action is even stronger, more one-sided: for the sheep will know the Shepherd's voice; there is a response, however ineffective; but a coin is entirely passive. And in both stories there is at least the suggestion of cost—of self-sacrifice—to the finder. The woman lights her lamp, and sweeps the house, and seeks diligently until she finds it; no trouble is too great for the tired housewife after her day's work has been done. And the Shepherd:

> But none of the ransomed ever knew
>   How deep were the waters crossed;
> Nor how dark the night that the Lord passed through
>   Ere He found His sheep that was lost.
>
>   .   .   .   .
>
> "Lord, whence are those blood-drops all the way,
>   That mark out the mountain's track?"
> "They were shed for one that had gone astray
>   Ere the Shepherd could bring him back."

The finding means sacrifice; and the joy in the finding, as well as the sacrifice in seeking, is at once a revelation of the sorrow of God over sinners and of the value that He sets upon them. The love of the Father is not passive, but active: it contains, from the beginning, not only the readiness to welcome home but the willingness to bear the Cross, the resolve to save—if we may not yet use the word "redeem"—at His own cost. These are, in truth,

all three—and not the Prodigal Son alone—parables of
Fatherhood. St. Matthew's version of the Lost Sheep
(Mt. xviii. 12-14) fitly ends with "Even so it is not the will
of your Father which is in heaven, that one of these little
ones should perish". It is, indeed, not only in the parallel-
ism of the Lord's prayer that "lead us not into temptation
but deliver us from evil" is the corollary, for our own
needs, of the petition that the Father's will may be done;
in the crisis of the Lord's own life the human prayer "that
the hour might pass away from him" turns at once to the
thought of the Father's will: "Abba, Father . . . not what
I will, but what thou wilt"; and immediately, to the three
disciples, He says "Watch and pray, that ye enter not
into temptation" (Mk. xiv. 35-38). The supreme mark
of the Divine Fatherhood, for Him and for us, is the Will
to protect and to deliver; but it is a Will which does not
stop short until it has led to the Cross, and with it our
wills are meant to co-operate. God does His part first, and
the self-exiled sinner is won to do his. That is the full
teaching of the three parables.

But the parable of the Lost Sheep does not stand alone.
There lies behind the whole of the "shepherd" language of
the Gospels the "shepherd" language of the Old Testament, some of the implications and connections of which
have been traced, or suggested, in Part I. And this parable
itself is a summary of Ezekiel xxxiv. In that chapter
Yahweh speaks of the faithless shepherds who did not seek
or feed the sheep: after their failure, "I myself, even I,
will search for my sheep, and will seek them out . . . and
I will deliver them out of all places whither they have
been scattered. . . . And I will bring them out from the
peoples, and gather them from the countries, and will
bring them into their own land; and I will feed them upon
the mountains of Israel. . . . I myself will feed my sheep,
and I will cause them to lie down, saith the Lord God. I
will seek that which was lost, and will bring again that
which was driven away, and will bind up that which was
broken, and will strengthen that which was sick." Is it
too much to say that here is not only the picture outlined

in the Lost Sheep but also, once the metaphor is stripped away, some of the very thought, and indeed the language, of the kindred parable of the Prodigal Son?

Nor are we far from the language and imagery of Deutero-Isaiah. There is at least a reminiscence of Isaiah xl. 11: "He shall feed his flock like a shepherd, he shall gather the lambs in his arm, and carry them in his bosom"; and of Isaiah liii., itself (verses 4-6): "Surely he hath borne our griefs, and carried our sorows. . . . But he was wounded for our transgressions, he was bruised for our iniquities: the chastisement of our peace was upon him; and with his stripes we are healed. All we like sheep have gone astray; we have turned every one to his own way; and the Lord hath laid on him the iniquity of us all." And when this latter passage moves on in its thought to the sacrificial lamb, as it does in verses 7 ff., we are precisely at the point where, in John. x. 11, we come to the "good shepherd [who] layeth down his life for the sheep".

The whole connection of thought, therefore, in these parables of forgiveness—and the point might be further illustrated from the parable teaching about debts—is, firstly, that God has an essential part to play in the restoration of the sinner. He is lost, starving, exiled from home, broken, sick—as well as in debt. He must be found, fed, restored, healed, forgiven. There is of course also the need of a movement on the sinner's own part: but of the two agents God comes first, and is the more active. If we had any desire to press the Lost Sheep and the Lost Coin and the cancelling of debts, as the Prodigal Son has been overpressed on the other side, it would be possible to say that, as compared with God's part, the sinner's is almost passive. But the truest and the fairest summary is the Johannine: "Herein is love, not that we loved God, but that he loved us, and sent his Son . . ." (1 Jn. iv. 10).

Secondly, the Old Testament language upon which our Lord is drawing speaks of Yahweh as the Good Shepherd. In these parables we may say at most that Jesus is not yet Himself the Shepherd. That identification emerges, even in the Synoptic record; but, in connection with the

Shepherd language, it is not explicit until we reach the
Fourth Gospel. The identification lies, it is true, near at
hand. We are not far from it, if we are not already there,
in the case of Zacchaeus. There, as we have seen, the
seeking and saving, which in the Old Testament is the
work of Yahweh Himself, is the work of the Son of man.
So in Mk. ii. 17 Jesus speaks of Himself as the healer of
the spiritually sick, as He has shown Himself already the
healer of men's bodies; and again there He is doing
Yahweh's work (Ez. xxxiv. 16; see above).

Such combinations of thought raise, indeed, the central
problem of Christology. It is not my purpose to discuss
that, and it is only relevant here to bring together some
of the many passages which show the position of our Lord
Himself in the deliverance which God effects. In that
deliverance or restoration He assumes a central or necessary part. It is just at this point that He differs, fundamentally, from the prophets. Modern Jewish writers, such
as Mr. Claude Montefiore and Mr. Israel Abrahams, are
at pains to show, on the one hand, that His teaching of the
free forgiveness of God to sinners, and of God's readiness
to welcome repentance, in itself is in line with, and indeed
goes no farther than, the best Jewish teaching, whether
in the Old Testament or among the Rabbis. Man has
direct access to the Father. On the other hand, "the prophet—whether John the Baptist or another—might bring
men to forgiveness; he did not bring forgiveness to men;
it was not his to bring".[1] The same might be said of God's
other gifts, and of God's "claims", as they are sometimes
called, with a suggestion of hardness which is really out
of place, and is not intended. But "the Son of man hath
power on earth to forgive sins"; He calls the weary and
heavy laden to come to Him, to receive God's own gift of
rest or refreshment; He would have gathered the children
of Jerusalem together for protection under His wings
(Mt. xxiii. 37; Pss. xci. 4, xvii. 8). To obey His sayings is
to build upon the rock (Mt. vii. 24). He re-enacts the Law,
and assumes an authority above that of Moses (Mt. 5).

[1] Israel Abrahams, *Studies in Pharisaism and the Gospels*, Series I., p. 140.

In His victory over Satan the Kingdom of God is come (Mt. xii. 28; Lk. xi. 20). He is Lord of the house of man's life, the city of man's soul—He or Satan (Mt. xii. 43-45; Lk. xi. 24-26). The centurion's trust in His power He accepts as faith: the faith is in Himself (Mt. viii. 5-13; Lk. vii. 1-10). It is not the language of a prophet. And the more we accept the attempts of such writers as those to whom I have referred to equate with His central teaching the existing religion of His own time, the more impossible is it to suggest, as the same writers do, that He is assuming a position of mediatorship of the kind that is at once superhuman and sub-Divine. Such a position He must have claimed, or must have been represented by His followers as claiming, if the reduced Christology of the modern Christian scholars through whom most modern Jewish scholars[1] have formed their impressions of Christianity is a true account of Him. But the more clearly we see Jesus as a true Jew, the more we find the spirit of the Old Testament alive in Him, the less does any Arian answer to the problem of His person become possible. The $\theta\epsilon\hat{\iota}os$ $\ddot{a}\nu\theta\rho\omega\pi os$ is a plant native to the soil not of Judaism, at its best or even at its worst, but of Hellenism.[2] Jesus speaks neither in that capacity nor as a prophet. The closer His affinity with the Old Testament, the more impossible is it to ascribe to Him any position less than that of the Catholic Christology.

It is in view of this relation of Jesus to the Father, or, since that phrase really is an anticipation of later dogmatic thought, in view of His self-identification with the Yahweh of His and His hearers' inherited religion, that His teaching, first about His own death and then about the consequent call to self-surrender for His followers, is of supreme importance. It is not only that from the moment of Peter's confession of His Messiahship at Caesarea Philippi, He says that He will suffer (Mk. ix. 31; Mt. xvii. 22 f.; Lk. ix. 44; Mk. x. 33 f.; Mt. xx. 18 f.; Lk. xviii. 32 f.), but that He must ($\delta\epsilon\hat{\iota}$) suffer (Mk. viii. 31;

---

[1] See, e.g., Mr. C. G. Montefiore and Dr. Klausner, passim.
[2] Dr. A. E. J. Rawlinson, New Testament Doctrine of the Christ, p. 70.

L

Mt. xvi. 21; Lk. ix. 22; Lk. xvii. 25). His death is a necessary part of His work. And it is not an end, but a means to
an end: "I have a baptism to be baptized with; and how
am I straitened till it be accomplished!" (Lk. xii. 50);
"I cast out devils and perform cures to-day and to-
morrow, and the third day I am perfected" (Lk. xiii. 32):
for each time that the sufferings and death are spoken of
by Him, He includes the rising again on the third day
(except in Lk. ix. 44 and Lk. xvii. 25). What, in His view
at the time, the death and the rising again meant is a
further question. That there is in it an element of judgment appears from the parable of the Wicked Husband-
men: their killing of the son is the signal for their overthrow; but it is also the signal for the founding of a new
community, and in some discussions of the bearing of
the parable that is overlooked. Its climax is not an end
but an end of which the purpose is a beginning, and the
story suggests as plainly the victory of the Son as His
death: "The stone which the builders rejected, the same
was made the head of the corner" (Mk. xii. 1-11). The
death is also the prelude to His entry upon His Messianic
Kingdom: the close connection between Peter's confession and the first foretelling of the death involves that:
"If I am the Christ, then know that I must suffer". The
way to Messiahship is suffering, death, and resurrection.
So the request of the sons of Zebedee follows immediately
upon another prediction, and assumes that however the
disciples misunderstood what He had said (Lk. xviii. 34)
He meant what would be the prelude to His "glory"
(Mk. x. 37) or "kingdom" (Mt. xx. 21). This story indeed, in St. Matthew and St. Mark, is replaced in St.
Luke by the general statement, "They understood none of
these things; and this saying was hid from them, and they
perceived not the things which were said"; and the probability is, therefore, that the key to the bewilderment or
despair of the disciples after the Cross is not so much
their failure to realise the fact that He had foretold His
death, as their persistent misunderstanding, which continues until the Ascension, of His ultimate destiny, and of

the real meaning of His Kingdom. There is also, in His language, evidence of the sense of destiny, or rather of fulfilment; the death and the new life must come because "it is written of him" (Mk. xiv. 21; Mt. xxvi. 24; so Mk. x. 32; Lk. xviii. 31; Mk. xiv. 27; Mt. xxvi. 31; Lk. xxii. 37; Lk. xxiv. 25-27).

It is of course disputed how far in these passages, which for the most part only suggest a summary of Old Testament interpretation, or in other parts of the Synoptic record, Jesus is to be taken as applying to Himself the language used in Isaiah liii. about the suffering Servant. One passage is undoubtedly quoted (Lk. xxii. 37 = Is. liii. 12, "and he was numbered with transgressors"). The great passage in Isaiah lxi. 1 ff. is the text of our Lord's sermon in the synagogue at Nazareth (Lk. iv. 18 f.), and it is clearly in His mind as a description of His ministry in His answer to the Baptist (Mt. xi. 5; Lk. vii. 22); and there are reminiscences or quotations of other verses in Deutero-Isaiah. That this prophecy—and for our present purpose there is no need to discuss whether its authorship is composite or not—was in His thoughts from the beginning to the end of His ministry is clear; and it seems difficult to argue, as Dr. Rashdall does, that He used it, of set purpose, in fragments, and that if He quoted from the earlier part of Isaiah liii. He would not have followed it in the later part of the same chapter. Of the last words of Mark x. 45 (Mt. xx. 28)—"to give his life a ransom for many"—I say nothing at this stage. Their genuineness has been challenged, and their weight can only be allowed if the substance of what they imply appears to exist already in the rest of the Synoptic teaching. But no one will dispute the trustworthiness of the words which immediately precede: "The Son of man came not to be ministered unto, but to minister". These give the motive for the rule of Christian greatness which our Lord has just laid down. His is no earthly kingdom, with earthly standards of values, under which to rule means to lord it over others, and greatness is the exercise of the authority of outward or material power (Mk. x. 42). In the Christian kingdom the King Himself achieves His glory by the path of ministry; that is, in it, the secret of greatness, and His followers must be, like Him, the ministers and servants of all. Here, without doubt, is the conception of the Lord's Servant of Deutero-Isaiah. Does service, for the Master and the King, mean giving His life—whether the life so given is, in any of the later and technical senses which Christian theology has intended, a "ransom for many"—or not?

The answer to that is in other sayings. What is clear is that on this supreme issue the central teaching is that "the disciple is not above his master: but everyone when he is perfected shall be as his master" (Lk. vi. 40); "a disciple is not above his master, nor a servant above his lord" (Mt. x. 24); or, as it is repeated in the Johannine teaching, "a servant is not greater than his lord" (Jn. xiii. 16 ; xv. 20). For the servants, or the disciples, the secret of following the Master is "let him deny himself, and take up his cross, and follow me" (Mk. viii. 34; Mt. xvi. 24; Lk. ix. 23; Mt. x. 38; Lk. xiv. 27). It may indeed be said that the mention of the Cross in these passages, even in Q, in which some of them occur, must be due to later associations; but the substance of the saying lies in the call to surrender life for the sake of securing life. The Cross, whether our Lord used the word or not, does no more than describe the method of surrender: it is, whether used in anticipation or in retrospect, a symbolic way of describing a death that is neither self-inflicted, as in suicide, nor merely accomplished by *force majeure*, as in murder, but voluntarily accepted in self-surrender for the Master's cause. And that principle is the very heart of our Lord's message: "Whosoever would save his life shall lose it; and whosoever shall lose his life for my sake (and the Gospel's, Mk.) shall save it" (Mk. viii. 35; Mt. xvi. 25; Lk. ix. 24; so Mt. x. 39; Lk. xvii. 33; and also Jn. xii. 25).

The principle, therefore, for the Master and for His disciples, for the Lord and for His servants, is the same. He cannot be thought of as exacting a demand from them, or laying down an objective for them, which are not a demand and an objective for Himself. If the servant is to suffer and to achieve as his Lord, so the Lord is to suffer and to achieve as the servant. For both, death or self-surrender, the surrender of life, is demanded; but always with a view to the life that is to follow it. If Jesus foretells His death, He also foretells His resurrection: if life is lost, it is that it may be found, or saved.

We have, therefore, an outline of what seems to be expressed or implied in the generally accepted body of the Synoptic teaching as to sin, and the recovery or deliverance from sin, and our Lord's own share in the deliverance. Men are, like the prodigal son, exiles in the far country of their sins. They are like sheep wandering and lost upon the barren hills, wounded and sick from exposure and the attacks of their natural enemies. They are God's treasure, lost in dark corners and hidden beneath dust and dirt. It is the traditional and inherited belief that He has all through His people's history revealed Himself to them in redeeming them from a foreign country, in leading and feeding them like a shepherd, in bringing them to a home which is both His and theirs. And in all this He was with them: Yahweh, the God of personal self-revelation, in Whose dealing with His servants there was the living personal touch of friendship as well as the direct contact of personal intercourse, entered Himself into their experience. He is not "coldly sublime, intolerably just". "He was their saviour. In all their affliction he was afflicted, and the angel of his presence saved them: in his love and in his pity he redeemed them; and he bare them, and carried them all the days of old" (Is. lxiii. 8, 9). It is this Yahweh, so known and inherited by our Lord and by all those who had, or to whom He gave, the key to the history which He fulfilled, who is the Father of the Prodigal Son, the Shepherd who searches at whatever cost for the lost sheep, the householder who spares no pains for the recovery of His treasure. And as the teaching goes on, by word and by act, in the ministry of Jesus, the outlines of the unseen God take shape; as Jesus Himself is found seeking and saving and healing, nothing is said, by Him or by His followers, to force a conclusion, but, equally, there is nothing to suggest any of the conventional methods by which the invisible God is supposed to be revealed. It is significant that as He himself does not use the style or method of the prophets, so He is never in any sense regarded as an angelic mediator—and these were the accepted channels hitherto of God's direct agency among men. He is only thought of as one of the old prophets by those who confessedly misunderstood Him. He is neither prophet nor angel nor, again, is He King in the accepted sense, any more than it occurs to them that He is acting as a priest. Nothing is said or suggested; but something is there, which makes itself felt, and which grows, alike in His teaching, and, though at an almost immeasurable distance, in the hearts of His followers. "They were in the way, going up to Jerusalem; and Jesus was going before them: and they were amazed; and they that followed were afraid" (Mk. x. 32). That is a description not only of the outward scene at the moment, but, inwardly, of the whole course of His ministry. "Man lives first and thinks afterwards." It is not the time, as yet, for theories; He goes too deep for the use of ancient labels for His action—either those of established prophecy or of earthly Davidic Kingship, or of the sacrifices of bulls and goats whose blood could not take away sin. For the present He gives a revelation to the eye of faith, while He is setting a problem for the theology of later times. But the revelation is barely apprehended. He has taught of seeking and saving. He has shown Himself to them as doing God's work. He has led them, at first by word only, to the implications of what the act of deliverance means both to God and to Himself, and in the end to them. He must die and live again. They, if they are to be His own, must lose their lives to save them. And in the end the death and the new life come, for Him, in the Passion and the Resurrection. That is the message of the Synoptic Gospels: and nothing shows the emphasis upon death and new life as the method and the purpose of His work so much as the actual proportion of the narratives which is

given to them.[1] Death, voluntarily accepted that life may
be found, is at once the secret of His Kingship, and the
revelation of the Father's character and will; and it is so
because it is the way in which He seeks and saves His
sheep and His treasure. He has Himself gone into the far
country of His people's sins. They come back, not alone
but in His company, following Him, borne by Him. He
has taught them that in doing this He must die; and that
they must share His Cross; and that for Him and for
them that means life.

The whole action is too near for them to see it yet in
its true bearings; too much a part of their experience for
them to think it out and give it the appropriate names.
But the reality is there of the first stages of a sacrifice:
there was no mistaking it for the writers of the Epistles,
for there is the approach to the presence of God of the
sinners who had been exiled from Him; with the sinners
there is One Who has made His life one with theirs, for
He has come with them from the far country, has shared
their human experiences alike in birth, in childhood, and
in manhood;[2] has faced their temptations, and shared
alike in joys and sorrows; and in the end the sinners take
His life, as He surrenders it, and in the surrender of life,
life is released, is found. So had been sketched out in
ancient times, however imperfectly, by human instinct,
or by Divine revelation, or by both, the return of the
sinner to his home, and the escape from the guilt of sin.
So the action has been interpreted from the earliest times
in the ancient language as the first stages of the perfect
sacrifice. It becomes, surely, a small and an immaterial
question after this, whether He could have called this
giving His life as a ransom for many. What we know is
that He quotes from a verse in Isaiah liii. immediately
following (verse 12), that, not once or twice only, He

---

[1] Mr. Selwyn has rightly stressed this in his analysis of the Gospel materials
in his *Approach to Christianity*, pp. 127 f.

[2] I avoid at this stage, purposely, the more definite or technical language of
the Incarnation doctrine; but the story, however simply told, is the story of an
identification between Him and those who come with Him, that is no longer
symbolic only and superficial, but profound and complete.

thinks of sinners and of the multitudes to whom He has been sent as those who like sheep have gone astray (verse 6); that at His trial He "opened not his mouth", like the lamb that is led to the slaughter (verse 7); that He regarded Himself from the beginning to the end of His ministry as the anointed messenger of Isaiah xl.-lxvi., who wins his Kingdom by ministering and serving; that it is precisely in this chapter (liii.) that the greatness and supremacy elsewhere foretold for the Messiah is seen to be achieved by the Servant's suffering for others; and that such a deliverance as He effects by His whole work of seeking and saving is by common tradition in Jewish history called "ransoming" or "redeeming". That He was to die is clear; that His death was a necessary and not an incidental part of His work is clear; that His work was, at whatever cost, to bring back to their Shepherd's fold, to restore to their true use, to win back to their Father's home, the sheep, the treasures, the children of God, is admitted: and these principles put together can mean nothing else than that between the giving of His life, on the one hand, and the "many" for whose sake He came, on the other, there is a connecting link, already lying to hand for His use, in the historical term "ransom".

CHAPTER III

LIFE TRANSFORMED

"LEAD us not into temptation, but deliver us from evil (or, the evil one)". We have seen that this is the corollary, in human experience, to "Thy will be done". And the Temptation of our Lord, whatever the precise bearing of the individual assaults of Satan, is in essence His consecration of Himself to the doing of the Father's will. The story of it is part of the introduction to the story of His public life, and like other introductions it is also a summary. It represents what in the language of modern religious experience is sometimes called a "decision for God": it is a crisis, not because it is necessarily an isolated or unrepeated phase in His life, but because the decision once taken was adhered to. There are indications that He was tempted again: Peter's "Be it far from thee, Lord: this shall never be unto thee", was to him the voice of Satan (Mt. xvi. 22 f.); and His own answer to His prayer, "Remove this cup from me", was "not my will, but thine, be done" (Lk. xxii. 42). At the Last Supper He seems to lift the veil from an inner side of His experience which is hardly revealed in the stories as we have them: "Ye are they which have continued with me in my temptations" (Lk. xxii. 28). His earthly life, in fact, is in no way so completely human as when He reveals it as a continual struggle against the tempter; and the completeness of His triumph is before everything else the measure of His self-dedication. "Lo, I come to do Thy will, O God" is the secret of it.

It would be easy, but it is unnecessary, to summarise

alike His example and His teaching in terms of obedience
to the will of God. The Fourth Gospel, whatever its
value as history, is at least the earliest direct commentary
on His life during the ministry, and what is often only
implicit in the first three Gospels is there constantly made
explicit. "My meat is to do the will of him that sent me"
(Jn. iv. 34); "I seek not mine own will, but the will of
him that sent me" (*ib.* v. 30, so vi. 38): these sayings are
summaries of the life recorded in the first three Gospels.
So for His followers: it is doing His Father's will that gives
entrance into the Kingdom of heaven (Mt. vii. 21); it is
those who do His Father's will who are His own true kin
(Mt. xii. 50; Mk. iii. 35).

What is significant, for our purpose, is not, however,
the mere fact of the life which He lived Himself, and
which He enjoined upon His disciples, being a dedicated
life, but the further fact of the setting in which that life
is found as soon as it is realised. We have come in fact
to the completion of the process which in the Old Testament we have traced. There has been from the beginning
a widening of horizons. It was always a history of life;
but the life has deepened in meaning; its implications
have been more and more clearly seen, in exact proportion to the extent of the social unit in which it was realised. In primitive times the unit was the family, or the
blood-clan.[1] The horizon was limited to the scope of the
clan's experience; and, so limited, the life was barely
more than what we should call physical. The unit grew
into the nation, with a wider and higher idea of God, and
new demands upon His people; there was a new widening
of the horizon. It grew again, in the teaching of the prophets and the experiences of the Babylonian Captivity,
from the nation to the whole human race. That was for
the Old Testament period the final widening of horizons.
The Apocalyptists made a new departure: in despair of a
Kingdom of this world, they looked to a Kingdom not
of this world but of Heaven. It was a change of standpoint and of outlook; it brought heaven, as it were, into

[1] See above, pp. 34, 39 ff., 52.

the picture—the unseen or the future world—but it left
out hope for this life. Our Lord recovered, as He always
did, what had been lost. He goes back, not without the
Apocalyptic vision, to the point from which it started,
and combines the old ideal with the new. He inherits the
whole tradition of the people of God: He comes not to
destroy but to fulfil. Once more, and finally, He widens
the horizon. The scope of the life that He lived, and into
which He would lift those who follow Him, is extended.
The unseen and the eternal are brought within it. The
kingdom of God, or of heaven, is, in the language of time,
both "here" and "hereafter"; in the language of space,
both "here" and "there". More accurately, the language
of time and space only fits a part, and that immeasurably
the smaller part, of what, taken as a whole, is outside
both space and time. We are familiar with such phrases
as "heaven is not a place, but a state"—however in-
adequately they express our meaning, or however little
we are able, under the limitations of human thought, to
conceive the meaning which we try to attach to them.
But the language of our limitations is, in fact, the only
language which, for the most part, we can use: and therefore much of the teaching about the new life of the Kingdom, whether of God or of heaven, is, in its wording,
local, spatial, and temporal. It is only in two directions
that we can escape from these hindrances—in the pictures or expressions that are admittedly symbolic, and
in the direct language of personal intercourse. And of
this latter the key-words are "love" and "fear". For both
express, taken together, the supreme development of the
distinctive idea of the Divine which traces back through
the various stages in the sense of Holiness to the earliest
beginnings. It is the idea which has become familiar in
recent years under the term "numinous". In its primitive
form it is known, under the limitations of the earliest
phases of religious life, almost as a physical "contagion".
But, early or late, it means that double feeling of attraction and of awe combined which distinguishes and expresses man's sense of contact with his Creator. And in

the Synoptic story itself this double feeling is indicated
for us by our Lord in the terms of love and fear. To love
God is the first commandment of the Gospel as of the
Law; and He forewarns us Whom we shall fear: "Yea,
I say unto you, Fear him" (Lk. xii. 5).

This contrast, sharply stated, is by itself, indeed, an
overstatement in one sense, and in another an incomplete
statement of the actual teaching. But it is there, in our
Lord's words, and it represents, as it were, the opposite
poles of the revelation which He gives. Between the two
extremes, there is His constant reiteration of "Fear not",
"be not afraid". But it remains true that, even for the
disciples, there are other conditions, the existence of
which they must face, and which under certain circumstances they must accept. Under these, God, Who desires and offers love, must be feared.

We have seen, in Part I., that the problem which the
Old Testament left unsolved was that of bringing Holiness—the power and character of God—into human life,
of expressing it in terms of practical righteousness. In the
Gospels we find that problem on its way to a solution. We
are, during our Lord's earthly life, in an intermediate
stage, preparatory to the completeness of what we find
after Pentecost. It has often been noticed that in His
recorded teaching there is singularly little about Holiness, and in the Synoptic Gospels singularly little about
the Spirit. We find, as before, in the Fourth Gospel something in the nature of a commentary on this reserve. The
true text of the passage (Jn. vii. 39), with which we are
familiar as "The Spirit was not yet given", seems to be
οὔπω γὰρ ἦν πνεῦμα: "it was not yet Spirit"—much as we
might say, "it was still night", "it was not yet day", "it
is still winter and not yet spring". And the reason given
is, in the light of the ultimate understanding both of the
limited conditions of the Ministry and of the fullness of the
later experience, "because Jesus was not yet glorified". To
His hearers, during the Ministry, Holiness, whether
directly felt or mediated through men, meant so much
that if He had deliberately and expressly made use of the

idea or attached it to Himself they could never have been natural with Him. It appears therefore, where it does appear, in His teaching, not as belonging to Himself but in relation to the Father, as the disciples are to approach Him—"Hallowed be thy Name"—and in relation to the Spirit. Otherwise He uses the idea as part of the accepted material of religious thought: "Give not that which is holy unto the dogs" (Mt. vii. 6); or in the more significant passage in which He speaks of the holiness of holy things and places as derived from God (Mt. xxiii. 16-22). Here, indeed, He seems to be correcting popular and formal, or magical, views of holy things not by denying their holiness but by reversing the common direction of approach. The gold of the Temple is holy, and the gift upon the altar is holy, but the holiness is not an external quality inherent in gold or gift, but a derived quality belonging more essentially to the Temple, and ultimately to God, Who dwells therein, and to the altar upon which, presumably, God accepts the gift, as the heaven is holy because it contains God's throne, and the throne because God sits thereon.

The opening words, indeed, of the Lord's Prayer[1] have a significance in our Lord's teaching about God which is altogether out of proportion to their length. To us, in modern times, Fatherhood and Kingship are familiar conceptions: they do not necessarily connote, but rather seem to exclude, the conception of God as God, and with that the thought of the "numinous" or of Holiness. But "Our Father which art in heaven", in the language natural to Jews of the first century, meant more than the almost purely ethical idea of Fatherhood to which our Lord's teaching is now commonly reduced. "Heaven" is the dwelling-place of God, as God; and the value, or the appeal, of the tender and familiar picture of the Father loses precisely what must, at the time, have given it its chief force on our Lord's lips if it is forgotten that this Father of infinite care and infinite mercy, Whose love is individualised in infinite detail, reaching even to the birds

---

[1] Otto, *Idea of the Holy*, p. 87. I have dealt with other passages below on Dr. Otto's lines.

and flowers, is Himself, first and foremost, the God of the
unspeakable Name. It is not for nothing that Jesus
observes, without exception, the rule that forbade Its
very pronunciation. He uses one of the established peri-
phrases—"Our Father in heaven"—other equivalents of
which were "the Merciful" (Lk. vi. 36); "the Holy One,
blessed be He" [*E. R. E.*, vol. ix. p. 177, *s.v.* "Name of
God" (Jewish), by I. Abrahams]. And the "sanctification of the Name" was the regular Jewish expression for
the moral consequences which were to flow from true
reverence for the Holy God; for the imitation of Him as
prescribed in Leviticus xix. 2 ("Ye shall be holy: for I
the Lord your God am holy"); for the vindication of God's
honour among men by conduct of which the characteristic idea is cleanness, the quality of the sanctuary, as
opposed to ugliness, the quality of the conduct which
profaned the Name; for the heroism which could issue in
martyrdom for His sake (*ib.* pp. 177 f.). The Lord's
Prayer gives us, indeed, a conception of God which begins
in the sanctuary. If we are made welcome as children in
our Father's home; if we are made citizens or sons of His
Kingdom; we lose the central meaning of home and
Kingdom alike, and their force as changing our lives, if
we do not begin by recognising the Father and the King
as before everything else the God Whose Holiness is the
first secret alike of awe and of love, before Whom, as our
Creator, we fall down in worship. To pray the Lord's
Prayer implies what is not fully expressed until after the
period with which the Synoptic Gospels deal. There is
contained in it the faith that the Holiness of the God of
Israel can be ours, and the pledge that we will make it
ours, so far as in us lies, by consecrating our lives.
Sanctuary and kingdom and the daily life which is the
field of moral effort meet, alike in the opening petitions
in which we dedicate ourselves to God, and in the closing
petitions in which we ask for the satisfaction of our needs
under these three heads—the food, which God the
Creator and Preserver of life alone can give; the forgiveness of our sins with the readiness to forgive others, which

is at once the chief characteristic of the King, and the
supreme law alike of admission to and of continuance in
the Kingdom; and the deliverance from evil and the safe-
guarding from temptation, which we have seen to be the
corollary in our Lord's mind of doing the Father's will.

But apart from our Lord's actual teaching there is an
element in the narrative about Him which is too constant
to be overlooked, but which from some modern points
of view is difficult to interpret. The formulation of the
precise bearings of the Synoptic story on later doctrinal
problems has tended to concentrate on the theology of
His Person. We have been too much accustomed to forcing
the Synoptic material into evidence, for example, either
for a "metaphysical" or for an "ethical" idea of His Sonship. We have expected it to show Him as mediating, or
revealing, the Divine Nature in one or other of these ways.
But the classification is not exhaustive; and neither the
ethical nor the metaphysical conception of Sonship, true
as each undoubtedly is in its proper connection, belongs
really to first-century thought, either Jewish or Greek. The
Jews, at least, and to some extent other nations also, were
in those times accustomed to the idea of a more direct
manifestation of God, which had not then been thought
out either on ethical or on metaphysical lines. Immediate
contact with the Divine—or the sense of the numinous—
was more familiar to them than we realise. The Eastern
"holy man", as Otto[1] reminds us, is in one sense a key to
much that is left otherwise unexplained in the Gospels:
for it is Eastern mentality with which, in the interpretation of the Bible records, we are concerned; and there are
phenomena in the New Testament, as well as in the Old,
which are so foreign to the ideas to which we, in the West,
are accustomed, that it helps us to visualise them, and to
estimate their true significance, if we can replace them
in their own characteristic Eastern setting. I do not, of
course, suggest that the typical "holy man" of the modern
or of the ancient East is comparable in moral worth or in
religious value to the Hebrew prophets, or still less to the

---

[1] Otto, *op. cit.* pp. 161 f.

Lord. But the phenomena of prophecy itself cannot be understood apart from the unworthy manifestations of it among those who are called in the Old Testament "false prophets"; and in the same way what we have to realise is that prophets themselves are part of a wider class, not confined to the Bible alone, but familiar throughout the sphere of Oriental religion as a whole. And with these men, rightly or wrongly, worthily or unworthily, it is an established fact of experience that they convey the sense of the direct action of God. They evoke, in those whom they affect, precisely that combination of attraction and of fear, of awe and fascination, which throughout history is the characteristic mark of man's sense of the Divine. Now in the Synoptic record by itself there are many passages which convey just this sense of the impression which our Lord produced. They cannot be eliminated from the story: it is easy to miss their significance; but, taken together, they appear to lead both towards the first form of the beliefs which His disciples reached about Him, and to some of the most distinctive elements of His own teaching.

We have sometimes the more general impressions. "They were astonished at his teaching; for his word was with authority" (Lk. iv. 32; so Mk. i. 22; and Mt. vii. 28 f.); or, after the prediction of His death and resurrection, when they "understood not the saying and were afraid to ask him" (Mk. ix. 32; Lk. ix. 45). In the case of the "miracles" the impression is more vivid. Nowhere does the unfortunate use of the word "miracle"[1] as the English equivalent for the δυνάμεις of the Synoptic Gospels, convey

---

[1] The general English term "miracle" covers three Greek words: (1) δύναμις, a [work of] power, used regularly in Matthew, Mark, Luke. (2) σημεῖον, a sign, the Johannine word for our Lord's "miracles", used also in the same sense Luke xxiii. 8; Acts iv. 16, 22, viii. 6; and once with δυνάμεις—σ. καὶ δ.—Acts viii. 13. (3) τέρας, a portent, a thing to be wondered at = miraculum, the strict equivalent of the English "miracle". This is only used once of our Lord's "miracles"—Acts ii. 22—and then qualified by its combination with not σημεῖον only but also δύναμις. Otherwise it is used in Acts, always with σημεῖον, of the Apostles' and Old Testament miracles. In the Gospels σ. καὶ τέρατα is used (a) of the works of the false Christs and false prophets (Mt. xxiv. 24; Mk. xiii. 22), (b) of the kind of σ. καὶ τ. which our Lord would not perform (Jn. iv. 48).

Thus in the New Testament our Lord's miracles are either acts of power, or revelations of what He is or does, acts of which the point is either greatness or significance rather than strangeness.

a more misleading impression. To us a "miracle", a thing to be wondered at, suggests an act for which there is no intellectual explanation. To the first eye-witnesses what we have misnamed "miracle" was a "mighty work", an act of power. It was not an enigma, but a revelation. Whatever problems the various kinds of these acts may present to our minds, to those who first witnessed them they were immediate manifestations of the Divine presence. Hence they were "amazed" (Mk. i. 27; Lk. iv. 36; Mk. ii. 12; Lk. v. 26); or they were "afraid" and "glorified God, which had given such power[1] unto men" (Mt. ix. 8); or "they were filled with fear, saying, we have seen strange things to-day" (Lk. v. 26). So after the raising of the widow's son at Nain, "fear took hold on all: and they glorified God, saying, A great prophet is risen up among us: and, God hath visited his people" (Lk. vii. 16); and after the raising of Jairus' daughter "they were amazed straightway with a great amazement" (Mk. v. 42; so Lk. viii. 56). So again, after the walking on the sea, St. Mark (vi. 51) says "they were sore amazed in themselves", adding a hint, the value of which we shall see later, "for they understood not concerning the loaves, but their heart was hardened"; while St. Matthew interprets the same mood in words which lend themselves to, or perhaps express, later theological interpretation, but may be wholly in a line with the Lucan language just quoted as a description of their sense of a direct manifestation of God: "They that were in the boat worshipped him, saying, Of a truth thou art the Son of God"—or, more literally, "a son of God" (Mt. xiv. 33)—as indeed is suggested after the healing of the demoniac boy: "They were all astonished at the majesty of God" (Lk. ix. 43).

Once more, in the healing of the woman with the issue of blood, there is the fear, as elsewhere, in the woman; and the definite mention of the "power" which the "miracles" suggested: He perceived in Himself "that the power proceeding from him had gone forth" (τὴν ἐξ αὐτοῦ δύναμιν ἐξελθοῦσαν—Mk. v. 30).

---

[1] ἐξουσία, authority; i.e. it produced the same impression as His teaching.

M

If such impressions were recorded only in connection with miracle, and led to no apparent consequences in the direction of either character or conviction, their significance, for our present purpose, at least, would not be great enough to make it worth while to dwell upon them. But we have seen even in this survey that the impression produced by our Lord's teaching is described in similar terms to that produced by the miracles: both suggest "authority", and inspire fear as well as "astonishment"; and one of the most arresting of the miracles turns the witnesses' thoughts at once to the ancient prophets. It is along that line of approach that teaching and miracle alike produce the sense of the nearness of God. They have about them what was to a Jew the unmistakable quality of the Divine, without necessarily suggesting at the moment any precise interpretation of what later theology calls the "Person" of Christ.

It is, in fact, from this side of the Gospel history that we approach the New Testament solution of the problem of bringing the Holiness of God effectively into the moral life of man; and in doing so we find ourselves at the point where, as I have said, our Lord finally widens the horizon of human activity. For there are further indications of the direct experience of God which He gave during His earthly life without transgressing the limitations which He had imposed upon Himself. There is, indeed, in the reality of the experience which He caused, a difference of degree between Himself and the greatest of the prophets; His teaching could override that of Moses; and "the power proceeding from Him"—I am careful, in this connection, not to anticipate the results of later thought and faith and say "His" power—produced results never once attributed to John the Baptist; but it was, in the sense which I am now emphasising, a difference of degree and not of kind. He reveals, to put it in another way, not so much Himself, the Second Person of the Holy Trinity, as God, the Yahweh of Jewish religion.

And this revelation is found on two main directions, in His dealings with "devils", or "demoniacs", and in the effects which He produced upon His actual followers, or upon the better type among those with whom He came into contact. In each case significant elements of His actual teaching are found to emerge.

I need make no attempt here to discuss the nature of demoniac possession as it appears in the Gospels. Whatever its causes were, one fact has ample evidence in the narrative. The person possessed, or the evil spirit possessing him, is constantly described as exceptionally sensitive to the aspect of our Lord's work and character which we have been discussing. One after the other has the instinct of repulsion and of fear which is one side of the normal reaction to the felt presence of God's Holiness. However little the concept of Holiness may emerge in the story taken as a whole, in this connection it provides the normal and typical language in which the occurrences are described. The spirits are repeatedly called "unclean" (Mk. i. 23, iii. 11, v. 8; Lk. viii. 29; Mt. x. 1; Mk. vii. 25): it is the defilement of the sanctuary, the quality which stands over against holiness. "What have we (I) to do with thee?" (Mk. i. 24; Lk. iv. 34; Mk. v. 7; Mt. viii. 29; Lk. viii. 28); "I adjure thee by God, torment me not" (Mk. v. 7; so Mt. viii. 29). There is the repulsion, and the fear of the Holy God Who is a consuming fire, of purer eyes than to behold iniquity. And there is the language of direct recognition, not only of the Messiah (Lk. iv. 41), or, apparently in the "numinous" and not in any metaphysical sense, of the Son of God (Lk. iv. 41; Mk. iii. 11; Mk. v. 7; Mt. viii. 29; Lk. viii. 28), but actually of "the Holy One of God" (Lk. iv. 34)—the exact words, though arrived at from the opposite direction, of St. Peter's confession in John vi. 69, our Lord's response to which is in complete harmony with the connection of thought which I have traced: "Did not I choose you the twelve, and one of you is a devil?" (ib. 70).

And it is just when the contact with "unclean spirits" or "devils" is in question that our Lord breaks through His ordinary reserve and speaks of the Spirit, or the Holy Spirit. He was accused of casting out devils by Beelzebub,

and in the face of that accusation He speaks out. The
alternative is that He casts them out by the Spirit (Mt.
xii. 28) or 'the "finger" (Lk. xi. 20) of God; that is to say,
life has been brought within the sphere of Holiness, and
therefore "is the kingdom of God come upon you" (*ib.*).
He has been challenged, and He makes us feel that to
Him it was a challenge not of Himself but of the
Holiness of God—for what He says about blasphemy
against the Holy Spirit followed in St. Matthew and
St. Mark as the immediate outcome of the charge that
He is possessed by Beelzebub; and St. Mark adds
"because they said, He hath an unclean spirit", as providing the connection of thought, then obvious, in the
contrast between uncleanness and Holiness (Mt. xii.
31 f.; Mk. iii. 28-30). In St. Luke the "blasphemy against
the Holy Spirit" comes in a different context; but the
connection of thought is the same: for it follows upon the
"Fear Him" which, as we have seen, is one extreme of
Jesus' teaching about God, and the "Fear not" which
we shall find to be His constant welcome to those who
come within the Kingdom instead of remaining outside it.
And in St. Luke it leads at once to the promise of the
Holy Spirit to the disciples in their hour of need (Lk. xii.
5-12).[1] This promise, again, in St. Matthew is directly
connected with the thought of casting out devils: it was
partly for that work that the twelve were sent out upon
their mission (Mt. x. 7 f.; so Lk. ix. 1, more emphatically,
and Mk. vi. 7, more emphatically still, as if it were their
sole work, "he gave them authority over unclean spirits").
He gave them, that is, His own "numinous" "authority"
over what was unclean and incompatible with the Holy;
and therefore it will be the Spirit of their Father that
speaketh in them (Mt. x. 20). So our Lord's mind reverts
in the immediate sequel to the charge about Beelzebub
(Mt. x. 25), and there follows the same saying about fear-
ing God, which in St. Luke directly precedes the promise
of the Holy Spirit (Mt. x. 28). And, lastly, it is significant
in this connection that when St. Luke, at the end of his

---

[1] See below, p. 174.

Gospel, and at the beginning of the Acts, records the immediate promise of the Spirit, it is not only as being one of the "things concerning the kingdom of God", but specifically as "power", or "power from on high" (Acts i. 3-8; Lk. xxiv. 49), that the Spirit is described.

It is therefore, on the one hand, out of the contact with evil recognised as "unclean" that the evidence of the Synoptic Gospels as to contact with God's Holiness becomes irresistibly clear; and, on the other hand, the sense of Holiness is one of the characteristic marks of the apprehension of the Master by the disciples. It is not only that the centurion at the Cross—if we may combine the versions respectively of St. Matthew and St. Mark (Mt. xxvii. 54; Mk. xv. 39: "Truly this man was a Son of God") with that of St. Luke (Lk. xxiii. 47: "Certainly this was a righteous man")—felt the presence of God, and felt it as a revelation of moral goodness; and, so feeling it, had the typical experience (he "feared exceedingly", Mt. xxvii. 54; "glorified God", Lk. xxiii. 47); but Isaiah's classical experience of God's Holiness is repeated. The centurion whose servant was healed felt himself unworthy to receive our Lord into his house, and even to come to Him himself (Mt. viii. 8; Lk. vii. 7). And, more vividly still, after the draught of fishes St. Peter is "amazed"; "falls down at Jesus' knees", and says "Depart from me; for I am a sinful man, O Lord" (Lk. v. 8 ff.). There is no explanation of this confession, unless the story defines for us the "amazement" so often chronicled in similar cases: it can only mean that the power which has been seen at work is felt instinctively to be the Holiness itself of God. So it was with Isaiah: he saw God, in His Holiness, as worshipped by the seraphim, and he became conscious of sin: "Woe is me! for . . . I am a man of unclean lips" (Is. vi. 1-5). That is the fundamental Jewish conception of the nature of God: it is only the pure in heart who can endure the vision (Mt. v. 8); without purity of heart, before redemption and reconciliation, no man can see God and live (Ex. xxxiii. 20).

It is striking that the apprehension of Holiness by the

disciples is exactly parallel to the apprehension of it by evil spirits. St. Peter's shrinking, and the centurion's, correspond not only to the "What have I to do with thee?" of the demoniacs, but also to the request of the Gadarenes that Jesus should depart out of their borders (Mt. viii. 34; so Mk. v. 17; and Lk. viii. 37). On both sides there is the feeling that man cannot be too near God: the difference lies in the reason for the feeling; and wherever there is the right reason—viz. either a sense of moral unworthiness, or, as we shall see, "faith"—our Lord's answer is "Fear not". So it is at the Transfiguration (Mt. xvii. 7), where there is first the natural fear of the Divine. So it is with St. Peter: "Fear not; from henceforth thou shalt catch men". He will, as it were, be within, and not outside, the sphere of the Holy; the same "power" which in the draught of fishes he has recognised as the power of the Holy will be his for the work of a fisher of men (Lk. v. 10).

Similarly, at the stilling of the storm they marvelled, were afraid, feared exceedingly (Mt. viii. 26; Lk. viii. 25; Mk. iv. 40 f.), and were rebuked for want of the faith that should have made them at home in the wider world of the Kingdom of heaven.

The exact position, therefore, in which, during the ministry, the conception of Holiness is found is transitional. Afterwards, when "it was Spirit", and it could no longer be said "it was not yet Spirit", the power of the Holy has become the mark of the normal life of the Christian society. In the time before Pentecost the disciples are in touch with it, on the border-line, half afraid. They are not yet at home in the presence of God: so after the Transfiguration, when His glory and their fear are gone, the story conveys a sense of relief in the simple ending, "they saw no one any more, save Jesus only with themselves". They are back again where they know where they are; all is once more familiar and normal. Nothing shows so clearly the reasons for our Lord's ordinary reserve. He has to train them for a new life in a new setting; to be citizens and subjects of a kingdom not of this world but of "heaven"; to look for home and kindred and

fatherhood in "heaven", not on earth; and to live in the
unveiled presence of God. They must learn that such a life
can only be found by surrender. They must take the
measure of the new area in which they are to move. They
must acquire a wholly new sense of value and of proportion. They have inherited a faith in a God Who may not
be seen; Whose presence is at once wholly desirable and
fatally dangerous; Whose life in the surrendered and
accepted blood of the sacrificial victims is too holy to be
received; Whose power is known and felt, but acts on men
only from outside, and has never possessed their hearts or
passed into their lives as their very own. They must be
trained and fitted, by the cleansing of the heart, to see the
vision and live. Defilement is not from without, a matter
of unwashen hands, but from within—that is the corollary of "blessed are the pure in heart: for they shall see
God", and the two sayings together make up the new, and
final, Law of Holiness. They must be taught that where
there is faith there is admission to a Presence which is a
Father's home, over the door of which is written "Fear
not". They must be led on through the lesson of the surrendered life, first in teaching and in example, and finally
upon the Cross, to receive the Life which conveys the full
Holiness of God; and they must become themselves part
of that Life, so that its power, still in outward action but
normally and most truly in inward influence, becomes
their own possession.

In the history of this process during our Lord's visible
life on earth we see their gradual training; partly, though
least effectively, in character—for that cannot be transformed until "it is Spirit", and the teaching which their
Oriental memories had enabled them to retain can become operative; partly in mental grasp, though that,
again, can only be reached when the Resurrection and
Pentecost have explained the Cross; and partly in the
strange borderland between the seen and the unseen, the
normal and the supernormal, where they have learnt to
feel the immediate presence of God. They were slowly
being introduced into a new world, which was to be to

them at once sanctuary, kingdom, and home. In a sense—
for it is clearly told as a critical turning-point in the
history—the training in the third of these lessons, the
sense of and contact with the Divine, had reached a point
from which a new departure could be made in St. Peter's
confession. The actual wording of what St. Peter said has
come to us in three forms: Thou art the Christ (Mark
viii. 29); the Christ of God (Luke ix. 20); the Christ, the
Son of the living God (Matt. xvi. 16). And as St. Matthew
gives the fullest form of the confession, so he alone gives
the words of our Lord's reply.[1] Peter has not arrived at his
confession by any process of instruction or of reasoning—
by what we should call, in our limited estimates, normal
experience—but by direct revelation: "Flesh and blood
hath not revealed it unto thee, but my Father which is in
heaven" (Matt. xvi. 17). The faith which has brought him
into personal contact with the Father is therefore the
foundation upon which the new society that is to be
heavenly as well as earthly can be built.[2] The sphere of life
is extended until it is at last complete, and the same law
runs throughout it. The earthly "keys" admit to or exclude from the whole; what is bound or loosed on earth is
bound or loosed in heaven. "Heaven" and "earth" may,
separately, still be used as exclusive of or contrasted with
one another, but the "kingdom of heaven" includes both.

It is at this point, therefore, in their training, and as the
immediate consequence of the direct experience of God
revealed in St. Peter's confession, that the Master can
begin to teach (Matt. xvi. 21; Mark viii. 31) the lesson of
the life that must be first surrendered, and will then be
transformed: "The Son of man must . . . be killed, and
after three days rise again" (Mark viii. 31). And it is
characteristic that here again, as in the cases already
noted, the sense of the nearness of the Divine and the

---

[1] It should be noted that we must not assume that St. Mark's or St. Luke's
record imply here what may be deduced from St. Matthew's. That stands by
itself. What follows from Mark and Luke is the fact that our Lord's teaching
about His death follows on St. Peter's confession.

[2] But if the point of our Lord's answer is the similarity of Πέτρος and Πέτρα,
it is Peter himself, not his faith, that is the "rock foundation".

sense of the personal power of evil go together; for Peter's
rebuke is an utterance of Satan himself and a temptation.

The disciples, therefore, are not yet, and indeed they
never were, during the ministry, at home in the new
world. They only saw glimpses of it, and at their highest
moments of contact, as at the Transfiguration, their footing was uncertain. In the last journey to Jerusalem there
was a characteristic moment. "Jesus was going before
them", in the loneliness of the Way of the Cross: there
was that in Him which had the typical effect of His
words, of His acts of power, of His glory at the Transfiguration: a silence, it would seem, that brought to them
the sense that the "silence in heaven" of the Apocalypse
adds to that vision: "They were amazed; and they that
followed were afraid" (Mk. x. 32). And at the end, before
the Ascension, they seemed even to have lost the horizon
to which at last the Cross and Resurrection, as well as
His constant teaching, should have extended their view:
they still thought of an earthly Messianic reign: "Lord,
dost thou at this time restore the kingdom to Israel?"
(Acts i. 6).

But although the disciples, until Pentecost, neither
grasped the scope of the Kingdom of heaven, nor permanently entered it; and although they had barely learnt
to recognise the Holy, and were not truly at home in Its
Presence, and much less had received Its power into
themselves, they had had enough contact with the Master
to recognise the Holy Spirit when He came, and they had
had enough teaching to enable them, once they had received the power, to realise what the Kingdom in fact
was to be. They could understand at length what our
Lord had meant. They saw things at last in their true
proportions in the new perspective.

For the Lord's words and acts, which at first they remembered rather than understood, had meant a new
sense of values, and had given a new scope to life. It was
this that had marked much if not all of the distinctive
teaching of the Sermon on the Mount. The tendency of the
day in Jewish religion, if we are to trust the Gospels,

was to rest upon the external, the concrete and the literal. The horizon was limited, and within its limits poverty, hunger, sorrow, persecution are what they are and no less; but in the new and transformed life they find their place in the scheme of heavenly or eternal values, and spell inheritance, satisfaction, comfort, and victory. The law, while it remains a law of outward conduct, is inchoate and incomplete; it is not fulfilled unless it is written in the heart, and becomes the new law of the life that is unseen even more than seen. The three great duties that were soon to become for the Jews the expression and the embodiment of, rather than the substitutes for, their sacrifices, almsgiving, prayer, and fasting,[1] are transferred from the sphere of outward performance and worldly reward to that of the Divine presence and acceptance. The treasure of earth, passing and insecure, is as nothing when seen in the light of the treasure of heaven, eternal and inalienable, and "where thy treasure is, there will thy heart be also". So in the new life there will be singleness of outlook, light instead of darkness, for those who are to be the light of the world; and singleness of aim, when allegiance is no longer divided, but there is perfect service of God. And there is the perfect satisfaction of all needs; for true life is attained, and the life is more than food. All such things, food and drink and clothing, only belong to a part of life, so far from being the whole that it cannot be called life in the true sense at all; but once the full scope is reached, once the Kingdom of God and the full consecration of man's powers in the search for righteousness are achieved, in the true life so found, "all these things shall be added unto you".

And the key to all this is to each man the remaking of his own character, in the humility that is penitence: "Judge not, that ye be not judged"; first "the beam out of thine own eye" before there is any vision to cast out "the mote that is in thy brother's eye". So the man is

---

[1] Note that in these three duties is found the fullness of sacrificial thought: (1) fasting, *i.e.* self-denial in self-surrender; (2) almsgiving = righteousness, *i.e.* the dedicated, and therefore transformed, life ; (3) prayer, the oneness of the life so transformed with God.

changed; and once he is changed, in the new world he has
only to ask, and He who is God as well as Father—"your
Father which is in heaven"—will give him the right food.
For the end to be attained is always life: narrow though
the gate be that leads by the way of self-surrender and
self-dedication and obedience, it is a Life that no outward disasters can take away; it is eternal, for it is
founded upon the Rock (Mt. v.-vii.).

The contrast, marked so clearly in the Sermon on the
Mount, between the surface values of the partial life,
within which the outlook had hitherto been confined, and
the ultimate or absolute values of the complete life of the
Kingdom, is of course found elsewhere. This at least
appears to be the meaning of the parable of the Unjust
Steward. As he plans for immediate and worldly needs,
so should the disciples of Christ plan, not so much for the
future beyond this world in time, but for the needs of the
whole of the new sphere in which they are to move: and
the interests and motives of the two spheres struggle for
the predominance. They conflict; and the choice must be
made between them: "No servant can serve two masters"
(Lk. xvi. 1-13). So with the story of the "rich young
ruler", and the words that follow it: if earthly riches
mean that the outlook is limited to this world, no obedience to an external law avails; nothing but self-surrender
can admit to the wider life of the new world which is
called heaven, the life that is eternal (Mk. x. 17-31), or
as in 1 Timothy vi. 17-19, with the same connection of
thought, "the life that is life indeed". On the other hand,
where the motive of outward obedience is a love that
goes deeper than the mere observances of contemporary
sacrifice, our Lord can say, "Thou are not far from the
kingdom of God" (Mk. xii. 32-34).

Similarly there is an underlying note in the Synoptic
stories of the feeding of the multitude. These stories
indeed appear to have a wider bearing still, especially in
St. Mark's version. For it is at least possible that a part of
the secret of the multiplying of the food lies in the preface
to the incident as given shortly by St. Luke (Lk. ix. 10),

and more fully by St. Mark (Mk. vi. 30-32), in their
accounts of the feeding of the five thousand. The disciples
had come back from their mission: our Lord saw that
their first need was rest and refreshment; and He takes
them apart into a desert place. They took with them what
was presumably a supply of food sufficient for their small
party: that is suggested by the mention of the insufficiency
of the one loaf only that they had after the feeding of the
four thousand (Mk. viii. 14). The crowds came and demanded the Master: they gave up their quiet day with
Him, and the rest to which they had looked forward; but
at least there would be the evening meal when the crowds
had gone. And in the true spirit of the self-surrender
which admits to the wider life of the Kingdom they gave
their food also, willingly, at the Lord's word. So surrendered He can take it in His hands, and bless (or "give
thanks", Jn. vi. 11)[1], and break it; and what is surrendered
to be broken is accepted as it is offered, and, in acceptance
transformed; it receives the new values and feeds the
multitude, and after that, not scantily but abundantly,
the disciples also. So, "My meat is to do the will of Him
that sent me" (Jn. iv. 34).

It is, indeed, clear, whether there were in fact two
feedings or one,[2] that St. Mark and St. Matthew both
suggest that our Lord intended, by what He did, not only
to minister to the outward wants of the people, but to
convey a further truth at least to the disciples. The feeding was, in fact, as in St. John, a sign of something beyond
itself. After the first narrative there follows the storm,
the disciples' panic, the coming of the Lord upon the
water, the stilling of the storm, and the "numinous"
amazement. They had had their experience of the new
life, with its new powers and values, but they had fallen
back within the limitations of the old: "They understood
not concerning the loaves, but their heart was hardened"
(Mk. vi. 52). After the feeding of the four thousand the

---

[1] For the true sequence of thought in the "blessing" or "giving thanks" see
below, pp. 287-295, 339.
[2] The argument which follows remains, whether the distinction suggested
between the "baskets" and the "hampers" below be pressed or not.

suggestion goes further. There had been, at once, a typical
conflict with the Pharisees (so Mk. viii. 11; in Mt. xvi. 1,
with the Pharisees and Sadducees). Afterwards, they
crossed the water, found that they had not enough food
for the day's needs, and were worrying about it. Jesus
warns them against the leaven of the Pharisees and the
leaven of Herod (Mk. viii. 15; Mt. xvi. 6, the leaven of the
Pharisees and Sadducees). They think that He is, on their
own level, discussing the merits of different kinds of bread.
His answer takes them back to the two feedings, both
fresh in their experience, both still not understood. Look
away, He says, from the partial views of life—the life of
superficial obedience of the Pharisees, of the letter without the spirit; the pure worldliness of the Herodians (or the
Sadducees): those views leave them just where they are;
they have no reward; they mean worrying about food and
clothing. He pleads with them, encourages them, reproves
them: "Do ye not yet perceive, neither understand? have
ye your heart hardened? Having eyes, see ye not? and
having ears, hear ye not? and do ye not remember?"
Twice, He says, you had the secret within your grasp: you
gave Me your own food, and I broke it. The first time you
had each a whole basket left over for yourselves (κόφινος),
and the other time the seven loaves you gave became for
your own joint use seven hampers (σφύριδες); you had both
an individual and a corporate experience. Surely you can
see? The Kingdom of heaven in its full expanse, with its
limitless life, is open to you; you have at your feet the
land that is very far off; the King in His beauty is waiting
for you to recognise Him; the Bread of Life—He has
almost said it to them in this story of St. Mark's—is yours.
Surely you know now that, if you do not worry, all these
things shall be added unto you? "Do ye not yet understand?" (Mk. viii. 14-21).

There is the same connection of thought in Luke xii.
There the warning about the leaven of the Pharisees—
here expressly defined as "hypocrisy"—seems to have
been given à *propos* of something that had been caused by
the presence of an overwhelming and unmanageable

crowd, and it is given to the disciples in their absence; it
may be that at this point Luke touches the narratives of
Matthew and Mark at the moment of the feeding of the
four thousand which they record and he does not. The
leaven of the Pharisees, as a limited view of life with a
restricted horizon, reaching only to the outward and not
the inward, in which the dominant thought of God must
be fear, is contrasted at once with the wider outlook in
which everything hidden shall be known, the light shall
penetrate the darkness, earthly death shall have found its
measure, and God is the Father Who cares, even more than
the awful Being Who is feared.

The wider life indeed includes the narrower: acts done
in this world are valid in the other. But the contrast continues, and leads directly to the Lucan narrative of the
teaching about the Son of Man and the Spirit which in
the other narratives we have seen to arise at the thought
of Beelzebub. "It is not yet Spirit", and nothing of the
"numinous" attaches as yet to the Son of Man; He is still
straitened, moving within a confined and limited sphere,
until His "baptism" be accomplished (Lk. xii. 50); but
when the time comes the Holy Spirit—the full power of
the new life—will be known, and blasphemy against the
Spirit shall not be forgiven; in that time the disciples will
have received power from on high, and will be taught by
the indwelling Spirit Himself.

Hence, at once, in St. Luke's context, the parable of
the rich fool, with its contrast between the riches of the
old life and the new, treasure for the old self and treasure
toward God. Hence, again, in an obvious connection,
the teaching found in St. Matthew in the Sermon on
the Mount about food and clothing and wealth—and the
values of such things, on the one hand, among the nations
of the world, and, on the other, in the Kingdom which is
also the Father's home.

The Sermon on the Mount ends upon the note of obedience as leading to life: "everyone therefore that heareth
these words of mine, and doeth them, shall be likened
unto a wise man, which built his house upon the rock"

(Mt. vii. 24). It has been the purpose of this chapter to gather together characteristic teaching of our Lord, and characteristic elements in the narratives about Him, in such a way as to bring out, not only His own obedience and that which He required from His followers, but the new world, or life, into which such obedience was the path. I have called His obedience self-dedication; for "Lo, I come to do Thy will, O God" is at once the key-note of His own earthly life, and the inner spirit of the offering of self which the old "burnt-offering" was intended to express. We have seen in Part I. that the burning of this offering was, to the Israelite, a symbol, not of its destruction in God's honour by the offerer, but of its acceptance, and transformation, by God.[1] Life, in the death of the sacrificial victim, was not ended, but surrendered; and surrendered in order that it might be accepted, and, in acceptance, lifted from its earthly limitations into full association with God in heaven.

It is precisely this lifting of the earthly into the heavenly that is presented to us in the Synoptic Gospels. It is here that our Lord once for all completes what had been left in the old days incomplete. I have attempted to indicate, both in Part I. and in the course of this chapter, two ways in which the incompleteness of the Old Covenant may be formulated. Life had not been grasped as a whole. Its horizon had been, by successive stages, enlarged: one great attempt had been made, in the Apocalyptic period, to solve its problem, not by enlarging its horizon, but by shifting its scene. It remained for our Lord, during His earthly ministry, to describe, and afterwards to achieve, the final enlargement. The description at first, and the experience later, were in the terms of the conceptions of Fatherhood and of the Kingdom. Neither were new; but both were, by our Lord's teaching, transformed.

It is only when both the ideas are given their full scope that either the moral standards of perfect righteousness or the true character and possibilities of the life of the children of God can be achieved. And the possibility of

[1] See above, pp. 13, 19.

this is brought for the first time within reach when the final interchange between heaven and earth is accomplished. The Holiness of the Divine, at first, as we have seen, so imperfectly apprehended that it is not what we could call either a spiritual or a moral quality, is throughout the history understood as God's direct personal action in human life. It is self-communicating power; and as it gradually reveals itself in terms of moral and of spiritual character it becomes at once more compelling, more truly awe-full, and more inaccessible. In the old dispensation, its power still operated on the surface of life alone. It left character untouched. It was not yet grace. In our Lord's earthly life it was within reach, half-recognised, more often than not most baffling and perplexing just when it was most clearly seen. But it plays round Him before the gathering of the storm like the lightning in a summer sky when all else is normal. It is the indications of it at this stage that we have now traced. The storm gathered, as He drew near the Cross; and Pentecost, prepared for by the Resurrection and the Ascension, is the flash that fused together what had hitherto in growing tension lain apart: "It is expedient for you that I go away: for if I go not away, the Comforter will not come unto you".

The dedication of human life in perfect obedience was accomplished in Himself as our first-fruits. He offered our human nature which He had made His own. It was accepted; and the Gospels close, as Acts begins, with the transformation which is God's way of accepting what we offer. The body of His humiliation becomes the body of His glory: the material is taken up into the spiritual; His baptism is accomplished; He is no longer straitened. Human life, in Him, at last finds its true scope. And with the coming of the Spirit the power from on high comes into the lives of ordinary men, and the transformation, effected for the Lord and described by Him in the Gospel story as waiting for His followers, is at last, in the New Testament Church, the daily experience of their own lives.

CHAPTER IV

LIFE SHARED

WE have seen in Part I. that the key-note of the pre-Christian history is Life: life as given and renewed and shared in a society, whether the blood-clan, the tribe, or the nation. It is life that underlies the ideas of the Divine Fatherhood, alike in its primitive and rudimentary, and its later and more spiritual form. Life—its recovery, uplifting, and communication—is the ruling conception of sacrifice: life as shared between God and man, and between man and man; and the same thought of the common life as shared is in the images of the wedlock between Yahweh and His people, and of the tree. And the thought of the maintenance of life by God's gifts of food and drink, sacrificial in their origins, extends, not altogether without association with ideas of sacrifice, or of God's blood as His life, not only to living water, but, in what we are inclined to call metaphor, to the maintenance of life in its more spiritual sense; and the thought is never absent from the familiar Old Testament image of God as the Shepherd of His people.

We have seen also in the last two chapters that much of our Lord's most characteristic "Synoptic" teaching and some of the most characteristic features in the Synoptic portrait of Him gather round Life. His first and last secret is that it must be surrendered to be won; and His own surrender is an integral part of His work of seeking and saving the sinners to whom He has come. Once so surrendered, it is given to God in obedience and service; and as so given it is transformed into the complete life of the new Kingdom.

There is yet another association of ideas in connection with Life. It is a conspicuous element in the later books of the New Testament; in St. Paul's thought about Christians as "in Christ", and Christ "in us"; in his teaching about the Body and its members, and the spiritual house or temple into which we are built; as well as, in St. John's language, about indwelling generally, and in particular about the Bread of Life and the Vine.

It is not always recognised that there is the same element in the Synoptic Gospels. The Synoptic teaching is, in a sense, throughout anticipatory. None of it could be fully grasped until the crisis of our Lord's work, from the Cross to Pentecost, had been surmounted. Not all of it could during the Ministry be equally developed. It was, obviously, only when the Christian society had begun its distinctive history that the thought of life as given, maintained, and shared could be understood from direct experience. But in the Synoptic story we have to remember both the background of inherited conceptions which our Lord and His hearers had received from the past and the developments of later times. We shall be prepared to find continuity in the story of the Ministry, not discontinuity; a bridge, and not a gap. We shall expect to find neither a vital part of the inherited religion ignored nor the later teaching and experience without its germs.

It is difficult, and indeed impossible, either to classify methodically or to summarise completely the material of the Synoptic Gospels. We can only take key ideas, and use them to find our way to this aspect of the living portrait that they give, or to that. I shall attempt no more in this chapter, as I know that I have neither attempted nor achieved more in the last two. And I am fully conscious that where evidence consists, as in some cases it must, of hints and allusions, it may be overpressed. But the evidence is, in its nature, cumulative, and there is room, I think, for suggestions as to underlying principles which have been, in this connection, perhaps too frequently overlooked.

In the first place, it is beyond dispute that, if one topic

is more characteristic of our Lord's message than another, it is that of the Fatherhood of God. And Fatherhood means, as He taught, that God's children are brothers. One life, or, as it would have been expressed in earlier days, one blood, runs through them all. Citizens of a kingdom, subjects of a king, worshippers of a God, they are one family. Their life comes from their Father; it is their Father—God—to Whom they look for the food for its continuance (as in the Lord's Prayer), and to Whom Jesus trains them to look for Fatherly care and providence through all the risks and mischances of experience. It is to the Father's home that He teaches them to return when they have sinned, and to the Father's love that they are to trust for their forgiveness; it is to God as Father, and as thereby akin to them and understanding them, that He leads them to pray.

And this relationship, this bond of kinship, is so strong that, in comparison with it, the smaller earthly kinships and relationships hardly deserve the name. "Call no man your father on the earth; for one is your Father, which is in heaven." [1] "Whosoever shall do the will of my Father which is in heaven, he is my brother, and sister, and mother." [2] The obedience which is the character of the new life, with the resistance to temptation which it implies, and the escape, by surrender, from the old life upon which it follows, reveals or creates the closest of all blood-relationships in the family of which Christ Himself is the elder brother.

With the language of Fatherhood, there goes that of shepherding; and the Shepherd, like the Father, feeds. The ideas of shepherding and feeding go together as in the old days. Jesus was sent, as He told the Canaanitish or Syro-Phoenician woman, to the lost sheep of the house of Israel, and in a moment He passes from the thought of the Shepherd's sheep to that of the Father's children, and their food: "It is not meet to take the children's bread. . . ." [3] So, in the stories of the feeding of the multitudes, on the first occasion "he had compassion on them, because they

[1] Mt. xxiii. 9.   [2] Mt. xii. 50.   [3] Mt. xv. 24-26.

were as sheep not having a shepherd",[1] and again, with
the four thousand, though there is no mention of the
shepherd, there is the shepherd's "compassion";[2] and He
teaches them (in the former story) and feeds them. There
was more here than the actual feeding of their bodies.
He was trying to train His disciples; and we saw that He
was near, indeed, to the teaching set out fully in the
Fourth Gospel about the Bread of Life. Here I need only
emphasise the fact that food is, in such a context, as
much the need of the new life as of the old, though food
of a different kind. Life is the end to be attained, and
food is the means of preserving it: the bread of God,
which gives life, is contrasted with leaven, which was
excluded from the old sacrifices because its fermentation
spelt death, and therefore is the right name, in this connection of thought, for hypocrisy and worldliness.[3]

Once more there is one passage in which He definitely
identifies Himself, as He had not done previously, with
the Shepherd of the Old Testament. He has finished the
last meal with His followers: He has given them their
food, blessing and breaking it in the old familiar way,
but with a new meaning, as we believe, and as the beginning of what was to be His new way of giving the food
in the Kingdom; and He speaks of the interval that is to
come. "I will not drink henceforth of this fruit of the vine,
until that day when I drink it new with you in my
Father's kingdom."[4] In the interval He had another cup
to drink—the cup of death and not of life; and the shepherd's work is, for that interval, suspended (until the
Lamb can feed them as the Good Shepherd from the
throne, and lead them to the waters of life[5]); "It is
written, I will smite the shepherd, and the sheep of the
flock shall be scattered abroad".[6]

"Blessed is he that shall eat bread in the kingdom of
God."[7] This is the prelude to St. Luke's parable of the
Great Supper. Our Lord's fellow-guest was full of the

[1] Mk. vi. 34.
[2] Mt. xv. 32; Mk. viii. 2.
[3] Mt. xvi. 5-12; Mk. viii. 14-21.
[4] Mt. xxvi. 29; so Lk. xxii. 18.
[5] Rev. vii. 17.
[6] Mt. xxvi. 31; Mk. xiv. 27.
[7] Lk. xiv. 15.

spiritual experience of the supper at which he had been
present: for it is clear from what we know both of Jewish
habits and of the associations which gathered round our
Lord's meals with His friends that the talk had been
on the things of God. The man thought at once of the
Messianic banquet: and our Lord's answer accepts and
assumes the conception of the Messianic life as maintained by food; His parable is directed towards another
issue—that of the conditions of admission, of the character of those who shall enjoy the banquet. And in the
Jewish circle of ideas which He thus takes for granted,
there are associations which we cannot ignore. It was not
only that banquets of all kinds had been originally sacrificial feasts,[1] and that in the Deuteronomic injunctions
about the blood there was always at least a ceremonial
reminder of their origin; but the devout Jews' discourse
on religious themes at their meals led to more or less
spiritual conceptions of the banquet in the world to
come. The food there was to be "the heavenly bread, or
manna"; "ambrosial milk and honey"; "the wine prepared from the beginning of the world"; and the banquet
would mean "sitting at the table of the Messiah". "But
while this eudaemonistic view is the popular one" (and
in any case, at its lowest, it has a far less materialistic
setting than is conveyed to modern ears by the mere
phrase "Messianic banquet"), "there is also the higher
and more spiritual view taught by Rab: 'In the world to
come there is neither eating [nor] drinking . . .; but the
righteous sit with their crowns on their heads and enjoy
the splendour of the Shekinah, for it is said, And they
saw God, and did eat and drink; that is, their seeing God
was meat and drink to them'." [2]

The Rabbinic idea of meals was, in fact, as Mr. Israel
Abrahams says,[3] not mere physical satisfaction; the meal
was a service as well, consecrated by benediction. He
quotes R. Simeon (Aboth iii. 3): "Three who have eaten

---

[1] See Part I. p. 36, and Kohler in *Jewish Encyclopaedia*, vol. ii., art.
"Banquets".

[2] The quotations are from *J. E.* vol. v., art. "Eschatology", also by Kohler.

[3] *Studies in Pharisaism and the Gospels*, Series I. p. 55.

at one table and have not said over it words of Torah, are as if they had eaten sacrifices of the dead (idols), for it is said: All tables are full of vomit and filthiness without *place* (*Maqom* = place: here, in its secondary sense, the Omnipresent, *i.e.* God). But three who have eaten at one table, and have said over it words of Torah, are as if they had eaten of the table of God (*Maqom*), blessed be he, for it is said: This is the table that is before the Lord (Ezek. xli. 22)." The "table" here in Ezekiel is the "altar" in the Holy Place in his vision of the reconstructed Temple; and, as it is the only table or altar there mentioned by him, is probably the table of the shewbread, both words being used,[1] as elsewhere.

This Rabbinic conception, says Mr. Abrahams,[2] "is exemplified also in the table discourses of Jesus to his disciples, and lies, to some extent, at the bottom of the institution of the eucharistic meal. In Jewish life this idea that the table is an altar gained a firm hold and led to a whole system of learned readings, devotions and, most remarkably, of hymns during meals, the Passover home-rites being but a conspicuous example of a daily Jewish usage. Just, then, as later on Christians would not share the Eucharistic meal with notorious evil-livers, so the Jewish Rabbi at various periods would (with less consistent rigidity) have objected to partake of any meal with men of low morals. So, also, Jesus' disciples are exhorted (Mt. xviii. 17) to treat certain offenders as 'the Gentile and the Publican', with whom common meals would be impossible." I say nothing of the historical authority of this particular passage in St. Matthew. But I have quoted Mr. Abrahams at length, because he reveals so clearly the Jewish attitude to food, and throws what is, to most modern Christians, so wholly unexpected a light upon what must have been in the minds of our Lord and of His hearers in the type of passage which we are considering.

It was for this reason that I passed, above, abruptly from the indications of the idea of spiritual feeding con-

[1] A. B. Davidson, *Ezekiel*, note *ad loc.*   [2] *Ibid.*

tained in the stories of the feeding of the multitudes to the "Messianic banquet". With the Messianic banquet should be grouped also the wedding feasts of the corresponding parable in St. Matthew,[1] and of the parable of the Ten Virgins.[2] The truth is that in the spiritual exegesis of later Judaism—of the best religion of our Lord's time —, whatever may have been the case in earlier days, the connection of thought between the sacrificial meal and the inward receiving of everything that the Life, at once Divine and communal, could mean was real. We have seen reason, indeed, for thinking that the connection was real in the Temple worship for the writers of some of the Psalms.[3] And the passage from R. Simeon, quoted above, shows that the Rabbis viewed the parallel between the table of God and the table of heathen deities exactly as St. Paul did. But whatever the precise degree of "communion" associations which actually attached in New Testament time to the peace-offering—and I have no desire to overpress that—it seems, at the least, clear that the sustenance of bodily life by bodily food provided for our Lord and for His contemporaries the natural language for the sustenance of the whole of life—however completely or incompletely conceived—by "heavenly" food. Whatever God has to give, whether character, or knowledge, or the Divine power which we call grace, is summed up under the general idea of life; and the means of the sustenance of life is food. Food must be given, received: it is broken in the act of receiving, and destroyed, so far as its original form and separate existence are concerned; but its destruction is for a further end: it is incorporated in the body that receives it, and transformed; it becomes a part of each body and lives again in a myriad new forms. The individuality of each receiver remains, but the whole substance of each is gradually built up out of the food which all have received: his life is his own, but shared in the common life which belongs to all his fellows, and came to him as to them from God. Hence the Jewish thought provides the material for Christian experience. Our Lord

---

[1] Mt. xxii. 1-14.   [2] Mt. xxv. 1-13.   [3] Part I. pp. 93-96.

sets an example to be followed. He gives us teaching to be listened to, accepted by our minds. But neither of these is effective by itself. He did more than to lay down a rule of moral conduct, or to deliver a system of truth. He enters into our own self. It is a Life given, broken, and surrendered; so transformed as to be universally accessible; that can enter into any life that has caught His spirit, has surrendered itself, allowed itself by dedication to be transformed, and so entering can become part of each life and the common possession of all. Here, as we have seen, lies the meaning of the supreme and otherwise disproportionate emphasis, in the simple Synoptic stories, on the Cross and the Resurrection. Here also lies the significance of the idea of food in the earlier parts of the narratives.

To "hunger and thirst after righteousness",[1] therefore, is no mere metaphor. Righteousness means the doing of the Father's will; and that, as we have seen, constitutes the closest imaginable "blood-relationship" with the Master Himself. Those who hunger and thirst are filled with His life. He becomes their food. It would appear that for this also there is Jewish precedent, or at least a Jewish parallel. Dr. Denney[2] says that, according to Rabbinic and Apocalyptic writers, in the Messianic Supper the good to be enjoyed is the Messiah Himself. So it is in His own experience: "My meat is to do the will of him that sent me";[3] "in that day ye shall know that I am in my Father, and ye in me, and I in you".[4] Once again the Fourth Gospel provides the interpretation of the earlier record.

It will have been observed that Mr. Abrahams refers, in the same connection, to that eating and drinking with publicans and sinners which was one of the ways in which our Lord challenged the limited Judaism of His day. We can see now why it caused so great offence, and what was the precise issue which it raised. The common meal had for the Jews, as for Him, so great a religious significance that for them His eating with such persons meant almost

---

[1] Mt. v. 6.
[2] *The Death of Christ*, p. 46, quoted in Rashdall, *Idea of Atonement*, p. 42, note 1.   [3] Jn. iv. 34.   [4] Jn. xiv. 20.

what we should call "admitting to communion". On that
He seems, if we can trust the passage in St. Matthew
referred to by Mr. Abrahams,[1] to have shared their views:
in the inner life of the Christian community circumstances might arise in which the Church must refuse a
share in the common food. Where He is, fundamentally,
at issue with His critics is on the qualification for admission to the common meal. They think that they alone
possess it; they are still under a form, though a later form,
of the limitation which excluded from the virtue of the
atoning sacrifices those who by sinning, with a high hand,
had cut themselves off from the true community of Israel.
He says, on the other hand, that the qualification is that
of felt and realised need: hence the Lucan parable of the
Great Supper, and St. Matthew's parable of the Wedding
Feast: the poor and maimed and blind and lame, the people
in the highways and the hedges, are the people whom He
came to bring into the Kingdom of God, and, when He
had brought them in, to feed with the food of the Kingdom.

It is not, however, only in connection with the thought
of food that the Life is spoken of as shared. There is at
least one other image, again inherited from older Jewish
and Israelite language. Not once or twice only our Lord
uses the figure of the Bridegroom. In one case He uses
it definitely of Himself; and the disciples are the "sons of
the bridechamber":[2] and indeed He seems to have in His
mind already the time when He shall be taken away, and
they will fast—the interval between the first gift of the
new food and His sharing it again with them in the Kingdom.[3] But the Messianic future is in His mind in the parable of the Ten Virgins, and again in that of the Wedding
Feast. As with the figure of the Shepherd, we may notice
in passing that He takes to Himself language that in the
Old Testament is used of Yahweh. But I speak of it here
because the figure of the Bridegroom and the Bride had
a clear implication in the old days of the common life
shared in wedlock. And that conception of marriage is

[1] See above, p. 182.   [2] Mark ii. 19.   [3] See above, p. 180.

retained, and indeed emphasised, by our Lord, in His teaching about divorce. He quotes Genesis ii. 24, "and the twain shall become one flesh", and adds to the quotation His own words, "so that they are no more twain, but one flesh":[1] flesh, according to the old Semitic idea, having the corporate or communal sense in which those who share the same life-blood are, in the one flesh, organically one.

Of the one life as shared, if not directly as derived from God, the familiar thought of the Kingdom of God as a crop or harvest, or a tree, is yet another illustration. It grows and multiplies as any other living organism. But of this I shall have something to say later.

I have touched already upon some of the more direct sayings of our Lord about His own close relationship with His true followers, in connection with the thought of spiritual food: those who do His will are His own kindred, and those who hunger and thirst after righteousness are filled with the heavenly food which is, in effect, Himself. Elsewhere qualification for the Kingdom, even before accomplishment of the character which it is to produce, means identification with Him: "Whosoever shall receive one of such little children in my name, receiveth me: and whosoever receiveth me, receiveth not me, but him that sent me",[2] or, in another connection: "He that rejecteth you, rejecteth me; and he that rejecteth me rejecteth him that sent me".[3] The former of these passages, indeed, is almost verbally identical with John xiii. 20; and, through that, the whole of this group of Synoptic sayings brings us into the normal Johannine outlook. So it is with His promise to the disciples against the days of persecution: "Whatsoever shall be given you in that hour, that speak ye: for it is not ye that speak, but the Holy Ghost";[4] or, in St. Matthew's version, "The Spirit of your Father that speaketh in you";[5] or, in St. Luke's, "I will give you a mouth and wisdom".[6] They will be one with Him in the Holy Spirit.

---

[1] Mt. xix. 5 f.; Mk. x. 8.   [2] Mk. ix. 37; Lk. ix. 48; Mt. x. 40.
[3] Lk. x. 16.   [4] Mk. xiii. 11.   [5] Mt. x. 20.   [6] Lk. xxi. 15.

We have found therefore, in what is admittedly Synoptic material, indications which, though of varying directness and force, amount, cumulatively, to clear evidence of the old idea of Life as shared. The new world, into which He has brought them, is, far more than the old, a world of Life. It is won by the surrender of life: it is found and realised in its transformation: it is maintained and developed by its communication. It is, indeed, a fatally superficial view of the Synoptic Gospels, though it is one which we have allowed ourselves under the stress of constant repetition too much to take for granted, which sees in their story and their discourses little more than an example of a perfect character and the words of a perfect teacher. Once we see Him against the background of contemporary Jewish life, or as inheriting the central ideas of Israelite and Jewish history, we find another and a deeper meaning both in His sayings and in His actions. The time for their interpretation had not yet come during the Ministry; and what the Gospels record is the story of the Ministry almost without interpretation. But the sayings themselves remain; and it is for us, as it was for the other New Testament writers, to see what their import is.

There are indeed two typically Synoptic parables of which the common interpretation seems hardly to discover the full meaning: and I shall venture to suggest something about each of these which will illustrate what I have said.[1] The parable of the Good Samaritan[2] is so commonly taken as teaching simply the duty of neighbourly kindness, and at the same time lies admittedly so close at the heart of what Jesus came to teach, that in an age impatient of dogmatic language, and in particular of the technicalities of soteriology, it is often claimed as if it were almost a proof that in the Gospel as He proclaimed it there is no dogma, but only charity in the philanthropic sense. The parable of the Sower[3] seems

---

[1] If, in what follows, I assert my suggested interpretation somewhat positively, it is for the sake of clearness. I offer it as no more than a suggestion of what the indications in our Lord's words seem to lead to, if thought out.

[2] Lk. x. 25-37.   [3] Mk. iv. 4-20.

as if it were merely a parable of preaching: the seed is the spoken word, and it falls now on this kind of human heart and now on that, so that it is for us to see that the soil of our own heart is like neither the hard path, nor the stony ground, nor the ground choked with thorns, but the good soil which can receive the word.

If we look closer—though these obvious lessons remain—more appears.

The prelude to the Good Samaritan is a question from a lawyer. It is a typical lawyer's question: "What shall I *do* to inherit eternal life?" Our Lord makes him answer himself from his own authority: "What is written in the law? how readest thou?" It is a test at once of the Law and of himself; and it makes the sequel all the more forcible that in his answer the lawyer shows at once the Law at its best, and himself as of the best of his own kind: "love . . . God . . . and thy neighbour". Our Lord's answer seems final, but there is an irony in it which points to the failure both of the Law and of its disciple : "This do, and thou shalt live". Do it: do it if you can; but can you? There is the difficulty. And the lawyer falls back on the typical expedient, under the Law, for at once evading the ultimate moral issue and appearing to oneself and to others to have satisfied its claims. He asks "Who is my neighbour?" He wanted, that is to say, a list of neighbours, classified, in concrete form; and he hoped, no doubt, that such a list would cover obvious claims of kindness and of service, and that he would be able to say, "All these have I loved from my youth up". He wished—and the word is central in this passage in a Gospel compiled by a companion of St. Paul and in a story which he alone records—to "justify" himself. And the tone of his question obviously suggests that in seeking for neighbours to "love" he meant people in a position to require kindness from himself. There is at least the suggestion of superiority: "Tell me who are the people to whom I am to do good: I am expert in the law, and it will be for me to help others".

And the answer to that is the parable. It is a picture, as vivid as any that our Lord ever painted, of one whose home was in Jerusalem, and who was going down to Jericho: Jerusalem, the city of God, the scene of His presence with His people, the home of the Law, high up on the barren hills, with its bracing air and its wholesome, disciplined life; Jericho, the city under a historic curse, where no true Israelites should live, with its soft and enervating climate, and its soil out of which life could be maintained without effort in the tropical heat. And the way from Jerusalem to Jericho—the *facilis descensus*—leads on from the city of selfish ease to the bitter sea of eternal Death. The traveller had turned his back on God, and was treading the downhill way; and, moving in that direction, is a prey to the enemies waiting about his path. He lies wounded, starving, half dead. For such an one the old Law has no remedy. The priest and the Levite fail him. But there comes one, to whom no legally minded Jew would look, despised and rejected of men. He has compassion: he heals the stricken man, takes him to the shelter of a roof which he provides, where he will be refreshed, restored, and fed; and it is all at his own cost. There follows the interpretation. The lawyer had asked to be shown the people to whom he was to do good: that was the direction from which he saw neighbourliness. Our Lord says to him, in effect, Here is a picture which will show you how to learn what love is: there are four figures in it; you shall guess which is the neighbour. But you would at once choose the man by the roadside. I will help you. You will not find love first in one to whom you are to do good: it is in one of the other three. The man in trouble is ruled out. "Which of these three, thinkest thou, proved neighbour unto him that fell among the robbers?" There is only one answer: "He that shewed mercy on him". That is the turning-point of the parable: it means more than the obvious thing that the neighbour whom you are to love is anybody whom you may find in real need. It means that; but first of all love must be learnt by being loved. You cannot set out to do good, unless you first learn that of all the world you need more than anyone to have good done to you. The lawyer is bidden to see himself in the picture as the man by the roadside: naked, wounded, starving. He must learn that he must first be clothed, healed, housed, and fed. Then, not from a pedestal of superiority, but as one who has himself repented, and suffered, and received all that he has that is worth having, he can go and do good to others.

The "surface" interpretation would have been the whole if the question had been "Which of these three knew best who was his neighbour?" The question is reversed: and the parable, retaining all its ordinary meaning, becomes in its deeper sense a parable of grace. The man is saved, is fed, even before he is changed. But we are left with the certainty that when his Redeemer comes again he will set his face, in the Redeemer's foot-steps, towards his cross and the city of God. The parable, indeed, contains the whole of St. Paul's doctrine of salva-tion; we can almost imagine St. Luke's finding it during the long stay at Caesarea, and St. Paul saying, "Whatever you leave out, you must put in that, with the picture of the lawyer for its key". And it is summarised, as is indeed the whole of the Gospel of Christ, in "Herein is love, not that we loved God, but that He loved us".[1]

Or the parable of the Sower. Here again the key may lie in an unexpected, and often unnoticed, turn given in the interpretation, most explicitly in St. Mark's version. What we should expect to be compared is the different kinds of soil. What is compared is the result of the sowing. Only in the first case, when the ground is too hard for the seed to penetrate at all, is the soil alone in the picture. In the other three cases the seed can begin its work: it pene-trates and grows. And what is compared in those cases is neither the seed nor the soil, but the plant. The seed is the word of God. It is God Who sows it. The soil is human nature. If that is in no way broken; if it is hard and un-touched; if it knows none of the discipline of the plough, the seed is wasted: it might never have come. But, though the results still vary according to the degree of discipline that the human heart receives, once the soil is broken, and

[1] 1 Jn. iv. 10.

the seed can enter beneath its surface, the purpose of the coming of the word can take effect. The seed, to the ignorant eye, has no possibilities; the soil is dead, and shapeless, and foul, with no promise in it; but once the seed in its first form has been broken and has perished, there is a life in it which cannot be quenched: its power is set free in the breaking of its outward form; it draws into itself hidden possibilities in the hopeless material into whose lower darkness it has come down; and by the unimaginable alchemy of eternal nature as it grows it takes yet more of the hidden treasures of the soil into itself; and there comes into the upper air a new body, with an undreamt-of beauty of form and of colour, and a gift of fruitfulness and of reproduction, to be watered, as it grows, with the dew and the rain from heaven, braced by the wind from the everlasting hills, and strengthened and cherished by the light and warmth of the sun of righteousness. The Word of God is not given merely to be copied or to be listened to. He comes to be broken among those whom He is to redeem; to draw them into living union with Himself; to reveal the Divine possibilities in them that none could have foreseen or believed; to transform their life and lift it from earth to heaven. And, once more, it is to the Fourth Gospel that we turn for what is both the summary of the parable and its interpretation: "Except a grain of wheat fall into the earth and die, it abideth by itself alone; but if it die, it beareth much fruit".[1]

[1] Jn. xii. 24.

CHAPTER V

TEMPLE, SYNAGOGUE, AND SACRIFICE

In the last three chapters we have been concerned with
what I have called the untechnical side of the narrative
and the teaching of the Synoptic Gospels, with their
bearing on the underlying principles of sacrifice rather
than with express references either to contemporary
Jewish usage or to sacrifice itself in a Christian sense. I
propose in this chapter to discuss, first, our Lord's general
attitude to the religion of His own day, so far as it bears
upon our subject; and, secondly, His own use of direct
sacrificial language.

I

I have spoken of our Lord's attitude to contemporary
religion generally, and not, as might be expected, to the
Temple and its cultus alone, because it is so commonly
said that He represents the Synagogue as against the
Temple. It is more often assumed than argued that there
was a distinction between these two sides of first-century
Jewish religion which reaches down to principle, as if one
side were living and the other dead: one representing a
recent tradition happily freed from sacrificial cultus and
ready to provide the non-sacrificial religion of the future;
and the other, a ceremonial survival of observances to
which none of the better Jews, and least of all our Lord
Himself, could be seriously attached. It is true, of course,
that the Synagogues provided opportunities for prayer
and for preaching of an independent kind, and that they

were also used as schools. But even as regards prayer they
originated in the Temple, which as early as the time of
the writer of Isaiah lvi. 7 could be called a House of
Prayer, and in the "liturgies" of which prayer and the use
of Psalms always played a large part; and there was
throughout the history an organic connection between
the Temple and the Synagogues: the Temple was indeed
the real model for the Synagogue both in Palestine and
among the Jews of the Dispersion. Nor was the Synagogue,
either in origin or in later character, anti-sacrificial, or
even unsacrificial. I need not repeat here what has already
been said on this point in Part I.[1]

In the light of the true character of the synagogue much
of the force of the plea that our Lord's own practice
favoured the synagogue rather than the Temple must
disappear. But even apart from this the familiar theory
is hardly borne out by the Synoptic narratives. What is,
of course, true, is that in the first three Gospels He is far
more often found in synagogues than in the Temple. But
there are obvious reasons why this must have been the
case, even if the narrative of the Ministry in the Fourth
Gospel is combined with that of the Synoptists; if, that
is, it is assumed, as I assume it here, for the purposes of
argument, though I believe it also to be in accordance
with fact, that there were visits to Jerusalem not described by the first three Evangelists as well as the last
visit for the final Passover. In any case, the Ministry was
mainly in Galilee; and our Lord had far more opportunities, as the Sabbath days came round, for those two years
or more, of worshipping in the synagogues than in the
Temple. Even so, however, it does not follow in the least
that He can be said, merely on that fact, to have "taken
sides".

What are the facts?

In the first place, we cannot entirely overlook the conditions under which He was brought up. In these days,
whatever our own personal convictions, we may not
build too much upon the two first chapters in the First

[1] Pp. 105 ff.

O

and Third Gospels. But the force of negative criticism on
the Birth and Infancy narratives bears, in the main, upon
specific passages in them which in our present text attest
the actual manner of His birth. It will hardly be denied
that the circle of relations and friends which appears
in those chapters was, in fact, as it is described. They
represent the "quiet in the land", who held the best and
purest Old Testament tradition. There is no touch in
Mary and Joseph, Zachariah and Elizabeth, Simeon and
Anna, of the type of Judaism with which Jesus afterwards was in conflict. We may be fairly certain that we
have a true description of the religion of His home and
of His early years. And in that circle there is evidence at
once of a faithful observance of the Law and of a deeply
spiritual attitude towards it. An overwhelming spiritual
experience—whatever its exact nature—would hardly
have come to a country priest on the unique occasion of
his offering the incense while on duty with his course,
unless it was to him an occasion of profound inward
significance. Both John and Jesus are duly circumcised
on the eighth day. Jesus is presented in the Temple, with
the sacrifice appointed in the Law; and Simeon and Anna
are both devout Temple worshippers, moved, naturally,
by the Spirit in the home of their spiritual life. Joseph
and Mary keep the Passover at Jerusalem every year:
and in due course they bring the Child with them to take
His own part in its worship.

The story should not be overpressed; but it is at least
one indication that, so far as home surroundings were
concerned, our Lord was brought up in a life naturally
centred in the Temple, and in the due observance of the
Law. Nor does His later speech or action indicate any
reversal of the attitude of His home.

Into the great question of what actually happened at
our Lord's baptism I cannot now go; but it would be
agreed that St. Mark's version of the story[1] seems to give
what the experience meant to our Lord Himself. There
is evidence for the connection between the Bath-Qol, or

[1] Mk. i. 9-11.

Heavenly Voice, and the symbolic figure of a bird—even actually of a dove—in Jewish literature, as well as in reflections upon Genesis i. 2 ("and the Spirit of God 'brooded' upon the face of the waters") for a symbolic connection between the Holy Spirit and the dove. And the dove, in Rabbinic literature, "is for the most part an emblem of Israel, its gentleness, fidelity, its persecution, its submission"; and the suggestion of the dove goes further still: "All other birds, when they are about to be slaughtered, wince, but the dove holds out its neck to the slayer".[1] The dove has its own association with sacrifice: it is the poor man's offering in the Law;[2] and the dove at the Baptism in the Synoptic Gospels is therefore not far in its suggestiveness from the Lamb of God in the Baptist's testimony in John i. 29, 35. To this we may add the associations of both parts of the Heavenly Voice. The classical example of the "beloved son" for Jews was Isaac: "Thy son, thine only son, whom thou lovest";[3] and the sacrifice, or "binding", of Isaac was probably even in the first century, as it certainly was later, almost central in Jewish thought. It was the "perfect burnt-offering", both as an act of redemption and as an example to be followed.[4] And the second part, "in whom I am well pleased", belongs to the opening words of the first description of the Servant of Yahweh in Isaiah xlii. 1—whose character in the following verses is in exact accord with the gentleness and submissiveness of the dove. I need not elaborate these associations; and I have no desire to lay undue emphasis upon them. But they cannot be ignored if we are to estimate the direction of our Lord's own outlook from the first. He begins His ministry with the gift of the Spirit in a form that suggests sacrifice—and that the sacrifice of the poor, as well as the age-long sacrifice of Israel; and with a message from the Father which links Him both with the supreme type of

---

[1] I. Abrahams, *Studies in Pharisaism and the Gospels*, Series I., pp. 47 f.

[2] I find that my suggestion of the dove as sacrificial was anticipated by J. L. Johnston (*Some Alternatives to Jesus Christ*, p. 190), to whom I owe the reference to Isaac. The dove was used both for burnt-offerings and for sin-offerings.

[3] Gen. xxii. 2. [4] I. Abrahams, *op. cit.*, Series II., pp. 162 f.

the true burnt-offering and with the mission and destiny of the Servant who is to suffer and to die for sinners.

The Temptation follows the Baptism. It is impossible, however we may interpret the actual event, or whatever the precise meaning that we may attach to each of the three temptations, not to regard them as in some way revealing what, under the impulse of the Holy Spirit, had been in our Lord's thoughts during His solitude. The Kingdom is there, as we should expect; but the other two directions in which His mind had been moving are equally significant. There is the food idea: the same contrast, when food is thought of wrongly, between food only for the body—the leaven of the Pharisees and Sadducees, or Herodians, as He called it later[1]—and food, as, before everything else, the symbol and the veil of God's communication of Himself: "Man shall not live by bread alone, but by every word that proceedeth out of the mouth of God".[2] And there is the temptation to use what would generally be called His Divine power, but what I should prefer[3] to call the "numinous" power, with which He had just been freshly endowed in the gift of the Spirit of Holiness, to enforce an instant acquiescence in His "claims"; I use the word "acquiescence" because such an acceptance would not have meant real "belief"; and I use the word "claims", unworthy of Him though it be, because it will be understood in this connection. And the natural scene, for Him, of the problem and the fact of the immediate power of Holiness is in the Temple, as the supreme sanctuary.

There are some passages in His teaching which ought not to be overlooked, if it is at all true, as I believe it to be, that the Temple was not far from His thoughts. They occur mainly in the first chapter of St. Matthew's Sermon on the Mount, though the same associations would exist, in a measure, for all the sayings with which I dealt in Part II. Chapter III. about holiness and the "sanctuary" idea of God, as in the Lord's Prayer and elsewhere. The two Beatitudes already noticed, the promises to the pure in heart and to those who hunger and thirst,[4] rest on con-

---

[1] See Part II. Ch. IV. p. 173.   [2] Mt. iv. 4.
[3] Above, pp. 159 ff.   [4] Mt. v. 6, 8.

ceptions belonging to the sanctuary; as we know from
another passage the ancient persecutions of the prophets
culminated, in His mind, with the last act of the kind in
the Jewish Bible, the murder of Zachariah in the Temple
courts; and the last Beatitude[1] therefore ends with
Temple associations. There follows, "Ye are the salt of the
earth".[2] Elsewhere our Lord also uses the figure of salt:
"Everyone shalt be salted with fire. Salt is good: but if the
salt have lost its saltness, wherewith will ye season it?
Have salt in yourselves, and be at peace one with another".[3] The gloss, in the familiar text, on the first of
these sayings in Mark, "and every sacrifice shall be salted
with salt", provides the key to them all. Salt was the invariable accompaniment of the sacrifices:[4] it symbolised
life, as being a natural preservative (so Philo: "Salt is one
emblem of the duration of all things, for it preserves
everything over which it is sprinkled").[5] The thought is
therefore sacrificial. In St. Mark "everyone shall be salted
with fire" follows immediately upon a passage about the
destroying fire of hell; the two uses of fire—to destroy, as
in the Valley of Hinnom (Gehenna), and to transform,
as in the burning of the sacrifice—are contrasted. The salt
in the dedicated life of Christians, in their burnt-offering
of themselves, is the fire of the Holy Spirit with which
the Baptist said that his successor should baptize.[6]
So they are to have salt—the secret of the life which
issues from self-dedication—in themselves, and that is a
common life in them all, and will mean being at peace
with one another. And they are the salt of the earth—the
fire which He came to cast upon it:[7]—the earth depends
upon them for its hope of being drawn one day into the
general self-offering of Christ Himself, of His followers,
and ultimately of all the world. For He also has to be
baptized in the same transforming fire: "I have a baptism
. . ."[8] follows upon "I came to cast fire . . ."; and His
disciples are to be baptized with the same baptism.[9]

---

[1] Mt. v. 10-12.   [2] Mt. v. 13.   [3] Mk. ix. 49; so Lk. xiv. 34 f.
[4] Lev. ii. 13.   [5] Philo, De Victimis, 3.
[6] Mt. iii. 11; Lk. iii. 16. See Swete's notes on Mk. ix. 49 f.
[7] Lk. xii. 49.   [8] Lk. xii. 50.   [9] Mk. x. 39.

They are also to be the light of the world: like a city set on an hill.[1] Here is certainly the thought of Jerusalem, conceived by the Jews as the light of the world because of the presence of the Holy One: the disciples are, at the least, the "new Jerusalem". But the idea of the light was connected also with the olive oil in the Temple lamp; and the phrase, "the light of the world" is used for the Temple itself.[2] The connection of thought may be illustrated indeed, though not quite directly, from John viii. 12, where the same symbolism used by our Lord of Himself ("I am the Light of the world") is probably suggested by the blaze of light from the special illuminations of the Temple at the Feast of Tabernacles, to the time of which the saying belongs.

There follows upon these suggestions of the sanctuary the passage about the Law: "I came not to destroy, but to fulfil". And the Law, especially when as here it is distinguished from the Prophets, means the whole law, "ceremonial" as well as "moral".[3] Here we are only concerned with what must have been in our Lord's mind when, early in His ministry, as a Jew, He spoke about the Law to Jews. His ultimate attitude to the obligation of the Law in part or in whole is not, at the moment, to the point. We may recognise the difficulty of reconciling this with His apparently unqualified support of every jot and tittle in St. Matthew's account of His teaching. But of the connection of thought throughout the first chapter of the Sermon on the Mount there can be no doubt. The sanctuary and its significance are to Him living things. So in His exposition of the commandments He can naturally use as an example of His meaning the presentation of a gift at the altar.[4] Like the old prophets, He does not attack such an action; but He is concerned with the spirit that lies behind it. A man cannot profess, by a symbolic act, to dedicate himself to God—cannot say "Lo I come to do Thy will, O God"—while he is at variance with his

[1] Mt. v. 14.
[2] I. Abrahams, op. cit. Series II. p. 16.
[3] H. F. Hamilton, People of God, vol. i. p. 247; C. G. Montefiore, The Teaching of Jesus, p. 25.   [4] Mt. v. 23.

brother, still less if, as the words imply, he has been wronging his brother.[1]

And, in the end, it is nothing less than God's own character at which He would have them aim. The God of Israel was never, in the Old Testament, so perfectly revealed as in His mercy: "There is mercy with Thee: therefore thou shalt be feared".[2] And "Ye therefore shall be perfect, even as your heavenly Father is perfect". St. Luke's version of this saying, following as it does the same teaching as in St. Matthew—"love your enemies"—keeps more closely to its context: " . . . he is kind toward the unthankful and the evil. Be ye merciful, even as your Father is merciful".[3] But the difference between "merciful" and "perfect" is only on the surface. The normal Jewish formula for the "Imitation of God" was, "Ye shall be holy: for I the Lord your God am holy"; and there is no Jewish parallel for St. Matthew's substitution of "perfect" for "holy".[4] But the two ideas of "holiness" and "perfectness" are closely akin, alike in their earlier and less ethical, and in their later and more ethical, connections: for perfect ($\tau \acute{\epsilon} \lambda \epsilon \iota o \varsigma$: תמים) ranges in meaning from "without blemish" in the sacrificial sense to that moral perfectness which qualifies for the vision of God; it does not lose its sanctuary associations. In the Old Testament "perfect" is used with "walking before God" (God says to Abraham before the sacrifice of Isaac "walk before me, and be thou perfect").[5] And mercy and perfectness as going together in God and man are parallel terms. The ideas of Matthew v. and of

[1] This is exactly in the spirit of Philo, *De Victimis*, 2 (C. D. Yonge's translation): "And the accuracy and minuteness of the investigation (of the victims offered) is directed not so much on account of the victims themselves, as in order that those who offer them should be irreproachable; for God designed to teach the Jews by these figures, whenever they went up to the altars, when there to pray or to give thanks, never to bring with them any weakness or evil passion in their soul, but to endeavour to make it wholly and entirely bright and clean, without any blemish, so that God might not turn away with aversion from the sight of it". I quote this at length because it illustrates the moral quality which was felt to be all-important in the offerer; and also the way in which the inward purity of the heart—moral goodness itself—was thought of, in connection with the sanctuary, in terms of cleanness, as fitting man to come into the presence of God. The thought is, indeed, not far from our Lord's "Whatsoever from without goeth into the man, it cannot defile him; . . . that which proceedeth out of the man, that defileth the man" (Mk. vii. 18, 20).   [2] Ps. cxxx. 4 (P.B.).
[3] Lk. vi. 35 f.   [4] I. Abrahams, *op. cit.*, Series II. p. 151.   [5] Gen. xvii. 1.

Luke vi. 36 are indeed found together in Psalm xviii. 23 ·
26 (= 2 Sam. xxii. 24-27).

23. I was also perfect with him,
    And I kept myself from mine iniquity.
24. Therefore hath the Lord recompensed me according to my
    righteousness,
    According to the cleanness of my hands in his eyesight.
25. With the merciful thou wilt shew thyself merciful;
    With the perfect man thou wilt shew thyself perfect;
26. With the pure thou wilt shew thyself pure.

To be perfect is to be merciful; both mean the quality
which makes it possible to walk in the presence of God:
they suggest that side of moral goodness which is felt as
cleanness or purity, and the whole of Matthew v. therefore, from beginning to end, becomes in sense a commentary on "Be ye holy, for I am holy", and in its highest
sense reflects the thought of the sanctuary.

I pass to various passages in which there is more direct
reference to our Lord's attitude to the Temple. We have
noted one side of His general view of the Law, taken as a
whole—He came not to destroy but to fulfil. And His own
actions are consistent with that principle. He is no
iconoclast. He sends lepers to offer the proper sacrifices in
the normal way after their cleansing.[1] As we have seen,
He assumes the offering of "gifts" at the altar, and only
cares that they should be offered in the proper spirit; and
He assumes that it is to the Temple that the penitent
sinner will go to seek forgiveness.[2] He pays the Temple
tax regularly, though there is a challenge, as regards His
own personal relation to it, in "therefore the sons are
free".[3] It is from the ancient and classical tradition of the
Temple that He argues against the burden of later rules
about the Sabbath.[4] It is the true traditions of offering, in
the saying about Corban, that He vindicates against the
Pharisees, who have made them void.[5] It is to the Temple
that He goes after the triumphal entry on Palm Sunday;
and to the Temple that He returns each day, as He makes

[1] Mt. viii. 4; Lk. xvii. 14.
[2] Lk. xviii. 9-14. See above, Part II. Ch. II. p. 140.   [3] Mt. xvii. 24-27.
[4] Mk. ii. 23-28; Mt. xii. 1-8; Lk. vi. 1-5.   [5] Mk. vii. 1-23.

it the scene for the whole of His work during the earlier part of the last week. And His cleansing of the Temple—at the end of His public activity in the Synoptic Gospels, as it is at the beginning in St. John—is a solemn vindication of its sanctity against its desecration by contemporary custom. The Servant of the Lord is a true servant of the sanctuary, as indeed the Hebrew word for "servant" suggests by use and association.

We saw that on close examination the passages from the prophets, commonly cited as showing that they were whole-hearted opponents of the principle of sacrifice, in reality only show that they attacked its wrong use. It was their tradition which our Lord carried on. He also is thought to be an opponent of the Temple cultus on principle. Twice He quotes,[1] with approval, "I desire mercy and not sacrifice", from Hosea. But the context makes His meaning plain. Once, He had already quoted (see above) the true spirit of the ancient use against its modern corruptions; on the other occasion, it was a question of His eating and drinking with publicans and sinners, and we have seen[2] that in that connection the issue between Him and His critics was not the principle of God's feeding His own in their sacred meals, but the qualifications for admission. It is the limitation of the power of sacrificial food to those who are in the least need of it, and the exclusion from it of those who were in "deadly" sin, which was at once the condemnation of the existing system and the habit of its exponents. He had come, once more, not to destroy—not to contradict its fundamental character —but to fulfil; to make good its deficiencies; to vitalise its impotence. Hence "I desire mercy and not sacrifice; for I came not to call the righteous, but sinners".

There are, indeed, these passages in which He criticises the spirit in which His contemporaries used the Temple. But they are not attacks upon the Temple as such. If it were right so to interpret them, there are many more passages which should be taken as equally attacking the synagogues. For it was in the synagogues that the conflict

---

[1] Mt. xii. 7; Mt. ix. 13.   [2] Part II. Ch. IV. p. 181.

between our Lord and His opponents began and developed.
He was cast out at Nazareth.[1] At the healing of the man
with the withered hand He "looked round about on them
with anger":[2] after the healing of the woman with the
spirit of infirmity, His answer to the ruler of the synagogue
began, "Ye hypocrites. . . ."[3] It was a picture of the
typical synagogue service that He had in mind when He
denounced the wrong kind of alms and prayers,[4] and the
ostentation of the scribes in the "chief seats".[5] If he foretold the ruin of Jerusalem it was in sorrow that moved
Him to tears; but there is no such feeling in the woes that
He pronounced upon Capernaum, Chorazin, and Beth-
saida, the scenes of His own synagogue ministry.[6] When
He foresaw the persecution of His followers it was the
synagogues that He thought of as its natural scene.[7]
There is an almost unrelieved gloom over His attitude to
the synagogues of the time.

I do not for a moment suggest that He was fundamentally hostile to the synagogue system as such. But,
if we weigh His language about the Temple against that
which He used about synagogues, there is no question as
to the greater severity of the latter. It probably means
no more than that His visits to synagogues were more
frequent, and the occasions for conflict in them more
obvious. In the Old Testament we find the prophets condemning unreal prayer as severely as unreal sacrifices;
and I only stress the exactly parallel situation in the
Gospels because of the inconsequence of the familiar
assumption that the prophets objected on principle only
to sacrifice, and our Lord only to the Temple. If the
words used by the prophets or by our Lord can be so
pressed on the one side, they should be equally pressed on
the other. The Temple and its sacrifices, however, have
few friends among modern interpreters; and, happily,
prayer and preaching and Bible reading have many. It is
not that we need to picture our Lord as less at home in the

---

[1] Lk. iv. 28; cf. Mt. xiii. 57.   [2] Mk. iii. 5.   [3] Lk. xiii. 15.
[4] Mt. vi. 2, 5.   [5] Mk. xii. 39.   [6] Mt. xi. 20-24; Lk. x. 12-15.
[7] Mt. x. 17; Mk. xiii. 9; Lk. xxi. 12.

synagogue than we have always thought Him, but as more at home in the Temple. He was the child and the friend of both, when they were properly used, and the enemy of neither. His censures, on either side, are directed not against the systems—or the system, for in truth it was the same system everywhere; the synagogue was the adaptation of the Temple to local needs—but against the misuse of the system.

This is not to say, of course, that He ever contemplated the continuance of the Temple. He spoke clearly enough about its end. "One greater than the Temple is here" in itself may mean no more, though it certainly means no less, than "the Son of man is lord of the Sabbath" in the same passage.[1] But at the end, He definitely foretold its overthrow.[2] So He is able to override the authority of the Law in the same passage in which He speaks strongly about its complete validity.[3] Unless the writers of the Epistles were wrong, and unless the evidence which we have found in the last three chapters goes for nothing, He was even at the time in the earlier stages of another, and at last a complete, sacrifice. The blood of bulls and of goats could not take away sin. Our question in this chapter. as in Part I., has been as to the place of the Temple and its worship not in the Christian system but in the preparation and the training for it. I hope that we have found reason for concluding that our Lord would have adopted St. Paul's summary, that the Law had been our "schoolmaster", or tutor, to bring us to Him; and that the "commandment", in its day and place, was "holy and just and good"; and that to Him, as well as to St. Paul and to any other Jew, "the Law" meant the Law with everything that it contained. The distinction between the ceremonial, the civil, and the moral law has its place in the XXXIX Articles of the sixteenth century; but it has been a tragedy of the history of interpretation that we have read back their language into the first.

---

[1] Mt. xii. 6-8 (Gk. μεῖζον—R.V.m., "a greater thing"; but the meaning does not seem to be substantially different).

[2] Mt. xxiv. 2; Mk. xiii. 2; Lk. xxi. 6.　　　　　　[3] Mt. v. 17-20, 22.

II

I have attempted to show that much of our Lord's Synoptic teaching contains the principles of sacrifice. It was, necessarily, untechnical: for the associations of the technical terms could not but have been fatally misleading during His ministry, and indeed for some years after the Ascension and Pentecost. To the Jews, and to Jewish Christians, before the implications of His life and death, of the Resurrection and Ascension, and of the gift of the Spirit, had been thought out, a priest could only mean an Aaronic priest in the Temple, and a sacrifice one of the actual Temple sacrifices.

It is not therefore until the last moment of His earthly life, and as it were in the sheer necessity of explaining what was to happen, that He uses strictly technical language. (I refrain deliberately from stressing the sacrificial sense of "ransom" in Mark x. 45, for reasons already given, though we have seen that it adds nothing but a familiar historical term to the thoughts underlying the whole passage.) This language is confined to the few verses which describe the Institution of the Eucharist at the Last Supper.

I know that in saying even so much as this I am seeming to prejudge a difficult problem. What did our Lord actually say at the Institution? We are bound to accept, at least in argument, the possibility, or, as most critics would call it, the probability, amounting in some minds to certainty,[1] that the true text of St. Luke speaks not, as in our English versions,[2] of two cups, but of one only,[3] and that before He took the bread: "And he received a cup, and when he had given thanks, he said, Take this, and divide it among yourselves: for I say unto you, I will not drink from henceforth of the fruit of the vine, until the kingdom of God shall come. And he took bread, and when he had given thanks, he brake it, and gave it them, saying, This is my body". That is the whole of the

---

[1] But see Batiffol, "Études d'histoire et de théologie positive", IIᵉ Série, L'Eucharistie, 3rd ed. pp. 21-28.
[2] A.V. and R.V. text, not R.V. margin.   [3] Lk. xxii. 17 ff.

Lucan Institution narrative that we can be sure of. It omits "This do in remembrance of me"; and "This cup is the new covenant in my blood, even that which is poured out for you".

The other materials are St. Matthew's and St. Mark's accounts, and St. Paul's. I give the substance of the evidence, for clearness' sake, in detail. (P. = St. Paul.)

				Mt.	Mk.	Lk.	P.
I.	First	a.	He took bread	Mt.	Mk.	Lk.	P.
	"Consecration".	b.	. . . blessed . . .	Mt.	Mk.		
			gave thanks			Lk.	P.
		c.	He brake it	Mt.	Mk.	Lk.	P.
II.	First	d.	. . . gave (it) to (them)	Mt.	Mk.	Lk.	
	"Administration".	e.	And said (saying)	Mt.	Mk.	Lk.	P.
		f.	Take, eat	Mt.			
			Take ye		Mk.		
		g.	This is my body	Mt.	Mk.	Lk.	P.
		h.	Which is for you				P.
		i.	This do in remembrance of me				P.
III.	Second	j.	And he took a cup	Mt.	Mk.		
	"Consecration".		In like manner also the cup after supper, saying				P.
		k.	And gave thanks	Mt.			
			And when he had given thanks		Mk.		
IV.	Second	l.	And gave to them	Mt.			
	"Administration".		He gave to them		Mk.		
		m.	Saying, Drink ye all of it, for	Mt.			
			And they all drank of it		Mk.		
			And he said unto them		Mk.		
		n.	This is my blood of the covenant, which is shed for many	Mt.	Mk.		
			This cup is the new covenant in my blood				P.
		o.	Unto remission of sins	Mt.			
		p.	This do, as oft as ye drink it, in remembrance of me				P.

(There follows, in Matthew and Mark, the verse which follows the giving of the [first] cup in Luke, "I will not drink henceforth, . . ." in almost identical words.)

I have given this in perhaps excessive detail; for it is not necessary for my purpose here to make an exhaustive examination of the text or of the history. But it will be well to see, in the first place, what the accounts have in common, or substantially in common, and what are the parts of the record for which there is less attestation.

I. The actual "consecration"—if we may, for convenience, use the later technical term—of the bread is in all four accounts: He took bread, blessed (εὐλογεῖν)—Matthew, Mark—or gave thanks (εὐχαριστεῖν)—Luke, Paul—and brake it.

II. The *act* of the first administration is only given expressly in Matthew, Mark and Luke, and is left to be understood in Paul.

The *words* of the first administration in their shortest form, "This is my body", are in all four accounts.

Paul adds "which is for you: This do in remembrance of me".

III. The consecration of the cup is described in Matthew and Mark, who here use "gave thanks" instead of "blessed"; it is not mentioned, but seems implied, in Paul: "In like manner also the cup after supper".

IV. The *act* of the second administration is again only given in Matthew and Mark, but is implied, like the consecration, in Paul.

The *words* of the second administration vary in the central point, but all three accounts connect "the blood" with "the covenant": "This is my blood of the covenant" (Mt., Mk.); "This cup is the new covenant in my blood" (P.); Matthew and Mark add "which is shed for many", recalling Isaiah liii. 11 (so "to give his life a ransom for many", in Matthew xx. 28 and Mark x. 45).

Matthew adds further, "unto remission of sins". Paul adds words corresponding to his account of the first administration, but adding nothing to it: "This do, as oft as ye drink it, in remembrance of me".

Thus in the accounts of the *consecration* there is, in substance, complete agreement, if we may take it that "blessed" and "gave thanks" are for practical purposes interchangeable. (The familiar Jewish practice was to "bless"; in the later Christian associations the more natural word would be "give thanks"; at the feeding of the five thousand Matthew, Mark, Luke use "bless"; John "gave thanks". But here Matthew, Mark use "bless" for the first consecration, "gave thanks" for the second.)

It is with the words of *administration* that we come to variations. The two elements common to all accounts are, as I have said, "This is my body", and (except in Luke's shorter text) the definite and explicit connection of the blood with the covenant. The additions to the latter in Matthew, Mark are explanatory, and their importance depends upon the implications of the covenant-blood. The additions in St. Paul are of first-rate importance historically; for, apart from the possible meanings of "which is for you", "do this", and "in remembrance of me", they alone give the Lord's express authority for the continuance of the rite.

I have put St. Paul's account side by side with those of the Synoptic writers. I know that it has been urged that the shorter text of Luke is the most historical of the four. I cannot examine the evidence at length. I will only say that in spite of the possibility of St. Luke's independence, as a Gospel writer, of St. Paul[1] it is hard to believe that he was consciously contradicting the eucharistic tradition which St. Paul had written down many years before, with which he had been so long familiar, and which must have governed the use at least of the Pauline churches. I may not press the suggestion, though I venture to make it, that St. Luke's shorter text does not necessarily exclude the familiar words of administration for the cup: if the suggestions in the last chapter hold good—that the story as St. Luke gives it, passing at once from the eucharistic cup to the future drinking in the Kingdom, suggests in itself the thought of the Messianic food and drink, and that, in the last analysis, it is Christ Himself Who is the drink as well as food of eternal life—

---

[1] See Streeter, *Four Gospels*, pp. 553 f.

we may perhaps safely assume that St. Luke is merely summarising what he knows to be familiar to every Christian, and perhaps, deliberately abstaining from specifying what he knew must still be a stumbling-block outside Christian, or rather in Jewish, circles. If he were writing partly for T. Flavius Clemens [1] and his family, and if Clemens' wife was at the time a Jewish proselyte, there was a definite reason for such silence. The difficulty in that case is the order of the story: why does he give the cup first and the bread second? The answer to that may lie in the uncertainty which we know to have prevailed as to whether the Last Supper was or was not the actual Passover. St. Luke, like the other Synoptists, seems to have thought that it was: he would have known of the fact that there were four cups at the Passover meal, and might easily have assumed that on that occasion it was one of the earlier cups which the Lord blessed.

Whatever may be the case, however, with St. Luke's shorter text, I shall assume that it is difficult on historical grounds to pass over the combined evidence of Matthew and Mark and of St. Paul. Canon Streeter suggests that Matthew took its present form not later than A.D. 85, and that Mark's date may be A.D. 65. 1 Corinthians was written A. D. 55-57. St. Luke may have finished his Gospel between 80 and 85. If there had been clear reasons for dating Luke's account earlier than any of the other three. it might reasonably be argued that it is the most reliable. But it must require strong pre-suppositions on the part of a historian to show that the latest of the four accounts is the only one which we can trust; and as Matthew, in the essential point of divergence as to the cup, is following Mark, Luke is on this point nearly twenty years later than the other two Synoptists, and at least thirty years later than St. Paul.

We may return, then, to the definite agreement about the blood and the covenant. It cannot be denied that on the lips, and in the ears, of those who were Jews and

[1] See Streeter, *The Four Gospels*, pp. 535-539.

had only Jewish associations in their minds, this is the
language of sacrifice. It has been little short of a disaster
that so much labour has been spent on attempts to prove
or to disprove a sacrificial reference in "do this", or in
εἰς τὴν ἐμὴν ἀνάμνησιν (in remembrance of me), and that
attention has thereby been diverted from the far stronger
and more certain sacrificial language of the blood and the
covenant. We may well be content to leave these other
issues "unproven", or even to say, for argument's sake,
that no sacrificial meaning can be attached to the words
at all. I should certainly be prepared to admit this if they
stood alone. But the dominating words are "blood" and
"covenant". We may, for our present purpose, pass over
the question of the variations in the actual saying in
Matthew and Mark on the one hand, and Paul on the
other. What matters is the evidence that our Lord used
both words, and in close connection with each other.
There can only be one meaning in that. He might indeed
have thought and spoken of a covenant alone, meaning
a new covenant in the heart, and taking Jeremiah's
supposed meaning of a covenant in a purely metaphorical
sense, without sacrifice. But, as we have seen in Part I.,[1]
no Jew ever thought of a covenant apart from sacrifice:
and the evidence is that "covenant" spelt "sacrifice" to
Jeremiah himself as much as to any other Jew. And in the
case of the Last Supper, our Lord does speak of blood as
well as of covenant, of His blood as the covenant-blood.
He is saying, in other words, that there is a new covenant
to be ratified, with a new sacrifice. It is to be interpreted
—He interprets it Himself—in the terms of the first
covenant and its sacrifice. There they offered burnt-
offerings and peace-offerings—there were as yet no sin-
offerings, and the element of atonement, so far as it was
realised, was contained in the existing sacrifices. Moses
sprinkled part of the blood on the altar, gave the people
the covenant, which they promised to obey, and sprinkled
the other part of the blood upon them, ... "and they
beheld God and did eat and drink".[2] Those were the tradi-

[1] P. 22.   [2] Ex. xxiv. 4-11.

P

tions which our Lord was assuming; and as Moses, before
the people entered into the full fellowship of the covenant,
went up the mount with Aaron and the elders into the
open presence of God, so (to use St. John again as a "commentary") the discourse in the Fourth Gospel begins
with "Now is the Son of man glorified, and God is glorified in him"; ("glory" meaning, fundamentally, not so
much what God is in Himself, as God manifested), "and
God shall glorify him in himself, and straightway shall
he glorify him. Little children, yet a little while I am with
you. Ye shall seek me" (so, when Moses was in the mount,
the people said, "We know not what is become of him");[1]
"and as I said unto the Jews, Whither I go, ye cannot
come; so now I say unto you. A new commandment I
give unto you, that ye love one another. . . ."[2]

There, in fact, is the picture—the only picture—which
gives the background to the essential part of our Lord's
words at the Institution. Its elements are deliverance in
the sacrificial surrender of life; self-dedication symbolised
in the offering of the sacrificial victim and expressed in
the assent by the offerers to God's law of the dedicated
life; and the vision of the presence of God in sacrificial
communion. It is an act both single and complex; and in
all its parts, when it is renewed in commemoration, it is
an act which begins with "blessing" and is, throughout,
"giving of thanks".

It is round this central or key-idea of the blood and the
covenant that all the other elements of the record fall into
their place. The breaking of the bread, an act so dominant
in the minds of the first witnesses, so bound up with their
earlier experiences, that it is given in all four accounts,
and was the first specific name for the whole rite in the
earliest Church, implies, even if we may not build upon
St. Paul's words, "which is for you", that the simple
"This is my body"—again, in verbal identity, in the four
records—meant "my body broken for you in sacrifice".
St. Matthew's and St. Mark's "which is shed for many",
and St. Matthew's "unto remission of sins", are natural

[1] Ex. xxxii. 1.   [2] Jn. xiii. 31-34.

expansions of what is already contained in the idea of the covenant-blood.

I have no desire to dwell upon the possible meanings of "do" in "do this". Too much has been said on this matter already; and if the sacrificial meaning "offer this" cannot be proved, it is equally clear that the other, and in itself non-sacrificial, meaning—"perform this action"—cannot invalidate the conclusions already drawn.

Nor, again, need anyone desire to press "in remembrance of me". The offering of incense with, or in, the *minḥah* or meal-offering,[1] was a marked feature of the ancient system: and a portion of the *minḥah*, called the *'Azkārāh* or "memorial", was burnt upon the altar. With this action it seems (as noted above)[2] that Psalms were sung; and it would appear that Psalms xxxviii. and lxx. were used for this purpose. Both are prayers for deliverance from trouble, pleading that God will not fail the offerer: "In thee, O Lord, do I hope";[3] "Make haste, O God, to deliver me;[4] ..." and they end with closely similar words: "Forsake me not, O Lord: O my God, be not far from me. Make haste to help me, O Lord my salvation";[5] "I am poor and needy; make haste unto me, O God: thou art my helper and my deliverer; O Lord, make no long tarrying".[6] So the prayer of the *'Azkārāh* Psalms is echoed in Isaiah lxii. 6, in a passage contemplating the deliverance of Jerusalem from her troubles: "Ye that are the Lord's remembrancers, take ye no rest, and give him no rest, till he establish, and till he make Jerusalem a praise in the earth". Incense was the symbol of prayer: and, so far as the *'Azkārāh* is concerned, there is evidence enough that its associations are with that form of prayer for help which may be called "reminding" God, a pleading of His promises in the hour of His servants' need. But the link with the *'Azkārāh* is weak: for the Greek word generally used for it in the LXX is μνημόσυνον. On the other hand, ἀνάμνησις is certainly used once, in Leviticus xxiv. 7, in a passage about the *minḥah*; and it is also used of the blow-

---

[1] A.V., meat offering.   [2] P. 93.   [3] Ps. xxxviii. 15.
[4] Ps. lxx. 1.   [5] Ps. xxxviii. 21 f.   [6] Ps. lxx. 5.

ing of the sacred trumpets on various occasions in the
sense of a reminder to God: "They shall be to you for a
memorial before your God".[1] So far as the actual Greek
word goes, no final or decisive conclusion can be reached.
ἀνάμνησις may mean "memorial before God": μνημόσυννον
would probably mean it. The verdict will depend upon
the general views of the meaning of the Institution story.
All that we can be sure of is that the idea of "memorial
before God" was a familiar part of the ancient sacrificial
thought: and if we adopt that interpretation here it will
be just so far as we are convinced on other grounds that
it is the ancient sacrifices that our Lord has in His mind.
It may also be well to ask whether the supposed distinction between "reminding ourselves" and "reminding
God" is ultimately valid, as regards Christian prayer. In
fact, whenever we end a prayer with "through Jesus
Christ our Lord" we are both reminding ourselves that it
is only through His redeeming work that we can pray,
and pleading the merits of His sacrifice before God, *i.e.*
making a memorial before Him.

I have said "the ancient sacrifices". I wish to stress the
plural. It has often been assumed that the Last Supper
was the Passover meal, as indeed the Synoptic writers
assert, though not altogether consistently. And the connection of the Institution with Jewish sacrifice has therefore sometimes been sought too exclusively in the Passover
rite and ceremonial. Or, sometimes, in other connections,
in view of the absorbing centralisation of our Lord's
sacrifice on redemption from sin, that sacrifice has been
interpreted as a sin-offering only. I have indicated that
the immediate point of contact between the new and the
old is rather the initiation of the first covenant. There, as
we have seen, what was offered was the complete range of
Israelite sacrifice as practised in early times, the burnt-
offering and the peace-offering. It cannot be too emphatically asserted that, in normal usage, the different kinds of
sacrifice went together. Sin-offering, burnt-offering, peace-
offering, with the *minḥah*, in the fully developed system,

---

[1] Num. x. 10.

were combined as were the burnt- and peace-offerings in earlier stages. In Part I. I have emphasised, as giving the key to the meaning of sacrifice as a whole, the six cere-monial actions which, with some omissions, run through all three special kinds. The three are generically the same: each illustrates, with varying emphasis, a single idea; just as there is a single idea, or plan, which is in our minds when we think of a complete Gothic cathedral, though in actual fact one individual cathedral may lack this part, and that another, or the nave may be the glory here, and the choir there, and again, in a third, a Lady Chapel. If the New Testament is concerned with ancient Jewish sacrifice, it is with its broad principles, not with the repetition of specific cases. There will be associations with stages differently emphasised in different forms of sacrifice, and in that sense we may be reminded now of one and now of another. The same is true of the connections of thought which we shall see to have existed, at least for St. Paul, with pagan sacrifice. But neither with pagan nor with Jewish sacrifices must we be betrayed, by our own neces-sarily artificial and entirely technical and antiquarian study of ancient religions, into assuming that in practice the classifications were so real to the actual worshippers. Sacrifice was their way of approach to God; its object at all times was to consummate that approach so far as might be possible. There were various steps in the ap-proach; and all that the distinction of special forms of sacrifice really means is that emphasis was laid, at special moments, now on this step and now on that.

In the analysis of the four accounts of the Institution, I used, in anticipation, the modern terms "consecration" and "administration" to distinguish its different parts. In view of some present-day issues in the Church of England, let me add that this distinction, which I believe to be accurate, is of importance. In the historical practice of the Church, the words "This is my body", and the corre-sponding words about the cup, have become a part, and an essential part, of the Canon, or Prayer of Consecration. And in the *Book of Common Prayer*, until the recent revision, they have been given an emphasis which they do not, in themselves, possess in other rites (I am speaking of the "rites", *i.e.* the words of the liturgies, not of the ceremonial which has in some outstanding cases come to be attached to them). All other liturgies give these words as part of a rehearsal of the whole of our Lord's redeeming work, including always the Resurrection and Ascension, and, in effect, in some families of Liturgies, the thought of Pentecost in the invocation of the Holy Spirit. In the English Prayer Book there is, indeed, the same rehearsal, but it is summarised in the words about "the full, perfect, and sufficient sacrifice, oblation, and satisfaction" at the beginning; and the detailed rehearsal which follows, by stopping short where it begins at the record of the Last Supper, throws this record into a special prominence. That prominence, or emphasis, is further marked by the provision for repeating the record of the Last Supper by itself in reconsecrating. And we have come, therefore, to think of "This is my Body", "This is my Blood" as the words of Institution by themselves. The Consecration Prayer does not, actually, imply this: for it includes what is really the record of consecration with what were, in fact, the Lord's words of administration. But the practical result is as I have described; and it is of vital importance that we should recognise that the original narratives leave us to infer the Lord's actual words of "consecration". The "president" or "celebrant" at the primitive Eucharist "gave thanks", as we know, in his own words. The "eucharistic" prayer was at first what we should call "extempore". But we know, from the general similarity of the earliest forms of "canon" which have come down to us in writing, as we should indeed have supposed from our own experience to be probable, that these prayers followed in the main the same general lines. We have therefore some indication of the practice of the time before "liturgies" were fixed in these earlier written forms.

Can we, from the later forms or from any other source, form an idea of the substance of our Lord's "blessing" or "giving thanks" which correspond at the Last Supper to what we now call the "consecration"? The answer turns partly on the difficult question as to the actual day of the Supper. As is well known, the Fourth Gospel states, with its characteristic accuracy and precision, that it was not the Passover meal. It was held on the "day of prepara-tion". That is to say, Nisan 14, beginning at 6 P.M. on what we should call the previous day, the Thursday, and ending at 6 P.M. on the Friday, was the day, the beginning of which found our Lord and His disciples at supper in the Upper Room: it was in a later part of the same day— what to us would be Friday—that He was crucified, and the Passover lambs were slain. On the Friday evening, at 6 o'clock, the Passover proper began, and the actual Passover meal was held.

I cannot here attempt to discuss the problem in detail. I give what appears to be the most likely solution.[1] Dr. Oesterley finds good reason for the conclusion that the Last Supper was the "social, semi-religious meal" nor-mally held by "*Chaburôth*" (parties of friends) on the afternoon before each Sabbath began; the time passed in spiritual talk until the moment of the opening of the Sabbath arrived, when the presiding member took a cup and said a fixed "blessing" or "sanctification" (*Kedūshah*) over it; and, after the cup, took bread and blessed it with another "*Kedūshah*"—or later, when the ceremony was transferred to the synagogue, "*Kiddūsh*". When a feast coincided with the Sabbath (as the Passover did in the year of our Lord's Crucifixion), the *Kiddūsh* made mention not only of the Sabbath but also of the leading idea of the feast. And as the afternoon of Nisan 14 was occupied with the slaying of the Passover lambs, and the evening that followed it must be given to the Passover meal, the gathering for the Passover *Kiddūsh* must have been held on the previous afternoon and evening, at the end, accord-ing to Jewish reckoning, of Nisan 13, and the beginning of Nisan 14.

Our Lord's words of blessing therefore would have been

---

[1] It is worked out fully in Dr. Oesterley's *The Jewish Background of the Christian Liturgy*, which I am here following (chs. vi., vii.).

those of the Passover *Kiddūsh* in some form; and we can estimate, with a fair degree of certainty, at least what their leading ideas must have been. The Jewish Passover *Kiddūsh* is of undoubted antiquity.[1] I give its text, summarised at the beginning:

[Commemoration of Creation, and, as its climax, God's rest on the seventh day, and institution of the Sabbath.]

(The words said over the cup) "Blessed art thou, O Lord our God, King Eternal, who createst the fruit of the Vine."

Blessed art Thou, O Lord our God, King Eternal, who hast chosen us from all peoples, and hast exalted us above all tongues, and hast sanctified us by Thy commandments. And Thou hast given us in love, O Lord our God, Sabbaths for rest, and appointed times for gladness, festivals, and seasons of joy; this Sabbath day and this feast of Unleavened Bread, the season of our freedom.

Blessed art Thou, O Lord our God, King Eternal, who hast kept us alive, and hast preserved us, and enabled us to reach this season.

(The words said over the bread) "Blessed art Thou, O Lord our God, King Eternal, who bringest forth bread from the earth."

Though I am anticipating here, I must refer, for a special reason, to the Johannine discourses in John xiii.-xvii. They represent the kind of conversation which would have taken place at such a meal. And their contents are in remarkable agreement with the view which we have outlined. Our Lord and His disciples were, in effect, a *Chabūrah*; and He says to them, emphasising the name, "Ye are my friends, if ye do the things which I command you".[2]

The Passover *Kiddūsh* is a memorial of Creation, and of the redemption from Egypt. The cup is blessed as the fruit of the vine. It speaks of the election and sanctification of Israel, of the freedom and joy which the Passover brings with it. All these topics find their place—not systematically, as if a list were being worked through, but naturally as the talk proceeds—in the "discourses". There is the Vine, which the three first Gospels represent our Lord as mentioning at the central part of the Supper,

---

[1] Oesterley, *op. cit.* p. 81.　　[2] Jn. xv. 14.; *op. cit.* p. 172.

worked out in the great allegory in John xv. The thought
underlying Creation and the Sabbath is that of completed
work: and John xvii. 4 f., if we may take it as going, in
the author's mind, with the picture of the Eternal Word
and His share in Creation in John i. 1-3, has the same
thought about the new Creation: "I glorified thee on the
earth, having accomplished the work which thou hast
given me to do. And now, O Father, glorify thou me with
thine own self with the glory which I had with thee
before the world was". There was in the *Kiddūsh* the
deliverance from Egypt for the journey to the promised
land. In John xiv. 2 there is "In My Father's house are
many mansions; if it were not so, I would have told you:
for I go to prepare a place for you". The *Kiddūsh* speaks
of election and sanctification—and making holy, sanctifying, means ultimately separating—; three times over there
is the Lord's choosing His own (Jn. xiii. 18, xv. 16, 19),
and in the last passage there is also the thought of the
separating which is sanctifying: "Because ye are not of the
world, but I chose you out of the world, therefore the world
hateth you". *Kiddūsh* again strikes the note of freedom; in
John xv. 15 they are no longer bondservants but friends.
And the note of joy is found three times over—"my joy",
"your joy"—in John xv. 11, xvi. 22, xvii. 13.[1]

This is, in a sense, anticipation. I am not using the
Johannine material with any assumption about the historical character of the discourses. But, if the *Kiddūsh*
hypothesis is at all secure, there can be no doubt that this
remarkable coincidence of thought at the least illustrates
it, even if it does not, as I venture to think, provide an
illustration of the fundamentally Jewish outlook of the
Fourth Gospel, and therefore of its claim to a more real
historicity than could be found for it before the Jewish
origins of New Testament ideas had been so fully studied,
and while it was assumed that the foundations of Johannine thought were not so much Judaic as Hellenic.

We may observe that on this theory of a *Chabūrah*
meal, with its Passover *Kiddūsh*, two significant results

---

[1] *Op. cit.* pp. 184 ff.

follow. On the one hand, as we have seen, we have good grounds for supplying what is in our records the chief gap in the history of the Institution. We have, that is, an indication of our Lord's own "consecration prayer". It was, if we are right, a rehearsal, cast into the form of thanksgiving, for Creation and Redemption, and striking the fundamental note of Commemoration. It gives us an obvious link with the eucharistic passages in the *Didache*. There the cup comes first, and the bread (that which is broken, τὸ κλάσμα) second. And the words about the cup are a manifest adaptation of the *Kiddūsh* for the cup. But the *Didache* may be taken more as a book of private instruction or devotion for the worshipper than a fragment of a Liturgy. So far as it goes, its evidence is of value as preserving the *Kiddūsh* associations of the Eucharist. Justin Martyr, on the other hand, tells us that the content of the Consecration Prayer at the Eucharist in his time was thanksgiving for creation and redemption, and commemoration (of our Lord's Institution); and these are most certainly alike the substance of the *Kiddūsh* and the framework of the later, written, Canons.

We arrive, that is, at a way of interpreting the story of the Institution which at once fills up its gap, and links it, historically, with the development of the Liturgies which we know. And that is valuable evidence, both as regards an understanding of the Institution, and in justifying the use of later liturgical development as illustrating our Lord's original intentions. It means that such developments are in no way out of line with the earliest practice of the Church.

On the other hand, we have evidence of the utmost value for the understanding of the whole rite, as regards its original connection with the Passover. It was, first, not the actual Passover meal. Certain real difficulties are thereby solved: for it is hard otherwise to explain the fact that the Passover lamb is not mentioned, nor the four cups—both together the central features of a true Passover; or to account for the bread being spoken of as ἄρτος, *i.e.* bread simply—the wider term—and not as ἄζυμα, the unleavened bread of the Passover feast.[1] But the chief import of this severance from the Passover—and it is for this reason that I have stressed Dr. Oesterley's argument—is that is sets us free to see the sacrificial reference in our Lord's words as general and not specific. The Passover was a sacrifice, including a sacrificial feast; but it is only one of the special applications of the general sacrificial idea; and to confine the sacrificial bearing of the Eucharist to what happened at the Passover is fatally to restrict the significance of sacrifice in the Christian system.

But, secondly, if the key to the understanding of the Institution is the *Kiddūsh*, it was the Passover *Kiddūsh*. We know—even before we reach the precise chronology of St. John—that St. Paul felt strongly the connection between our Lord's sacrifice and the Passover. He is not, indeed, confined to these associations, as we shall see. He, like our Lord, viewed sacrifice, or the sacrificial idea, broadly, and as a whole. But to him "our passover also hath been sacrificed, even Christ".[2] And he knew that on the second day of the Feast the Sheaf of the First-fruits was offered, in the morning. That would have been Nisan 16, the first day of the week; and to him Christ rose from the dead on that morning as "the first-fruits of them that are asleep".[3] Thus in the Church of his days the way was being prepared for that close connection of thought between the Last Supper and the Passover which gave us the apparent Synoptic identification of the two. I have given reasons for adopting this theory. It is always, however, possible that the Passover itself was anticipated by our Lord on this occasion.

It is hard, in any case, not to believe that Passover thoughts were in our Lord's mind at the Supper. We read that at the end, before they went to the Mount of Olives, they sang a hymn. The closer the association at that moment with the Passover the more impossible is it to think that this could be other than the Hallel,[4] the Pass-

---

[1] The Eastern Church, in using leavened bread for the Eucharist, is therefore, here as elsewhere, more primitive than the Western.   [2] 1 Cor. v. 7.
[3] 1 Cor. xv. 20; *op. cit.* pp. 183 f.   [4] Pss. cxiii.-cxviii.

over hymn. Its use was, indeed, not confined to the Passover. It belonged to the rite of all the great feasts in the
Temple. It was inseparably bound up with the whole
system of sacrifice. And that system, or rather its underlying principles, had been the foundation of much of our
Lord's teaching. Its central historic occasion had been
expressly recalled by Him that night. I cannot but end
by recalling some of the thoughts which, with the Hallel
upon His lips, He took with Him to Gethsemane, and
the Cross, and the Glory. "The Son of man must suffer
many things . . . and be killed, and after three days rise
again." [1] "This cup is the new covenant in my blood." [2]

Psalm 113 is a burst of praise to God enthroned in
heaven, the protector of the lowly and the poor:

> 5. Who is like unto the Lord our God,
>   That hath his seat on high,
> 6. That humbleth himself to behold
>   The things that are in heaven and in the earth?
> 7. He raiseth up the poor out of the dust,
>   And lifteth up the needy from the dunghill;
> 8. That he may set him with princes,
>   Even with the princes of his people.
> 9. He maketh the barren woman to keep house,
>   And to be a joyful mother of children.

Or Psalm 114—which commemorates the redemption
from Egypt and tells how God fed His people with the
water of life—

> 8. Which turned the rock into a pool of water,
>   The flint into a fountain of waters.

Psalm 115:

> 9. O Israel trust thou in the Lord:
>   He is their help and their shield.
> 11. Ye that fear the Lord, trust in the Lord:
>   He is their help and their shield.
> 12. The Lord hath been mindful of us; he will bless us:
>
>   .   .   .   .   .   .
>
> 13. He will bless them that fear the Lord,
>   Both small and great.

---

[1] Mk. viii. 31.   [2] 1 Cor. xi. 25.

14. The Lord increase you more and more,
    You and your children.
17. The dead praise not the Lord,
    Neither any that go down into silence;
18. But we will bless the Lord
    From this time forth for evermore.

Psalm 116:

1. I love the Lord, because he hath heard
   My voice and my supplications.
3. The cords of death compassed me,
   And the pains of Sheol gat hold upon me:
   I found trouble and sorrow.
4. Then called I upon the name of the Lord;
   O Lord, I beseech thee, deliver my soul.
5. Gracious is the Lord, and righteous;
   Yea, our God is merciful.
6. The Lord preserveth the simple;
   I was brought low, and he saved me.
7. Return unto thy rest, O my soul;
   For the Lord hath dealt bountifully with thee.
8. For thou hast delivered my soul from death,
   Mine eyes from tears,
   And my feet from falling.
9. I will walk before the Lord
   In the land of the living.
12. What shall I render unto the Lord
    For all his benefits toward me?
13. I will take the cup of salvation,
    And call upon the name of the Lord.
14. I will pay my vows unto the Lord,
    Yea, in the presence of all his people.
15. Precious in the sight of the Lord
    Is the death of his saints.
16. O Lord, truly I am thy servant:
    I am thy servant, the son of thine handmaid;
    Thou hast loosed my bonds.
17. I will offer to thee the sacrifice of thanksgiving,
    And will call upon the name of the Lord.
18. I will pay my vows unto the Lord,
    Yea, in the presence of all his people;
19. In the courts of the Lord's house,
    In the midst of thee, O Jerusalem.
    Praise ye the Lord.

Psalm 118.

1. O give thanks unto the Lord; for he is good:
   For his mercy endureth for ever.

5. Out of my distress I called upon the Lord:
   The Lord answered me and set me in a large place.

6. The Lord is on my side; I will not fear:
   What can man do unto me?

8. It is better to trust in the Lord
   Than to put confidence in man.

13. Thou didst thrust sore at me that I might fall:
    But the Lord helped me.

14. The Lord is my strength and song;
    And he is become my salvation.

17. I shall not die, but live,
    And declare the works of the Lord.

18. The Lord hath chastened me sore:
    But he hath not given me over unto death.

19. Open to me the gates of righteousness:
    I will enter into them, I will give thanks unto the Lord.

20. This is the gate of the Lord;
    The righteous shall enter into it.

21. I will give thanks unto thee, for thou hast answered me,
    And art become my salvation.

22. The stone which the builders rejected
    Is become the head of the corner.

23. This is the Lord's doing;
    It is marvellous in our eyes.

24. This is the day which the Lord hath made;
    We will rejoice and be glad in it.

25. Save now, we beseech thee, O Lord:
    O Lord, we beseech thee, send now prosperity.

26. Blessed be he that cometh in the name of the Lord:

[These three clauses were repeated by the people, in the Temple, after the Levites. "Blessed be he that cometh in the name of the Lord" is, therefore, the key-note of the Psalm.]

We have blessed you out of the house of the Lord.

27. The Lord is God, and he hath given us light:
    Bind the sacrifice with cords, even unto the horns of the altar.

28. Thou art my God, and I will give thanks unto thee:
    Thou art my God, I will exalt thee.

29. O give thanks unto the Lord; for he is good:
    For his mercy endureth for ever.

CHAPTER VI

THE IDEA OF SACRIFICE IN THE NEW TESTAMENT

THE Old Testament, as we have seen, leaves us with certain general principles underlying the approach to God, and at the same time with a developed "technique" in the sacrificial worship by which, in spite of abuses and misunderstandings, it was assumed that that approach was to be made.

We have attempted hitherto to test the Synoptic picture of our Lord's life and teaching as regards the principles. We have found that, both for Himself and for His followers, the approach to God begins with the surrender of life for the sake of others; and that in such surrender is revealed God's desire, in Him, to "seek and to save" sinners. Through that surrender He first, and His followers after Him, pass into a new and transformed life. It is the life of obedience to God's will, or of self-dedication. And it is, in effect, the entry upon a new world. He has finally enlarged the horizon of human life. The kingdoms of this world have become the Kingdom of God and of His Christ. There are new powers, and new values. Man has at last been admitted into the Presence of God: for the Life is found to be at once that of children in their Father's home, of subjects in the heavenly kingdom, and of worshippers in the heavenly sanctuary. And, finally, the life, first found in self-surrender and then transformed in offering, is shared. It is the life of an organic unit, running through each member and the whole; and it is communicated by food.

Of technical language there is, as we should expect,

but little. What there is belongs to the story of the Institution of the Eucharist or Lord's Supper: but we have seen reason in that story for believing that in the supreme moment of our Lord's earthly life, as in His general attitude during the ministry, His mind turned easily and naturally to the thought of the Temple and its cultus. He gathers up the sacrificial tradition in Himself, as, indeed, He passes to His death with the hymn of the Temple worship on His lips.

We pass from the Synoptic history of our Lord's work on earth to the rest of the New Testament. It will, I hope, help, both in clearness and in brevity, if I say here from what points of view I propose to deal with the evidence of the Acts, the Epistles, and Revelation.

I shall not attempt an exhaustive treatment. My object is not so much to draw out the whole of the New Testament teaching on sacrifice as to emphasise two features in it, viz.: (1) That the redeeming work of our Lord, taken as a whole, did, for the writers, both as Jews, and in their purpose of explaining Christianity to Gentile contemporaries, naturally fall under the dominant conception of sacrifice; and (2) that in the sacrificial language and ideas that we find in their writings there is, at least so far as they use exact language, accuracy as regards what I have called "technique". They assume in their readers the familiarity which they possessed themselves with the ordinary procedure of sacrifice. And, in particular, I may anticipate what I shall have to say in Part III., by stressing the undoubted fact that they never conceived of sacrifice as limited to the death of the victim. They knew that sacrifice consisted of a succession of acts, of which the slaying of the victim was only one.

I

We saw in Part I. that the Old Testament leaves an unsolved problem. On the one hand there is the sanctuary idea of God and of His holiness, and as the working out of that idea a complete scheme of approach to Him by sacrifice. Its purpose was to convey Holiness to man: for in Holiness there lay the whole principle at once of purity and cleanness, and of the communication of God's power. But it failed: for the Holiness which it succeeded in imparting was hardly more than external. It could not deal with any but trivial sins. The blood of bulls and of goats could not avail for complete redemption.

On the other hand, there was the ideal of God as a righteous King, requiring His own perfect righteousness from His people. That, again, as the history showed, remained an ideal: its failure is nowhere more vividly expressed than in St. Paul's account of his own experience of the Law.

What was needed was the effective combination of the two methods. The holiness—that self-communicating power of God which the study of the dawn of human religion has shown as hardly more than a physical contagion, and which we know in Christian language as "grace"—must be brought into human life in such a way that the ideal of righteousness may be at last achieved. The arena of the sanctuary must be so widened as to include, effectively, the whole moral content of life; and the power to obey the moral law must be found in God's gift of Himself. The Temple area must become the Kingdom —the scene of the life of the Divine commonwealth; and the Kingdom must become the Sanctuary. Worship can never be complete until it includes service; service will only be effective when it is, itself, worship.

I have attempted to show that the beginnings, at least, of this fusion—of the solving of the problem left by the Old Testament—are found in our Lord's teaching, and in the records which we have of some of the phenomena of His life. But it was during the Ministry only a beginning. "It was not yet Spirit."

With the story of Pentecost in the Acts the whole scene is changed. At once "it is Spirit". The new life has begun in earnest. We still come across traces of what, for the Christian society, had passed away: there were Apollos, and the other disciples at Ephesus who could say that when they became believers, "we did not so much as hear whether there is a Holy Ghost".[1] That incident only shows up the new conditions in clearer relief. The Spirit came at Pentecost: He came, or was given, to new believers, normally, after, though in the case of Cornelius before, their baptism. He is felt to be a living presence in the society.[2] Where the Church is, there is the Spirit: it was to Him that Ananias and Sapphira lied;[3] and the story of their deaths is exactly on the lines of the Old Testament stories of sins against the "numinous". It is in the sanctuary service of the Church at Antioch that the Spirit designates Barnabas and Saul for their missionary work, and it is in the language of holiness or separation that He speaks ("as they ministered to the Lord"—λειτουργούντων = performing the service of the sanctuary: "*Separate* me Barnabas and Saul . . .").[4] So at once the epithet "holy" is applied to our Lord in the early "speeches": He is the "Holy and Righteous one" (the two characteristic ideals of the old dispensation are combined, in human experience, for the first time), and in the same sentence the Prince, or Author, of life, as well as, just before, God's servant (παῖς—עֶבֶד—the word which was as familiar in the sense of servant of the sanctuary as in the more general sense which alone it preserves in English, and itself belongs to Isaiah liii. with its sacrificial strain);[5] and again, "Thy holy Servant Jesus".[6] They are able, in fact, at once to find a word for their experiences of Him during the ministry,[7] just as in St. John's Gospel Peter's confession, in the light of their later realisation, is "Thou art the Holy One of God".[8]

I cannot attempt to give full materials for the language of the Epistles; and there is certainly no need to lay fresh emphasis upon the place given to the Holy Spirit by the New Testament writers, outside the Synoptic Gospels. But it must be observed that the epithet—the "Holy"— ought not to be allowed to lose its force. We are so accustomed, in the language of theology, to speak and think of

---

[1] Acts xix. 2, R.V.m. [2] Acts iv. 31. [3] Acts v. 3.
[4] Acts xiii. 2. [5] Acts iii. 13-15. [6] Acts iv. 27, 30.
[7] Part II. Ch. III. pp. 165 ff. [8] Jn. vi. 69.

the "Spirit"; and the distinctive sense of "holiness", "the
holy", and the associations which, in New Testament
times, such words carried with them, has become to us so
weak in our common ethical use of them as merely con-
noting perfect character, that there is danger of our
treating the epithet as if it were purely conventional.
What we have to remember is that "Holy", when used of
the Spirit, as elsewhere, must, in New Testament times,
have precisely that reference to the "numinous" and to
the religion of the ancient sanctuary which it has in its
other uses. It is still separation: St. Paul is "called to be
an apostle, separated to the gospel of God"; and the
exact parallel to this is κλητοὶ ἅγιοι, "called to be holy,"
five verses later, of the Romans to whom he is writing: [1]
the "calling" of Christians is therefore indirectly itself a
thought of the sanctuary. Or, Christians are a temple:
"Wherefore come ye out from among them, and be ye
separate, saith the Lord, and touch no unclean thing. . . .
Having therefore these promises, beloved, let us cleanse
ourselves from all defilement of flesh and spirit, perfecting
holiness in the fear of God." [2] So the virgin, separated
from the cares of matrimony, "is careful for the things
of the Lord, that she may be holy both in body and in
spirit". [3]

On the ethical side it is still contrasted with uncleanness; it has the "aesthetic" element which we have found
in it before. "Quench not the Spirit" suggests "hold fast
τὸ καλόν", the good in the sense of the beautiful. [4] So
"God called us not for uncleanness but in sanctification"; [5]
"But ye were washed, but ye were sanctified, but ye were
justified in the name of the Lord Jesus Christ, and in
the Spirit of our God" [6] (righteousness, with its forensic
associations, is definitely brought into the sphere of the
sanctuary in the sacramental action of the Church). Or
again, as above, cleansing ourselves from defilement of
flesh and spirit is "perfecting holiness".

And it is the Spirit which gives power, just as our

[1] Rom. i. 1, 6; so 1 Cor. i. 2.   [2] 2 Cor. vi. 16-vii. 1.
[3] 1 Cor. vii. 34.   [4] 1 Thess. v. 19, 21.   [5] 1 Thess. iv. 7.   [6] 1 Cor. vi. 11.

Lord's "numinous" quality was felt in His acts of power,
or "miracles", and as He promised to the disciples.[1] God
"supplieth to you the Spirit and worketh miracles among
you"[2]—and the word for "miracles" is "powers", δυνάμεις.
So our Lord "was declared to be the Son of God with
power, according to the spirit of holiness, by the resurrection of the dead"[3]—a phrase, which, as we shall see, is
central in the conception of the stages of the Christian
sacrifice. Or again, the Gospel came not "in word only, but
also in power and in the Holy Ghost";[4] it is the Holy Spirit
—the power of Holiness that issues from the Holy God—,
which in the old days made His presence effective for
death or for life, that makes the difference between a mere
delivery of a spoken message and the communication of
active grace: the gospel "is the power of God unto salvation",[5] and the Kingdom of God, now become the Eternal
Sanctuary, is therefore "not in word but in power".[6] And
the whole of the great eighth chapter of the Epistle to the
Romans is, in effect, a hymn of victory in praise of the
new power of holiness which the Spirit has brought in
place of the weakness of the Law.[7]

Or, in another aspect, the Spirit's power is shown in His
gift of life: He is the Spirit of life, through Whom God
raised up Christ Jesus from the dead, and shall quicken
us;[8] so much so that, in the same chapter, He is Himself the
living sympathiser, helper, and intercessor,[9] sharing our
Lord's own heavenly work for us. And the life that He
gives is the life of God. He makes us realise our sonship
and our place in the family of God.

I have dwelt upon some of the aspects of the Holy
Spirit in St. Paul's Epistles—and they might be paralleled
from the other writings—because they bring out the
truth that the new world into which Pentecost had been
the entrance and of which our Lord had spoken—the
world of new powers, new character, new outlook, and of
new life—was throughout, and in the first place, a

---

[1] Acts i. 8.   [2] Gal. iii. 5.   [3] Rom. i. 4.
[4] 1 Thess. i. 5.   [5] Rom. i. 16.   [6] 1 Cor. iv. 20.
[7] Rom. viii. 3.   [8] Rom. viii. 11.   [9] Rom. viii. 26 f.

sanctuary. The members of the Kingdom are a holy
nation: like the old Israel, they are a priesthood, at once
holy and royal;[1] a kingdom, and priests.[2] Hence the constant use of ἅγιοι " the holy people"—inevitably translated "the saints", but none the less wholly misunderstood
by the uninstructed reader—for Christians generally. As
members of the people of God, of Christ's body, as branches
of the Vine, as stones in God's house or temple, they share
God's holiness. They are called out of the world, separated
from it, set apart, and, with that, given a power by which,
for the first time, if they will only use it, they can achieve
righteousness. Christ Jesus was made unto us righteousness and sanctification:[3] and sanctification means to
dedicate to God; to sanctify a people to Him means "to
consecrate them to Him as a worshipping people".[4]

And if it be asked what is the new sanctuary, which is
to be the scene and arena of the new life, the answer may
be given from many passages. It may be pictured as in the
visions of Heaven and its worship in Revelation—and in
that it is perhaps the widest, because in its ultimate perfection it includes all created nature—or in the vision of
the Holy City, where all life is both worship and service,
and the whole City is itself the presence-chamber of God;
or as the heavens, or the heavenly and perfect sanctuary
of the Epistle to the Hebrews, the Holy of Holies, within
the Veil, the City which is, spiritually, Mount Zion and
the heavenly Jerusalem, where are, as in Revelation, the
"angels and archangels and all the company of heaven";
or, as with St. Paul, "our citizenship is in heaven",[5] in the
Jerusalem which is above, and is free, which is our mother.[6]

Or, in other terms, the sanctuary is thought of as built
of living stones. St. Peter could not forget how he and the
others, with the Master, at the end of their last hymn together on the last night, sang of the chief corner-stone,
and he sees the spiritual house built round or about Him
of living stones.[7] So St. Paul constantly says that we are a

---

[1] 1 Pet. ii. 5, 9. [2] Rev. i. 6; see also Ex. xix. 6. [3] 1 Cor. i. 30.
[4] A. B. Davidson, *Hebrews*, p. 206. [5] Phil. iii. 20. [6] Gal. iv. 26.
[7] 1 Pet. ii. 4-6.

temple—always the ναός, the innermost shrine; "know ye not that ye are a temple of God, and that the Spirit of God dwelleth in you . . . the temple of God is holy, which temple ye are";[1] "we are a temple of the living God".[2] Or, with his own unique power of finding new possibilities in old language, he can see every individual as a temple of the Holy Spirit;[3] or the old Temple, with its varied buildings, reproduced in the separate buildings of the new community and growing, like a living thing, into a single "holy temple in the Lord", "builded together for a habitation of God in the Spirit".[4]

He is indeed carrying on into the new life the thoughts upon which he had grown up in the old. It is in the same terms that he summarises the privileges of Israel in the past. They had the sonship—the life of God communicated and shared; the glory, the Shekinah, in the Holy of Holies; the covenants, first instituted and then renewed, always in sacrifice; the giving of the Law, which included for him as for all Jews the law of worship as well as the law of conduct; the service of God—λατρεία, the service of the sanctuary—, as well as the promises of the Messianic future, whether of the Kingdom, always centred round Zion and the Lord's house, or of the Servant, who was to be the perfect offering for sin.[5] He sees his own ministry in terms of temple service (λατρεύω),[6] when he speaks of his intercession for the Roman Christians; and even in terms of priesthood when he pictures himself officiating as a priest (ἱερουργοῦντα) of the gospel ministry, "that the offering up of the Gentiles might be made acceptable, being sanctified by the Holy Ghost".[7]

II

It is not surprising that, with these thoughts of the Spirit, of Holiness, and of the Sanctuary, the different writers are found to turn to the category of sacrifice when they speak both of our Lord's work for us, and of our

[1] 1 Cor. iii. 16.   [2] 2 Cor. vi. 16.   [3] 1 Cor. vi. 19.   [4] Eph. ii. 21 f.
[5] Rom. ix. 4.   [6] Rom. i. 9.   [7] Rom. xv. 16.

life in Him. I have dwelt upon this group of ideas in some
detail, though I might have worked it out more fully,
because, as I have said before, the tendency of discussions on sacrifice has been to begin, and too often to end,
with specific "sacrificial" terms. What gives the strictly
sacrificial passages their value is the basis of tradition and
of thought, of inherited religion and of conscious Christian development, which lies behind them, and it seemed
worth while therefore to form some estimate of the scope
of the "sanctuary" conception of Christian life which we
find in the New Testament.

Of the three fundamental principles which we have
traced in the Synoptic Gospels I need not attempt even
such an outline as I have given in the last section. No one
will dispute that alike for St. Paul, the writer to the
Hebrews, St. Peter, St. John, and the writer of Revelation, Life surrendered, Life dedicated and transformed,
Life communicated and shared provide three headings
under which all, or nearly all, their teaching might naturally be grouped.

There is no question of the "cruciality of the Cross", in
Dr. Forsyth's phrase. "We preach Christ crucified"[1] is
for St. Paul the starting-point of the Gospel. He "gave
Himself up for us";[2] He "came into the world to save
sinners";[3] "The death that he died, he died unto sin
once";[4] "God, sending his own Son in the likeness of sin-
ful flesh and as an offering for sin ($\pi\epsilon\rho\grave{\iota}\ \dot{\alpha}\mu\alpha\rho\tau\acute{\iota}\alpha\varsigma$—the LXX
equivalent to "sin-offering"), condemned sin in the flesh";[5]
It is by His blood that we are justified;[6] in Him "we have
our redemption through his blood, the forgiveness of
our trespasses".[7] It is the same with the other writers as
with St. Paul. And with the surrender of His life there is
inseparably bound up the surrender of the life of His
servants, of those whom He redeems. As in the Gospels,
it is with the servants as it is with the Master. They are
buried with him in baptism: their membership of His
body depends upon their dying with Him in order that

---

[1] 1 Cor. i. 23.   [2] Eph. v. 2.   [3] 1 Tim. i. 15.   [4] Rom. vi. 10.
[5] Rom. viii. 3.   [6] Rom. v. 9.   [7] Eph. i. 7.

they may live with Him. St. Paul can say, "I have been crucified with Christ"; and this not in a mystical or doctrinal sense alone, but quite literally and simply in the doing of His work and the following of His example: "Always bearing about in the body the dying of Jesus"; "We which live are always delivered unto death for Jesus' sake".[1]

And the purpose and vindication of the surrender, for Him as for them, is the life which follows upon it. I need quote no separate passage. To St. Paul and to St. Peter, to the writer to the Hebrews and to St. John, and equally in the Apocalypse, the new life of the Resurrection is what gives its value to the Cross and to the blood. However we may interpret the Resurrection records in the Gospels, the life of Christ Who passed through death is transformed. God has accepted His surrender: the Spirit has touched the body of His humiliation, and it has become the body of His glory. He is nearer to His followers, present in a more intimate way, than He was in the days of the ministry. And as He is transformed, so are they. They are alive with Him; they can walk in newness of life; if any man is in Christ, he is a new creature. We have only to think of the eighth chapter of the Epistle to the Romans; of what St. Paul wrote to the Ephesians; of the heavenly life and work of the perfected Christ, in His High Priesthood in the Epistle to the Hebrews; of the teaching of the last discourses in St. John; of the visions of the Priest, and of the Lamb standing as it had been slain, in Revelation; of the new capacities of the Apostles after Pentecost, and of the felt experience of the new realities throughout, which made the Apostolic Church what it was: the dedicated life, in Him and in them, is the life of new powers and new values which He had pictured to them in the old days.

Once more, the life, so surrendered and transformed, is shared. The Christian knows what sonship is. He knows Whose Blood is in his veins. It is, indeed, the supreme gift for which all else is but preparation. The Pauline "in

---

[1] 2 Cor. iv. 10, 11.

Christ", "Christ in me", "in you"; the Johannine indwelling of the Son in us, and the Father in the Son; the Spirit Who is at once the atmosphere which we breathe and the dweller in the temple, whether of each man's own self or of the whole redeemed community: these are only other ways of interpreting the Vine, the olive tree, the Body. And the life so shared was given in Baptism, and is renewed, as it were by food, in every gift that goes to maintain it.

III

It is upon this material that the special language of sacrifice is used. It is easy to find examples. The surrender of life is the underlying principle, or the chief point of emphasis, of the sin-offering. I have already quoted one passage[1] in which St. Paul says that God sent His Son περὶ ἁμαρτίας, as an offering for sin. So the burnt-offering: "He gave himself up for us, an offering and a sacrifice to God for an odour of a sweet smell";[2] and the "living sacrifice" of the dedicated and transformed life of the new Christian character in Romans xii.; and the same language of the burnt-offering is used of the new life of Christians; in fact in one case the two uses of fire, so distinct to the Hebrew mind, seem to be contrasted as they are in the Gospels:[3] "For we are a sweet savour of Christ unto God" (we are, as it were, recognised as part of Christ's offered and accepted Body), "in them that are being saved, and in them that are perishing; to the one a savour from death unto death, the other a savour from life unto life";[4] "yet now hath he reconciled (you) in the body of his flesh through death, to present you holy and without blemish and unreproveable before him".[5] Or St. Paul speaks of himself and of the Philippians: "Yea, and if I am offered upon the sacrifice and service of your faith, I joy, and rejoice with you all":[6] he will be the drink-offering poured about the altar on which their offering of faith, the dedication

---

[1] Rom. viii. 3.   [2] Eph. v. 2.   [3] Above, p. 197.   [4] 2 Cor. ii. 15 f.
[5] Col. i. 21 f.   [6] Phil. ii. 17; cf. 2 Tim. iv. 6.

of themselves, is being presented; and their gifts to him are part of that same burnt-offering, "an odour of a sweet smell, a sacrifice acceptable, well-pleasing to God'.[1]

Once more St. Paul sees our Lord as the Paschal Lamb: "Our passover also hath been sacrificed, even Christ",[2] and, as we have already seen,[3] he thinks of Him, rising from the dead on the third day, as the first-fruits of them that sleep, the first-fruits being offered on that same day, the second day of the Passover feast.[4] The Passover stands to some extent by itself in any classification of the ancient sacrifices that may be made. In connection with the Last Supper it is commonly spoken of as if it were only a meal, at which there is no more required in the way of priest-hood than the informal priesthood of the father of a household leading the family worship and presiding at the family meal; or, similarly, if sacrificial language is used, it is distinguished as a feast upon a sacrifice rather than an actual sacrifice. Both these ways of looking at it are inaccurate. The lamb had been slain, and its blood had been used in the ordinary way; the priests had done their work; and the whole meaning of the subsequent meal in each household or group was not that it was a feast, more or less ordinary, following upon a previous sacrifice, but that it was the concluding stage of the sacrifice itself. It is upon the Passover as sacrificed, therefore, that St. Paul lays stress: to him it was that—the stages through which the Lamb had passed before the meal—which made it what it was. So too to St. John the Paschal significance of Christ is brought out in his story of the Cross: "They brake not his legs. . . . For these things came to pass, that the scripture might be fulfilled, A bone of him shall not be broken."[5]

With the peace-offering, and therefore the whole circle of ideas which went with it in the Rabbinic tradition with which St. Paul was familiar, the connection is definitely made in the passage in 1 Corinthians x.,[6] where the Eucharist is treated as the parallel in Christianity to the

---

[1] Phil. iv. 18.   [2] 1 Cor. v. 7.   [3] Above, p. 219.   [4] 1 Cor. xv. 20.
[5] Jn. xix. 33, 36, quoting Ex. xii. 46.   [6] 1 Cor. x. 14-22.

sacrificial meals alike of Jewish and of pagan religion. The argument is, of course, that to converts from paganism the act of eating food already killed and offered in sacrifice may retain associations of communion with gods who are indeed non-existent,[1] but who, if they retain for some of their former worshippers any lingering semblance of reality, are for them powers of evil. The Christian act of communion therefore is assumed to stand to the whole Christian sacrifice in the same relation as the eating by pagans stands to pagan sacrifice; and the peace-offering of Israel is given as an analogy to both which will explain the argument to those among the Corinthians who are familiar with, and were perhaps, like St. Paul, brought up upon, the Jewish worship. Here we have the one passage—and it is therefore of supreme importance—where the Eucharist is definitely brought by St. Paul into its place in the Christian conception of sacrifice. The same thought seems to be intended in the Epistle to the Hebrews, in "We have an altar, whereof they have no right to eat which serve the tabernacle".[2] I am aware that this reference is disputed. But I think that it will be found that the difficulty turns upon the overwhelming strength of the habit of interpreting the Cross as the ultimate Christian altar. Of this I shall have to speak later; though, so far as this passage is concerned, even writers who, like Bishop Westcott and Dr. A. B. Davidson, say that the altar intended is the Cross recognise that the meaning is that, in Dr. Davidson's words, we have a sacrifice of which we partake. He says, indeed, that "there seems no allusion in the expression 'we have an altar' to the sacrament of the Supper". Bishop Westcott, on the other hand, and I think Dr. Davidson also, say clearly enough that the writer means the participation, by way of a feast, in the Christian sacrifice, and we may safely leave it that the only uncertainty is whether the actual eucharistic table was as early as this sometimes spoken of as an altar also.[3]

---

[1] 1 Cor. viii. 4.   [2] Heb. xiii. 10.

[3] St. Paul's phrase, "the table of the Lord", in 1 Cor. x. 21, comes from Mal. i. 7, where it is expressly a synonym for "mine altar"

What is evident is that in Hebrews, as well as to St.
Paul, the Christian sacrifice involved communion, as did
the older sacrificial systems. In fact the argument in
the Epistle to the Hebrews seems to stress this. For the
writer's point is not so much that those who serve the
Jewish tabernacle are as such "out of communion", as
we should say, with Christians. It is rather that he has
been stressing the analogy of our Lord's sacrifice with
one special aspect of Jewish sacrifice, namely, the sin-
offering, and in particular the great sin-offering of the
Day of Atonement. What he seems to say, therefore, is
that it is just at the point of communion that the sin-
offering breaks down. Those for whom it was offered
might not eat of the sacrifice; and when the priest offered
it for himself, or for the people including himself, even he
might not eat of it. The flesh of the victim was burned
without the camp: it was too holy to be received as food.
And to that extent let us use to the full, the writer says,
the symbolism of our Lord having suffered without the
gate. Let us go out with Him from the old sanctuary, the
earthly Jerusalem, with its fatal limitations, its imperfect
sacrifice: for we seek after the city that is to come—
where indeed we have already arrived. There we have an
altar-table; the ministers of the Jewish altars, as he has
already said, on the theory of their own system, may not
have a right after a sin-offering to the act of communion
which would have made their offering effective; but let
us, on our altar, through Christ, offer up a sacrifice of
praise continually. It is the true sacrifice that comes from
a thankful heart. It is the reality to which the old thank-
offering—a form of the peace-offering—had pointed. He
uses the LXX phrase θυσίαν αἰνέσεως [1] (sometimes περὶ
αἰνέσεως), familiar alike in the Law and in the peace-offering Psalms: [2] it means, in the Hebrew idiom, not a sacrifice
in which we offer praise and nothing else, but a sacrifice
in which we offer a victim in a spirit of thankfulness.
And therefore when we eat from our altar in the new
City-sanctuary we shall remember, as the writer may well

[1] Lev. vii. 12, xxii. 29.   [2] See above, pp. 93 ff.

have had in mind, that even the Jewish tradition taught
that the one sacrifice that should continue in the Messianic
age would be the peace-offering. Christ is no mere sin-
offering. He fulfils the idea of sacrifice in all its forms.
He gives Himself as our food: His flesh, no longer too holy
for the forgiven sinner to receive, becomes part of ours;
and, as might have been added, even His Blood itself,
the very Life of the sacrifice, too holy in the old days
ever to be received, and never imparted to any offerer,
priest, or layman, more closely than by an external sprinkling, is given to every Christian worshipper to drink.
Through Him therefore let us offer up our sacrifice continually. It has meant already the leaving the old world,
the losing of our old life, in going with Him in His sin-
offering without the gate; but at this stage, the writer
says, it will resemble not the sin-offering but the peace-
offering; and such an offering is not outward only but inward; it means a thankful heart; and, even more, it means
a practical life, like Christ's, Who went about doing good,
and giving everywhere all that He had to give. That life
of doing God's will, of self-dedication, is part of our own
offering, as it was of His. And with such sacrifices God is
well pleased. He accepts them, and He transforms them.

I have dwelt upon this passage because it illustrates
more than one feature in the New Testament language
about sacrifice. That language assumes an understanding
of its meaning in the readers to whom the Epistles were
addressed. It is therefore allusive, not explanatory. It is
incidental to an argument, not a deliberate exposition of
Jewish, or pagan, or even Christian sacrifice as such. Even
in Hebrews, which is so full of sacrificial thought that it
sometimes seems as if the subject of the Epistle is sacrifice,
the treatment of sacrifice is really subordinate to the
main thesis of the Incarnation and Redemption. And once
the contrast, so fully drawn out, between the Jewish and
the Christian sacrifice is reached there is still no full
treatment of either. That is, I believe, the key to the
difficulties created by some of the passages in the Epistle
which seem to assert that whatever our Lord's sacrifice is

it is finished: *e.g.* "But he, when he had offered one sacrifice for sins for ever, sat down on the right hand of God".[1] The one special form of Jewish sacrifice that is dwelt upon in detail is the sin-offering in its fullest form on the Day of Atonement; and the treatment of our Lord's sacrifice corresponds to that. But the language of the Epistle must be taken as a whole; and the full scheme of Jewish sacrifice must be seen behind even that. If this had been always done there would have been less controversy, and, what matters more, less apparent reason for controversy. The Epistle, indeed, if it insists on anything, insists on the continuance of our Lord's High Priesthood. He is a Priest for ever, and a Priest of a fuller kind at once older and newer than that of the Aaronic priesthood, with the limitations with which in its very growth and improvement it had been made ineffective. Melchizedek belongs to the days before specialisation had narrowed the functions either of priest or king. Our Lord's Priesthood belongs to the later time when, with all the gains which specialisation had brought, the offices of king and priest, as well as of prophet, could only find their perfection in One in Whom they were once more combined. But His Priesthood in becoming perfect cannot cease to be real. It cannot be a mere memory. Like His Kingship, it continues. He has entered into the holy place—once for all, it is true. He does not need to re-enter every year, like the Jewish priest; and there His work is to sanctify, by bringing His outpoured life before the face of God, as the blood was sprinkled on the mercy-seat. But the old entrance was a momentary act, to clear off the ceremonial—or hardly more than the ceremonial—defilements of a year. His entrance is to cleanse the human conscience from dead works to serve the living God. That needs doing every day, and every year, while time lasts. It avails for every new act of sin; it gives the power for every further act of dedication, of the doing of God's will. It is no longer only negative, as removing some of the sins of the past; it is, what the old sacrifices never were, positive, constructive,

[1] Heb. x. 12; so i. 3, viii. 2.

grace-giving. It looks forward as well as backward. It is
the living force without which the new life cannot be
lived. He entered, "now to appear in the presence of God
for us": the "appearance" is not merely His being there
(παρεῖναι), but ἐμφανισθῆναι, "a being made manifest, a
presenting Himself". His intercession therefore is that of
a priest; and if to intercede is to remind God, to make a
memorial before Him, as we have seen;[1] if that conception
was familiar to the Jewish mind; if it was bound up, in the
ceremony of the 'Azkārāh, with the idea of sacrifice, we
have again an illustration of the way in which the fragmentary treatment of sacrifice in the Epistle can be filled
out—must indeed be filled out, if we are to find a meaning
for its language as a whole. For He is expressly described
as still a λειτουργός, a ministering priest; and the function of priesthood is described as to offer gifts and sacrifices for sins. For those expressions we have to find a
content. The general sense of the Epistle must govern
the interpretation of individual passages; and, further,
the general sense of the New Testament must govern the
interpretation of an individual book. And, in regard to
sacrifice, since all New Testament language is fragmentary
and allusive, the ultimate factor in our decision, whether
as to separate passages or as to separate books, must be
our knowledge of Jewish sacrifice as a whole. We cannot
so stress the passages in Hebrews which describe our
Lord as sitting, as to explain away those other passages
elsewhere which show Him as standing,[2] any more than
we may use the latter to explain away the former. Both
are the language of symbol; and it should in these days be
abhorrent to us so to literalise or materialise heaven as to
think of them in any other way than as expressing different
sides of our Lord's eternal activity.[3]

Again, much, if not all, of the difficulty as to the
beginning and the ending of our Lord's priestly work
disappears if we remember the normal procedure of

[1] Above, p. 21; pp. 211 f.　　　　　[2] Acts vii. 55; Rev. v. 6.
[3] See for a full treatment of the supposed ending of our Lord's sacrificial work,
S. C. Gayford in J. T. S. vol. xiv. pp. 458-467 (a review of Dr. A. J. Tait's *Heavenly
Session of our Lord*).

contemporary sacrifice. The Epistle speaks of the Jewish High Priest as "officiating" throughout the sin-offering. But the occasion is the Day of Atonement; and on that day, in apparent exception to the "rule", the High Priest himself slew the victim. The rule is that the work of the priest, as priest, does not begin until after the death. The victim is killed by the person on whose behalf the offering is made; in the case of the sin-offering, the sinner. The High Priest kills on the Day of Atonement because he is offering for the whole people, of whom he is one. It is therefore natural, when the Epistle is taken by itself, to regard our Lord's High Priestly work as beginning with the Cross. Hence the discussions as to His supposed Aaronic priesthood on earth, and His priesthood after the order of Melchizedek in heaven. On the other hand, the Epistle says quite definitely that He was a Priest after the order not of Aaron but of Melchizedek; and upon that Priesthood He entered after His earthly work was finished. First come the days of His flesh, of His prayers, His strong crying and tears, His learning obedience by the things which He suffered; and then He is made perfect, becomes the author of salvation, and is named of God a High Priest after the order of Melchizedek;[1] or, "as a forerunner Jesus entered for us" within the veil, "having become a high priest for ever after the order of Melchizedek."[2]

The Priestly work proper begins, therefore, after the Death. The sacrifice indeed begins before the work of the Priest. But the Cross is not itself the Sacrifice. It stands in its place—and that an essential place—in the whole course of the sacrificial action, but is not either its beginning or its end. If we could once "write off" the later error, of which I shall attempt to draw out the consequences in Part III., which made the Christian world identify sacrifice with death, there would be no need to challenge the continuance of our Lord's sacrificial work in Heaven. Once the fatal association of sacrifice with death is established, such a challenge, indeed, becomes a

[1] Heb. v. 7-10.   [2] Heb. vi. 20.

necessity. At all costs the Cross itself must be vindicated. The Cross is all-sufficient. By His death our Lord
achieved His final victory. That Death cannot be repeated. It cannot, by any fresh suggestion of His dying,
be supplemented. It does, once for all, all that His Death
can do. The common use of the word "crucial" is theologically accurate; the Cross is decisive; it is the turning-
point in human history and in the conflict between right
and wrong, between man's better self and his lower,
between God and all that is against God. But once the
idea of sacrifice is concentrated upon the death of the
sacrificial victim, the Cross becomes the Altar, Christ's
sacrifice is finished at His Death; and loyalty to the Cross
compels a reading of the Epistle to the Hebrews; which
excludes for Him all priestly and sacrificial work from
that moment onwards.

What the writer to the Hebrews has in mind, and with
him the other writers of the New Testament, is a world
in which such an error as the equating of sacrifice with
death would have been inconceivable. He, and they, use
the language of sacrifice—the language of the whole
world, Hebrew and pagan alike, of their own times—
with an accuracy which passed in later days almost completely from Christians of every school of thought. I have
already shown that they have in mind the later stages of
sacrifice which came after the death—the use of the blood,
the offering upon the altar, the meal. And they use the
language appropriate to each—not with the definition of
a technical treatise, but as men speak of things with
which they are by habit familiar. I hesitate to lay stress
upon one aspect of this accuracy more than upon another. But in one sense the supreme test of it is in the
place which is occupied, in all the writers who touch the
subject—and it is only St. James and St. Jude who do not
touch it directly at all—, by the blood in relation to the
death. I cannot here give detailed evidence. That has been
done, convincingly, by Dr. W. Milligan.[1] "It is a fact

---

[1] W. Milligan, *The Resurrection of our Lord*, 3rd ed., Note 56 and Appendix,
pp. 274-304.

R

worth noting", he says,[1] "that the almost uniform practice of the Sacred Writers (exceptions can be easily explained) is to ascribe our salvation to the 'blood', not to
the 'death' of Christ; and the two terms, blood and death,
are not synonymous." For the blood is the life. The work
of our redemption was accomplished, it is true, by death;
but nowhere, either in the Synoptic Gospels, or in the rest
of the New Testament, is the death regarded as an end in
itself. Christ dies in order that He may live. The victim
was killed in the old sacrifices, but never that it might
simply be destroyed. Sin brings death as its consequence:
the offerer's, or the penitent sinner's, slaying of his own
victim means that he accepts that consequence; but he
does it in order that, through the death to the old life,
he may live to the new: else sacrificial death were symbolic suicide. The blood, in fact, needs to be dissociated
from the idea of death. To us, with our modern associations, it is merely the evidence, the revolting evidence, of
slaughter and destruction. To the men of the ancient
world it was not revolting, but precious. It was life, once
prisoned and misused, now released. It was more than
that. It was the life which was at once their own and
God's, the holiest thing, therefore, that they knew. And,
once alienated from God by sin, in its shedding it was
released. It could be taken to Him, and the life, once
reunited with Him, could be, in a measure only, it is true,
by sprinkling, but still in a measure, imparted to them.
The Cross therefore looks both backwards and forwards.
It means, as regards the past, death; as regards the future,
since the blood is poured out, it is the surrender, and
therefore the release, of life.

That there should be confusion, to some extent, in the
mention of the Cross, or of the death, of our Lord is inevitable. We owe indeed all that followed on his death to
the fact that He died. It is right therefore that we should
"preach Christ crucified". No one can always analyse the
meaning of the Cross whenever he mentions it or thinks
of it. We cannot blame Christian writers of the period

[1] *Op. cit.* p. 281.

when the fatal identification between sacrifice and death began for their mistake. When they were speaking of the Cross they were speaking of something which, taken as a whole, was the critical part—the turning-point—in the sacrificial action; and since the process of the death is also the process of the surrender of life there is a sense in which the further stage of the sacrifice, the dealing with the blood, is already, in the death, beginning. But the death is only made effective when the work of the blood begins, and after, or with, it the further stages also.

But in the New Testament writers the blood is given its full force. They know their subject. They may sometimes speak of the death without distinguishing its backward from its forward look. But where they do distinguish—as they most commonly do—their meaning is plain. St. John, for instance, thinks of our Lord in the opening verses of the first Epistle, in the terms of the sin-offering: "He is the propitiation for our sins";[1] and it is "the blood of Jesus his Son" which "cleanseth us from all sin".[2] So it is the blood upon which he throws the emphasis at the end: "This is he that came by water and by blood, even Jesus Christ; not with (or in —R.V.m.) the water only but with the water and with the blood".[3] So St. Peter: "in sanctification of the Spirit, unto obedience and sprinkling of the blood of Jesus Christ";[4] "Ye were redeemed . . . with precious blood, as of a lamb without blemish and without spot, even the blood of Christ".[5] So St. Paul—bringing out the backward look of death, as death, and the forward look of blood, as life—"while we were yet sinners, Christ died for us. Much more then, being now justified by His blood, shall we be saved. . . ."[6] So, again, four times over, in Revelation; e.g. he "loosed us from our sins in His blood".[7]

All this—and other passages might be quoted—bears on the atoning aspect of the surrendered life. But the use of the blood goes further. It is the means by which

---

[1] 1 Jn. ii. 2.   [2] 1 Jn. i. 7.   [3] 1 Jn. v. 6.
[4] 1 Pet. i. 2.   [5] 1 Pet. i. 18 f.   [6] Rom. v. 8 f,
[7] Rev. i. 5, R.V.m. See also v. 9, vii. 14, xii. 11,

we appropriate to ourselves the full life of the new community. That is its significance in the Eucharist—implied in the accounts of the Institution, and drawn out in St. John's Gospel. Here, at least, we need not stay to discuss how far either the words or the substance of the teaching in St. John vi. are our Lord's own and how far they embody the interpretation and reflection of the writer. I should myself accept them as giving the substance, and in some cases more, of what our Lord actually said: for it is difficult otherwise to account for the apparent ease with which the disciples a year afterwards could receive His words about His Blood at the Last Supper. But they are, at the least, evidence for what the writer, and through him the Apostolic Church in sixty or seventy years' experience, had found to be the ultimate meaning of the blood. It is upon it that the setting of the story throws the emphasis. The feeding of the multitude was a sign of something beyond itself. There is, first, a summary of a simple conversation, arising, naturally enough, between the Lord and some of those whom He had fed (verses 25-34). He gives them, in its simplest form, in the first "discourse" (for the narrative distinguishes three, to different audiences), the teaching which we have seen to be implied in St. Mark: its key-note is, "I am the Bread of life" (verses 35-40). An inner ring of the general multitude, those who had known Him as a boy at Nazareth, and whom we can almost see pushing up to the front places in the first discourse with a natural sense of proprietorship in the new prophet, are heard challenging something that to them, of all people, was an obvious puzzle: "How doth he now say, I am come down out of heaven?" To them, because they ought to have understood Him better than the rest, He takes His teaching, in His own and the traditional prophetic method, alike in mercy and in judgment, one step further; and the climax of the second discourse is "the bread which I will give is my flesh, for the life of the world" (verses 41-51). That proved a new problem, that we may call sacrificial, or theological; and it became a matter for controversial and critical discussion among those who would reflect on such things: "The Jews . . . strove with one another (were striving—ἐμάχοντο), saying, How can this man give us his flesh to eat?" They were accustomed to the idea of eating sacrificial flesh, but the flesh only of animals. This sounds like human sacrifice: does he mean that he is another Isaac? and even the human sacrifices in the dawn of Hebrew history stopped short at the burnt-offering stage: the fathers knew nothing of eating human flesh. And the simple answer to that, if our Lord had been minded to give it at once, would have been in the thought of the Ascension: "It is the spirit that quickeneth; the flesh profiteth nothing". But before He could say that, there was more to be brought out; and it comes in the third discourse (verses 52-59), delivered as a synagogue sermon while these discussions were in the air. These theological disputants ought to have understood;[1] and therefore again, both in mercy and in judgment, He develops the former teaching. "You are held", He says, "in the limitations of your own sacrifices. For the true sacrifice you need what they cannot give. You eat the flesh: you know, up to a point, what that ought to mean, for what your sacrificial victims are worth; but you cannot drink the blood. But the climax, the meaning, the purpose, of sacrifice is life. That is what my sacrifice will give, and alone can give. Except ye eat the flesh of the Son of man *and* drink his blood, ye have not life in yourselves": the flesh of representative manhood, in which— for flesh always has the sense of the common nature as shared[2]—they will realise their corporate unity alike with all the children of God and with their Father; and still more the blood, which is the Life of mankind, and will be theirs, not in mere outward sprinkling, but in themselves by the act of drinking. It is to be, in the experience of perfect sacrifice, not the flesh only but the

[1] Cf. John iii. 10 to Nicodemus: "Art thou the teacher of Israel, and understandest not these things?" So He might have said in the synagogue at Capernaum.
[2] So St. Paul in Romans xi. 14, in speaking of Israel: "If by any means I may provoke to jealousy them that are my flesh, and may save some of them". And see above, pp. 35, 186.

blood: "He that eateth my flesh and drinketh my blood hath eternal life".

That was the climax. And St. John remembers its effect. He says nothing of its reception by the Jews. That, no doubt, was hostile. It marked a new and a more serious crisis. It was a challenge to all the ideas upon which friend and enemy alike had been brought up. To drink blood! That is to tamper with the Holy: that is either a supreme achievement or it is a blasphemous venture into the forbidden. They dare not even listen. "Many therefore of his disciples, when they heard this, said, This is a hard saying; who can hear it?" And to them He could give, hoping this time that mercy would prevail over judgment, the final answer: "Will you be able to understand my ascension? That will show you what I mean. I am to be transformed. I am to pass into the new world where, indeed, I am already, and pray God that you may be one day, at home. The blood of the new sacrifice will make that possible for you. It is the spirit that quickeneth: the flesh profiteth nothing: the words that I have spoken unto you are spirit, and are life."

And to many these were, indeed, as to the Jews, words of judgment. But not to all. It was a crisis out of which the twelve, at least—all of them as it seems—came triumphant. Peter was their spokesman. His answer shows that, so far as they could, in the exaltation of the moment, they were feeling their way to what He meant. "Thou hast the words of eternal life. And we have believed and know that thou art the Holy One of God." There lay the solution. Others may fear Holiness still. But they know Him Whom they have believed. If Jesus *is* Holiness, "fear not" takes the place of "fear". He is the Life. And, with perfect naturalness, the words in which He sadly says that not even all the twelve are safe, take the form which is in the Synoptic Gospels appropriate to the moments of the revelation of the Holy: "One of you is a devil"[1] (verses 60-71).

Here, indeed, as in many other cases of the use of actual

---

[1] See above, p. 163.

sacrificial language, the technical terms carry with them, expressly, the fundamental principles of the Gospel. We are brought through the sixth chapter of St. John to a point where sacrifice proves a conception around which at once much of his apparently untechnical material must be grouped. As with his picture of the Good Shepherd, who lays down his life for the sheep, so with his interpretation of the Bread of Life as the flesh and blood of the Son of Man. To these two sacrificial passages is directly related all that he says elsewhere about the Spirit, about Life, about Light which is the condition of Life, and stands contrasted with the darkness of the sin from which we are delivered, about incorporation and indwelling. So it is with the sacrificial language of the other writers. When they thought of our Lord's work and of the Christian experience in terms of sacrifice they were not precluded from using other language about it in whole or in part; but to them, whatever else it might be, it was sacrifice. And the idea of such sacrifice, when they used it, covered the whole range of what they taught and felt. Christianity in them, like the religion of the Old Testament in its earlier stages, is not yet specialised. They were not consciously formulating a theology, still less any one or more of the departments of modern theology. They were not working out a system of personal or social ethics. They were not deliberately framing a cultus to express truth or conduct in terms of worship. What they have left us provides material out of which the Church in after years found all these, and more than these. That progress was inevitable, unless Christianity were to become in the wrong sense a religion of a book, tied to the letter and not freed by the spirit. Hence the later developments in the direction of sacrifice, which we shall have to trace.

But in one sense the relating of principles to formal expression, of truth and life to worship, is at least prepared for. If the Church from the first saw the new life as a sanctuary; if sonship to the Father, and membership of the Kingdom, were only other terms for service in the presence of God, it was inevitable that the content of the life should at once be expressed in terms and acts of worship. And since no worship in a sanctuary could be conceived of in those days in any but a sacrificial way, it was to be expected that from the first the language and, so far as possible, the acts of sacrifice should find their place in it. What I have attempted to show is therefore, in the first place, that sacrificial thought and language, and the underlying principles of sacrifice, were at once the inheritance of our Lord and the New Testament writers from the past, the material for much of their own thoughts and words and actions, and were capable of expressing the whole content of the Christian revelation. I have said nothing of, nor do I now propose to dwell upon, the popular theory that St. Paul's sacramental teaching was imported by him into a religion that was neither sacrificial nor sacramental from the mystery-cults of the Graeco-Roman world. It is possible that that theory is less popular than it was, and at least in its extreme form has had its day. In any case, there are many books in which it is discussed and criticised. I shall venture to hope that we have found enough evidence to justify us in saying that no such theory is needed to account for the character of Pauline and of subsequent Christianity. The religion of Jesus implies sacrifice. He instituted at least one sacrament—that of sustenance—and the evidence is indeed strong enough to justify us in still believing that He also instituted the other—the sacrament of initiation, or, as we commonly call it, of baptism. The inner meaning of the Eucharist lay already to hand in the contemporary religion of the Jews. Baptism was a Jewish rite. It had been linked with Christianity by the work of the Baptist, and in particular by our Lord's own Baptism. It seems certain that proselytes were baptized in New Testament times; and baptism as early as that meant repentance, through the natural Jewish symbolism of cleansing. And Mr. Abrahams quotes sayings that suggest new birth, though these may be later than the Christian era.[1]

---

[1] I. Abrahams, *op. cit.*, Series I. ch. iv.

And in the second place, we have tested the sacrificial language and thoughts of the New Testament by the norm of sacrifice as understood by contemporary Jews. We have found that Jewish sacrifice is, on the one hand, realised in practice under three main forms; the sin-offering, representing the idea of the surrendered life; the burnt-offering, that of the life dedicated and transformed; the peace-offering, that of the life bestowed and shared. And, on the other hand, in the general conception of sacrifice, of which each of these are special expressions, there is a well-understood sequence of significant actions or stages. It begins with the approach—the drawing near, which we have in Hebrews[1]—of the sinner with his victim. The second action is the identification of the sinner with the victim by the pressing of his hands upon its head. The third is the killing of the victim, not by the priest, but by him on whose behalf it is to be offered. Then, and not before then, the priest begins his work. He takes the life, voluntarily surrendered, into the presence of God, and thereby atonement—at-one-ment—is made. And the fifth stage is the offering upon the altar, and the acceptance by God in the fire from heaven which, so far from destroying, transforms; and the last, with which alone the sacrifice is complete, is the meal in which the worshipper is fed by the food from heaven.

That was the Jewish outline. And St. Paul found something not unlike it in the Greek world. The typical procedure of the Greek blood-offerings bears at least a sufficient resemblance to that of the Hebrew sacrifice to make his conception of the Eucharist in 1 Corinthians x. and xi., both expressed and implied, intelligible to Greek as well as to Jewish readers. The altar is the point of contact with the god. The victim is brought near; and a living touch between it and the god is effected, both by throwing some of its hair into the altar-fire and by throwing forward barley stalks (οὐλόχυται), which have been placed on the altar so that they strike it on its forehead. It is killed: the blood is caught in a vessel; parts of the flesh

---

[1] Heb. x. 22; so iv. 16, vii. 25, x. 1, xi. 6, xii. 18, 22.

are placed on the altar and burnt; other parts provide a sacred meal for the worshippers. The salient points appear to be the approach; the killing before the victim is placed on the altar; the dealing with the blood; the offering on the altar through fire; and the communion feast.[1]

By such a test we find that the sacrificial language of the New Testament is proved accurate. It is in such language that it prepares the way for the later expression of worship in terms of sacrifice. And in such a scheme of sacrificial thought the stages of our Lord's work for men naturally find their place. The approach and the identification are blended in the Incarnation: in the picture of the prodigal son drawing near to his father's home, and the Good Shepherd returning with the lost sheep. The sinners slay the victim: the High Priest Caiaphas, who took the lead in bringing Him to the Cross, prophesied, in the sense of speaking more truly than he knew, when he said that it was expedient that one man should die for the people. He who is both Victim and High Priest passes with His blood—the life of man, now released from its exile in the far country of his sins—through the Veil, the torn and broken body of the limited life in which we dwell apart from God, into God's presence in the Heavenly Sanctuary. There He pleads, intercedes, atones. His Body —the human nature which He came to redeem and to dedicate in the doing of God's will—is offered in its perfect obedience, and transformed by the Spirit, in Resurrection, Ascension, and Session, into the body of His glory: it is freed from the limitations of its earthly life, when it was the body of His humiliation, and becomes spiritual and heavenly. It is only so that it can henceforth exist, or be known, in heaven or in earth. And, in the end, He gives His new manhood to His own in the gifts of His new Body and of His blood which is His and their eternal life.

That, and nothing less, is His Sacrifice. Not the Atonement only, however we may define that, but the Incarna-

---

[1] *Encycl. of Religion and Ethics*, vol. xi., art. "Sacrifice" (Greek), p. 15 (a description of Homeric sacrifice; but see the whole article).

tion also, in the fullness of its meaning, belong to it in all
its stages. The Sacrifice is not the Death alone; nor the
pleading with the blood alone; nor the offering upon the
altar "in heaven"; nor the act of Communion alone. Later
language may speak of the Death as sacrifice, or of the
offering; and in the limitations of speech and of thought
such words may be allowed. But it would be equally
accurate to call our Lord's coming into the world and His
earthly life, or the communion feast, sacrifice. We do not,
it is true, commonly so speak of them. Each stage is
sacrificial. All together make the One Sacrifice. We shall
presently trace the point at which what is excusable,
though technically inaccurate, becomes disastrous alike
for doctrine and for worship.

In the New Testament we are not within sight of that.
It leaves us with truth and life conceived, and accurately
conceived, in terms of sacrifice; and with both from
beginning to end conceived, and vitalised, in terms of the
sanctuary and of worship. And, without doubt, it leaves
us with the Eucharist in so many words described as
constituting, for us, at least the last of the six stages in the
Sacrifice. It has brought us, through the general conceptions of intercession, of unity in the Body through
baptism and in the new life of self-dedication, as well
as in the thought of joy and thanksgiving—Eucharist,
εὐχαριστία—to the point at which the earliest writings
outside the canon, and the earliest liturgies, develop its
underlying thought. It is to that development, and to its
faithfulness or its unfaithfulness to the standard once for
all laid down, that we now turn.

PART III

AFTER THE NEW TESTAMENT

CHAPTER I

INTRODUCTORY

THE purpose of the last part of this book is strictly
limited. I am not attempting a history of eucharistic
developments as a whole; nor indeed any complete
account either of the idea of eucharistic sacrifice, or of the
different controversies which arose about it in the course
of time. I desire now to assume, after what has been said
—with what degree of justification the reader must judge
—that the fundamental principles of sacrifice, whether
called by that name or not, as well as a certain degree of
use of sacrificial language, were part of the true New
Testament tradition. I have attempted also to show that
if the New Testament writers did think of the category
of sacrifice as providing a way, if only one way, of expressing what our Lord does for us, it could only be on the
general lines to which they were, by their own Jewish
training, accustomed; and in Part I. my object was to
describe what those general lines were. I shall now only
touch upon enough of the history to show that, as time
went on, the ideas of sacrifice changed. Ultimately they
took a form wholly unlike that which they bear both in
the Old Testament and in the New. We shall see first then
how this change occurred; and what its results were when
it did occur. My purpose is one of reconciliation. I hope
that it will become clear that both the modern recoil from
the idea of sacrifice in connection with the Atonement,
and the whole of the controversies and divisions about the
eucharistic sacrifice, which have vexed the Church since
the beginning of the Reformation, are due to the change;

that, granted the theory of sacrifice which came to prevail, they were inevitable; and that, if we return to the true and original scheme or idea of what sacrifice really was, they are no longer necessary. I shall not be pleading for a compromise. I shall aim at showing, mainly with regard to the Eucharist, that neither side in the great controversy need be ashamed of its part, or seek to explain it away.

But the change will, I think, be better appreciated if we review the position in the early centuries. I cannot trace the development in detail; and the suggestions which I may have to make as to the reasons for it may not commend themselves. But of the fact of the change there is no doubt.

It may be well that I should offer, as an introduction to this part of our study, some general observations on the problem of sacrifice, and indeed of the Eucharist generally, as it presents itself to us at the present day. For the Church of England, at any rate, the problem is immediate and urgent.

There are, it will be agreed, three statements of the problem, or, as I should prefer to say, three aspects of it, which are familiar, and all of which, as I at least believe, are necessary.

(1) "I will have mercy and not sacrifice." It would be agreed on all hands that this is one fundamental principle of God's dealings with men. For it we have the authority of a long tradition, reaching back to the highest moral teaching of Prophets and Psalmists, and confirmed unequivocally by our Lord Himself. It is confirmed, moreover, by the conscience and the thought, the heart and the reason, of every Christian. Whatever may be the external expression, in doctrine or in worship, of man's duty towards God, or of God's redeeming work towards man, the inward requirement is obedience; and of obedience in the inward sense of conformity to the will and character of God: "Lo, I come to do Thy will, O God". The motive in man for the fulfilling of that requirement is love; and the motive for man's motive is God's love for man. That is the teaching alike of the Old

Testament and of the New: pictured, for the former, in the story of Hosea and his wife; summed up for ever, in the latter, by St. John's "We love, because He first loved us".

(2) "Christ was once offered." I take this as a typical statement of the all-sufficiency of the redeeming work of Christ. The sacrifice of Christ, whatever that phrase actually proves to mean, cannot be anything but unique. It is "the full, perfect, and sufficient sacrifice, oblation, and satisfaction for the sins of the whole world". I need not elaborate this: for, whatever way may be found of stating the atoning work of our Lord—on any theory, that is, of the Atonement—it is all-embracing and all-sufficient.

(3) "This our sacrifice of praise and thanksgiving." It is difficult to find a phrase as typical of the third element in our problem as those which I have given for the other two. But if what I have said elsewhere as to the Hebrew usage is true, these familiar words from the English Prayer Book cover all possible views of it. Whether what we offer in the Eucharist is praise and thanksgiving, or something—or Someone—offered by us in praise and thanksgiving, it cannot be disputed that from the first the idea of sacrifice is bound up at least with the corporate expression of Christian life. Even in the New Testament, as we have seen, the idea itself is linked with the Eucharist, at least so far as the act of communion is concerned. And from the earliest times after the New Testament, the associations of sacrifice, first as offering, then as propitiation, gather with increasing definiteness round the whole of the eucharistic action. I am not prejudging here the sense in which the common phrase, "the eucharistic sacrifice", should be interpreted. What I venture to assert is the simple fact, in the widest sense, of the sacrificial character of eucharistic tradition from the beginning until the time when that side of eucharistic belief appeared to conflict with the other two vital aspects of the faith.

The question before us to-day, as for so many centuries,

S

is whether the third, or even the second, of these aspects conflicts with the first, or the third with the first and second. In the language, and with the associations, of controversy, ancient and modern, they have sometimes been distinguished as respectively the ethical, the Evangelical, and the Catholic views of our Lord's work and of the Christian response to it. But I dare to hope that my readers, at any rate while they follow what I have to say in the rest of this book, will forget both the associations of controversy and the limitations which controversy has imposed upon these three great conceptions. None need, if properly understood, exclude the others: nothing can claim to be truly Evangelical unless it be also ethical; and nothing has a right to the full meaning of the name of "Catholic" unless it is also both ethical and Evangelical.

All three of these fundamental ideas are indeed not only primitive, but, as properly understood, necessary to each other, and each is incomplete without not one only, but both of the others. No solution of our present difficulties can be satisfactory which fails to do justice to each and to all.

We have passed, or we ought to hope that we may pass,[1] from the habit of mind which sees no end to a controversy but the elimination, or the suppression, of one side or the other. That, as Dr. Mozley pointed out in his celebrated passage in the Essay on Development, which Dr. Holland said should be hung as a charm round the neck of every English Churchman troubled with antinomies, is not the spirit of the Catholic, but of the heretic. The Catholic[2] faith accepts a paradox, and gives full value to both its sides. The heretic is too logical to be complete. The controversialist, as such, asserts that he may deny: the Church of Christ in the fullness

---

[1] I had dared to say this with less qualification when I wrote the first draft of this passage before the last stages of the *Prayer Book* discussions.

[2] Dr. Mozley in the passage referred to used the word "Catholic" as describing the spirit and tradition of the ancient and undivided Church, the Church of the Councils: it is the sense in which all English Churchmen would accept it, and in which I use it here and elsewhere in this context.

and breadth of her teaching only denies that she may assert.

The issue may, indeed, be avoided. It is true that controversy may grow into bitterness: heretical logic may lead to denial; the condemning of heresy may lead to the rending of the Body of Christ; but bitterness, denial, and schism may be wounds willingly incurred in the battle for truth. To avoid the issue may be to prefer peace to truth. Compromise is less Christian than controversy: Christ said "I am the Truth": He did not say I am the Peace, but, actually, "I came not to send peace on earth but a sword".

In the present case the three points of view of which I have spoken provide us with two antinomies. The Christian religion knows no sacrifice; and yet it is sacrificial through and through. That is one; and the other is apparently as insoluble. There is no sacrifice but that of Christ our Redeemer; and yet the Eucharist is a sacrifice.

How can we hold, as true Catholics,[1] with equal loyalty to both sides of these two antinomies? We cannot in either case avoid the problem, or solve it by removing one of its two factors.

That is the situation which we have to face to-day, and to the facing of which these pages are an attempt, in some small measure, to contribute.

Both antinomies are concerned with the doctrines of the Atonement and of the Eucharist. I say this in order that we may see where we stand. But perhaps a caveat may be entered at the outset against over-classification. To isolate a particular head of doctrine is undoubtedly helpful for the purposes of the theologian, but it is a process of the laboratory or of the dissecting-room, not of actual life.

Such classification is only safe while that is remembered and the results are tested at every stage in the living body itself. We have to remember that we are studying the Living Christ, Who is Himself the Truth. No one part of Him, as Truth, is itself except as an organ of a body in its place in the whole. And I believe that this is

[1] See footnote 2 on preceding page.

especially true of the Atonement and the Eucharist. It is familiar to students of theology, but I doubt if it is widely realised by other Christians, that there are many of the ordinary headings of doctrine upon which there is as yet no authoritative pronouncement by the undivided Church. The doctrine of the Holy Trinity, of the relation of the Father to the Son and to the Holy Spirit, received its formulation at the Council of Nicaea (A.D. 325), and the doctrine of the Incarnation at that and at the three General Councils which followed it (Constantinople, A.D. 381; Ephesus, A.D. 431; Chalcedon, A.D. 451). But, great as has been the volume of theological writing upon them, there has been no corresponding formulation of the doctrines of the Atonement, the Sacraments, the Church, the Ministry, or of Inspiration.

Is it too much to say that the Church has known three great dogmatic ages? The first was that of the Holy Trinity, or of the Father. The second was that of the Incarnation—of the Son. Both these doctrines were, at least for the time being, completely formulated, and that formulation stands, except so far as in the light of further achievement there may be scope and demand for further analysis. There remains the dogmatic age of the Holy Spirit, which began, in one sense, with the Pelagian controversy, and in which we are living now. It is in the understanding of the Person and work of the Holy Spirit alone that the problems of the Atonement and the other undefined branches of Theology can find their solution; and it is upon these that Christian thought has consciously exercised itself since the period of the Great Councils. The relation of the saving work of Christ to society and to the individual; the relation of Christ, in Sacraments, through the Spirit, to ourselves; the relation of the outward and visible to the inward and spiritual, alike in the Sacraments, the Church, and the Ministry—all elements of the study of the spiritual Body of the glorified Christ—; and the way in which the Church is led into all truth by the voice of those to whom God has spoken ; all these are parts of the study of the Holy Spirit. As the thinking out

of the implications of the facts of Christian experience
continues, as it passes from the Godhead to the Incarnation, and from the Incarnation to the Spirit, it moves
inevitably into regions in which at every stage the concrete has to be considered more and more alongside the
abstract. It was of course the distinguishing mark of
Christian speculation from the beginning, that metaphysical thought was based upon data mediated through
physical experience. It begins with the historical fact of
the Word made flesh, or, if some prefer to regard that
formula as itself the product of speculation, with the
historical facts of the earthly life of Jesus as known from
the first in the experience of those facts, and with the
deductions drawn from them by His first disciples. Those
facts, so mediated, together with the Apostolic traditions
about them, are, at every stage, the touchstone and guide
of theological speculation. But it will not be denied that,
as speculation advances from the Eternal Being of God to
the union of God with man in Christ, and from that to
the manifold phases of the work of God in Christ through
the interplay of the Spirit with human individuals and
societies, the field of experience, the data for inductions,
the tests to be applied to deductions, widen with the
centuries. The records of religious experience, the actual
growth of the Church, the infinite variety of new exigencies which the movement of human history produces—
all these increase the raw material of concrete evidence
which has to be taken into account, side by side with
increasing knowledge of the deep things of God which
the Spirit, as our Lord promised, is always bringing out
of the welter of human life to those who know Him. It
is not surprising that we sometimes fail to see the wood
for the trees.

There were times in the history of the Old Testament
Church when the voice of prophecy seemed lost for ever.
No "word of the Lord" broke through the silence of the
long years between Isaiah, with his contemporaries in the
prophetic office, and Jeremiah and the other prophets of
the Decline and Fall of the Kingdom of Judah. But the

work of the Spirit of the prophets was being done; and the public crisis which produced Jeremiah, Nahum, and Zephaniah revealed also in Deuteronomy the result of the silent work of the intervening time. In the Exile the corporate life itself of the Church-Nation seemed to have been destroyed; and in the disillusionments of its first renewal again there seemed no hope of a prophetic revival. But there came not only the formal utterances of the post-exilic prophets, but the perfect flower of the prophetic spirit in the post-exilic Psalms, and with them the fruition of the silent thought and study of the Jewish institutions which the Exile had made possible. And the same alternation goes on. The great men of the eighth and seventh centuries, and the lesser men of the period of the return, had not yet made the world ready for the Christ. But the later centuries had each their part to play, and in the ecclesiastical and corporate decadence—as it seemed —of the intervening period, the work of preparation was still being done, as really, if not as manifestly, as by Isaiah and Jeremiah. We have only in recent years come to know how vital a part in the necessary developments was played by the teachers and seers of that time, and by the unknown and humble saints of whom was Jesus Christ according to the flesh.

"These things were written for our edification, upon whom the ends of the ages are come." We can look back, look out around us, and look forward, and take heart. We shall shrink, as in the light of the history of the Jewish Church we try to understand the history of the Christian, from the disheartening contrasts which we are accustomed to make between the Apostolic Age and the age of the Fathers, the age of the Fathers and the age of the Doctors, and the pessimistic implication, to which we are so given, that in our days even the age of the Doctors is gone by. The saying is often quoted that the heathen look to the past for their Golden Age and the Jews to the future. To-day neither the Christian Church as a whole, nor any part of it, can adopt the pagan outlook in this respect instead of the Jewish. "The old men that had seen the first house, when the foundation of this house was laid before their eyes, wept with a loud voice."[1] That was an alien cry: it was the pagan spirit. And it needed the prophet's answer: "The latter glory of this house shall be greater than the former, saith the Lord of hosts: and in this place will I give peace, saith the Lord of hosts".[2] We can no longer allow ourselves to look back to any period of the past for the golden age of the Christian Church—to Puritan times, to mediaeval, to the time of the Great Councils and the Fathers, even to the Apostolic Age itself. We look forward to the vision of the last two chapters of the Apocalypse. We have our part to do, in our day, a part which could not have been done by our forefathers, and which we dare not leave neglected to our children, in the building of Jerusalem.

It is nothing less than this that we are called to. We need to see ourselves as helping to work out the doctrine of the Holy Spirit. Decisions upon the Eucharist are nothing less than that. They become parts of the vital dogmatic development of the central positions of Christianity. That is at once the encouragement and the responsibility of the work to which the Church of England has now been called—is, indeed, called the more clearly by the apparent failure of one great attempt. We have to prove that "I believe in the Holy Ghost" is something that we really mean.

The two antinomies—or paradoxes—which have been stated above, connected as they are with the relation of the inward and the outward, and with the fundamental character of one of the two great Sacraments, must therefore be regarded as bearing directly on, and likely to be affected by, our belief in, and our conception of, the Holy Spirit. "Belief in, and conception of": because the faith which we are attempting to formulate is not a purely intellectual thing. It is an attempt to know a living Person, as all living persons are known, in the contact of daily life, and, from first to last, in that form of contact in which love and self-surrender have the same meaning.

[1] Ezra iii. 12.   [2] Hag. ii. 9.

We pledge ourselves, each of us, every time that we repeat the Creed, to a personal movement towards, and self-dedication to,[1] Him in Whom we believe, Father, Son, and Spirit. And if we can only put ourselves in, or ask Him to lead us into, this position, we have the first and best guarantee of a solution of our problems. The bitterness of controversy, and the desire for victory for our own views, disappear: we are at once a band of brothers, each and all seeking the same end, each with a contribution to make, and a cause which is not that of one individual or of a section, but nothing less than the whole cause of God. That, and that alone, is loyalty to the King and the Kingdom; that, and that alone, is the ancient Catholic motive.

And as we cannot separate love from thought, our faith from our conceptions about our faith, so we shall gain immeasurably if we keep in our minds the vital relations between specific problems such as those of the Atonement and the Eucharist and the progress of Christian thought about the Holy Spirit as a whole. It is because the study of sacrifice is vital to such special problems that it too has its bearing, and largely depends for its right understanding, on the belief in the Holy Spirit. And it is for this reason that I have attempted, at the outset of the last part of my book, to survey the field as a whole, that we may see where we stand. I believe that such a survey may help, both as giving in some degree the measure of our responsibility for what we are doing, and even more as an encouragement which, at the moment, we appear to need. For, unless I am wrong, there is far more reason to hope than we sometimes allow ourselves to realise, that the supposed contradictions in the three convictions outlined at the beginning of this chapter are not contradictions at all; and that without compromise or concession, without the removal of parts of each in order that the remainders may be ingeniously dovetailed into an unreal unity, we can arrive at a eucharistic settlement which gives full play to all three. Such a settlement, if it

---

[1] *"Credo in Deum"*, not *"Credo in Deo"*.

is to be accepted with equal readiness by us all, must bring out to the full the "ethical", the "Evangelical", the "Catholic" conceptions of our religion. It must give us a form of worship which expresses a genuine and inward self-dedication, and neither in ceremony nor in rite externalises religion into magic. It must do full justice to the fundamental Christian truths for which the reformers strove, and to which those who feel themselves to be the trustees of their tradition can never be disloyal. And it must be in the full stream of the historical inheritance of the Church from the earliest times; it must be unhesitatingly and uncompromisingly Catholic.

It is because I believe that in expressing our faith we commit ourselves to the belief that this thing is possible, that I ask my readers to follow me to the end of this study of sacrifice, especially in its bearing on the problems of the Eucharist.

Under the conditions in which these pages are written, such a study cannot be complete. To some the facts will be familiar, and, for them, it will be unnecessary. But I believe it to be true that for many centuries there has been, and in many quarters, and not least among convinced and comparatively well-instructed Christians and Church people, there is to-day at once a wide familiarity with sacrifice as an idea, and a strangely inadequate knowledge of the meaning of its terms. In view of this I make no apology for traversing what is in some respects familiar ground. But there are, at the same time, aspects of the use of the sacrificial idea which I believe have largely escaped notice. It has been to them that I have attempted already to draw attention; and in what follows I hope to show their bearing upon our present disagreements.

In any department of thought and study which has a long history it is, of course, necessary to test the meaning of the words which recur at different periods. No student is unaware that language shifts in its use, and that the same term may have one content at one time and a different one at another. This is as true of Christian theology as of any other subject. But it is, I think, more easy to recognise where the terms involved are specifically philosophical, or specifically historical—such as the philosophical terms which underlie the definitions of the Councils on the Holy Trinity or the Incarnation, or, to take a different example, the meaning of the word "bishop" in the literature respectively of the first, second, and third centuries.

Eucharistic theology, and, so far as the technical terms of sacrifice are concerned, the theology of the Atonement, have been less fortunate in this respect. The language of sacrifice has always been part of the popular, as well as of the scientific, stock of religious terminology. It has been taken too much for granted that what everyone used everyone must understand. Like every other branch of theology the eucharistic belief and doctrine of the Church has had a history of growth. It began, in the New Testament, as something taken for granted. Its implications (on any of the subsequent theories of its nature) were not realised. Whatever were the latent truths about the Eucharist, they were, in Bishop Gore's phrase about the Holy Trinity, "overheard rather than heard". "Men live first and think afterwards": experience and practical use precede analysis and formulation.

As we have seen, in the case of eucharistic theology the period of analysis and formulation was long deferred. The doctrine, whatever it was, was held unconsciously rather than consciously, for many centuries. The self-conscious period, in this case, did not begin until after Charlemagne's resettlement of Western Europe once more gave the Church freedom to think. She had long before, in the stress of questions and controversies, defined her beliefs on the Trinity and the Incarnation. There remained, as we have seen, the problem of the Holy Spirit. It was to this, in effect, that she addressed herself from one point of view in the controversy about grace, and from another, and that with which we are immediately concerned, in the eucharistic controversies which began with Paschasius Radbertus in the tenth century. From that time to this

the issues have been in doubt. There has been precisely
the procedure with which we are familiar in the fourth
and fifth centuries. God is One, and He is Three: it was
an illogical paradox which courted the logical solution of
escaping one of its sides. Christ is God, and He is Man—
and the logical answer was to explain away either His
Godhead or His Manhood. So with the Eucharist. There
are, in the language of our Catechism, the outward and
visible sign, and the inward and spiritual grace. There are
at once bread and wine, and the Body and the Blood. It
was the obvious difficulty. And the history of Christian
thought on this fresh form of the paradox of our faith has
been that of successive attempts to impugn the reality of
the one or the other—a history which has continued for
a thousand years, and is not complete yet.

Large as has been the place occupied in eucharistic
controversy by the problem of the eucharistic sacrifice,
it is undoubtedly true to say that the sacrificial question
has never been so thoroughly faced as the question of the
Presence. The causes of this difference are no doubt
manifold; but among them in particular are two. As I
have already suggested, there has been a half-conscious
assumption that the language, at least, of sacrifice was
familiarly understood. And there has also been the inevitable tendency to divide theology into separate subjects,
and to pursue them independently of each other. So far
as the idea of sacrifice was concerned, it belonged both to
the Atonement and to the Eucharist. It has therefore,
in a sense, fallen between two stools; its meaning has
been assumed under both headings and not studied
fully for its own sake. As a result, both departments of
theology have suffered. Sacrifice tends to be a difficulty
in each, although, properly understood, it should be a
help.

It is not that eucharistic theology begins with the
tenth century. Contributions had been made to it con-
tinuously, though not deliberately, from the New Testament onwards. It covers therefore a period of nineteen
hundred years. Terms connected with the Presence came

into use by degrees. None of them, as technical terms, belong to the whole history. There has therefore been less time for change in their meanings; and under the conditions of the scholastic theology, in which most of them were produced, there has been less possibility of change. But the terminology of sacrifice was inherited by Christianity from older religions: it had nine centuries to pass through before the deliberate study of the Eucharist began, and it has had a history of ten centuries since. There has therefore been a third difficulty through which the category of sacrifice has passed. Not only has it been assumed that its terms are generally understood; not only has it never, until recent years, received adequate study for its own sake; but there has been an unexampled length of time in which, under the cover of both these disadvantages, men have in fact unconsciously changed the meanings attaching to those terms.

Behind the normal and recognised history of eucharistic thought, there lies therefore a continually shifting background. Theologians and ordinary Christians spoke of sacrifice in connection with the Eucharist from the earliest times; but while such phrases as "the eucharistic sacrifice" have persisted, sacrifice has meant now one thing, and now another. Not only the idea of sacrifice itself has changed, but the content of the idea has changed also. What was taken for granted as belonging to it at one time has been less emphasised at a later period, ignored later still, and in the end often excluded from its scope. And for the most part such changes have been unrecognised. It follows therefore that at each stage, if we are to form accurate judgments on the eucharistic sacrifice itself, we must be alive to the varying senses in which words are used.

The sacrificial language of the Christian Church has suffered under two further disabilities, neither of which could have been avoided.

Its first period—that of the New Testament and of sub-Apostolic times—was one in which the Church was challenged, as it has never been challenged since, by other religions largely based on sacrifice. At first all, and for a long time most, Christians had been won over as adults from Judaism or paganism. They had been brought up amid sacrifices of another kind. The first instinct therefore of their new teachers was to insist that such sacrifices as they had known, whether Jewish or pagan, had no place in their new life. The earliest Christian writers could not use the language of sacrifice without grave risk of misunderstanding. Under these conditions their courage in adopting the sacrificial language which they did use— restrained and reserved as it was—is itself a vindication of the view that, whatever we are to find that sacrifice in itself really means, they regarded it as of the essence of the new religion. What is surprising, considering the difficulty under which they laboured, is not that they said so little about sacrifice, but that they said so much. But the fact of their reserve makes a special difficulty for, and gives a special direction to, our study of their meaning. Here less than anywhere—and it is dangerous everywhere —can we be content with the search for technical or half-technical terms. We have to go behind the concordance to the conceptions underlying what the writers said, to fundamental ideas of sacrifice.

The second disability has already been partly touched upon. The language of sacrifice as applied to the Eucharist, and with it other eucharistic language as well, has long passed from the schools of theology into the everyday use of practising Christians. Eucharistic controversy has touched ordinary people. They have felt that it concerns them more directly than, except here and there at a few periods, other branches of theology. Controversies change in tone so far as they become popular. They can pass, on their popular side, into the hands of those whose zeal outruns both their discretion and their sense of responsibility. In such a setting the issues can seem to become trivial. The line between the expert and the faddist can be passed; great principles soberly maintained become the war-cries of partisans. And they tend, in proportion, to be neglected by those whose hearts are set on the things that really seem to count. They become, like Silesia, not worth the bones of a Pomeranian Grenadier. There has been, without doubt, in the not very remote past, a banality in some forms of English controversy on the Eucharist, which, for some time, and too often, has blinded many of the best and most serious men, especially among the laity, to the real gravity of the principles at stake, and to the infinite possibilities that lie ready to be seized in the eucharistic life. A subject that was cradled in a half-silence, however necessary, that matured in controversy, and has sometimes sunk into triviality, is easily misunderstood.

Yet the very popularity of eucharistic controversies, in spite of the pettiness, the cheapness, the superficiality that it can bring in their train, is significant. And it is all the more significant because in a controversy there must be two sides. It means that, from whatever point of view the Eucharist is approached, it touches personal religion, and the religion of the common people, almost more widely than any other religious topic. For it is the point at which the central truths, as we call them, become operative on the individual soul. In the dust of battle the great Figure at the centre of the rite is obscured, and He may even pass out of sight.[1] But the very dust is evidence of the fact of Christ. It is because it is in the Lord's Supper, in the Holy Communion, in the Mass, that the plain man is face to face with Him, that the plain man cares so intensely what kind of presence He may be believed to vouchsafe, or what its connection is with His Cross, or how we may be said to join in His Sacrifice. Even the most disheartening details of eucharistic theology, the worst phases of eucharistic controversy, are witnesses in spite of themselves to the vital importance of the Eucharist for Christian faith and Christian life.

---

[1] "But, alas! how sad is the present condition of Christians, who have a communion disuniting. The Lord's Supper, ordained by our Saviour to conjoin our affections, hath disjoined our judgments. Yea, it is to be feared, lest our long quarrels about the manner of His Presence cause the matter of His absence, for want of charity to receive Him,"—Thomas Fuller, *Mixt Contemplations*, ii.

CHAPTER II

EUCHARIST AND OFFERING

WE have seen reason, in our study of the fundamental principles of sacrifice, as well as of the grouping of the Old Testament rites, to distinguish three main stages or ideas. There is first, in order of thought, the surrender of life; secondly, the offering of the life so surrendered, and its transformation in God's acceptance; and, lastly, the union between God and man, and man and man, by communion in the life so transformed. It is upon these three ideas respectively that the chief emphasis is laid in the Jewish sin-offering, burnt-offering, and peace-offering. In the Christian sacrifice no one idea receives emphasis at the expense of the others. "The full, perfect, and sufficient sacrifice, oblation, and satisfaction" contains them all; and includes, indeed, within its scope not only the three fundamental principles which we found (whether in direct reference to sacrifice as a technical category of religious thought or not) in our Lord's central teaching, but also the full sequence of the various sacrificial actions of the old cultus. It takes up, that is to say, what is indicated, or striven after, in each: the approach and the laying on of hands, in the Incarnation; the slaying of the Victim, on the Cross; the use of the blood, in that heavenly pleading and "sprinkling" of which the Epistle to the Hebrews and other New Testament books draw out the meaning—the "Atonement" proper; the transforming of our Lord's manhood into the Body of His Glory in Resurrection and Ascension, and with it, at every step of our own self-dedication, of the Body of redeemed mankind; and, finally, the indwelling of God in man and of man

271

in God, and the fellowship of man with man, in the meal upon the spiritual Body and upon the Blood, which is the Life, of the glorified Christ.

The task upon which the Church sets out, from Pentecost onwards, is the appropriation to herself, and through herself to the world, of what our Lord has thus made possible. So far as her earliest teachers used, as they did use, the language of sacrifice, they made it clear, at least in St. Paul's case, if not also in that of the writer to the Hebrews and of the author of the Fourth Gospel, that as regards the last of the six stages the appropriation is made, so far as it can be concentrated in, or expressed or "symbolised" by, a single act, in the "Breaking of the Bread". The Jewish tradition, which they inherited, knew the sacrificial meal as the sacrifice of praise or of thanksgiving. It is at this point that the New Testament breaks off, and the post-New Testament literature begins. The link between the two is the word εὐχαριστία, Eucharist. A communion-feast *is* a Eucharist. The *thing* is in the New Testament: the *name*, not expressly applied to the communion-feast, is there; and the earliest literature outside the Canonical books does no more than make the inevitable connection.

As we should expect, there is a transition stage. The Epistle of Clement of Rome to the Corinthians is the link between the first century and the second. In the second century, from Ignatius onwards, "Eucharist" becomes the characteristic name for what the New Testament calls "the breaking of the bread". Clement continues naturally enough the fundamental ideas of the New Testament writers. He uses the language of holiness, with the corresponding thought of goodness in terms of cleanness and purity: "Approach Him in holiness of soul, lifting up pure and undefiled hands unto Him";[1] "The holy of holies shall come forth from that nation";[2] "Seeing . . . that we are the special portion of a holy God, let us do all things that pertain unto holiness".[3] He understands the special meaning of the blood: "Let us fix our eyes" (not, on the

---

[1] Clem. Rom. i. 29 (Lightfoot's translation).   [2] *Ibid.*   [3] *Ib.* 30.

Cross, but) "on the blood of Christ and understand how precious it is unto His Father, because being shed for our salvation it won for the whole world the grace of repentance"; [1] "Thereby" (*i.e.* by Rahab's scarlet thread) "showing beforehand that through the blood of the Lord there shall be redemption". [2] He quotes Isaiah liii. [3] He understands the inner meaning of the burnt-offering: (Abraham) "by obedience offered him" (Isaac) "a sacrifice unto God". [4] He quotes a psalm [5] about the sacrifice of praise, the sacrificial meal. Such passages show that he inherits and uses what had already been made familiar in the New Testament; as indeed he more than once speaks of our Lord as our High Priest.

But at this point, so far as language is concerned, he goes further than his predecessors. Christ is the High Priest of our offerings: [6] that may be new language; it is hardly a forward move in thought. But in a later chapter the development begins, for he speaks of "those who have offered the gifts of the bishop's office unblameably". [7] Here, and in another passage, in which he says, "Let each of you, brethren, in his own order give thanks (εὐχαρι-στείτω) unto God . . . not transgressing the appointed rule of his service (λειτουργίας)", [8] we have a picture of what is undoubtedly the public worship of the Church. Lightfoot says that the "Eucharist" here is chiefly, though not solely, to be taken of the principal act of Christian thanksgiving, the celebration of the Lord's Supper. λειτουργία, which we have already found in the New Testament, is the regular word for worship in its sacrificial sense. The gifts are the "sacrifices of praise" of the psalm that he quotes, with the prayers, the thanksgivings, the alms, the eucharistic elements, and the contributions to the *agape*. That grouping of ideas, then, reveals the conception of offering, admittedly in its widest sense, as already attached, if to other services also, [9] yet inevitably and pre-eminently to the Eucharist.

[1] *Ib.* 7.   [2] *Ib.* 12.   [3] *Ib.* 16.   [4] *Ib.* 10.   [5] *Ib.* 35 (Ps. l.).
[6] *Ib.* 36.   [7] *Ib.* 44.   [8] *Ib.* 41.
[9] I use this expression in order not to seem to prejudge the case; but the idea of a public non-eucharistic Sunday service at this date is probably an anachronism.

T

It is with Ignatius that the word Eucharist (εὐ-χαριστία) becomes definitely attached to the service itself, in the later sense,[1] and, indeed, as in Justin Martyr afterwards, to the consecrated Food. The eucharistic gift is the "flesh of our Saviour Jesus Christ, which flesh suffered for our sins, and which the Father of His goodness raised up".[2] He also brings the "altar" within the sphere of worship, with the Eucharist, and the bishop as celebrant, though it is probable that he only uses it either of the Church as the sanctuary within which the bread of God is given, or of the heavenly and spiritual, not the earthly, "altar" of later times.[3] Like Clement, he knows the meaning of the blood; for it is love,[4] as Jesus Christ is "our inseparable life";[5] and he distinguishes between it and the Cross: "Nailed on the cross of our Lord Jesus Christ, . . . and firmly grounded in love in the blood of Christ".[6]

In the *Didache* again, as expressly in Ignatius, and intermediately in Clement, the general idea of Christian thanksgiving is concentrated in the Eucharist, which is the Food received, as well as the action of giving thanks.[7] And, further, the Eucharist is definitely spoken of as a sacrifice (θυσία) which is offered, and in that connection the passage in Malachi, so frequently used of it later, is quoted, though not fully or accurately: "In every place and at every time offer me a pure sacrifice; for I am a great King, saith the Lord, and my name is wonderful among the nations". And the moral preparation for the Eucharist is described in the appropriate terms of the sanctuary: "Confess . . . that your sacrifice may be pure (clean, καθαρά)". Disputes must first be reconciled in accordance with our Lord's injunction,[8] taken literally of the Christian altar, or at least the Christian offering, "that your sacrifice may not be defiled".[9] It is noticeable, indeed, that this reference to our Lord's words about reconciliation, which begin "if therefore thou art offering thy gift at the altar, . . ." can only mean that in the

[1] Ign. *Phil.* 4 *al.*   [2] *Ib. Smyrn.* 6.   [3] *Ib. Phil.* 4.   [4] *Ib. Trall.* 8.
[5] *Ib. Eph.* 3.   [6] *Ib. Smyrn.* 1.   [7] *Did.* 9.   [8] Mt. v. 23 f.   [9] *Did.* 14.

writer's mind the dominant conception of the Eucharist is offering—an offering, obviously, which implies receiving, but an action in which that which is to be received must be offered.

The Epistle of Barnabas has perhaps no direct reference to the Eucharist; but if, like other early writers, he says emphatically that the Jewish sacrifices are abolished with the rest of the old dispensation, it is "that the new law of our Lord Jesus Christ . . . might have its oblation not made by human hands",[1] and he quotes freely from Psalms li. 17, 19, as giving the inner meaning of the Christian sacrifice, alike in suffering and in oblation: "The sacrifice unto God is a broken heart, the smell of a sweet savour unto the Lord is a heart that glorifies its Maker:"[2] I say, "in oblation", for as the reference is apparently to the burnt-offerings of the last verse of the psalm, in which God shall delight (hence Barnabas' use of the familiar "smell of a sweet savour"), so the connection of thought, in a Christian sense, can only be with the giving of thanks which, as we shall see later, is the key-note to the whole Christian idea alike of offering and of reception. Barnabas is, however, only directly occupied with the redeeming work of our Lord: that he thinks of as sacrifice ("He was in His own person about to offer the vessel of His Spirit a sacrifice for our sins"),[3] and as fulfilling in various ways the sacrificial types of the Old Testament. With the scope and principles of the old cultus he is familiar. The cleansing from our sins is "through the blood of His sprinkling";[4] that is, he distinguishes, not expressly, but in his natural use of language, as a matter of course, between the death of the Victim on the Cross, which he mentions elsewhere, and His Blood; and he knows that it is the sinner, not the priest, who kills the victim, and in fact contrasts the sinners who slay Him, and after that have no more part, with the children who sprinkle the people with the hyssop, who are the Apostles who "preached unto us the forgiveness of sins and the purification of our heart".[5] So the

---

[1] Barn. 2.   [2] *Ibid.*   [3] *Ib.* 7.   [4] *Ib.* 5.   [5] *Ib.* 8.

Christian sacrifice ends with the transformation of its victim in the Resurrection and Ascension, and the day of the Resurrection is therefore kept by Christians for rejoicing. And, finally, by "receiving the remission of our sins and hoping on the Name we became new, created afresh from the beginning. Wherefore God dwelleth truly in our habitation within us":[1] we are, that is, a spiritual temple. It is, throughout, a picture of redemption in terms alike of sacrifice and of sanctuary.

I am conscious that, in brief and imperfect summaries such as these of the references to our subject in the earliest Christian literature, I am treading what is, at least to students, already well-worn ground. But it will be well to take two or three more authors in order to collect, with sufficient completeness, the materials for a general summary of the position in the early centuries. In Justin Martyr there are passages of the first importance as regards both the second-century teaching and also the early liturgical developments. Justin, in fact, touches both primitive and later conceptions and practices at so many points that the materials which he provides almost defy classification. He is at one with other early writers in repudiating carnal sacrifices, such as those of the heathen and of the Jews.[2] He uses the familiar language about the true sacrifice as an offering of prayer and thanksgiving.[3] But the Christian sacrifice which he contrasts with the Jewish, and which is the fulfilment of the repeatedly quoted passage in Malachi,[4] is also the bread and the cup of the Eucharist;[5] and it is indeed almost impossible to interpret his use of the word "do" (ποιεῖν) in connection either with praise and thanksgiving or with the elements, otherwise than as meaning to "offer".[6] With Justin the two thoughts of offering prayer and thanksgiving and of offering the elements are inseparably connected. In the passage in which he speaks, at first entirely in the manner of other writers, both of early and of later times, of prayer and thanksgiving as being the only perfect and well-

---

[1] Barn. 15, 16. [2] Apol. i. 9, 13 ; Dial. 28, 29. [3] Dial. 117 al.
[4] Mal. i. 11. [5] Dial. 41. [6] Ib. 117, 70.

pleasing sacrifices,[1] he goes on at once to speak of this
offering as part of what Christians have "received"
(παρέλαβον), and says that it is made in remembrance (ἐπ᾽
ἀναμνήσει) of their "solid and liquid food" (τῆς τροφῆς
αὐτῶν ξηρᾶς τε καὶ ὑγρᾶς), in which they remember the
Passion. Elsewhere[2] he describes this eucharistic "tradition" or παράδοσις. The food itself, he says, is called
"Eucharist": the elements are not "common" (κοινόν ;
i.e. they are holy, as in the Eastern liturgical phrase, τὰ
ἅγια τοῖς ἁγίοις); but, as the food over which thanks
have been given—the "thanked-over" (εὐχαριστηθεῖσα,
"eucharisted") food[3]—, they are "the flesh and blood of
that Jesus who was made flesh". For, he proceeds, the
Apostles delivered (παρέδωκαν ; so St. Paul of the eucharistic tradition which he received—παρέλαβον—and delivered—παρέδωκα—),[4] as had been enjoined on them,
the account of the Institution; "That Jesus took the
bread, and when He had given thanks (εὐχαριστήσαντα,
when He had done that which made the bread εὐχαρι-
στηθέντα, 'eucharisted', said, Do this for my memorial (εἰς
τὴν ἀνάμνησίν μου). This is my body; and He took the cup
likewise, and when He had given thanks, said; This is my
blood."

The Christian Church is therefore carrying out a
παράδοσις, or tradition, which is believed to have come
from the Lord, through the Apostles. The observance of
that tradition is the Christian sacrifice, which has super-
seded the various Jewish sacrifices (Justin has the whole
range of the Jewish sacrifices in mind, and not any one
variety; he expressly mentions the Passover, the sin-
offering of the Day of Atonement, and the meal-offering
—minhah—as in different ways fulfilled in Christ);[5] and
in the performance of the Christian sacrifice there are,
blended together, offering, remembrance, communion, as
well as conduct—the imitation of God[6]—all, as it were,
constituted, or effected, in the supreme act of thanksgiving, which gave the name of Eucharist alike to the

[1] Dial. 117.   [2] Apol. i. 66.   [3] See also Apol. i. 65.
[4] 1 Cor. ii. 23.   [5] Dial. 40, 41.   [6] Apol. i. 10.

whole and to its parts. Christ is the High Priest,[1] the
"eternal Priest of God", and the priesthood of the Jewish
people has passed to the Christians. It is therefore His
Eucharist, His giving of thanks, at the Last Supper,
which, in the "tradition", is carried on. We are in a
Jewish atmosphere: for if we are right in believing that
the words of our Lord's thanksgiving, or consecration,
were those, or like those, of the Passover *Kiddūsh*,[2] so we
find that the scope of the "president's" thanksgiving in
Justin is like that of our Lord's, viz., Creation and Redemption.[3] But the Christian Eucharist, offered, as the
Jewish, to God, is now Christ-centred; in fact, the redemption wrought for Israel by Yahweh in the Red Sea has
passed into the Redemption wrought by Christ for us:
specifically, therefore, the memorial is of His Passion,[4] or
of His blood;[5] but also of His Incarnation;[6] and, as Justin
implies in giving the reason for Sunday as the day of the
Eucharist, of His Resurrection.[7] It is, in fact, a memorial
of Christ.[8] The thanksgiving which makes it operative
covers the whole of God's work, from Creation in the
beginning to the holy food which we receive. The scope of
the thanksgiving is the scope of the sacrifice: Justin's
language therefore shows that his grasp of the principles
and method of sacrifice is as wide and complete as, in one
essential particularly at least, that of the function of the
blood, it is accurate; it is the blood of Christ that delivers
from death;[9] and He is the Rock, who gives those who are
willing to drink of the water of life.[10]

None of the writers of the period following Justin,
though they vary in their individual applications of the
typical language, depart from the general conception of
offering, and sacrifice, attaching to the Eucharist, which
has already become apparent. None of them—and the
same is true until a much later period, with certain exceptions to be mentioned later—approach the constricted
idea of sacrifice as mainly related to the death of Christ to

[1] *Dial.* 33, 42, 113, 116.   [2] See above, pp. 215 f.
[3] *Dial.* 41 f.; *Apol.* i. 13, 67.   [4] *Dial.* 41, 117.   [5] *Ib.* 70.   [6] *Ibid.*
[7] *Apol.* i. 67.   [8] *Ib.* i. 66.   [9] *Dial.* 111.   [10] *Ib.* 114.

which it is my primary purpose to draw attention. With
Irenaeus, who is writing against Gnosticism, it is natural
that a leading thought should be that the elements are
offered as first-fruits of God's creation;[1] but the eucharistic idea remains in general that of an oblation, covering
the oblation of our character and of our prayers: it is the
new oblation of the new Covenant;[1] and it is offered at the
heavenly altar.[2] What is conveyed by the receiving of the
elements—the "thanked-over" bread and wine (as in
Justin), which, as such, have two sides, an earthly and a
heavenly—is the Gift of God, which is life eternal; the
Body and the Blood of the Lord, so given and received,
have the hope of the Resurrection.[3] It is, in fact, in
Ignatius' phrase, the "medicine of immortality".[4]

Such conceptions of the Eucharist as these contain the
ruling ideas which, on the whole, are those of the earliest
centuries. There are specific developments, rather of
phraseology than of substance, to which I shall refer
later. But it is at this point that we may perhaps best
examine what the ruling ideas imply.

The two outstanding thoughts are those of offering
and of thanksgiving (Eucharist). We have seen that the
"Breaking of the Bread" in the New Testament is quite
definitely associated with the last stage of the complete
action of ancient sacrifice, the sacrificial meal. In the
first period after the New Testament, its associations are
realised with the last stage but one, with the act of offering, with which is to be understood God's acceptance, and
transformation, of that which is offered. Of the fact of
this association of the idea of offering with the Eucharist
there can be no doubt. But in view of later emphasis on,
and of still later restrictions upon interpretation of, the
Christian offering the outstanding feature of the early
language is the wideness of its scope. The burnt-offering
was a partial and imperfect expression of an inner moral
fact, of the unqualified dedication on the offerer's part,
not only of all that he possessed, but of himself; and of

---

[1] Iren. *Adv. Haer.* iv. 17. 4-6.   [2] *Ib.* iv. 18. 6.
[3] *Ib.* iv. 18. 5, v. 2. 3.   [4] Ign. *Eph.* 20.

himself in the sense of the inner motive of his life, his own
will. It was never more than partial, and it could be so
externalised and formalised as to become nothing more
than an outward ceremonial act with no moral meaning
behind it. In sharp contrast to this the Christian offering
is, as originally understood, nothing if not ethical. It
begins, as it were, from within: with the dedication of the
worshipper's whole life, first in conduct, and then in
conduct expressing itself. And this expression of the inner
will is first that of prayer and thanksgiving; then, by a
natural symbolism, that of personal gifts; of alms for the
relief of the necessity of others; of the bread and wine,
over which God is to be blessed or thanked, as representing the Creation. For in the wide outlook of the *Didache*
and of Irenaeus, as well as of other writers, "nature",
whether in obvious symbolism as illustrating the corporate life and universal character of the Church, or in
the range of theological thought, is bound up with the
redeeming and revivifying work of Christ, and included
in its scope.

With these wide and varied expressions of the idea of
offering there is always the act of remembrance, or
ἀνάμνησις. The rite, instituted on the night before our
Lord's death, cannot but be, and indeed is already in the
New Testament, at least a memorial of His Passion.
Whether it can be, as regards our Lord Himself, a
memorial of more than His actual Passion depends upon
the conception of what was His redeeming work. That
conception may, indeed, be limited. There were times, in
the later history, when so far at least as the Eucharist
was concerned, the Cross, if it may be so said, dominated
the whole of the current interpretation. But that was
not so in the earlier period. The mere fact that from the
first the Church celebrated the Eucharist on Sunday, not
on the day of our Lord's death, but on the first day of the
week, the day of His Resurrection, is evidence that the
Christ of the Eucharist was the Living Christ, not the
Lamb slain, but the Lamb standing—and therefore alive
—and in the midst of the throne. The memory of the

Cross is there: it is the Lamb "as it had been slain"; but it is a memory.

If these chapters were intended to give a full history of eucharistic thought, it would be necessary to examine the other writers of the period before, and during, the Great Councils in detail. But I venture to generalise. The immediate question before us is that of the accuracy, or the scope, of the sacrificial language of the period. There are evidences, to which I shall refer, of the tendency to emphasise the thought of our Lord's death in connection with His sacrifice. That emphasis prepared the way for the later concentration upon the Cross with which serious controversy upon the sacrifice became possible. But such evidences are partial and fragmentary. What is decisive as regards the general trend of sacrificial language is the fact that for the first four or five Christian centuries the range of the sacrificial idea is as wide as possible.

It was in this period that the main lines, as well as much of the wording, of the Liturgies, were fixed. And whatever may have been the later adventures in interpretation of eucharistic theology, or in experience of eucharistic devotion, the liturgies survive as unmistakable evidence of the earlier conceptions. It is not until we come to Liturgies drawn up at the time of the Reformation that, as in the Consecration Prayer of the second English Prayer Book, first issued in 1552, the commemoration of our Lord's redeeming work is limited to His death. That, for all its simplicity, was a mediaevalist conception. It is not primitive. Every primitive consecration prayer in every part of the Christian world; every Eastern liturgy, earlier or later; every form of the Canon in the Western Mass, including the present Roman Canon, preserves the width of the original outlook. The redeeming work of Christ is not His Death only, but also His Resurrection, and His Ascension, or, as the latter is often amplified, His Ascension and His Session at the right hand of God. Whether the picture of the redeeming work is expressly completed or not by the further mention of the Holy Spirit (I avoid, deliberately, at least at this point, the vexed question of the *epiclesis* or Invocation of the Holy Spirit in the act of consecration), the evidence is clear that in whatever way the Person and Work of Christ were associated with the eucharistic offering, it was, in worship, always the living, glorified, heavenly Christ who was thought of; always His work at its fullest, heavenly in the present, earthly in the past, mediated, in the power of Pentecost, by the Holy Spirit.

That is the evidence of worship; and the very permanence, in liturgical forms, of aspects of thought and belief which have sometimes almost disappeared from theological writing and from popular devotion is a proof, if proof were needed, of the value of liturgical evidence. We are gradually being enabled to bridge over the gap that separates the first century from the earliest written liturgies. But we know enough of the history to be sure that a written liturgy, or a written prayer—especially a consecration prayer—is no new creation of the actual date of writing. It represents innumerable earlier *ex tempore* prayers, gradually stereotyped by use; it reaches back therefore, at least as regards the ideas which it expresses, far behind its own first appearance in writing.

The evidence of the liturgies is decisive. Not only do they commemorate the whole course of the redemption, but they show that the sphere, or setting, of the Christian life is nothing less than that to which, as we saw in Part II., our Lord first trained, and then, at Pentecost, enabled, His followers to extend their view, and in which they learnt, in the new life of the Church, to move. The outward part of the worship of the Church is on earth, expressed in human words, and in earthly acts. But its inward, unseen, part is in heaven. It is the worship of heaven in which the Church on earth joins: hearts are lifted up to the throne of God; the angels are part of the worshipping throng; and the angelic hymn, the Holy, Holy, Holy, is the summary of the praise alike of earth and of heaven.

And the writers of the period bear this out. From

Clement of Rome[1] to Chrysostom in the East and to
Ambrose and Augustine in the West, there is the full view
of the heavenly worship. "We have our Victim in heaven,
our Priest in heaven, our sacrifice in heaven" (carnal sacrifices have given place to a "reasonable service"). "What
is the reasonable service? . . . 'God', it is said, 'is Spirit,
and those who worship Him must worship in spirit and
truth', things which need no body or instruments or
places, such as gentleness, restraint, mercy, endurance of
evil, long-suffering, lowliness of mind."[2] "Is not the altar
also of heaven? How? It has nothing carnal. All the oblations become spiritual."[3] I quote Chrysostom, because I
shall also have to refer to him later as one of the examples of the crude and almost materialistic tendency
which seems to link the idea of the sacrifice of Christ with
His actual death. If he is inconsistent, the explanation is
probably that he is rhetorical. But in the very moment
of what looks like gross materialism or literalising he
passes to the wider, higher, more spiritual thought: "When
thou seest the Lord sacrificed and lying as an oblation,
and the priest standing by the sacrifice and praying, and
all things reddened with that precious blood, dost thou
think that thou art still among men and standing on
earth? Nay, art thou not straightway translated to heaven
so as to cast every carnal thought out of thy soul, and
with unimpeded soul and clean mind to behold the things
that are in heaven?"[4] To him, it is clear that the blood of
Christ is the surrendered life, with which, as High Priest,
as in the Epistle to the Hebrews, He passes through the
Veil.

So St. Ambrose: "We have seen the High Priest coming to us; we have seen and heard Him offering His own
blood for us".[5] "He is offered as Man, as one taking on
Himself suffering—(*recipiens passionem*); and He offers
Himself as High Priest, that He may forgive our sins,

---

[1] Clem. Rom. i. 34, 59-61.
[2] Chrys. *In Heb. Hom.* xi. 2. 3 (quoted in Stone, *H. D. E.* vol. i. pp. 117 f.).
[3] *Ib.* xiv. 2 (Stone, vol. i. p. 118).
[4] *Ib. De Sac.* iii. 4 (Stone, vol. i. pp. 118 f.).
[5] Amb. in Ps. xxxviii. Enar. 25 (Stone, vol. i. p. 119).

here in symbol, in reality there where He pleads with the
Father for us as Advocate."[1]

So to St. Augustine the earthly altar is a symbol—and
an imperfect symbol—of the altar in heaven. There "the
Priest alone, yet clearly there the whole Priest, will stand,
that is with the body added of which He is the Head,
which has already ascended into heaven".[2] And he understands not only the heavenly character of the offering,
but the scope. The Body of Christ in the Eucharist is the
Body of many members, which is the Church itself: "If
you have received well, you are that which you have received";[3] and, after quoting St. Paul,[4] "Be what you see,
and receive what you are". He follows out, indeed, the
true interpretation of the ancient sacrifices; for, in becoming part of the Body of Christ, the Christian has been
kindled by the sacred fire: "When ye received the fire of
the Holy Ghost, ye were, so to speak, cooked".[5] He uses,
that is, the literal language of the fire-sacrifices. And he
knows what completes the sacrifice: the true sacrifice is
a contrite heart; and the inner meaning of all the old
sacrificial ordinances was love to God and to one's neighbour: "Therefore every work which is done in order that
we may be united in holy fellowship to God . . . is a real
sacrifice".[6] Offering is not complete without communion:
"Wherefore now Christians celebrate the memorial of the
same accomplished sacrifice by the most holy offering and
reception of the body and blood of Christ".[7] Augustine is
in effect summarising what is to be found throughout the
earlier literature. But nowhere is there a more complete
view of what sacrifice means as applied to our Lord's
work, or of what sharing in Christ's sacrifice means to
Christians. The action of the sacrifice does not stop with
His Death. It is heavenly, as well as earthly. It is only
consummated in communion; and alike in offering and

---

[1] Amb. De off. i. 248 (Stone, vol. i. p. 119).
[2] Aug. Serm. cccli. 7 (Stone, vol. i. p. 121).
[3] Ib. Serm. ccxxvii. (Stone, vol. i. p. 95).
[4] 1 Cor. xii. 27, x. 17.
[5] Aug. Serm. cclxxii. (Stone, vol. i. p. 96).
[6] Ib. De Civ. Dei, x. 6 (Stone, vol. i. p. 123).
[7] Ib. C. Faust. xx. 18 (Stone, ib.).

communion it gives direction, purpose, and meaning to the whole of human life: it is profoundly ethical. There is no summary more telling than in the famous passage in which Augustine uses the opening verses of the twelfth chapter of the Epistle to the Romans. "The whole redeemed City itself, that is the congregation and society of the saints, is offered as a universal sacrifice to God by the High Priest, who offered even Himself in suffering for us in the form of a servant, that we might be the body of so great a Head. For this form of a servant did He offer, in this was He offered; for in this is He mediator and priest and sacrifice . . . (Rom. xii. 1 ff.). . . . This is the sacrifice of Christians: 'The many one body in Christ'. Which also the Church celebrates in the Sacrament of the altar, familiar to the faithful where it is shown to her that in this thing which she offers she herself is offered."[1]

I have said above that in this period the association of the Eucharist with the sacrifice of Christ is linked with the last stage but one, as in the New Testament with the last stage, of the ancient sacrifices. It is not a contrast. The old link is not severed because the new link is forged. The passages last quoted show this. What this progressive, backward, association of the earthly rite and the historical and heavenly reality seems to indicate is the gradual learning, in practical experience and in thought, of the lesson of our appropriation and God's gift of our identification with what Christ did and does for us. If there is a permanently new element in such appropriation in this period marked by the idea of offering it is in the gradual clarifying of the idea of what is offered. As is often pointed out, the explicit language of offering is first used not of Christ Himself, or of His Body and Blood, but of the fruits of the redeemed life—conduct, prayer, fastings, thanksgiving, alms—the elements themselves as the first-fruits of the created world. But the transition to, if it be a transition, or the express inclusion of, the thought of the centre and key-note of all our personal offerings

---

[1] *Ib. De Civ. Dei*, x. 6 (Stone, vol. i. pp. 123 f.).

being Christ's own offering of Himself is near at hand
from the first. The record of the Institution, an integral
part of the rite, of necessity links up the prayer of the
officiant with our Lord's own "eucharistic prayer" at the
Last Supper; and if He be thought of as alive, and as
present with His later disciples at every "breaking of the
bread", as He was with the earliest in the upper room, it is
an inevitable step to Justin's difficult phrase, "through the
prayer of the word that comes from Him" (δι' εὐχῆς λόγου
τοῦ παρ' αὐτοῦ[1]). Whatever the precise translation of these
words may be, they represent our Lord as vitally connected with the eucharistic action: either He is the
author of the eucharistic prayer, or His is the actual
unseen power which makes that prayer effective. So
Irenaeus' phrase, "the new oblation of the new Covenant",
cannot be separated in thought from our Lord's own
language at the Institution. If He spoke of the "blood of
the new Covenant", He thought of Himself as the Victim
by Whose sacrifice the new Covenant was ratified; and to
say that the "new oblation" is confined in thought to
sacrifices made by His followers is to suggest that they, or
the Church, are the Victim and not the Lord Himself. If
we add to such passages as these the constant use of the
idea of our Lord's High-priesthood, the recurring thought
of the heavenly altar, and take with them the memorial
made in every Eucharist of all that He did and does in His
sacrificial work, we have the whole of the material ready
for what is often thought of as a new and alien element
introduced by Cyprian. The Jewish priesthood has, by his
time, long disappeared. The distinction between Christianity and paganism is so clearly marked that confusion
is impossible between the ministers of the Christian
sacrifice and of the heathen. Cyprian applies the obvious
words to that which was already familiar; indeed, the
words had already been used by Tertullian, as in the East
by Origen; and Cyprian's responsibility, if it can be so
called, or his achievement, is merely the clarifying and the
fixing, in what thenceforward became accepted terms, of

[1] Justin, *Apol.* i. 66.

what had always been implicit in idea, and had already been tentatively expressed in language.

I shall reserve to the next chapter such indications as there are in this period of the later identification of sacrifice with the act of killing the Victim, together with suggestions for the reasons of their appearance. Apart from these it remains broadly and generally true, whatever specific developments of language there may be, that in both the liturgies and the writers with whom we are concerned, even those writers who approach nearest to the perilous identification from which ultimately trouble came are accurate in the sacrificial language which they employ and in the sacrificial thought which underlies that language. The dominant idea of sacrifice is oblation, or, more accurately, of oblation and communion combined. With these two stages of the supreme sacrifice the earthly Eucharist is inseparably associated.

The idea of offering, however, does not appear in its full significance unless illustrated by the other characteristic thought of the period, that of thanksgiving or Eucharist. Recent studies of the Jewish background of early Christianity, such as those of the late Mr. Israel Abrahams from the Jewish side, and of Dr. Oesterley and, more recently, Dr. Gavin from the Christian, have thrown much unexpected light upon Christian origins. I have already referred in Part II. to Dr. Abrahams' *Studies in Pharisaism and the Gospels*, and, in connection with the Institution of the Eucharist, to Dr. Oesterley's *Jewish Background of the Christian Liturgy*. Dr. Gavin's *Jewish Antecedents of the Christian Sacraments*[1] takes us back to Dr. Oesterley's conclusions as to our Lord's "giving of thanks" or "blessing" at the Last Supper. We have seen that in all probability He used the Passover *Kiddūsh*. The *Kiddūsh* is a typical, if supremely solemn and important, example of the blessings with which the Jews met not the happiness only but also the "ills and cross-accidents" of

---

[1] See especially Lecture III. "*Berakha* and Eucharist", upon which much of what follows is based, and which I found to confirm conclusions at which I had already, in part, arrived.

life. To the Jew the name of God was, as we have seen in
Part I., more than a name is to us. It was, to him, God as
always revealing Himself, progressively with more and
more fullness, in His loving intercourse with, and care of,
His people. All life was governed by His will: even the
dark side of it, the evil, could be thought of as His work,
hard as the thought may be to us: and He is the Creator
and sustainer not of man only but of the whole universe.
There is no distinction in the Jewish mind between inward and outward, secular and sacred. Life, whatever it
is, and however from a later and Hellenic point of view
we may distinguish its various parts, calling one side of it
material and another spiritual, is one, and is His. Every
activity of our own depends upon Him, and must be
referred to Him. Every contact that we have with Him is
a fresh revelation of Himself, a fresh outpouring of His
power and of His Love. It follows that in every circumstance of life the approach to Him is that of blessing or
thanksgiving for what He does or gives, and that what He
does or gives is, as it were, a new outpouring of Himself, a
new manifestation of the Name. Hence what in primitive
times was in danger of becoming magical, the "calling of
the Name" of the Lord over that for which His power was
sought. But the Name was called in blessing. God is, as we
should say in our later language, a Person; and our dealings with Him are on the same lines as our dealings with
other personalities in ordinary life. In our intercourse
with human beings we know that the secret that unlocks
the hearts of others, that alone can stimulate their best
instincts, is just that combination of love and faith which
is the fundamental idea of the Jewish blessing of God
through His Name and in the end saves it from magical
use. For there is no love in one human person for another
without admiration or respect; and this, though at an
infinite distance, is in germ the sense of creaturely adora-
tion with which we approach God, the supreme Person.
Among ourselves, it is only when a man is met by the
confidence and trust which springs out of admiring love
that he is at his best and that he can unfold. The perver-

sion of such stimulating admiration is flattery, which is insincere admiration attempting to produce the effects of the sincere; but the very commonness of the flatterer's attempts is evidence of the underlying soundness of that which flattery perverts. It is only in the right atmosphere that a man, like a flower, can open out, and reveal and give the best that is in him. If we need our friend's help, we do not approach him with a long face or with a mere demand for what he can give. We come to him, if we come worthily or effectively, in the manifest enjoyment of his friendship, in the spirit which surrounds us both with the atmosphere of love, of appreciation of the friend for the friend's sake. It is so with the true approach to God. He has given what is best in us. He made us in His image: "Love I gave thee, with Myself to love". He needs our response, as He has made it possible. It follows that if we desire a special exercise of His power, a special gift of His grace, we shall under no circumstances, even the worst, approach Him in doubt or in depression. The Jewish instinct was right; our Lord's lesson in prayer was right; we begin by "glorifying" or "sanctifying" His Name. The Jew worshipped God the Giver over his food: our Lord taught us to begin our prayers for ourselves by the worship of the opening clause of the pattern prayer: before we ask for our daily bread we are to say "Hallowed be Thy Name".

This appears to be the fundamental principle underlying the characteristic Jewish idea that in blessing Divine power is released.[1] If we desire God to reveal or to give Himself to us, we put ourselves first into the attitude of praise and thanksgiving; we bless Him; we glorify Him. There are abundant illustrations of this mental, or moral, attitude in the writings of St. Paul and of St. Peter, especially in the paragraphs with which, after the opening salutation or address, the Epistles almost invariably begin. The Jewish formula begins "Blessed art thou, O Lord our God, King Eternal. . . ." Dr. Gavin has shown that since the blessing was a thanksgiving, the *berakha*

---

[1] Gavin, *op. cit.* p. 59.

(blessing) may be rendered in Greek either literally "Blessed be God" . . . or, in the active form which is more natural to the Greek language, "we give thanks unto Thee, O God". So, St. Peter, more conservatively, used the Jewish idiom, "Blessed be the God and Father of our Lord Jesus Christ . . .";[1] and St. Paul sometimes the one and sometimes the other. But, beyond the phraseology of the opening words, the content of these paragraphs is even more typical of the Jewish and early Christian habit. God is blessed or thanked for specific aspects of His work for all Christians, or for those to whom the letter is written; these aspects are sometimes developed into an orderly and logical commemoration as, in Ephesians,[2] of creation by the Father, and of redemption wrought through and in the crucified and glorified Christ, and sealed by the Spirit: and such commemorations and thanksgivings issue in prayer for those whom the writer is addressing. It is in the radiant joy of worship and thanksgiving that prayer finds its proper setting: such alone is the true prayer which cannot fail of its answer, for it is the prayer of faith.

The *Shepherd of Hermas* has striking illustrations of this principle. Hermas is going on the Campanian Way: "I entreat the Lord . . . that His great and glorious Name may be glorified, for that He held me worthy that He should show me His marvels. And as I gave glory and thanksgiving to Him, there answered me as it were the sound of a voice, 'Be not of doubtful mind, Hermas . . .'", and a great beast came to meet him, from which he was delivered: and the Church explains to him that he owes his deliverance to believing that he can be saved "by nothing else but by His great and glorious Name".[3] Further,[4] "doublemindedness" is contrasted with faith: and sorrow "is the sister of doublemindedness and angry temper": "sorrow is more evil than all the spirits . . . and crushes out the Holy Spirit": "put away therefore from thyself sadness, and afflict not the Holy Spirit that dwelleth with thee, lest haply He intercede with God

[1] 1 Peter i. 3.
[2] Eph. i. 3-14.
[3] *Herm.* V. 4. 1, 2 (Lightfoot and Harmer).
[4] *Ib.* M. 9, 10.

(against thee)"—that is to imply that with the opposite of sorrow in the heart the Spirit will intercede for us; "therefore clothe thyself with cheerfulness, which hath favour with God always"; "the intercession of a sad man hath never at any time power to ascend to the altar of God". I have quoted this teaching from Hermas both as typical of the Christian approach to God in the early part of the second century, and because it is exactly in harmony with the language of the most "Judaic" of the Epistles. St. James uses the same word for "double-minded" as Hermas (δίψυχος) and in the same sense; "let him ask in faith, nothing 'doubting'; for he that doubteth is like the surge of the sea, driven by the wind and tossed. For let not that man think that he shall receive anything of the Lord; a double-minded man, unstable in all his ways". And these verses occur between two typically Jewish sayings, "count it all joy, my brethren, when ye fall into manifold temptations"; "let the brother of low degree glory in his high estate: and the rich, in that he is made low".[1]

It is this instinct of blessing, of calling upon the Name, and therefore sanctifying it, of thanksgiving as the secret of the faith of effective prayer, that is the atmosphere in which the Christian sacrifice of praise and thanksgiving is offered. It is in this background that what we think of as the blessing of the bread and of the cup finds its true analysis and orientation. To us, far removed from the spirit of Jewish religion, the words pronounced "over" the elements appear to be a direct blessing of them, and, if we believe that they produce an "objective" effect, we are nearer magic than we sometimes realise, or, in the nervous fear of magic which is itself evidence of our nearness to it, we deny the effect and leave the words nothing but a mainly commemorative meaning. In the Jewish atmosphere in which the Christian Eucharist arose, it is not the elements that are blessed but God, Who has given us so much in the past and still gives Himself to us through them.

[1] James i. 2-19.

So our Lord at the feeding of the multitudes when He took the loaves and blessed, or gave thanks, blessed not the loaves, but God Who gives us our food. So at the Last Supper His "blessing" was not a direct blessing of the bread or of the cup but a blessing of, or a giving of thanks, a eucharist, to, God Who gave them, and Who was also Creator and the Redeemer of Israel. So runs the eucharistic prayer in Justin Martyr's account; it is a thanksgiving for Creation and Redemption. So run the consecration prayers of the Liturgies. They descend lineally from the "*Kiddūsh*", the "sanctification", of the Last Supper. So far as the substance of the eucharistic consecration prayers is concerned, there seems no break of historical continuity. In form and content they are Jewish; and the introductory dialogue between priest and people, beginning with "The Lord be with you", and continuing with "Lift up your hearts", and "Let us give thanks", seems to have, like the form of the following prayer, a Jewish background.[1] This dialogue is found in the "Egyptian Church Order", which Dom Conolly has shown to be the work of Hippolytus, and which apparently preserves for us the Roman rite as Hippolytus had known it in his youth, before the new régime in the early third century at the time of which he writes, and the changes brought in by it which he deplores.[2] It is therefore second-century evidence. It creates indeed one difficulty, the bearing of which has yet to be explored, but which does not affect the significance of the eucharistic direction of the consecration prayer: it omits, that is, the specifically Jewish element in the form of the prayer wherein creation is commemorated, and passes at once from the "*Sursum Corda*" to the Redemption. It has been argued that we have here evidence for a distinctively Christian eucharistic form, into which at a later time the Jewish Commemoration of creation, ending as it does with the "*Sanctus*" (Holy, Holy, Holy) was introduced. But Hippolytus' Canon is certainly not in other respects independent of Jewish origins: and we

[1] Gavin, *op. cit.* p. 87.   [2] *Ib.*, *op. cit.* pp. 44 f.

have evidence of the Christian use of the *Sanctus* in Clement of Rome, and a definite statement that God was thanked for creation as well as redemption, by Justin Martyr.

We have therefore, as it appears, a definitely fixed eucharistic tradition, continuous from Jewish times in form, and wholly Jewish in spirit. Of that spirit—the spirit of thankfulness and worship as the secret of effective prayer—I have given varied examples from early Christian writings, and I have attempted to trace both its source in Jewish religion and its reasonableness in our normal attitude towards God. It is unfortunate that the idea of the "Eucharistic" secret, or method, of prayer has become in our minds so exclusively associated with one great Sacrament. For it was the early tradition of the Church to use the eucharistic form, beginning indeed with the "Lift up your hearts" and its accompanying words, in other solemn forms of consecration. This tradition is best illustrated for English Christians of the present day by the happy return to it in the central prayers at Baptism and at Ordination in the *Prayer Book as proposed in 1928*. The value of these "Eucharistic" forms is that they tend, by the way of practical experience, without diminishing the effectiveness, or the supreme solemnity, of whatever we mean by the "consecration" in the Holy Communion, or Liturgy, to increase its naturalness and to remove that isolation in which the Consecration Prayer of our Liturgy has stood. It would indeed be well if we could realise, for the purposes alike of practical devotion and of intelligent understanding, that there is a sense in which the Consecration in the Liturgy is not unique: that it rests in its inner meaning upon a fundamental principle that underlies, safeguards, and in a sense justifies, not only other solemn consecrating acts of the Church, but also the best side of Jewish and of early Christian prayer as a whole.[1] For such "blessings" or

---

[1] See above (p. 290) for similar prayers in St. Paul and St. Peter. The prayer in Ephesians i. 3-14 might indeed have been St. Paul's own consecration prayer with the special reference to the Last Supper left out.

"eucharists", such "givings of thanks", for their very efficacy depend upon faith, and upon that answer of the human heart to the Divine of which the highest name is love. Once and for all such an approach, such a method of "consecration", rules out, so long as it is understood, anything that can be called magical. The instinct that leads man to glorify God and to thank Him for the disasters of life as well as for its triumphs, that can make of the Cross upon which, in Jesus, all humanity is for ever crucified, the material of the supreme Thanksgiving, is the instinct of the faith that can remove mountains. To its prayers the answer can never be withheld. It is as far as possible removed from the idea of a mere form of words which evokes the Divine action as such. That was not our Lord's method of consecration. It is not that of the Church.

It must not be supposed, however, that the Church's Eucharist is merely the continuation of the Jewish. I have tried to show how profound is the meaning of the Jewish idea, which the Church inherited, and how infinite, as regards effects, are its possibilities. But for Christians the method was from the first the method as used by our Lord. He is, in whatever sense, the centre of the Christian prayer. The "*Kiddūsh*", the "sacrifice of praise", the "offering", is His. The link with Him has never been broken. The very names employed for it in the East attest the continuity with the earliest times; the Greek "*anaphora*" (offering), the varied forms of the original word "*Kiddūsh*" that are still preserved in the liturgical languages akin to Aramaic, are evidence alike of its Jewish origin—since the "sacrifice of praise" was the peace-offering—and of the new element which He introduced into it. For the faith that lies behind every *Kiddūsh* is no less, in the Christian rite, than His, as well as the faith of the whole Church. And whatever it was, in the experience, at first dimly understood, of His earthly life; in the new vision of the Risen and Ascended Lord at Pentecost and after, that the first Christians found in Him; in the faith by which the first Jewish believers found in Him the God

of the Ineffable Name; whatever it was that made them
set a unique value for this life and for eternity upon the
redemption that He wrought; that could not but transform and transfigure for them at once the whole sense of
the power of the eucharistic prayer. Men in old days had
found, or been led to, the *method* of releasing the power of
God: but their faith was weak; their unredeemed heart
had not the purity for the unclouded vision. Now their
thanksgivings were not theirs, but His, Whose faith was
so strong that He could go to the Cross with the praise of
the Hallel upon His lips: Who taught them the Christian
Eucharist in the very moment of His Death: Who was
declared to be the Son of God with power by the resurrection from the dead. To the answer to His Thanksgiving
prayer there could be no limit. His Blessing could only
mean what it said. Hence the "realism", or as we should
say, in common speech, the "literalism", in early Christian language about the eucharistic elements, from
Ignatius onwards, naïve as it seems to us who are accustomed to technical and controversial distinctions and to
the use of later forms of thought. Hence the naturalness
with which, long before the time of eucharistic theories,
language is used of the Body and the Blood by Christian
writers of the early centuries. It is useless to fasten upon
such language the precision of mediaeval or modern technical terms. Christ is God, in the Christian faith, from the
beginning: and the blessing of the Lord's Name by Him
Who is Himself the Lord, as well as Man, must have a
power transcending all earthly limitations, as it transcends alike all early and all modern attempts at definition.

The Eucharist became the centre of Christian life and
worship before there was, or could be, a Christian theology in any technical sense. It is for this reason that the
early language about it is so wide as to baffle analysis.
It is above controversy. It begins, in a setting of offering
and of thanksgiving which embraces the whole Christian
life as well as the Person and work of Christ, as the communion-feast in the Christian sacrifice. In the early
centuries, the rationale of the communion feast is found

by experience to be precisely that atmosphere of self-dedication and rejoicing which is not only part of the Christian spirit, but is the Christian spirit. It is therefore at once the offering, of human life and property, of the fruits of the earth, of the First-fruits alike of man and of Creation, of Christ Himself: and the Eucharist, or Thanksgiving, for all that God has done in Nature and in Christ, in Creation and in Redemption, out of which alone the full gifts of God can come.

The conception of the Person and work of Christ is therefore central to the understanding of the Eucharist. While Christology is undeveloped, what we try to call, in the first centuries, eucharistic doctrine will be, in comparison with that of later times, vague and hard to capture. On the other hand, as Christology advances, we shall expect to find its reflections upon eucharistic language. The more the Christian mind dwells upon the meaning of what our Lord is to us and does for us, the more clearly will the vague outlines of the eucharistic vision be filled in. As with every religious development there is, at the time, in each stage, both loss and gain. The rite is from the beginning, with much else, the memorial of Christ's redemptive work. As the mind of the Church came to a clearer and more vivid understanding of what that meant, it was inevitable that new meaning should be found in the memorial. There came the time when it was impossible to make the memorial of the redemption without pleading for its results. The Eucharist could not but be the joining on earth with the intercession of the High Priest in heaven. And if His work was in any sense a propitiation, the eucharistic prayer must be propitiatory too. It becomes a pleading by the outpoured Blood. It is attached, as time goes on, brought into living association with, yet one more stage in the Perfect Sacrifice. It had from the beginning been consciously associated with the last stage, with the communion feast: we have seen how that association moved back to the stage of offering and transformation: and it moves back once more to the life surrendered and to the Cross upon which

the surrender was made. It is the appropriation to herself, by the Church on earth, of all that Christ gives and
does. And in these early centuries there is a sense in
which that appropriation is complete. Atonement, offering, communion, have each their place in the sacrifice as
properly understood. The complete association of the
Eucharist with the complete Sacrifice was inevitable, and
as long as the complete conception of the Sacrifice remained it was an immeasurable gain. It could bring the
whole of our Lord's work into the living consciousness
alike of the Christian society as a whole and of the individual worshipper; the Cross, the prevailing intercession,
the self-dedication alike of Him Who is offered and of
those who are offered in Him, and God's acceptance and
transformation of the offering, the union of God's life
with man's in the sacrificial receiving of the gifts.

But with the gain there came a loss. In the new clearness of the centre of the eucharistic vision the proportions of the vision as a whole were changed. It is this
change which we shall now examine. Its causes, or at
least some of them, lie in the period of which we have
seen the brighter side. Its effects are with us still.

CHAPTER III

SACRIFICE AS DEATH

My task is now, however briefly, to trace the change of which I have already spoken, and to examine some of its causes, and of its results. The fact of the change will not, I think, be disputed: it is written large over the history of eucharistic thought and of eucharistic devotion, and it still affects the religious and theological language in current use. I shall not, therefore, attempt to give the evidence for it in full detail. That may be found in any book which collects passages bearing on the Eucharist, such as Dr. Stone's *History of the Doctrine of the Holy Eucharist*. What is most relevant to my immediate purpose will be to indicate the beginnings of the new point of view; its ultimate extent at, and immediately before, the Reformation period; and its persistence to the present day.

The first reason for it I have suggested in the previous chapter. The earlier centuries give us, as we have seen, a wide and comprehensive range of eucharistic thought. So far as sacrifice is concerned, the writers are, substantially, accurate in their use of language. The scope of the Christian sacrifice is still as wide as that of the Jewish sacrifices in their full form, and corresponds in broad outline with the similar conceptions found in the sacrifices of the pagan religions. But upon this complete, though as yet undefined, background the progress of thought about the Person and work of Christ gradually brings His Figure into clearer relief. He is always in the mind in the eucharistic action. He is the High Priest, and therefore inevitably the unseen leader in it. It is His work of redemption that it commemorates. In the rite, He is present with His own as He was in the Upper Room. When the disciples are assembled on the first day of the week, He still comes, in His risen and ascended life, and stands in their midst. That is true from the beginning: but it is always the Risen Christ: and the setting of the worship is in heaven. The vision, indeed, of the heavenly worship in the Book of the Revelation, follows, in chapters iv. and v., the outline of the normal eucharistic prayer. It begins with God, surrounded by the host of Heaven and the living creatures, praised and worshipped for Creation, until the worship finds its climax in the Holy, Holy, Holy. It passes from creation and the *Sanctus* to Redemption—to the Lamb in the midst of the throne, alive through death, and the Spirit; and as the vision unfolds in the succeeding chapters it is seen to include the whole company of the Redeemed, the great multitude whom no man can number.

That picture is complete: and I am only recalling what I have already attempted to show in the earlier part of this book, and anticipating what I shall have to say in the concluding chapter, if I add that whatever may be the differences of emphasis at different times, no conception of the Christian sacrifice or of Christian worship can ever be adequate if it covers any smaller field. But, as first conceived, the various elements in its composition have not been defined, or thought out. During the period of the Great Councils, the Person and Work of our Lord takes, not a more central, but a clearer place in the whole. In the first two centuries there is but little attempt at definition. With the growth, first of a doctrine of God and then of a conscious Christology, while as yet there is little or no progress with the doctrine of the Holy Spirit or of His Work through Church and Sacraments, or with a deliberate study of Christian ethics, the central part of the original picture stands out more clearly than its setting or circumference. The Christian sacrifice still includes all its original parts. Its content is the same as before. The ultimate scene of its progress is, in the true sense of all Christian life, in the "Heaven" of which our Lord taught, and in which at any moment the seen and the unseen both have their shares, and still in due proportion. Christ's sacrifice includes that of Christians: His Body, which is offered, is the Church of which He is the Head. But the general sacrifice, as He is better understood and more clearly seen, comes to be thought of as the sacrifice of Christ. That sacrifice indeed still includes our prayers and thanksgivings, our gifts, our surrender of our lives. But He is seen more clearly as the motive force which alike inspires and enables the rest, and in Whom alone they are acceptable. The succession of acts which constitute the sacrifice are His acts. In them His people join, but in His acts it is He whom they know themselves to be offering, His intercession, by the power of the surrendered life which is His Blood, which they plead, as it has always been His Death, making offering and pleading alike possible, which they have commemorated.

As the years go on, and the conversion of the Roman Empire brings the world into the Church, a new moral situation is created. The problem of the sins of baptized Christians becomes more acute as the Church grows in outward size and strength. The instincts, alike of worship and of the prayer inseparable from worship, already concentrated upon the figure of Christ, in Whom God is revealed and brought into the world, and the world led to God, begin to dwell with a new emphasis upon the saving Death. It is a change, if it be a change, at once inevitable and evangelical: it witnesses to the agelong "Evangelical" core of all true Christianity. It uses whatever language may be current in connection with the Cross; much of the language of St. Paul and of St. John is rediscovered: and as the need of the Cross and its propitiation, of which the New Testament had spoken so strongly, is felt with a new poignancy, the direction of prayer in worship follows the new needs. If sin becomes an outstanding problem, prayer will be for the deliverance from sin which the Cross made possible: and the crowning act of prayer becomes "propitiatory".

It is sometimes said that this is a fundamental change, and that Tertullian and Cyprian in the West, and in a measure even Origen in the East, altered the original conception. The reason for this criticism is doubtless the fact that it was upon the definitely "propitiatory" use of the Eucharist that in later times so many practices and inferences were grafted which were rightly felt to need reformation. But a distinction must be made. It is one thing to use the Eucharist for prevailing prayer, and, since in all prayer there must be prayer for others, to use it in prayer for the sins of others. It is another thing when later definition, or speculation, has provided a purgatory, with its temporal sufferings, as the scene for the purifying of suffering souls, and practical demands as well as sacrificial theories have multiplied masses. It is round these developments that what many of us think of as the abuses of the propitiatory use of the Eucharist were gathered. They do not belong, of necessity, to the original instinct which led men to use it for prayer for salvation from sin through the Cross and the Blood.

What the earlier use of the Eucharist for propitiation really did was to carry one step further that backward linking of the earthly worship with the stages of the one Sacrifice of which we have already watched the beginnings. As it was from the first inseparably linked with the Sacrifice of Christ in the culmination of that sacrifice in the communion meal; as in the earlier post-Apostolic period it was found to be inevitably linked with the offering: so, once more, it becomes the earthly symbol of, and link with, the Blood and the Cross. Nothing now is added: indeed the conscious thought of Christians has gone back to features in the teaching of the Epistles which had in a sense lain dormant and unrealised. The new detail seen in the complete picture is, indeed, Scriptural. It was there, though hardly seen, from the beginning. And as long as the picture can be seen whole, and in its true proportions, every recovery, or discovery, of detail is a gain.

But the very greatness of the eucharistic picture was itself a danger. It is not in formal heresy alone that the

Christian mind fails to preserve the breadth of vision or of thought and the sense of proportion which are alone truly "Catholic". And there were practical causes for the loss alike of completeness, of proportion, and indeed of accuracy.

As long as the Church was a persecuted minority neither the need of discipline nor the lack of spiritual zeal interfered with the primitive habit of frequent Communion. Whatever else the Eucharist was discovered, and as I at least should say rightly discovered to be, its climax was the reception of the elements. As long as that continued, its further use as the Christian offering and the pleading of the Blood and of the Cross could not alter the idea of its full content. But the same circumstances which brought its propitiatory side into a new emphasis weakened it, in practice, on the side of communion. For many reasons, good and bad, for the sake of necessary discipline over the raw material brought into the Church, as well as through the lessening of spiritual intensity, communion became infrequent. It became possible for the ordinary worshipper, at what were increasingly, to him, the normal services which he attended, to throw the emphasis upon offering and propitiation rather than upon communion. That was one cause. And there is another to which I doubt if sufficient attention has been called. If there is any truth in what I have attempted to show in Parts I. and II., it is clear that the original Christian language about sacrifice was based upon the knowledge which teachers and taught alike possessed of the fundamental principles of ancient sacrifice. St. Paul could argue alike from Jewish and from pagan sacrifice to Christian. He and the other New Testament writers could assume a knowledge in their readers similar to their own, and their mentions of and references to sacrifice and sacrificial ideas could be fragmentary and allusive. They lived, as I have said, in a world in which the main principles at least of the technique of sacrifice were fully known.

So far as the Jewish sacrifices were concerned that knowledge could be assumed, at least among Jewish

Christians, not only until the destruction of the Temple in A.D. 70, but as long as personal memory and tradition could preserve the picture of the Temple worship. But after, in Christian circles, such memory and tradition had passed away, there remained throughout the Christian world, before the eyes of Christians, the public acts of Pagan worship. And in the broad principles of sacrifice the Pagan worship resembled the Jewish. It is not a question of how far the ancient religions of Greece and Rome were, as religions, alive. We need not, except in studying whatever appropriation there may have been of common and current religious terms, wander down the devious byways, or unravel the chronological maze, of the "substitutes" which the "mystery cults" offered, as religions, for whatever may have been lacking spiritually in the ancient and more official cults. It was to these that St. Paul appealed, in 1 Corinthians, for his argument. It was in their sacrificial meals that he found a parallel to the Christian Communion. And with their technique, as long as it remained, the early Gentile Christians were familiar, and for several centuries therefore the whole Christian Church. Writers who had themselves been converts from paganism had been brought up on it. Writers who had been brought up as Christians still lived in a pagan world. The life which Christians attempted to live was, as we can see from Tertullian and others, inevitably complicated by the daily use of pagan sacrifice in the common events of social and of public life. It was the constant challenge to take part, directly or indirectly, in such sacrifice that made consistent Christianity so difficult. It was the inability to take such part that made the Christians politically suspect, for the old religions were bound up, at every point, with the life of the State. It was because of the living persistence of pagan sacrifice that the martyrs met their deaths.

As long as these conditions continued, there was no likelihood of ignorance of what sacrifice meant. The fathers who lived and wrote before the extinction of the pagan worship, or at least before the toleration of Christianity by the Empire, knew it only too well. They could never dissociate one stage in the sacrificial action from another. They knew the place of the use of the blood, of the act of offering, of the eating of meats sacrificed to idols; they could not dissociate any or all of these from the victim's death.

It is only in the later part of this early period, when the life of the Church is becoming at least partially self-contained, that the first signs appear of a loosened hold upon technique. Here and there language is used, in the time when, for Christian reasons, emphasis is already being thrown in eucharistic worship upon our Lord's death, which anticipates the one-sidedness of later times. It is impossible altogether to dissociate such language from a gradual weakening of the general accuracy in sacrificial language which is otherwise the mark of the earlier centuries.

Cyprian (d. A.D. 258) says that "the passion is the Lord's sacrifice that we offer". In the same passage, however, he says that we offer the cup in commemoration of the Lord and of His Passion: and the Eucharist is to him not the celebration of the Last Supper, in the evening, but, because it is in the morning, a celebration of the Resurrection. Similarly he quotes the passage about Wisdom's feast [1]—thereby including the meal in the sacrifice: and the redemption is not by the Cross only but by the Cross and the Blood.[2] The first reference, often given by itself, would if it stood alone imply the equation of sacrifice with death: but Cyprian is too near the living pagan system; he knows what the idol feasts mean, as St. Paul does; and his words, like those of the other writers of the period whom I shall quote, must not be taken as expressing his whole meaning.

The outstanding passage—as anticipating later language—occurs in St. Gregory of Nazianzus. "Be not negligent", he says, "both to pray and to intercede for us, when by word you draw down the Word, when with bloodless cutting you sever the Lord's body and blood,

---

[1] Prov. ix. 1-5.　　　[2] Ep. 63.

using your voice as your sword."[1] If that were the whole of
his teaching he would stand with the mediaeval and later
writers who use the language of mystical immolation as
the explanation of the eucharistic sacrifice. But it is not:
to him it is the heavenly altar, not the earthly, which is
the true scene of our worship.[2] We join with Christ in all
the stages of His sacrifice, not in worship only but in life.
"By sufferings let us imitate His suffering. By blood let
us honour His blood. With ready mind let us ascend His
cross. . . . Keep the feast of the Resurrection. . . . If He
descend into Hades, go down with Him. Learn there also
the mysteries of Christ. . . . And if He ascend into heaven,
go up with Him."[3]

It is so with St. Chrysostom. "Him who was nailed to
the Cross we are to see as a Lamb slaughtered and sacrificed. . . . When thou seest the Sheep sacrificed and completely offered . . ."[4] "Reverence this Table, of which we
all have communion, Christ slain on our behalf, the sacrifice that is laid upon it":[5] so also the passage quoted
above.[6] On the other hand, there is no question with him
of the repetition of the sacrifice, which the later language
of immolation came so near to making necessary: "we
do not offer another sacrifice, as the high priest of old,
but we ever offer the same; or rather we make the memorial of the sacrifice":[7] and, as we have seen, his whole
conception of the sacrifice is heavenly and spiritual.[8]

We are, in fact, with these writers, at the point where
familiarity with paganism, as a living system, is ceasing.
Gregory of Nazianzus and his successors had been brought
up as Christians. It is easy for them to use expressions
which in the earlier centuries would not have occurred
to those who were brought up on pagan sacrifices, or, at
an earlier period still, to those who were accustomed to
the Jewish. And in no case is it the language of careful
dogmatic exposition. Their phrases are often casual

---

[1] Greg. Naz. *Ep.* 171 (Stone, vol. i. p. 71).
[2] *Ib. Orat.* xxvi. 16 (Stone, vol. i. p. 116).   [3] *Ib.* xiv. 25 (Stone, *ib.*).
[4] Chrys. *De Coem. et Cruc.* 3 (Stone, vol. i. p. 115).
[5] *Ib. In Rom. Hom.* viii. 8 (Stone, *ib.*).   [6] See p. 283.
[7] Chrys. *In Heb. Hom.* xvii. 3 (Stone, vol. i. p. 117).   [8] See p. 283.

X

obiter dicta. And in some cases they are frankly rhetorical. Chrysostom is primarily a preacher: and Cyril of Jerusalem, who resembles him in what we might call crudity of language, but whom, as his expressions are more concerned with the nature of the presence in the elements than with the sacrifice, I have not quoted, is delivering popular expositions or catechetical lectures. What such language shows, with regard to the sacrifice, is that, as Bishop Gore says, "it is obvious that the language of dramatic representation easily slides into that of real repetition".[1] The Eucharist is the memorial of the passion. That language, so far as later inaccuracies are concerned, may mean anything. On the fullest view of sacrifice it is not only historical in fact, but wholly legitimate in theory. The Lamb in the midst of the throne is always the Lamb "as it had been slain". But all expressions about commemorating the Passion grow naturally into a vivid realisation of it. We speak and think, inevitably, every Good Friday, as if our Lord were, at the very moment of our thinking and speaking, actually upon the Cross. And there is a sense in which the Cross, not in memory only, but in the living experience of the sufferings of humanity, of men who are members, or who are made to be members, of Christ's Body, is an ever-present and continuing fact. If we are "crucified with Christ", it is upon His Cross: if we suffer, what makes suffering not bearable only but triumphant is our ability to make it, His grace that enables us to make it, a "suffering with Him". There is, in all the most legitimate language, late as well as early, ample material which, in the light of the later theory, spells "immolation". But throughout the period of the Fathers, such language, however near the line subsequently passed it may in some cases be, is more than safeguarded by the width of their conception of sacrifice.

It is different when the age of eucharistic theology, in the true sense, begins. By that time centuries have passed since even pagan sacrifices were known. It is an age in which there is nothing of what we should call the

[1] Gore, *Body of Christ*, p. 302.

historical sense. There is no desire for, or opportunity of, the study of religious origins. The data for speculation are the inherited and accepted doctrines and practices. The ancient technique of sacrifice has been forgotten. The tradition has already grown of associating the Eucharist as an offering, rather than as an offering and a communion, pre-eminently with the propitiatory pleading of the Cross.

It is not until we come to St. Thomas Aquinas' definition of sacrifice that anything that can be called a conscious theory is formed. From the time of the Fathers until St. Thomas what is being formed is a tradition, not a theory. The tradition is far from being unanimous or consistent. Writers can be picked out, like Bede and Alcuin, in whom the dominant idea is that of the heavenly sacrifice and of the glorified Body.[1] Others use language which often, from the points of view of later teachers, contradicts itself. Gregory the Great speaks of the "renewing" (*reparat*) of the death: the Son "living in Himself immortally and incorruptibly is again sacrificed on our behalf in this mystery of the sacred oblation"; and yet at the hour of the sacrifice the heavens are opened: earth and heaven, angels and worshippers, seen and unseen, are united. He "suffers again . . . ; as often as we offer unto Him the sacrifice of His passion, so often we renew His passion to ourselves to set us free": yet "without intermission the Redeemer offers a burnt-offering on our behalf, who without ceasing presents to the Father His Incarnation for us".[2] So in Florus (*d.* 860) there is the "altar of the Cross", but the altar and the offering of the perpetual sacrifice are also heavenly and spiritual.[3] Paschasius Radbertus (*d.* 865) has both the heavenly offering and the repeating of the Passion.[4] Ratramnus (*d.* after 870), the inspirer of Nicholas Ridley, seems to identify the sacrifice with the Death of Christ.[5] Fulbert

---

[1] Stone, vol. i. pp. 199 ff.
[2] Greg. Mag. *Dial.* iv. 58; *In Ev. Hom.* xxxvii. 7; *Mor.* i. 32 (Stone, vol. i. p. 195).   [3] Florus, *De expos. Miss.* 33, 66 (Stone, vol. i. pp. 215 f.).
[4] Pasch. Radb. *De corp. et sang. Dom.* viii. 1, 2; ix. 1, 2 (Stone, vol. i. pp. 220 f.   [5] Ratramn. *De corp. et sang. Dom.* 100 (Stone, vol. i. p. 232.)

of Chartres (d. 1029) speaks of Him as "sacrificed on the altar of the Cross": but He is, in the Eucharist, accessible to faith, as the worshipper may need, in any of the stages of His work, from His infancy to His heavenly session: and though he distinguishes the heavenly Body, which dieth no more, from the sacramental, which dies daily, the latter also rises daily.[1] Stephen of Autun (d. 1139) is clear about the heavenly action of the Eucharist, but he says that the act of killing is repeated (immolatio iteratur).[2]

There are one-sided expressions of the repetition of the death in other writers; but I only quote from Peter Lombard (d. 1160) because his authority tends to establish and to define the growing tradition on a new footing. "What is offered and consecrated by the priest is called a sacrifice and an oblation, because it is the memorial and representation of the real sacrifice and holy immolation which was made on the altar of the cross. On the cross Christ died once, and then was He immolated in Himself; in the Sacrament He is immolated daily, because in the Sacrament there is the commemoration (recordatio) of that which was done once."[3] I have here altered Dr. Stone's translations (which I have followed in other passages) of two words: in one case ("offered" instead of "presented" at the beginning) there is no serious difference of meaning; but in the other case it is, I think, significant that the word translated "offering, offer" by Dr. Stone, is in the original "immolatio, immolare". It is one thing to say that our Lord is "offered" daily: it is another, and, for our present purpose, much more serious and significant, to say as Peter Lombard does, that He is killed, or "immolated" daily. Such language, in restricting the idea of sacrifice to the death, leaves out the connection of the Eucharist with the rest of our Lord's redeeming work. It also illustrates the constant difficulty of the "immolation" language, which reappears through the history, in the impossibility of

---

[1] Fulbert of Chartres, Epp. v. and iii. (Stone, vol. i. pp. 243 f.).
[2] Stephen of Autun, De Sacr. Alt. cc. 9, 17, 13 (Stone, vol. i. p. 282).
[3] Peter Lombard, Sent. IV. xii. 7 (Stone, vol. i. pp. 306 f.).

saying that our Lord is slain afresh in every Eucharist, without in the same breath calling the action of the Eucharist a mere memorial. The conception of sacrifice is impossible; and the language used to express it breaks down.

It would have been easy to multiply illustrations of what happened: they may be gathered from almost any writers of the period. But there can be no doubt as to the trend of thought. The schoolmen accepted what they found and framed their definitions to include, and, so far as possible, to justify the current beliefs. What is put into words by St. Thomas Aquinas is therefore at once a summary of existing tradition, and a starting-point for new developments. "Sacrifices", he says, "are properly so called when something is done in regard to things offered to God (*quando circa res Deo oblatas aliquid fit*); as that animals were slain and burned, or that bread is broken and eaten and blessed".[1] Here we have at once a profound misconception of the Old Testament. We have seen in Part I. that the purpose of the burning was not destruction but transformation. But in the accepted tradition Christ's sacrifice was His Death. It is this that, on the scholastic method, defines the general idea of sacrifice: this, and the other use of sacrifice in the Eucharist, in which "something was done" to bread. We have not as yet, in St. Thomas, an express use of the word destruction as the key to sacrifice. But his phrase prepares the way for it, as it does for those various modifications of the destruction theory that were afterwards attempted. And, characteristically, the equation of sacrifice with death helps to define the purpose of sacrifice. It is something done to appease God (*ad eum placandum*).[2]

These definitions, or this combined definition, lead on to two other features of St. Thomas' eucharistic teaching of which mention must be made. He justifies the then growing practice of communion in one kind (finally sanctioned in 1415) on the ground that the priest both

---

[1] Aq. *S. T.* II.[2] lxxxv. 3 (Stone, vol. i. p. 324).
[2] *Ib.* III. xlviii. 3 (Stone, *ib.*).

offers and receives in the person of all:[1] and he says that
the perfection of this sacrament lies not in its use by the
faithful but in the consecration of its matter (*non in usu
fidelium sed in consecratione materiae*).[2] The restriction of
full communion to the celebrant, and the teaching that
his work as priest is complete in the consecration, throw
the emphasis of the meaning of the sacrifice upon the first
stage of the Eucharist, and upon the action of the priest
in "offering", rather than upon the complete action of
earlier times which included priest and people, offering
and communion. And, secondly, in close connection of
thought, it follows that a distinction is made between the
Eucharist as sacrifice and the Eucharist as sacrament. It
is out of this distinction that the habit grew of applying
the Mass "mechanically": for St. Thomas laid it down
that, as sacrament, it had its effect only in those who
already had spiritual life, but that, as sacrifice, it availed
for others for whom it might be offered even if their
spiritual life were only potential and not actual. It would
not be fair to impose upon St. Thomas the full meaning
read into this distinction in later times; and I am here
concerned not with what may be regarded as the misapplications of the Mass in detail, but merely to point out
how in both these respects such misapplications opened a
wide field for the effects of erroneous views of sacrifice. It
was the wrong theory of sacrifice which made these
developments possible. It was these developments which
produced the situation contemplated in the XXXIX
Articles (Art. XXXI). It was upon this background that the
language of Article XXXI about the "sacrifices of Masses"
was framed.[3] It may be said indeed that the description
of the Eucharist as partly sacrifice and partly sacrament
is the most concise as it is in some ways the most popular
statement of the mediaeval misconception of sacrifice. It
can only mean that with the act of offering the sacrifice is
complete. That would be untrue even if "offering" were
properly interpreted, if it were understood as in primitive

---

[1] Aq. *S. T.* III. lxxx. 12 *ad* 3.　　　[2] *Ib.* lxxx. 12 *ad* 2.
[3] See Dr. Kidd, *Later Mediaeval Doctrine of the Eucharistic Sacrifice*, pp. 51-57.

times as following, with the pleading, upon the "memorial" of the death. Even so, the true sacrifice only finds its goal and its culmination in the sacrificial feast. The whole procedure of redemption, beginning with our Lord's making Himself one with us in the Incarnation, and His sharing the conditions of our earthly life; continuing on the Cross, and in His passing through the Veil with the Blood with which He makes Atonement before God; issuing in His and our offering of manhood, His own and ours, and in God's acceptance and re-creating of it in the heavenly life; is left, so to speak, suspended in mid-air, ineffective, unfinished, without the union of God with man in the reception of the glorified Manhood and the enfranchised Life which are the Body and the Blood. At every stage the Eucharist is both a sacrifice and a sacrament. If a distinction is to be made, the truth can only be preserved by making its wording cumbersome: so far as it is a sacrifice, it is throughout a sacramental sacrifice; so far as it is a sacrament, it is equally a sacrificial sacrament. Even that goes too far, though it is perhaps technically possible. For in early times the peace-offering was as much a sacrifice as the burnt-offering or the sin-offering. It was only so far as in the imperfections of the old system, and under the limitations of its historical growth, they could be regarded as separate from each other that each could be regarded as "a sacrifice". In practice they were offered together: and if, under the exigencies of language the word sacrifice could be applied to each, it is still true that each contained several of the essential acts of the whole procedure. There is no warrant for applying the word "sacrifice" to the death of the victim alone, or to the use of the blood, or to the offering; but if there were, it would be equally applicable to the act of eating with which the complete sacrificial action ended.

We have arrived, therefore, at the later mediaeval period, which gave us the conditions out of which the Reformation, and our own controversies, arose. The equation "sacrifice = death" is universally accepted. The error is fundamental. I should be straying from my immediate purpose if I attempted to develop its results in other directions. But if it is, as I believe, the ultimate cause of the Reformation protest on its sacramental side, I cannot but suggest briefly what some of those results were.

We have already seen that it was through the growth of the ideas of purgatory that the propitiatory side of the Eucharist, at first and in itself Scriptural and "Evangelical", could be applied in new and dubious ways. We have to add to that temporal and spatial conception of the state of the soul after death the separation of the priest's part in the Eucharist from the people's, and the resulting multiplication of Masses, the idea of the possibilities of the "application" of the sacrifice which we have found, if only in germ, in St. Thomas, and the quantitative or numerical idea both of sins and of masses which marked the later Middle Ages: and the limitation of the sacrificial theory becomes on that side sufficient to evoke the manifold reactions of the sixteenth century, even apart from its own inherent difficulty. It is only in the light of these accretions and developments that we can estimate rightly what the Reformers had to face, and the bearing of what the Protestant world would call the abuses of the Mass upon the far deeper question of the true relation of the Eucharist to the Sacrifice of Christ and of Christians. We are indeed helped, on this side of the question as on that of the Presence in the elements, by the contrast between the mediaeval Western Doctrines and practices with those of the Eastern Church. In the East, these "abuses" have not arisen. There the primitive conception of the Eucharist has survived. Not only has the "heavenly" character of the worship been preserved, but the unity of the sacrifice, in its eucharistic form, has been maintained, because, in spite of infrequency of communion, the priest has never been separated, as in the West, from the people. The primitive form of the eucharistic service is that which brings out its corporate character. The Eucharist is the act of the whole body. Of this "High Mass" is in the West still the expression; and in the East that is the only way in which the Liturgy is used. The

whole of Eastern tradition is concentrated upon the one
Eucharist, in the sense that custom prohibits more than
one celebration each day, at least upon one altar. It is
the exact contrast to the Low Mass of Western practice,
with the whole of the action, or almost the whole, sufficiently performed by the priest. I am not pleading, here,
either for or against what is called full ceremonial in the
eucharistic celebration. But it is unquestionable that the
varied parts of the different assistants, from the officiating deacon and sub-deacon downwards, which to many
modern temperaments merely spell distraction and over-
elaboration, were meant to bring out, did in early times
bring out, and still do in the East, the true idea that the
Eucharist is the common and joint action of the whole
body in which each and all of the members play their
part. The "sacerdotalist" associations of the "Mass"
belong to the much later, and purely Western, traditions
of Low Mass. They are rooted in and inseparably bound
up with what all loyal sons of the Reformation regard as
abuses. It was one of the ironies of English Church history
that for several centuries made the Low Mass, often with
its single officiating priest, and always with no further
"assistance" from the laity than in the collection of the
alms by the church-wardens, the norm and even the
parent of the typical Anglican celebration of the Holy
Communion. It is not the only way in which the English
Church has, quite unwittingly, followed in her ordinary
practice, as well as in her formularies, a mediaeval, and
not a primitive, tradition.

It has often been observed, and I have already suggested, in an earlier chapter,[1] that far more attention has
been paid, in the working out of eucharistic theology, as
well as in popular devotion, to the Presence in the
Eucharist than to the Sacrifice. It has therefore widely
escaped observation that theories of the nature of the
Presence largely depend upon theories of sacrifice. Chronologically, controversy, and theory, about the Presence
come first. But they took shape upon a background at

[1] See Part III. Ch. I.

first of precarious uncertainty, and in the end of positive
error, about the meaning of sacrifice. Yet it is upon the
character and scope of the Sacrifice that the conception
of the eucharistic Body and Blood must be formed. Here
again the example of the East is of value. Apart from
tentative, and often rhetorical or picturesque, expressions, such as we have found in Gregory of Nazianzus,
and Chrysostom, the definite tendency of the East has
been in the direction of preserving the full idea of the
sacrifice, and consequently of the earthly act of worship
being thought of rather as the lifting up of the worshippers to Heaven than as the bringing down of the
Lord to earth. It has followed from this that the characteristic Western ideas of the Presence are not found in the
East. In the West, on the other hand, as the scope of the
sacrifice became narrowed to the "representation" of
Christ's death, and the altar became, however mystically,
the counterpart not of the altar in heaven but of the altar
of the Cross, it became inevitable that the conception of
the Presence should adapt itself to the new point of view.
If the sacrifice was thought of as in some sense an "immolation", then, however insensibly, it was bound to
follow that the Body and Blood should be thought of as
the Body and Blood of Christ as slain. The path was open,
to popular faith, for visions of bleeding hosts, and to
popular interpretations of the Presence which can only
be called materialistic. It was, indeed, to preserve a
spiritual view of the Presence that St. Thomas formulated his doctrine of transubstantiation:[1] and whatever
may be our attitude to the Roman doctrine we ought
never, in fairness, to forget the intention of its real creator.
But popular devotion, and the unphilosophical habit of
the popular mind, read into the metaphysical teaching of
St. Thomas as adopted by the Church what neither he,
nor the best theologians after him, intended. If in the
Eucharist, or in the Holy Communion, the Christ Who is
sacrificed, or Whose Sacrifice is commemorated, is the

[1] See an article by Mr. W. H. V. Reade in *The Guardian* of Nov. 25, 1927, on
"What Thomas Aquinas taught".

Christ as slain upon the Cross—if, that is, the Sacrifice is interpreted in terms of death alone—it is His Body as in death that we are concerned with either in the elements or in our Communion. It is His Body in its preresurrection state, the Body of His Humiliation. It is inevitable, therefore, that where the belief in the Presence is fully and unquestioningly accepted there should be danger of materialism, and that the very fear of materialism should create doubts about the Presence. Here again the wrong idea of sacrifice forces upon us impossible conclusions, and we have another case of the irony of later English developments: not only does Lancelot Andrewes actually use the word "corpse" (cadaver) of the eucharistic Body,[1] but Bishop Moule can say that the sacred Body in our Lord's thought is the Body as in Death: "that is", he continues, "as in the act and process of the One Sacrifice which is our Redemption".[2] It is small wonder that, under the domination of his idea of sacrifice, he needs must say in his memorable statement of our Lord's Presence at the Holy Communion that He is present not *on* the Holy Table, but *at* it.[3] For such a doctrine of the sacrifice drives us either to accept the risk of materialism in believing the Objective Presence, or to avoid the risk by refusing to believe it.

I have said that in the later mediaeval period the equation "sacrifice = death" is universally accepted. There are, it is true, indications here and there that some writers understood that more than the death of the victim was implied, or required, in the Old Testament sacrifices, and the word "offering" is freely used, as well as such words as "immolation". But of the tendency as a whole there is no doubt: and once it was established the word "offer" is regularly used of what happened on the Cross. Strictly speaking, the word "offer" connotes the word "altar", as the "immolation" or the "slaying" of Christ connotes the Cross. But once the idea of sacrifice is limited to the act

[1] Andrewes, *Sermons* (Anglo-Catholic Library), ii. 302.
[2] Report of a Conference held at Fulham Palace in Oct. 1900, p. 29.
[3] *Ib.* p. 73.

of death, the Cross becomes an Altar, and "offer" becomes equivalent to "immolate". Hence such inevitable phrases as "Christ was offered on the Cross", or "the Altar of the Cross", or even "the Sacrifice of the Cross". Such expressions have by long force of habit become so familiar that it may seem almost an impiety to question them; and it would be both hypercritical and unjust to suggest that in our own day they necessarily imply wrong ideas of sacrifice. "The sacrifice of the Cross" occurs, for instance, in the *Answer of the Archbishops of England (Dr. Temple and Dr. Maclagan) to the Apostolic Letter of Pope Leo XIII on Anglican Orders* issued in 1897.[1] In such a context, as in the modern use of such language in general especially in a devotional sense, it is, as a rule, not a question of conscious theorising about sacrifice at all, but of the unconscious repetition of what has become customary. The importance of these phrases lies not in individual instances of their use, but in the evidence which they give of the general acceptance, in the centuries from the late Middle Ages onwards, of an inaccurate, and therefore unworkable, conception of what sacrifice meant; of the wide prevalence of that conception; and of its persistent continuance. Under the influence of that conception it was inevitable that the controversies about the Eucharistic Sacrifice should arise, and, once they had arisen, it has been impossible to reconcile them. But the first step towards an end of controversy is the dispassionate examination of the terms in use. And of the history of those terms there can be no doubt.

It would be easy, but it would be wearisome, to give, at this point, a catena of extracts from theological writers from St. Thomas to the present day, showing the prevalence of the "immolation language", and of such apparently innocent phrases, arising from it, as those which I have mentioned. I shall, however, only give a few examples, taken almost at haphazard; I will ask any reader who wishes to verify what I have said to read the second volume of Dr. Stone's *History*, or almost any book

[1] P. 18.

which contains large collections of passages bearing upon
the eucharistic sacrifice. The examples which follow will
at least illustrate the completeness of the grip to which
the death-conception of sacrifice had attained, and perhaps also some of the difficulties and embarrassments
which it caused, as well as the impasse into which it has
led Western Christendom.

Many pre-Reformation writers might be quoted: but I
will only mention Duns Scotus and his follower Gabriel
Biel, because the Scotist school were regarded, from a
later Roman Catholic point of view, as unsatisfactory in
their teaching on the eucharistic sacrifice, and may be
held to have prepared the way for Protestant denials of
it. In Duns Scotus we find, as we should expect at that
period, "the offering made on the Cross" and "the offering of the passion":[1] and in Gabriel Biel, writing not long
before Luther's time, "the supreme sacrifice offered on
the Cross".[2] And to these perhaps John Colet may be
added, not as a systematic theological writer, but as a
typical representative of the New Learning writing immediately before the outbreak of controversy: "Jesus
Christ", he says, "was sacrificed and offered and died that
we may feed on this sacrifice until He come": "God Himself was offered on the altar of the Cross".[3]

The Reformers, both on the Continent and in England,
leave no doubt either as to their own idea of what sacrifice
was, or as to the ground on which they attacked contemporary teaching, or what they thought to be the contemporary teaching, about the Sacrifice in the Eucharist.
The Lutheran Confession of Augsburg speaks of the
passion of Christ as an offering:[4] and the Würtemberg
Confession of the "oblation once offered on the Cross".[5]
The Zwinglian Book of Articles of 1523 has "Christ, Who
offered Himself once for all on the Cross . . . the Mass
is not a sacrifice but a commemoration of the sacrifice once for all offered on the Cross".[6] Calvin again re-

---

[1] Duns Scotus, *Quaest. Quodl.* xx. (Stone, vol. i. p. 343).
[2] Gabriel Biel, *Sent.* IV. viii. 1 (Stone, vol. i. p. 390).
[3] Stone, vol. ii. pp. 4 f.   [4] *Ib.* p. 26.
[5] *Ib.* p. 34.   [6] *Ib.* p. 38.

gards the Christian sacrifice as completed on the Cross: "it was offered once for all, because the efficacy and power of that one sacrifice which was offered by Christ is eternal, as He Himself bore witness with His own mouth when He said that it was complete and fulfilled".[1]

The definite statement of the Confession of Augsburg that "there was added an opinion, which increased private Masses infinitely, that Christ by His Passion satisfied for original sin, and appointed the Mass in which an offering should be made for daily sins" goes with the definite references to the same "opinion" in our own XXXIX Articles. There (Art. II) Christ is "a sacrifice, not only for original guilt, but also for all actual sins of men"; and (Art. XXXI) "the offering of Christ once made is that perfect redemption, propitiation, and satisfaction, for all the sins of the whole world, both original and actual". It is clear that this last statement has the same bearing on the practical abuses of the day as the words of the Confession of Augsburg; for it continues *"wherefore* the sacrifices of Masses, in the which it was commonly said that the Priest did offer Christ for the quick and the dead, to have remission of pain or guilt, were blasphemous fables, and dangerous deceits". What the Reformers, in England and on the Continent, had in view was the whole system of the multiplication of masses, which had become, in modern language, a part of the financial system of the mediaeval Church, and which alike for moral reasons and for doctrinal meant a radical departure from anything that had been known in earlier days. The extent, and even the existence, of the actual teaching that the Cross availed for original sin and the Mass for actual, or post-baptismal, sins, has been disputed; and it was certainly repudiated, once it had been brought to light, and dropped, so that it cannot be said to have been, still less to be to-day, the official doctrine of that part of the Western Church which is in Communion with Rome. But, in spite of denials, on the Catholic side, of its very existence, there is sufficient documentary evidence to

---

[1] Calvin, *Inst.* IV. xviii. 13 (Stone, vol. ii. p. 55).

show that the opinion had been held, though the Reformers wrongly attributed it to St. Thomas Aquinas, and it may not have been as widespread as the prominence given to it in Reforming documents suggests.[1] But its value for our immediate purpose is that it could not even have arisen, nor could the Reformers' language have been used, if there had not been in the current ideas the implication that what was done on the Altar was of the same kind as what was done on the Cross. It is another vivid illustration of the habit of identifying sacrifice with death, and, with sacrifice, the oblation. That, at least, is shown by the title of our Article XXXI: "Of the one Oblation of Christ finished upon the Cross". There is one offering, as there is one Sacrifice: but only if death alone satisfies the meaning, and gives the full content, of sacrifice, does it follow that oblation is fully performed in the act of death. Granted that underlying idea, both the title and the argument of the Article are inevitable.

The language of Cranmer, Ridley, and Latimer, in incidental descriptions of what they meant by the sacrifice of Christ, is identical with that used by their opponents. Gardiner has, "His sacrifice of His body and blood done upon the Cross":[2] Latimer "the sacrifice which Christ Jesus our Redeemer did upon the Cross".[3] Or again, Gardiner: "the only immolation of Christ in Himself upon the altar of the Cross";[4] Cranmer: "the only offering of Christ whereby He offered Himself unto death to God the Father once for all on the altar of the Cross".[5] And Ridley uses the same language in an argument against the eucharistic sacrifice, at least as he felt it to be understood in the terminology then current: "Now, when we come unto the Lord's board, what do we come for? To sacrifice Christ again, and to crucify Him again, or to feed upon Him that was once only crucified and offered up for us?"[6] Here, clearly, "sacrifice" = "crucify" = "offer".

---

[1] See, for a full examination of the evidence, Dr. Kidd, *op. cit.* pp. 78 ff.
[2] Stone, vol. ii. p. 149.   [3] *Ib.* p. 198.
[4] *Ib.* p. 153.   [5] *Ib.* p. 181.   [6] *Ib.* p. 186.

So it is with the Council of Trent: "although He was about to offer Himself . . . on the altar of the Cross": "He instituted a new Passover, Himself, to be immolated by the Church through her priests under visible signs";[1] and "since in this Divine sacrifice which is accomplished in the Mass, that same Christ is contained and is bloodlessly immolated, who once offered (*obtulit*) Himself in blood (*cruente*) on the altar of the Cross":[2] and again in the Canons twice (Canons 3 and 4) "the sacrifice accomplished on the Cross".

The language of the Council of Trent governs, of necessity, all subsequent Roman Catholic teaching. The passages which I have quoted contain precisely the same triple equation which appears in Bishop Ridley's language. Sacrifice, immolation, and offering seem to be synonyms; and if there are added to them the three epithets "propitiatory", "true", and "proper" which the Council attaches to the word "sacrifice" as used of the Eucharist, it is easy to understand the attitude of the non-Roman writers of the sixteenth and later centuries. For the Mass from the Reformation period onwards was thus inseparably bound up by authority, as it had long been by common consent, with its special propitiatory use, and with most of the theories and practices with which that use had come to be associated; and as defined, in effect, by this special use was also bound up, on its sacrificial side, with the theory of sacrifice which postulated an immolation of some sort in every Celebration.

But doctrinal definitions are never as rigid as they seem; and if we are to do justice to post-Tridentine Roman theology as well as to the Council itself, we have to recognise that a surprising degree of latitude has been achieved, and allowed, in the interpretation of the Council's decisions. For the word "offer" can be extended beyond what happened on the Cross: moral conditions in the worshipper are attached by the Council to the propitiatory side of the sacrifice as a condition of its efficacy: and even the stricter and fuller epithets applied to the sacri-

---

[1] Council of Trent, Sess. xxii. *De Sacr. Miss.* cap. 1.   [2] *Ib.* cap. 2.

fice in the Canons—"true" and "proper"—are not actually defined. The essence of the teaching of Aquinas, that "something must be done to" what is offered in sacrifice, though it undoubtedly lay behind the more thorough-going and usual interpretation of the Trent decisions, and had been the motive force which led to all forms of the "immolation" language, left room, as the history showed, for the mildest form of interpretation also, such as we have in Salmeron, and in a less degree in Vasquez. For them, though in slightly different ways, the idea of "immolation" was practically confined to what happened on the Cross, and in the Mass the separate consecration of the two species is enough to give it its link with the one absolute sacrifice. And, following more or less in this direction, the French theologians, whose distinguished line begins with de Condren in the seventeeth century and is continued to Lepin and de la Taille in our own day, have been able, by extending the idea of the offering beyond what actually happened on the Cross, to bring back into the general idea of sacrifice much of what is apparently left out at Trent, and to give at least some meaning to the Heavenly Offering of our Lord in direct connection with the earthly offering in the Eucharist.

But the omission of all reference to the continued offering in Heaven is and must remain the most serious gap in the statements of Trent. The result has been the commoner and prevailing line of interpretation which, in its very varying forms, has emphasised change or destruction as the distinctive element in sacrifice, whether in the fraction (Melchior Canus, 1520–1560), or in the communion (Bellarmine, 1542–1621), or even in a modification of the victim by way of presentation rather than of destruction (Suarez, 1548–1617), or in the distinct and emphatic sense of destruction of some kind of the actual victim (the "lower condition"—*declivior status*—of the body of Christ produced by consecration, whereby it becomes mere food: de Lugo, 1583–1660, and, similarly, Franzelin, 1816–1886). In all these, in different ways, the "immolation" theory of sacrifice has been the dominant note in interpretation. It is only the more literal use of it that strictly justifies the active protest made at the Reformation; but even the "mystical immolation" theory which is on the whole dominant in the Roman Church of to-day[1] is enough to demand the continuance of the protest in non-Roman formularies.[2]

I have attempted, in fairness, to show how far the Council of Trent left the door open for a wider view of sacrifice than might at first sight appear. But it remains that the real difficulty lies in the sixteenth-century language which the Fathers of Trent were bound to use. Under it, even the most liberal and Scriptural theories of the French writers are bound to allow for at least the overlapping of the idea of offering with that of immolation. The truth is that under the mediaeval, and even earlier, emphasis on the place of the Cross in the complete sacrifice, and the ultimate concentration on the propitiatory element in the Eucharist, what were originally, and should be recognised to-day as, the successive stages of the sacrificial action are, as it were, telescoped. In the original history and in the true conception of sacrifice the death of the victim, and indeed the presentation of the blood, are as distinct from the offering as all are from the communion. We have traced the process by which the Eucharist was successively linked, in the gradual realisation of its meaning, with the different stages of the Christian sacrifice as a whole: first with the last stage, the communion; then with the last but one, the offering; and then with the preceding stages, the pleading with the Blood, and the Cross. We have seen how with the gradual loss of frequent Communion, and for other reasons, the Eucharist, as sacrifice, ceased to be linked with the last stage, and became concentrated more and more exclusively upon the Cross, until it was distinguished as sacrifice in its relation to the Cross, and as sacrament in what remained of its Communion side. But as the language

---

[1] *Dict. de Théologie Catholique*, *s.v.* Messe, cols. 1246 ff.

[2] For a fuller discussion of the Council of Trent and subsequent teaching see Dr. Kidd, *op. cit.* pp. 115 ff.

of offering was too firmly rooted in the traditional view of
sacrifice to be dropped, a meaning had to be found for it
in strict connection with our Lord's death: hence, in the
language of the period which we are considering, the
three stages before communion may be said to have over-
lapped, and, in fact, in the prevalent teaching, to have
coalesced. It became easy, therefore, to misread the
meaning of "burning" in the Old Testament sacrifices,
and to see in it not a transformation through offering,
but a destruction in death. Communion was no longer,
even for the priest (however essential, by our Lord's
command, it was to the service as a whole), regarded as a
part of the sacrificial action. And the fatal equation of
death with sacrifice, with all its consequences in theory
and practice, was the result.

There is, indeed, an almost pathetic side to the Trent
definitions and to their subsequent history. More than
once their authors insist that Christ once offered Himself;
that what is given in the Mass is only the fruit of what was
done upon the Cross, which the Mass represents, and the
virtue of which it applies; and that therefore the sacrifice
of the Mass in no way derogates from the sacrifice of the
Cross. It is the language of immolation, however, which
must remain the stumbling-block: in spite of the anathema
of Trent,[1] if, and so far as, that language is used in any
sense approaching to that of a real slaying of Christ upon
the altar, the word "blasphemy" in our Articles is justified.
Not once or twice only the peril of this is seen in Roman
language, and almost automatically corrected by a reminder that the Mass is not, after all, a real immolation
but a memorial of the one death. Yet a memorial is what
Zwingli taught: and the paradox, as well as the pathos, of
the more extreme developments of the Trent teaching is
always this strange oscillation between "blasphemy" and
Zwinglianism. I say this in no spirit of harshness, or of
controversy. It is only an illustration of the fatal disability, not of the intentions of the Trent theologians, but
of the language in which their times compelled them to

---

[1] Sess. xxii. *De sacr. Miss.* Canon iv.

speak. There is only one remedy, and it is one which I believe is the solution of the difficulties on the Reforming, as well as on the Roman side, of this otherwise irreconcilable controversy. We can translate the inadequate and inaccurate language of the Mediaeval theology into the complete' and accurate vocabulary of the Bible, of the early Church, and of the recovered knowledge of our own day, just as we can translate Hebrew language and ideas into English, or Greek into Latin, or the Elizabethan language of the English Articles into the English of the twentieth century. In such a translation the intentions of the Fathers of the Counter-Reformation can be preserved, as well as those of the Fathers of the Reformation itself. And once, in translating, the true proportions and the accurate technique of sacrifice are recovered, the actions merged in the language of Trent can be dissected out from one another, communion restored to its integral place in the full sacrificial action, the positive teaching of the sacrifice, of the place of the Eucharist in it, of its propitiatory character, can be admitted, the epithets "true" and "proper" can retain their force, and the anathemas may remain indeed on paper, but with no one left to anathematise.

I have dwelt at some length upon the Council of Trent and its consequences, because they carry us to the present day so far as the Roman Catholic doctrine of the Eucharist is concerned, and because they illustrate so vividly the nature of the deadlock to which the equating of sacrifice with death has brought us. That deadlock finds equally clear, though even more varied, illustrations in English theology. There is hardly any typical English writer, until the nineteenth century, who does not start from the same equation. With one school of thought the natural result is the repudiation of every, or almost every, sense in which the Eucharist can be called a sacrifice. The title of Bishop E. A. Knox's book, *Sacrifice or Sacrament*, illustrates in itself how strangely the acceptance of a wrong mediaevalism can influence the most anti-Roman teaching: for that antithesis is, as we have seen, mediaeval, and arises out of the very tendencies against which the author is protesting. It is as unhistorical as the mediaeval idea of sacrifice, from which indeed it emerged; and it is as fatal to the original conception of the communion-meal as the identification of sacrifice with death was to the original conception of sacrifice as a whole. For there is no basis, as we have seen, in the Bible, for a communion-meal which was not itself a part of a sacrifice. No covenant-meal was other than sacrificial. No memorial meal could have been a meal on flesh and blood, in any sense of those terms, unless it had been understood as a meal upon a victim offered in sacrifice. To Jewish Christians, as to us, feeding upon the Body and the Blood would have been so abhorrent as to be impossible unless it had been from the first understood by them as the spiritual appropriation of the living Christ, slain and offered for them first as a Covenant Victim.

But there are many attempts, throughout Anglican history, to find a real meaning for the ancient language of sacrifice in the Eucharist. They vary greatly from one another, but they are alike in one respect. They recognise that the Eucharist is a sacrifice of prayer and thanksgiving, of our alms, of the elements of bread and wine, it may be, and certainly of ourselves, our souls, and bodies. They admit, in different degrees, that so far as the sacrifice of Christ is concerned the Eucharist is more or less completely a memorial of it, or even, by a straining, sometimes, of language, a memorial sacrifice. Some writers go very near to the justifiable part of the mediaeval and Tridentine language of propitiation, for they recognise that the Eucharist is the supreme moment of intercession, and therefore, in Archbishop Bramhall's words, "impetratory". They cannot admit, with all this, that the Eucharist is an offering of Christ. For the obsession, and the restrictions, of the mediaeval idea of sacrifice continue. They speak, like their predecessors, of the sacrifice of the Cross; and if the Death of Christ is a sacrifice, He cannot be sacrificed again. The Cross is all-sufficient as an Atonement for all sin; and if the Cross is the sacrifice, a sacrifice of the Altar must be another sacrifice, and will impugn the uniqueness of the Cross.[1] That, again, under the limitations of the old language, is true. Yet it leaves a supreme difficulty wholly unsolved. I leave aside here the question of the true meaning, in its Hebrew models, of a phrase like "sacrifice of praise and thanksgiving", for I have already pointed out that in the Hebrew usage it must mean not a sacrifice in which praise and thanksgiving are offered, but a sacrifice of something which is offered in praise and thanksgiving. But our alms, the elements, our own lives: to say that these are worthy to be offered to God in themselves is either pagan or Pelagian. It is not Christian. Nothing that we have, no offering that we can make—no prayer indeed, or thanksgiving that we can utter, for what I am saying applies as strongly to the common interpretation of the familiar and beloved phrase of the Prayer Book—can be brought to God otherwise than "through Jesus Christ our Lord". So the ending of every prayer testifies. So we are bound to confess, if we accept St. Paul's language and the experience of Christendom, and recognise that nothing can be done worthily and purely that is not done "in Christ". Nor can we dissever ourselves, for the purposes of eucharistic worship alone, from the living Body of Christ of which by baptism we are members. What we do, the Body does; what the Body does, we try to do; and the Body can never act without its Head: the Body is Christ. Whatever we offer therefore, we offer in Him; offering it, we offer Him.

Once more the mediaeval language must be translated. Once we recapture the older language, we, like the Roman Catholic Church, can disentangle what we, no less than she, have merged. We cannot cut the knot. We must untie it; or we must disentangle, for the confusions which history has left us are rather a tangle than a knot. Only so can we pass, without repudiation of our forefathers, and without apology for any form of Anglican denial, however extreme, from misunderstanding and controversy into understanding and unity.

[1] Archbishop Bramhall: "a suppletory sacrifice": see Stone, vol. ii. pp. 341 f.

I have said nothing of the developments of Anglican teaching which began with the Oxford Movement. They have their unique value so far as they have forced upon us the solution of the problem of the eucharistic sacrifice, and made it, whether sufficiently explained or not, a real part of modern devotional life. In their earlier stages, without any abandonment of the Anglican tradition, they commonly assumed, though often with little conscious emphasis, the traditional language about the Sacrifice of the Cross; and to this extent they have recovered the truth of the ancient teaching of the Church without solving the difficulties which the traditional language created. To criticise or examine them in detail would only mean the repetition of much that has been already said. But in our own day there have been many expositions such as I have attempted in this book. The full conception of sacrifice, and the vision of the heavenly worship, have largely been recovered, and it is indeed only the strange persistence of the familiar theory of sacrifice, and the general failure to recognise what has been so often made clear, that can justify another attempt to say what has been better said before. The "man in the street", and many who are more familiar with theology than he, would still, if they were asked to describe a sacrifice, suggest an altar, with a living victim bound upon it, and a priest standing over it with a knife in his uplifted hand. Translated into the language of the Christian Sacrifice, that is the conception of Christ offering Himself upon the Altar of the Cross, of sacrifice as equivalent to, and completed in, death. And until that delusion, however venerable it may be, is dispersed, the truth must be stated and re-stated until it is plainly seen. It is such a statement that I shall attempt to give in my last chapter.

CHAPTER IV

THE COMPLETE PICTURE

"I WILL have mercy and not sacrifice." "Christ was once offered." "This our sacrifice of praise and thanksgiving." We have already seen that in these three familiar phrases there are contained principles, each of which must have its full value in any complete view either of Christian life or of Christian worship. The history of Christendom shows vividly enough how easy it is for the "ethical", the "Evangelical", the "Catholic" aspects of what should be a single whole to be so emphasised by controversy as to become isolated. Each, or each two, in turn can be pressed to the apparent exclusion of the rest; yet in isolation none is capable of being stretched to cover the whole content of the Christian tradition or to satisfy the demands either of Christian thought or of Christian feeling.

Or again, and more simply, it has proved fatally easy to allow life and worship to fall apart from each other. That which is offered, or received, in worship can be so conceived that it becomes unrelated to that which is done, or needed, in everyday conduct; and it is then that worship, if it is unattractive, becomes undesired, or, in proportion as it is made beautiful and satisfying, becomes to the very best men something that is itself undesirable. It can be made an end in itself, and the instinct for it can be so satisfied as to leave the moral side of our nature untouched. Or, on the other hand, the moral life, once separated from the stimulus of intercourse with the living God which is the secret of all specifically Christian character, can become cold, austere, abstract, impersonal,

328

the typical product of a moral philosophy rather than of a personal religion.

What we need is a conception of worship so framed that it touches, and includes, every department of human activity; and a conception of life which at every point is directed towards God, and consciously depends upon God, in such a way that the moments or the acts of worship are the points of contact between God and everything of which the worshipper forms part. And since life is corporate, and all outward acts of worship are corporate, life, so blending into worship, worship, so irradiating and energising life, are both safeguarded against selfishness, the great temptation, and loneliness, the great tragedy, of our experience. The City of God is also His Temple: worship and service, in the vision of the perfect life, are only two sides of an inseparable whole.

It is when worship and conduct, ceremonial and rite on the one hand, and character on the other, tend to fall apart that the place of what we call in the technical language of theology Christian dogma, and in the language of experience the characteristic Christian convictions, such as those of sin and of redemption, become uncertain and unstable. As in time-worn doctrinal controversies, so in the modern undoctrinal drift, it becomes impossible to give full play to the three fundamental elements of historical Christianity. Yet none can stand alone.

If I have written about sacrifice, it is on an assumption, for which I hope that I have already given enough ground to call it, at least for myself, a conviction, that the Christian sacrifice, properly understood, contains, as an idea, far more than is commonly supposed. As applied to the Atonement, it is more than a hard dogmatic theory, or an antiquated and outworn formula. As applied to the Eucharist, it is more than a type of ceremonial or rite, or a recrudescence of primitive or discarded superstition. It is the expression at once of the most fundamental and typical Christian convictions and also of the most characteristic and the simplest Christian morality.

It is precisely when, and so far as, the conception of

sacrifice becomes imperfect, or inaccurate, that what I have called the fundamental elements of Christianity, and what should be the inseparable conceptions of worship and life, become divorced from one another. And history, in recording such divorce, justifies it.

The theologians of the Reformation, whatever their defects, or the defects ultimately revealed in the systems of which they were the authors, had to face an accepted idea of sacrifice which, as used to interpret the Eucharist, seemed to them to impugn the all-sufficiency of the Cross. Under the limitations of the language which, in their days and for long after, all Western Christendom had unconsciously agreed to use, they were right. That which was done on the Cross was unique. It was all-availing. Its merits were infinite. If it had to be called the Sacrifice of the Cross, there could be no other. No refinement of words, no stretching of the convenient, because almost indefinable, word "mystical" could justify belief in a Sacrifice of the Mass. They were faced, or thought inevitably that they were faced, with a choice. The very heart of Christianity from the beginning had been up to their time, and is to-day, the conviction that in the Cross alone is salvation. That is "Evangelical" religion. It, and it alone, is literally true to the best and least controversial sense of that supreme, but ill-used, word, for it summarises the Gospel as preached at the beginning. It, and it alone, redeems the word to-day from the narrowing and degrading associations of controversy. For the "Evangelicalism" which is concerned first and last with the preaching of the Cross can never die. What it asserts is true: what hinders it is the denials, attached to it by the perversities of history, of other aspects of the Christian faith and life which have been made to seem inconsistent with its essential message. The Reformers believed that they had to choose between the preaching of the Cross and the preaching of "another gospel". So believing, could they have chosen otherwise? They chose, and many of them, leaders and followers alike, sealed their choice with their blood. They were martyrs for the truth; and, if we have

to say, "for the truth as they saw it", we do not diminish
the glory of their martyrdom. We only admit that our
circumstances are not theirs; that increased knowledge
means not blame for them but responsibility for ourselves. They could but speak the things which they had
heard and seen.

The defenders of the traditional doctrines, on the other
hand, were in an equally impossible position. Up to the
time of the Reformation, as we have seen, sacrificial
language had been attached to the Eucharist at all times
and in all parts of the Christian world. In the best and
widest sense of the word "Catholic", the eucharistic
sacrifice, whatever it meant, was a part of the Catholic
tradition. As it was legitimately possible to say, on the
one hand, that no tradition, however venerable or universal, could be allowed to interfere with the central
experience of the Cross that had made Christianity what
it was, so it was equally possible, and equally legitimate,
to say that, whatever the difficulties of terminology, no
part of the Catholic tradition could be surrendered. If
"sacrifice" was merely death or destruction, and was
therefore the right word for what happened on the Cross,
then some way must be found of explaining, without
abandoning, the Sacrifice of the Altar. It was not the
fault of the Mediaevalist, or "Catholic", theologians that
they, like the Reformers, were tied to language so inaccurate that it could not serve as a vehicle for truth.
With the means at their disposal, and at that of their
adversaries, the truth had to be divided. As the Reformers were right on the one side, so were the Catholics
on the other.

Or again, in more recent times and in our own, sacrifice
has been understood as implying something in the character of God that is either immoral or unworthy. We have
inherited from the ages of misconception, the history of
which I have attempted to trace, the belief that sacrifice
consists in the substitution of an innocent victim for a
guilty sinner, and, concurrently, though the second conception does not necessarily attach to the first, the belief

that sacrifice is destruction. Hence the inevitable, and wholly justifiable, recoil from the sacrificial interpretation either of the Eucharist or of the Atonement. Nothing can be conceivable in the character of God which would not be moral or worthy in the character of man. Morality is outraged by the idea of a God Who will punish the innocent in place of the guilty: and equally by the idea of a God Who takes pleasure in mere destruction. If sacrifice therefore means substitution or destruction, in the interests of morality itself, in our very reverence for the character of God, sacrifice must go.

Or worship, interpreted in terms of sacrifice, may be supposed to suggest magic. There is no doubt that there have been times, both in the history of primitive religion, and in that of some of the developments of Christian worship, when the mere performance of certain outward acts, or the mere repetition of certain words, have been supposed to produce effects upon the action of God. And because primitive religion was sacrificial, and the most conspicuous act of Christian worship has been interpreted in a sacrificial sense, magic and formalism are words easily used at the expense of the conception of sacrifice in general. I say, they are easily used, because they are so used with more ease than accuracy. Jewish and Christian history, as well as that of religion generally, show clearly enough that other religious actions, besides sacrifice, can be made magical or formal. Isaiah, as we have seen,[1] denounced formal prayer in the same breath as formal sacrifice; and no one would deny that in the most anti-sacrificial types of Christian worship it has proved possible to carry mechanical prayer to the point at which formalism passes into magic. But, allowing for this necessary care in the use of language, we have to recognise that sacrifice, as well as prayer, can be interpreted, and used, in a formal and magical sense. Such interpretation is as foreign to the true conception of sacrifice as the equation of it with death, or the explanation of it in terms of substitution or of destruction. But where it occurs it brings the in-

[1] See Part I. p. 69.

evitable recoil. We cannot, again, reverence a God Who is influenced by purely mechanical means; and a false conception of sacrifice, once more, in the very interest of true religion, at once causes and justifies the recoil from the idea of sacrifice itself.

Let me recapitulate, or summarise. What is the Christian sacrifice? Or what is the Christian conception of life as expressed in the true language of sacrifice?

I have tried to show[1] that in our Lord's "simplest" teaching there are three great principles which follow, the one from the other, in order both of thought and of action, and that these are, in fact, the underlying principles, or stages, of sacrifice. They emerge, in the teaching and practice of the early Church, as essential parts both of eucharistic worship and thought, of Christian doctrine and experience, and of the formulation of Christian character They are not less necessary or possible to-day.

"Follow Me." "Herein is love: not that we loved God, but that He loved us and sent His Son. . . ." Christ begins with a gift and with a demand. The gift is that He takes up His Cross; the demand that we should take up ours. Surrendering His Life, He asks, insists, that we shall surrender our own with His. That surrender is, for Him and for us, the acknowledgment of sin; on His side, the acknowledgment of the sin, not of Himself, but of the human family of which, in His love for us, He has made Himself a living part. Like the Prodigal Son, we, as a race, have wandered into the far country of our sins, into the outer darkness where we can neither see the vision of God nor hear His Voice. God cannot, will not, force us back, for our yielding to force would be morally worthless, and force would be, on God's part, the destruction of the freedom which He has given us, of His image in which we were made. The return to God must be our own. Man, who has sinned, and, in sinning, left his Father's house, must return. Yet none can make the first move, for all are tied and bound by the chain of their sins; blinded by long disuse to the heavenly vision, deaf to the heavenly voices;

---

[1] Part II. chs. II., III., IV.

unaware, by the force of agelong absence, of the heavenly country itself. Into the outer world Christ comes. He makes Himself bone of our bone, and flesh of our flesh. In the darkness He alone can see, for He alone has the vision of the pure in heart. Across the distance He alone can hear, for He has never ceased His perfect intercourse with the Father. To Him the heavenly country is the Father's house where He is at home. And on the other side, in sharing His brethren's exile, He knows, as they cannot, what they have lost. He sees, as they cannot, what it costs to be separated from God. He feels the pains that they cannot feel. He knows that the life which their sins have withheld from the service of God must be surrendered to Him again. He, and He alone, at first, knows what sin really is, and what the deliverance from sin will cost. He, and He alone, has a will that is not paralysed by long mis-use. He can make the move. "The Son of man must be killed." He takes up His Cross. And, taking it, He passes through the first stage of sacrifice. He is slain, as the victim in the old sacrifices was slain, not by the Priest—not by Himself, as God's representative—but by the sinners for whom He dies. And, so dying, so surrendering His Life, He passes with the Blood, which is the sur-rendered Life, through the Veil, which is His flesh, His own broken Body, into the Holy of Holies, the very Presence of God. The Life, which is His Blood, the life, that is, in the ancient belief, both of God and of all His children, and therefore His Life and ours, has been not destroyed, but set free. It is delivered from the prison house, the far country of sin, from the bondage of corrup-tion. That is His part in the first stage of the Sacrifice. It is His gift, and the Father's gift. It is that for which God, Who so loved the world, gave His Son, that whosoever believeth on Him may have everlasting life. That element in the Christian sacrifice, the Cross of Christ, stands by itself. It can never be repeated. It belongs, as we see it, to one moment of history and to one place in the world, and to no other: for we can only see it in time and space. It is only so far, and equally just so far, as we can use the language of eternity or of heaven, that we can also say that the Cross is an eternal fact. The Lamb, alive for ever, is always, before God, the Lamb "as having been slain in sacrifice". I do not dare, in this connection, to use, if it can be helped, language that is either technical or controversial. But it would be almost true to say that the Cross is eternally present and can never be re-presented. It is altogether true to say, as I have said, that it can never, "mystically" or otherwise, be repeated.

With Christ's gift comes His demand. He took the first step in man's return, in order that, joining ourselves to Him, we may, in His strength, under His guidance, seeing with His eyes, hearing with His ears, take the steps that follow. He bore His Cross, not that we might escape bearing ours, but that in Him we might be able to bear it. He was crucified, not instead of us, but that, as St. Paul knew, we might be crucified with Him. So, in the Johannine language, and in the thought, when properly understood, alike of St. Paul and of the Creeds, we "believe on Him in order that we may have everlasting Life". What He gives is the power to identify ourselves with Him, or, as St. Paul would say, to become members of His Body: What He demands is the surrender of ourselves to that fellowship. He warns us that it means the Cross; but He makes it possible by human intercourse and friendship. That is the story of the earthly ministry; and the experience of those who have been His since Pentecost only repeats the old story of His intercourse with the Twelve. That intercourse, with them and with us, leads to a double union with Him. As He looked forward in the old days, He spoke of it as constituting a blood-relationship. To the first Christians the union was clear, in its double aspect, from the beginning. For, to the adult newly won over in a heathen world, baptism inevitably meant the taking up of the Cross. As time went on the union becomes operative in one sense in Baptism; in another, and too frequent a sense, potential. For it is possible, as experience shows, once the Church has nominally Christianised society, to be one with Christ in Baptism, and yet to pass through life without any conscious acceptance of the Cross. Yet the demand remains, as does the opportunity. And the secret of taking the opportunity, of finding, or recognising, the Cross when it comes, sought, as in conscious and deliberate self-denial, or unsought, as in acceptance of the burdens and of the disabilities of life, is always in the realising of the Cross of Christ. He gives us, indeed, not only something to think about, or to understand, or to attempt, but something, supremely simple, to do. We are to be washed, in faith, and in that washing, or Baptism, we are brought into the living touch with Him which makes all things possible and gives us the powers of His life, which is our new life. We are to break the bread, as His Body was broken, and, in the memorial of His Cross, as in our Baptism, we are admitted into the new and eternal world in which He is known of us as the Lamb that hath been slain. But that act, if it is to have its meaning for us, means the conscious, daily, effort of self-surrender, in a thousand small acts of unselfishness, as well as in great self-denials, or in the acceptance of obvious and recognisable Crosses.

That is the first stage in the Sacrifice, for Him and for us; it is the self-surrender which is in the spirit of the Cross.

And the second is in the new field to which the Cross admitted Him, and admits us. Its key-note is the service of perfect obedience. "Lo, I come to do Thy will, O God." In Him that obedience had been without flaw and without reserve. His manhood had been offered in the body of His humiliation. So offered, with a perfectness to us inconceivably complete, it is accepted, and "on the third day", when He rises again, transformed. In Him manhood has passed, wholly and fully, into the new and wider world of which He had so often spoken. The whole of His human powers are for ever identified with the unhindered action of the Will of God. They are lifted into a new life, of new value; the life of the unimpeded Spirit. For a time His manhood is made known to human senses, but only when those senses are sufficiently touched and lifted by faith to enable them to apprehend it. He "appears", not to His enemies, but only to His friends. And in the short records of the experiences of the forty days, there is still enough of the old manner of living to make His friends sure that it is their own Master and Friend Who is alive with them. He allows them sometimes to recognise Him, and sometimes shows them how to find Him in other human forms, so that at first they do not know Him when He is there. But the marks of the Cross are present, and He is the same to-day as He was yesterday. At the Ascension the transformation, and, with it, the need for evidential appearances, are complete. And at Pentecost, and after, they know Him as truly as before, though only in the Spirit. They have discovered that when they come together on the first day of the week He is in their midst, and they have known Him in the breaking of the Bread. He has been offered, or offered Himself, and the offer has been accepted. The fire of the Spirit has come from heaven on his Manhood, and He has gone up, as did the burnt-offering, in symbol, in old days.

But He does not go, has not gone, alone. He is still the Body of which His own are members, or the Head of the Body, leading where they follow. In Him mankind has begun its return to the presence of God, is once more serving in the Kingdom of the King and at home in its Father's house. The service of His members is His service. He does not cease to obey because He has made obedience possible. In Heaven He is still Man; and as Man He works. There can, indeed, be no ultimate distinction between His glorified life and the life of redeemed humanity. His self-surrender is indeed complete; His own obedience is complete. But in Him and through Him alone mankind, so far as it is joined to Him, continues to offer its service of obedience to God. It is in this sense alone, but in this sense necessarily, that His offering of Himself continues. It represents, it embodies, indeed, the whole movement of humanity and of all Nature towards God. What we have learned to see, in the discoveries of the development of created life, in biology, in anthropology,

Z

in every other branch of "science", in the history of the upward movement of the human individual and of society, is indeed the picture of the ceaseless stream of created life towards God Who gave it. When that movement becomes conscious, wherever there is a deliberate choice of the better and the higher instead of the worse and the lower, we call it self-dedication. When it is fully self-conscious in the Christian sense it becomes a part of the offering of the Christian sacrifice. But the Christian, in this sense, as in others, is a priest. As man is Nature's priest, in the sense that he leads the movement of Nature towards God, so the Christian is the priest of all mankind, in the sense that in him is made explicit what is implicit in all unconscious human self-dedication.

It is this great stream of offering that is expressed, symbolised, summed up in the offering of the Eucharist. As the elements are made to express the breaking of the Body once broken, and the pouring out of the Blood once shed, so, in offering them thus broken and poured out, in the simple action that goes deeper than words, we join in, we gather up, the whole movement of Nature and of mankind towards the Throne. What is offered, at every Eucharist, may be expressed in praise and thanksgiving, may be represented in part by the gifts that we bring. but all these are what they are only as expressions, or representations, of the one offering that is always in process. We bring to the Altar, or we should bring, every part of our life outside the sanctuary. Every part of it is indeed the material which we present. It is only an arbitrary and accidental line that we draw at the church door. For the whole village street that leads up to the west door of the church standing at its head, the fields in which the village does its work, are as much God's house as the building of the Church itself. What is presented in symbolic and corporate act at stated times within the Church walls is what has been gathered, offered, achieved in street and field, in factory and school and playground and home.

For all that is worth doing, all that is well done, is

part of the supreme and single effort of Christ our Head.
If anything is perfect, it is from Him: if anything is imperfect, what is good in it is His, and we offer it to be
made good, or to be made whole, by Him. And everything and everyone, so offered, is, like Him, but by infinitely slower stages, because of our infinitely less perfect beginnings, accepted, and, in acceptance, transformed.
That, quite apart from *a priori* Christian teaching, is a
fact of daily experience. It is seen in the spiritualised
face, the growing refinement and delicacy and gentleness,
the growing moral strength of those who have lived obviously dedicated lives. It is seen in the unfolding of un-
suspected powers of head and heart in men and women
who in their early years appeared to have neither ability
nor character. It is seen in the outcome of all honest and
self-sacrificing work. God, here and now, reveals the new
values of the life of the Kingdom of Heaven into which
His servants try to enter and to bring their work.

So it is with the Eucharist. There, as we have seen, the
whole approach to God, alike with our offerings and our
needs, is covered, directed, uplifted by thanksgiving.
For thankfulness of heart, alike in achievement and in
failure, is the expression of faith; and the prayer for acceptance, for comfort, for power, for forgiveness, that
comes from a faith that is at all times and under every
stress an outburst of thanksgiving, is the prayer that God
must answer: "must", not because He is compelled by
magic, but because His nature is Love; and such thankfulness and faith spring from a love that His love must
answer, or deny itself. In the Eucharist, therefore, what
we offer is accepted, and what is accepted is transformed.
We offer Christ's Manhood, which we call His Body: our
manhood which has been made part of His, and which we
try daily to identify with His more closely by Christlike
living; our gifts, to be transformed, or transvaluated like
the widow's mite: and the elements in which all these are
gathered up and symbolised. Is it possible that when all
else that is concentrated in the eucharistic offering is
transformed we must say that to these only no blessing

is given, no power conveyed? Or can we think of them, once set apart and offered, as separate from, contrasted with, that which they represent? As symbols they have already, by breaking and pouring out, been made to "represent", or at least to "remind of", the breaking of the Lord's Body and the shedding of His Blood upon the Cross; and that intimate association with Him (I avoid purposely any of the possible technical terms) they must retain in all the stages, whatever those stages are, of the eucharistic action until they have been received in Communion. It was as symbols that they were always regarded; and we have to remember the often-quoted saying of Harnack:[1] "What we nowadays understand by 'symbol' is a thing which is not that which it represents; at that time [in the early Christian centuries] 'symbol' denoted a thing which, in some kind of way, really is what it signifies".

I only say so much as this about the elements, not to introduce the disputes about them at this stage, but because it is wholly impossible to consider the Eucharist as our point of contact with the offering of the whole Body of Christ, whether we think of it mainly as our offering of Him or as our offering of ourselves, without finding for them their own place in the eucharistic action. And all that I am saying at the moment is that if, and so far as, it is legitimate and, as I should myself say, necessary to give to offering, in some sense, an integral place in the whole action, the Elements must bear the same part in it which they bear in the commemoration of the Cross and in the act of communion. And if, with the idea of offering properly made, there goes in all Christian experience the idea of God's acceptance of what is offered and His transformation, or transvaluation, or lifting, raising, changing, spiritualising it in acceptance, then in some sense at least the Elements will be transformed with the rest of the whole offering of which they are both symbols, and, as symbols, actual parts.

---

[1] Harnack, *History of Doctrine* (Eng. trans.), ii. p. 144, quoted in Gore, *Body of Christ*, p. 89.

The third stage in the Sacrifice, once more for Christ and for us, is the sharing of the Life that has been set free in the surrender of the Cross, and offered, accepted, and transformed. It is the stage of the Communion-meal. The Life of the Body, and therefore of the Lord, whether we think of Him as the Head of the Body or as the Body as a whole, is to be made, more fully than ever, our own life. More fully than ever: for from the moment of our first admission to the Body we possess it; but our membership, in this stage of our existence, is but partial, incomplete, undeveloped. We are children, and a child's life needs food in order that it may grow: we are weak, and the weak need food to give them strength: we are diseased, and we need the right food, and not the wrong, that we may have health. So the Christian is said to be "in Christ", and Christ is "in him". To achieve that inward and outward unity of Christ with His own is the ultimate purpose of the whole work of Redemption, alike of the Incarnation and of the Atonement.

Here, more than anywhere, the accepted language of the New Testament and of devotional experience is found to be difficult. The ordinary man is apt to say that, for him, the idea of "mutual indwelling" is unreal, a thing, perhaps, for "saints", or for exceptionally religious people, but without meaning in the ordinary experiences of the world. Yet, as so often happens, it is precisely in the common intercourse of life that the highest truths of religion find at once their analogy and their justification. Because God is Personal, our intercourse with Him will prove to present analogies to our intercourse with human persons in the affairs of every day. And it is just in this intercourse that we can see most easily what mutual indwelling can mean. For the experience of life is that in friendship, and still more in friendship that has ripened into love, two living persons grow into each other's lives, or selves. Love, as we say, takes us out of ourself; and that is another way of saying that it takes us into the self of the person whom we love. Each self remains distinct, but each penetrates the other, and in this interpenetration a

common life is first created, then developed, which in turn
gives a new fullness to the individual selves, or lives,
which contribute to it. And the closer this union, the more
that thoughts, feelings, wills, actions, are linked together,
the more literally true is it that each lives in the other.
This is "mutual indwelling" in common human experience. And its nature, its possibilities, its value, are revealed
nowhere more clearly than in its absence. For it is again
a common element in experience that the wholly self-
contained, self-absorbed, selfish, personality is narrowed,
cramped, starved. It is in unselfish expansion into the
lives of others that personality is developed; in the instinct
of the love, and therefore of the service, of others; in
the sense of family, of social, civic, national, world-wide
obligations; in friendship in all its degrees; and, most of all,
in the intimate relationships of life between brother and
sister, parents and children, husband and wife.

It is therefore only on a line with our common experience that the Love of Christ means that His Life, that all
that He is, issues forth into ourselves. He and we describe
His relationship, and God's relationship, to us precisely
in terms of human relationships. He calls us to be, and
makes us, citizens of a City, subjects of a King, members
of a Body, and, more intimately still, He makes Himself
known to us as a Friend: He makes us children of a Father,
and is Himself our Brother; and alike in His own teaching,
and in St. Paul's development of it in the Epistle to the
Ephesians, He teaches us that the marriage, whereby two
human beings become in the full possibilities of love one
flesh, is the mystery, the secret revealed, of Himself and
His Church.

It is in this sense that He gives Himself to us in
Communion. He gives His flesh—His Manhood in the
corporate sense of manhood as organically shared—and
His Blood, which is His Life. Or if we speak not of His
flesh but of His Body, it is Manhood as it was meant to be,
a thing only realised in the corporate activities of a single
whole compacted of many parts. The Body, or the Flesh,
is spiritual, because it has passed through death, has been

offered and accepted and transformed. The Life is eternal, because in death it has been surrendered and brought into the presence and into the full stream of the Life of God. And the meal that we are given on earth becomes at once the meal in the Kingdom of which Jesus spoke at the Last Supper. It is the Messianic banquet, if we use the phraseology of our Lord's own Jewish religion; but because it is Jewish it is essentially also a sacrificial meal with the associations of spiritual eating and drinking which I have already traced.[1]

Here indeed the "allegories" or "metaphors" of St. John's Gospel fall into line not only with the sacramental meaning of the Eucharist, but, as is not so often seen, with each other. It is not only that Jesus is the Bread of Life. He is also the Living Water: for the idea of living water in the Old Testament is inseparably bound up with the blood, which is the life, of God, and that Life He gives us in the Living Water which is His Blood. He is the Good Shepherd; and the primary thoughts of shepherding, as we have seen, are those of feeding and of ruling. As He rules us, so He feeds us: "The Lamb which is in the midst of the throne shall be their shepherd, and shall guide them unto fountains of waters of life".[2] And in the figure of the vine He gives us the whole picture of the Body with its members, each and all depending upon the intercommunication of a single Life.

Nor, if we open our eyes to what the Eucharist reveals, can we fail to recognise that it is He Who is the Light which makes the vision possible, as He is the Light in which alone we can see the whole extent and character, the proportions and the values, of the Kingdom, the City, the home, into which we are admitted. And He is the Door through which the sheep go in and out and find pasture, moving from home to food, and from food to home; but the movement is always through Him. We pass, as He passed, through His broken flesh which is the veil, as in old days the sharers in the covenant sacrifice passed, with the light which represented God to

[1] See above, Part II. Ch. IV. pp. 180-184. [2] Rev. vii. 17.

Abraham, between the divided bodies of the victims. So, in another illustration, a ladder is set up by which the interchange between Heaven and earth, God and humanity, is maintained.[1] The truth that He is the Door, indeed, a part in the life both of earth and of heaven, helps to illustrate the two great aspects of eucharistic worship which are characteristic, though not exclusively in either case, of the Eastern and the Western Church. In the West, the tendency has been in the main to think of the worship as on earth, and of the Lord as coming down upon the visible Altar. The altar and the people are therefore naturally brought together: the altar is open and seen, and the whole action of the Eucharist takes place before the people's eyes. It is through Him Who comes to the altar, or to be in their midst, that they see the heavenly vision: He is the Door, so to speak, behind the earthly altar. There are, of course, the dangers or the limitations that accompany this view of the Eucharist, such as Bishop Gore describes in what he says about "Jesus-worship", and experience shows that in the West it has been only too easy to lose sight of the Heavenly worship altogether, and to see on the earthly altar only what happened, on earth, on the Cross. In the East, on the other hand, the altar is shut off from the people, except at the moments when the Royal Doors are opened, by the iconostasis, or screen. Yet no one who has taken part in the worship of the Eastern Liturgy can for one moment feel that to the people that means, as it would to us in the West, exclusion from the worship itself. Their part in it is not less real, and often far more real, than anything that we know. Is it not because the typically Eastern idea of worship is in exact contrast with the Western, in the sense that in the Eucharist, instead of heaven being brought down to earth, earth is lifted up to heaven? From this point of view, the Altar, or, as we should call it, the sanctuary —the whole space within the screen—*is* symbolically

---

[1] Gen. xxviii. 12; Jn. i. 51. For "the angels of God ascending and descending" cf. the Canon of the Latin Mass: "command them to be brought by the hands of Thy holy Angel unto Thine Altar on high".

Heaven; and the congregation knows that the Royal Doors are, like Christ Himself, the door between earth and heaven. The opening of the door is in that sense a reminder in a symbolic form that at no single Eucharist can it be ignored that in our earthly worship Heaven is opened to us.

Be this, however, as it may, these Johannine allegories all find their place in the full picture of the eucharistic, or, in its full and best sense, sacrificial life of the Church, in what is commonly called "life", and what is commonly called "worship". And, using them so combined, we are at once free from the old difficulty of attempting to interpret "I am the Bread of Life" in a different sense to the others. We used to be told, and with much reason, that in form the sayings were the same; and that since the rest were obviously metaphors and figures, we must not take literally the words about the Bread of Life. Seen, however, all of them, as bringing out, each in its own way, different sides of the same spiritual picture, they may still be treated as in form the same; but instead of metaphors, in the language of true understanding, they become all literal truths. We need no longer depress the meaning of "I am the Bread of Life"; but we enhance the meaning of the rest.

I have attempted, and no one can be more conscious than I how unworthily and imperfectly, to suggest in these pages both the content and the character of the Christian sacrifice. To see both content and character in full is the surest safeguard against those views of parts or aspects of it which, once seen out of their place in the whole, could be misunderstood, and out of the misunderstandings of which our worst divisions and controversies have come. I will only illustrate in two ways.

It is precisely the fear of either a literal or even a "mystical" repeating of the Cross which has caused, in effect, the difficulties felt about sacrifice in the Eucharist. It was the equating of sacrifice with death which naturally led—could not but lead—to the language of immolation. And it was the concentration, in the idea of Christian sacrifice, upon the Cross, to the exclusion of the thought of offering in its true character, and indeed of communion, which led to the "propitiatory" developments in the mediaeval Mass. The sacrifice of Christ comes, as wholly propitiatory, to be interpreted as a sin-offering alone, and the other aspects of the ancient, or complete, sacrificial process were lost sight of. Hence it is often thought, by writers who cannot, as they believe, accept the tradition of the Eucharist as really sacrificial, that to prove that it is not propitiatory, in the mediaeval sense, or even in the Tridentine, is to prove that it is not true sacrifice at all. They are concerned, and, under the compulsion of the inaccurate language which they have inherited, as I should say rightly concerned, to secure at all costs the central truth of the all-sufficiency of the Cross. Any theory of sacrifice which seems to challenge that must be repudiated.

I have, I hope, sufficiently shown, in all three parts of this book, that if sacrifice is properly understood, the whole of this danger goes. On the other hand, there ought to be no difficulty, and no risk, in seeing the Eucharist itself as a true and proper sacrifice, or, if it be preferred, in its true and proper place as an integral part, for us on earth, of the One Sacrifice in its fullness. It should be possible, at long last, to bury the controversy about the "Eucharistic Sacrifice". No possible way of abusing it remains. It can never be in any sense a repetition of, or a rival to, a supplement of, what happened on the Cross. We can enter freely into its full meaning.

And the second great topic of eucharistic controversy has been that of the Presence. There can be no one who does not wish to think of the living Christ offering Himself to us, entering into our lives. But the fear has been of His coming being thought of in a material sense. And that conception of His Body and Blood as in some way material emerged directly from the belief that the Christ Who was offered on the altar before His Presence could be given was offered in the sense of being slain. Once the sacrifice was interpreted in terms of death, no explanation, however careful, could prevent the Body and Blood of the Holy Communion being thought of in terms of the "body of His humiliation". That meant that they were "body" and "blood" in the sense in which we use those terms not only of Him before He died, and in His Death, but also in relation to our own present life. And it is this fear of materialism that has made men shrink, and—under the compulsion, as I should say again, of the inherited language, rightly shrink—from believing in a Presence bound up with the Elements. There could be no Presence which was "carnal" or "corporal" in that way. But, once more, if the sacrifice is rightly understood, and seen in its fullness, the Body and the Blood of the Eucharist are the Body and Blood of the glorified, not the crucified, Christ. They cannot be material. They belong to the time when "it was Spirit", because Jesus has been glorified. The reasons for the old protest go, and with them all reasons for explaining away the full reality of the Eucharistic Body and Blood. They are there, and indeed they must be there, if the Offering is a real Offering, and, even more, if the Communion-meal is a real Communion. Can we not, again, bury the controversies about the Presence, as we bury those about the Sacrifice?

I have one last suggestion to make. It will be remembered that I have said that our identification of ourselves with Christ, upon which for its completeness our offering in the Eucharist as in all life depends, is in our daily experience imperfect. It is begun in Baptism; but it can only be completed in such rare cases as St. Paul's, in which a man may dare to say, "I have been crucified with Christ". I go back, if I may, on behalf, as it were, of all who cannot yet say this, to the full scheme of the Old Testament sacrifice, the first stage of which is the approach to the altar, together with the laying, or pressing of the offerer's hands upon the victim's head. For a very real part of the practical difficulty felt in entering fully into eucharistic worship is that, as seen in its ideal and perfect form, at least as regards the stage of offering, it assumes too much. It therefore loses part of its reality; and where there is unreality there is, in the best and most honest men, discouragement. In fact, we are in a double position during this life. As baptized, we are in actual truth already identified with Christ, and members of His Body. We are ready and able to take our part in the great Offering; and it is indeed well, and necessary, that we should. But as "uncrucified", we have not yet reached that stage. We are still in the first stage of all, that of approach, and, once we take steps to make our approach a reality, already concerned with the second, the laying on of hands. For the approach demands, and consists in, the steady attempt, under the circumstances of ordinary life, to do our duty, to set our face towards God, to move towards the Cross of self-surrender, and the altar of self-dedication. That general moral effort demands self-knowledge, self-examination, repentance, and, in some form, acknowledgment of sin and its confession. These two processes, intertwined and, in fact, simultaneous, though in order of thought succeeding the one to the other, summarise the moral side—often "undogmatic", and not consciously connected with what is called "institutional" religion—of the normal life of a man who believes generally in Christian principles and is trying to live, however simply, a Christian life; or the double process may be begun and continued, on the one hand, with a clear grasp of Christian truth and its possibilities, in the open vision of the Cross and the altar that are waiting to be reached; or, on the other hand, in a character actually, but not in any sense consciously, Christian. In any of these cases we are at a definite stage of the complete sacrifice. For the process, as on its positive side, as an attempt at moral achievement, as the pursuit of an ideal, it is the "drawing near" or approach to the altar, is on its negative side, as the attempt to uproot and repent of bad habits, just what was expressed in the ancient laying on of hands. For that involved some definite self-diagnosis, some expression of repentance, some degree of confession, and it was in that spirit that the offerer by

laying, or pressing, his hands on the victim's head, identified himself with it.[1] In the Christian approach that
identification of the sinner with the victim is accomplished, indeed, in one sense, in Baptism; but it remains
to be accomplished in growing completeness in every
attempt that penitence and self-discipline inspire to make
ourselves more fully one with Christ as He surrenders
Himself to the Cross.

It is this "drawing near" which is still, under our double
position in this life—identified with Christ in one sense,
still not identified, or only half-identified, in another—a
very real part, to us, of the living sacrifice. In every
Eucharist the two conditions overlap. As one with Christ
we join in the climax of the worship: we are admitted to
the heavenly altar, to the fellowship of the angels and
archangels and the whole company of heaven; and as such
we offer the whole Body in all its constituent parts, and
under all the names of each and of the whole. And yet,
as still far from our perfect union with Christ, we ask for
mercy in the Kyrie; we ask God to make our imperfect
offering of our imperfect gifts, of our imperfect selves,
complete with Christ's completeness; and, in our English
service, this side of our approach is actually named and
identified in the technical phrase which descends straight
from the old Jewish approach, "*Draw near* with faith",
before the confession.

I have hitherto traced in the history of the Eucharist its
progressive identification or linking up with the different
stages in the complete sacrifice, beginning from the last
stage, the communion-meal, and working backwards,
through that of offering, to the stage of the propitiation
by, or pleading of, the Blood and the Cross. May it not be
equally true that there is yet another linking up waiting
to be made as conscious as the rest? The great need of our
time is to bring our common life into our worship: to see
the vital connection between religion and morals, cult and
conduct, the Eucharist and ethics. Here, surely, is the
link. In communion, in offering, in the pleading by the

---

[1] Büchler, *Studies in Sin and Atonement*, ch. v. pp. 416 ff.

memorial of the Cross, Christian experience has shown the vital connection of the Eucharist with the eternal truths, and with the historical facts, of our religion. It is, once sacrifice is understood in all its fullness, equally connected with the whole of man's practical and moral life from his birth to his grave. It has its bearing on, it has its place for, effort as well as achievement, failure as well as success. I have already pleaded that every phase of what can be called self-dedication and achievement, has its place, consciously and even unconsciously, in the great single offering in which the whole movement of man and of Nature towards God is summed up. What I suggest now is that every true moral effort, every acknowledged moral failure, is equally a part of the process of the full sacrifice of which the Eucharist is the symbol and the expression. By some the effort is made in a Christian consciousness already clear; and, for them, their part in the eucharistic approach is also clear. But there are many for whom the goal to which they are moving has not yet stamped itself in the recognised form of the Cross of Christ. It may be to them nothing more explicit than a general ideal of self-denial and self-discipline. The Church can make its approach along the first steps of sacrifice on their behalf, as it can make its offering also to include the unconscious offering and self-dedication of many who could not find for themselves the Christian words for the Christian things that they are doing. But in so far as this extension of the scope of the Eucharist can be made more consciously real, its own appeal will be the wider and the stronger. It can become the opportunity, the outlet, of the many, instead of the secret, or the privilege, or even the shibboleth, of the few. And, in this extension of its scope, its more dogmatic, more mystical, sides can be brought more into touch with common life, and, in that new and fruitful contact, be made more intelligible and more human, but not less Divine. For this last linking up will be, after all, a linking with Jesus not in His Glory only, not only upon His Cross, but in His earthly life. The Eucharist will have its appeal not only to those whose experience has given them the heavenly vision, or brought them to the foot of the Cross, but to those also who first find their contact of sympathy and grace with Him Whom they call the Jesus of the Gospels, or of "history". That contact may be imperfect, but it is real; and the lesson of Christian history, as of Christian experience, is that it matters little on which of Christ's many aspects we first fasten our gaze, from which we first find our help, provided that that one leads us to the rest.

It may indeed be realised, when we can see the history of our own times in true perspective, that much of the modern "undogmatic" trend of the concentration on practical ethics has all the time been the contribution of our own age to the gradual realisation of this part of the meaning and scope of the Christian sacrifice; just as the contribution of the Middle Ages was to the realisation of the part played in it by the Cross, and of the early centuries to the place in it of the offering.

My plea, therefore, is for the fullness of the Christian sacrifice. My argument has been that it was to absorption in one stage only of it—that of the Death—that we owe the tragedies of controversy both about the eucharistic sacrifice and about the Presence, as well as much misunderstanding of the Atonement. Absorption in any other one stage, or indeed, in anything less than the whole, is the sure way to disaster: whether it be to fasten merely upon the glory of worship and of offering, and to forget our own sin and the Cross, and the moral life; or to rest content with the human example and fellowship of Jesus in His Galilean life, and to refuse to follow Him to the Cross and to the Heavenly worship.

What I have attempted to set out is the scope of sacrifice, once really understood, and the bearing of each stage of it upon the rest; the place of the Eucharist in its relation, at every stage, to the whole process from beginning to end; and the vital connection between the One Sacrifice, so revealed in the Eucharist, and every phase and part of all human, and indeed all created, life. So understood, the Eucharist is the most illuminating, as it is the most effective and the most comprehensive, of all conceivable acts in which we can take part. It covers every phase and part of human activity to-day. It gathers up all Christian history. It gives us living touch with the Living Christ in every stage and in every aspect of His work for us and for the world. And in making us one with Him, it makes us one with every generation of mankind. He Himself made the dry bones live. He consecrated, as He cleansed and purified and completed, every earlier effort of man to find God or to serve Him; even what are to us the unthinkable coarseness of the primitive communion-meal on the living flesh and blood, and the unthinkable and perverted barbarities of human sacrifice, and the futilities of ceremonial atonement by the blood of bulls and goats. He sees in these not their coarseness, their barbarity, their futility, but the direct vision, the instinctive longings, of the childhood of the race; and He redeems them in restoring them. For us there is the Living Manhood in the Body and the undying Life of God and of man in the Blood; the perfect surrender and the unqualified, effective, acceptance of Manhood at its best in the complete offering of the dedicated human will to the will of God; the passing through death upon the Cross, with the surrendered Life, into the presence of God; as well as the simple life of human duty and sympathy, of human effort and friendship, in the days of His humiliation, in the streets of Jerusalem, and upon the Galilean hills. For us, therefore, in the Eternal Christ the past is alive, the present is intelligible, the future is known. He has made us heirs of the Kingdom of Heaven, and with it He has made us heirs of the world of Nature and of History, which both by Creation and by Redemption is His own.

I have greatly dared, in this chapter, in saying that if we so think of sacrifice we can bury the great controversies about the Eucharist. We shall bury them if we can follow, and grasp, the vision to which, however imperfectly, I have tried to point, not in any sense of controversial victory but by a simple tracing of their history, and a simple understanding of their language. We shall be able to look back, each of us, on our own past, and on the past of those with whom we or our ancestors have disagreed, without apology, without compromise, without withdrawal, and, above all, without bitterness or censure. We can accept on both sides the positions which were maintained. Neither side was wholly right, in so far as it denied a part of the truth. Neither side was wholly wrong, in so far as it asserted an essential part of truth. But that which was wrong, in each, was wrong through what was not its fault; and that which was right remains its glory and its pride.

That is the only possible method by which controversy can be healed. It is by that method that we must work for the healing of the many wounds in the Body of Christ that yet remain. May His Spirit lead us and enable us until each of us, and each section of our divided Christendom, can say that it is of His fullness that we have all received, and grace for grace

INDEX OF SCRIPTURE REFERENCES

2 A 2

INDEX OF NAMES AND SUBJECTS

Printed in Great Britain by
Billing and Sons Ltd., Guildford and Esher